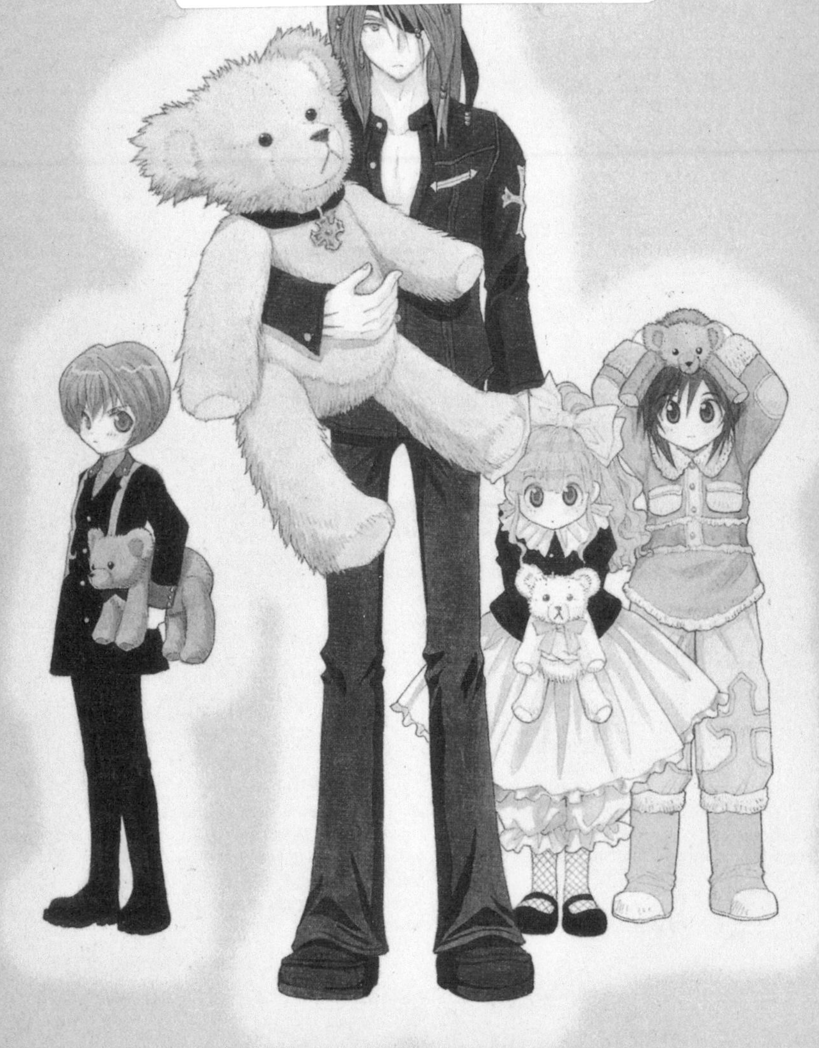

+ANIMA Volume 5
Created by Natsumi Mukai

Translation - Alethea & Athena Nibley
English Adaptation - Karen S. Ahlstrom
Copy Editor - Nikhil Burman
Retouch and Lettering - Star Print Brokers
Production Artist - Mike Estacio
Graphic Designer - James Lee

Editor - Troy Lewter
Digital Imaging Manager - Chris Buford
Pre-Production Supervisor - Erika Terriquez
Art Director - Anne Marie Horne
Production Manager - Elisabeth Brizzi
Managing Editor - Vy Nguyen
VP of Production - Ron Klamert
Editor-in-Chief - Rob Tokar
Publisher - Mike Kiley
President and C.O.O. - John Parker
C.E.O. and Chief Creative Officer - Stuart Levy

A  **TOKYOPOP** Manga

TOKYOPOP and 🐸 are trademarks or registered trademarks of TOKYOPOP Inc.

TOKYOPOP Inc.
5900 Wilshire Blvd. Suite 2000
Los Angeles, CA 90036

E-mail: info@TOKYOPOP.com
Come visit us online at www.TOKYOPOP.com

ISBN: 978-1-59816-351-3

First TOKYOPOP printing: September 2007

10 9 8 7 6 5 4 3 2 1

Printed in the USA

Volume 5
by Natsumi Mukai

HAMBURG // LONDON // LOS ANGELES // TOKYO

+ANIMA

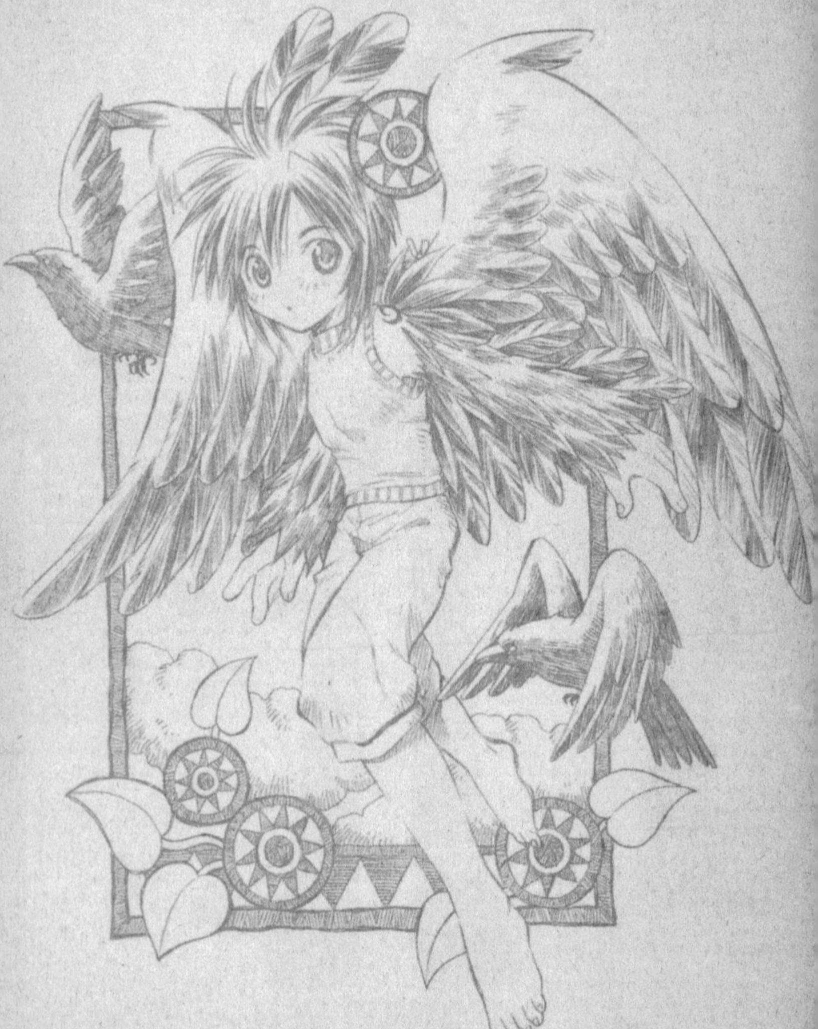

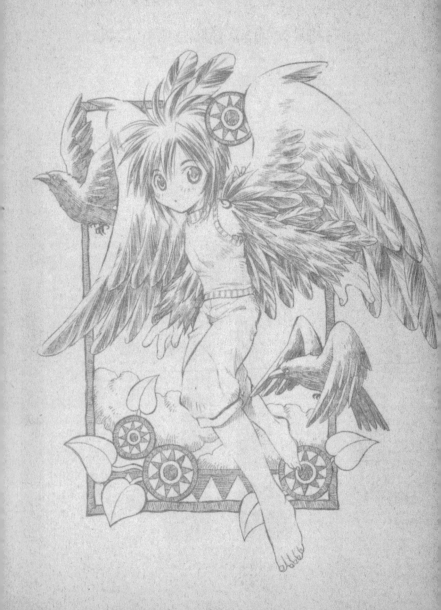

+ANIMA

プラスアニマ

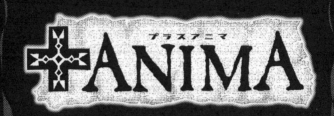

迎夏生

NATSUMI MUKAI

In this world, there are those known as +Anima: humans who have within them the powers of animals.

Cooro, a crow +Anima, meets Husky, a fish +Anima, at the circus. The two of them agree to travel together, and are later joined by new companions: Senri, a bear +Anima, and Nana, a bat +Anima. And so, the four children's adventures began.

STORY & CHARACTERS

With the help of Rose, who turns out to be a cat +Anima, they manage to calm things down and arrive safely in the next town.

ローズ[Rose]

Along with Rose, a peddler whom they meet on a mountain path, the four cross the mountains. Everything goes fine until they meet Igneous, an Astarian soldier who hates the Kim-un-kur mountain people (Senri's clan). The narrow mountain pass is thrown into confusion when Igneous finds Senri.

I'M SORRY I DIDN'T PAY!

クーロ[Cooro]
Crow +Anima. He spreads his pitch-black wings and soars to the sky. He's always on the lookout for something to eat.

ハスキー[Husky]
Fish +Anima. He can swim freely through water like a merman. He's a little stubborn, and doesn't like girls.

THE +ANIMA-SENRI!

センリ[Senri]
Bear +Anima. His sharp-clawed arm is amazingly strong. He doesn't talk very much.

ナナ[Nana]
Bat +Anima. She can fly and has an ultrasonic screech. She loves pretty clothes and is scared of forests at night.

ローズ[Rose]

Meanwhile, Rose discovers that her younger brother Pinion, who was supposed to have been living with relatives, has been taken away from them and brought to this town...

ピニオン[Pinion]

SEE, LOOK!

マグダラ[Magdala]

With Rose, the party arrives at Maggie Vil. This city has been led by generations of women called Maggie. The main entertainment in town is a fighting tournament. The children are told that, if they participate in a match and win, they can get a large sum of money. Having differing opinions about participating in the Games, they meet the wealthy girl Magdala, who guides them to the coliseum where the Games are held.

Rose follows Pinion, but loses sight of him. We find out that the people who took him are Astarian researchers. They decide to stay at Maggie Coliseum for a while and resume their experiments with Pinion...

シノン[Sinon]

It turns out that Magdala is the only daughter of the town headwoman. She invites Nana to her rooms and introduces her friends. All of them flock to Magdala, but things begin to seem strange when Magdala ignores one girl and looks coldly at Sinon, a young boy who says he wants to go home...

Husky and Cooro end up participating in the Games. Looking more serious than usual, Husky wins an overwhelming victory. But Cooro flies into the sky in the middle of his match and disqualifies himself.

After their matches, Husky and Cooro refuse to be Magdala's bodyguards, so she throws them into the dungeon. There they find Sinon, who was also in the dungeon for trying to leave Magdala...

Meanwhile, Nana tries to leave Magdala's room, but the other girls stop her. They tell her that everything here is decided on Magdala's whims, so she'll be in terrible trouble...

The morning after they're locked in the dungeon, Sinon escapes. He is chased into the coliseum's arena where Magdala's pets, two big cats, set upon him. When they do, he suddenly becomes a swan +Anima and flies away.

Then Senri runs in carrying Pinion. Rose, Cooro and the others fight the researchers and some athletes from the coliseum who are trying to get Rose's brother back. Magdala learns for the first time about the powers that exist outside of Maggie Vil.

With Magdala's guidance, Cooro and the others make it out of Maggie Vil. Rose, with Pinion at her side, resumes her peddling and bids farewell to Cooro and the others.

Nana feels hurt when Husky, who himself has valuable gems, tells her that she is more suited to acorns and flowers. To make her feel better, Husky attaches a stone he found at the bottom of a pond to a flower-shaped pendant that Senri made and gives it to Nana.

Many adventures still await the four on their journey...

CONTENTS

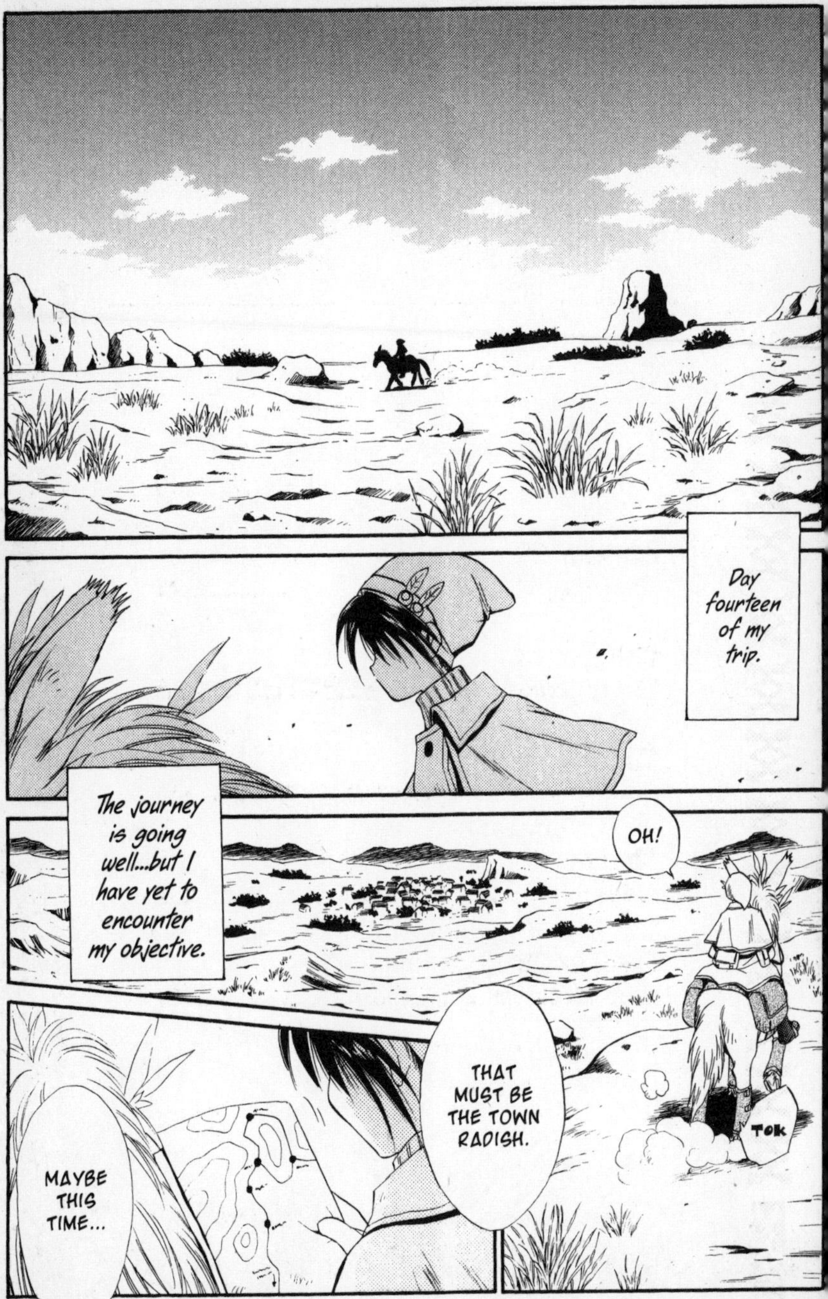
Day fourteen of my trip.
The journey is going well...but I have yet to encounter my objective.
OH!
TOK
THAT MUST BE THE TOWN RADISH.
MAYBE THIS TIME...

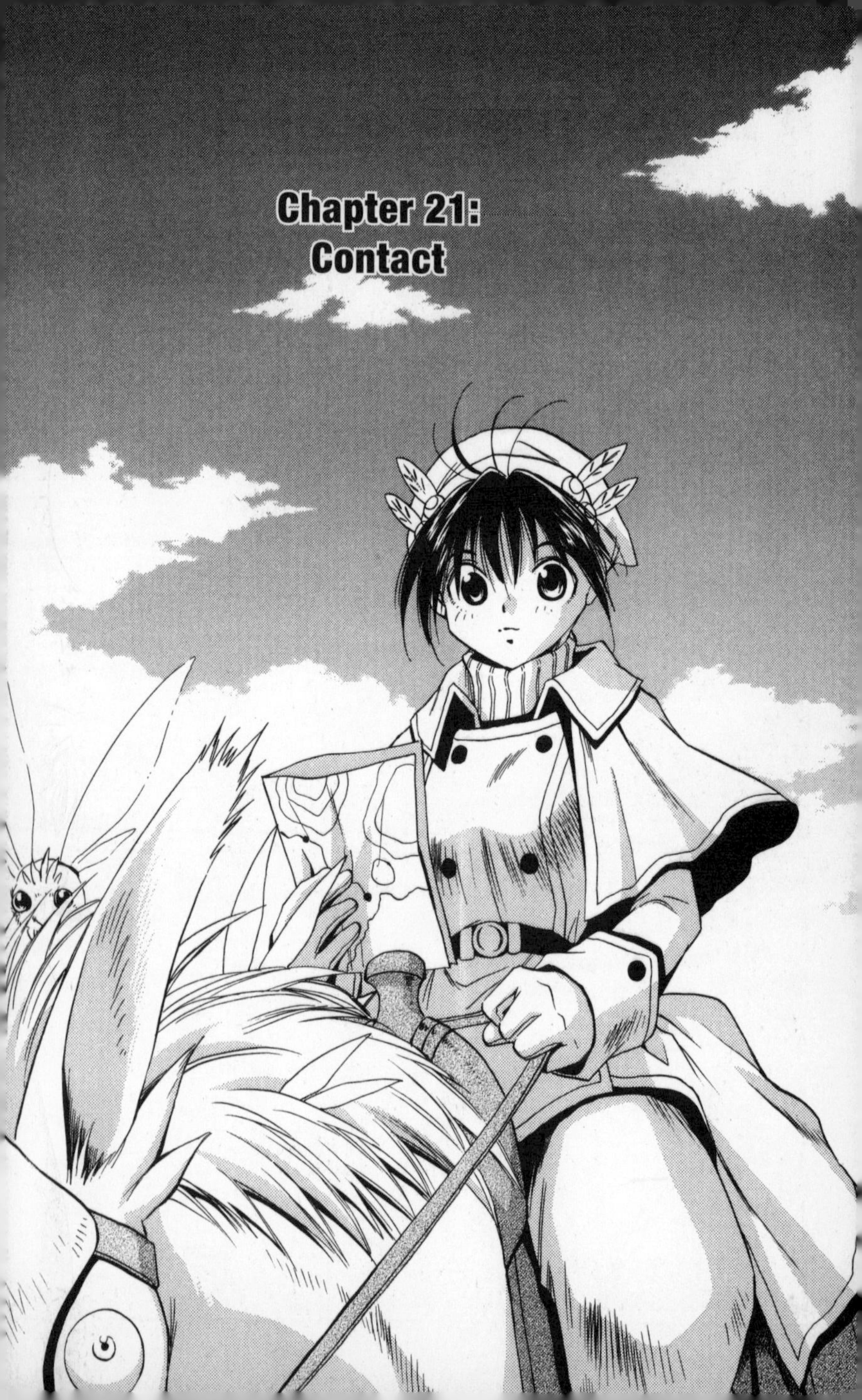
Chapter 21:
Contact

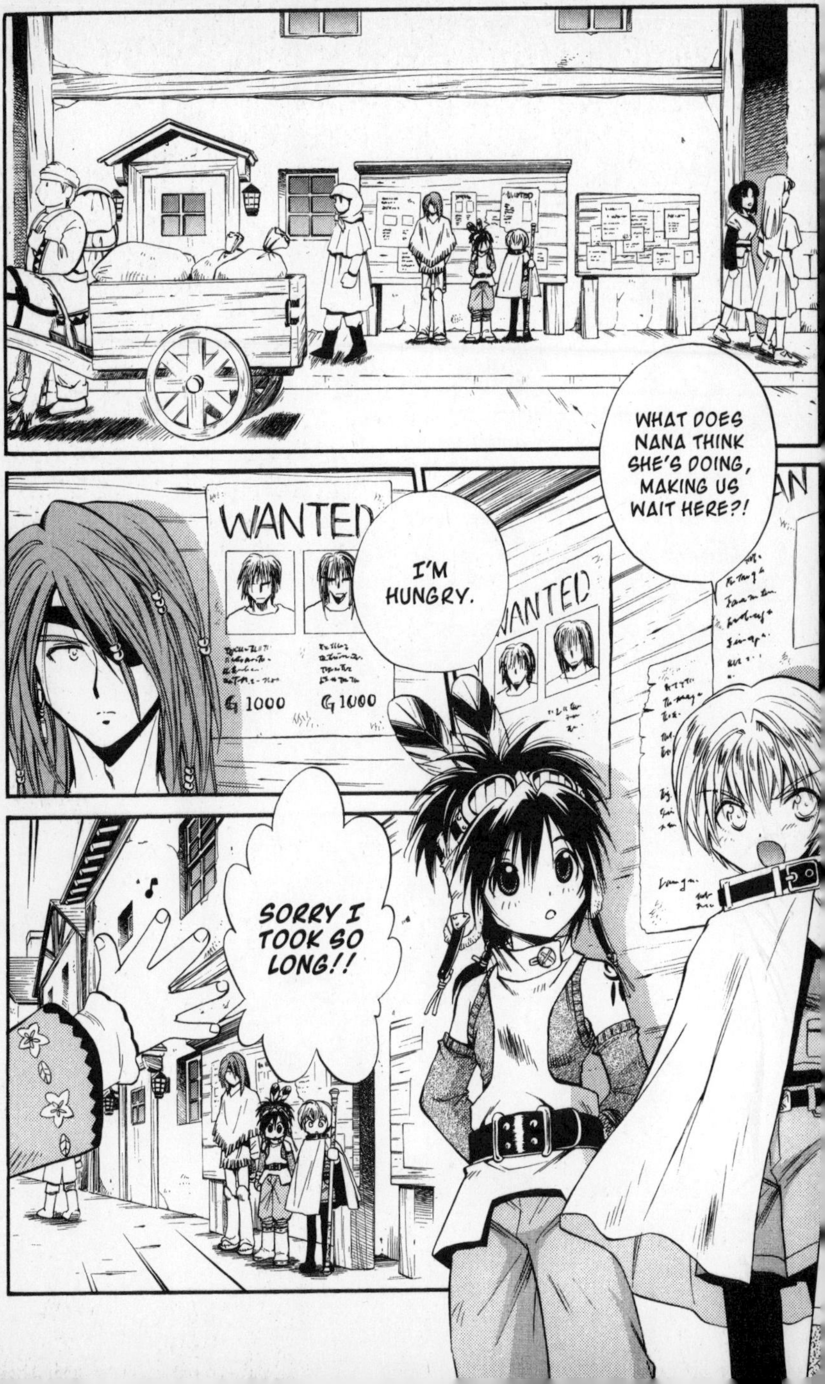

WHAT DOES NANA THINK SHE'S DOING, MAKING US WAIT HERE?!
I'M HUNGRY.
WANTED
G1000
G1000
SORRY I TOOK SO LONG!!

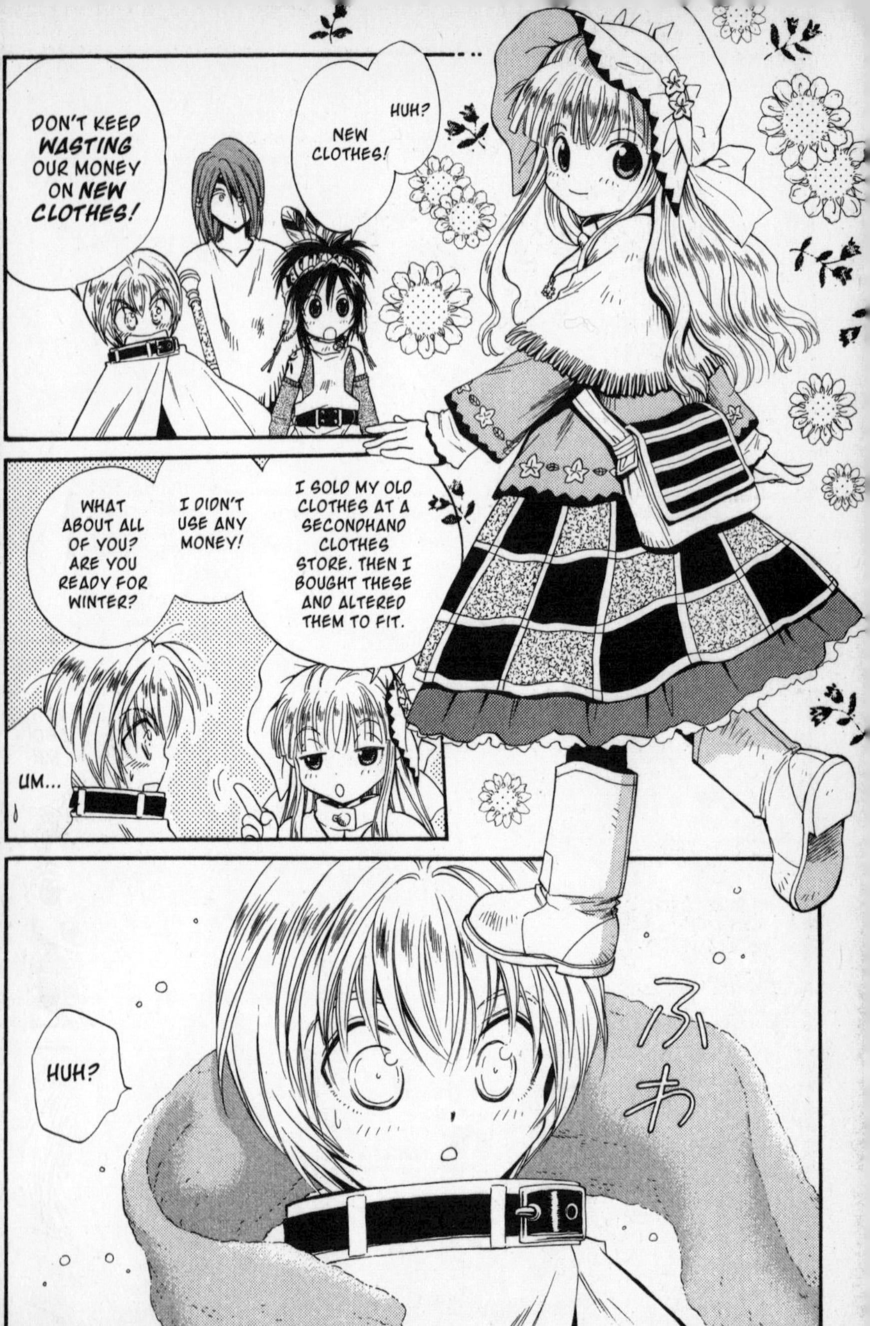
HUH?
NEW CLOTHES!
DON'T KEEP **WASTING** OUR MONEY ON **NEW CLOTHES!**
I SOLD MY OLD CLOTHES AT A SECONDHAND CLOTHES STORE. THEN I BOUGHT THESE AND ALTERED THEM TO FIT.
I DIDN'T USE ANY MONEY!
WHAT ABOUT ALL OF YOU? ARE YOU READY FOR WINTER?
UM...
ふわ
HUH?

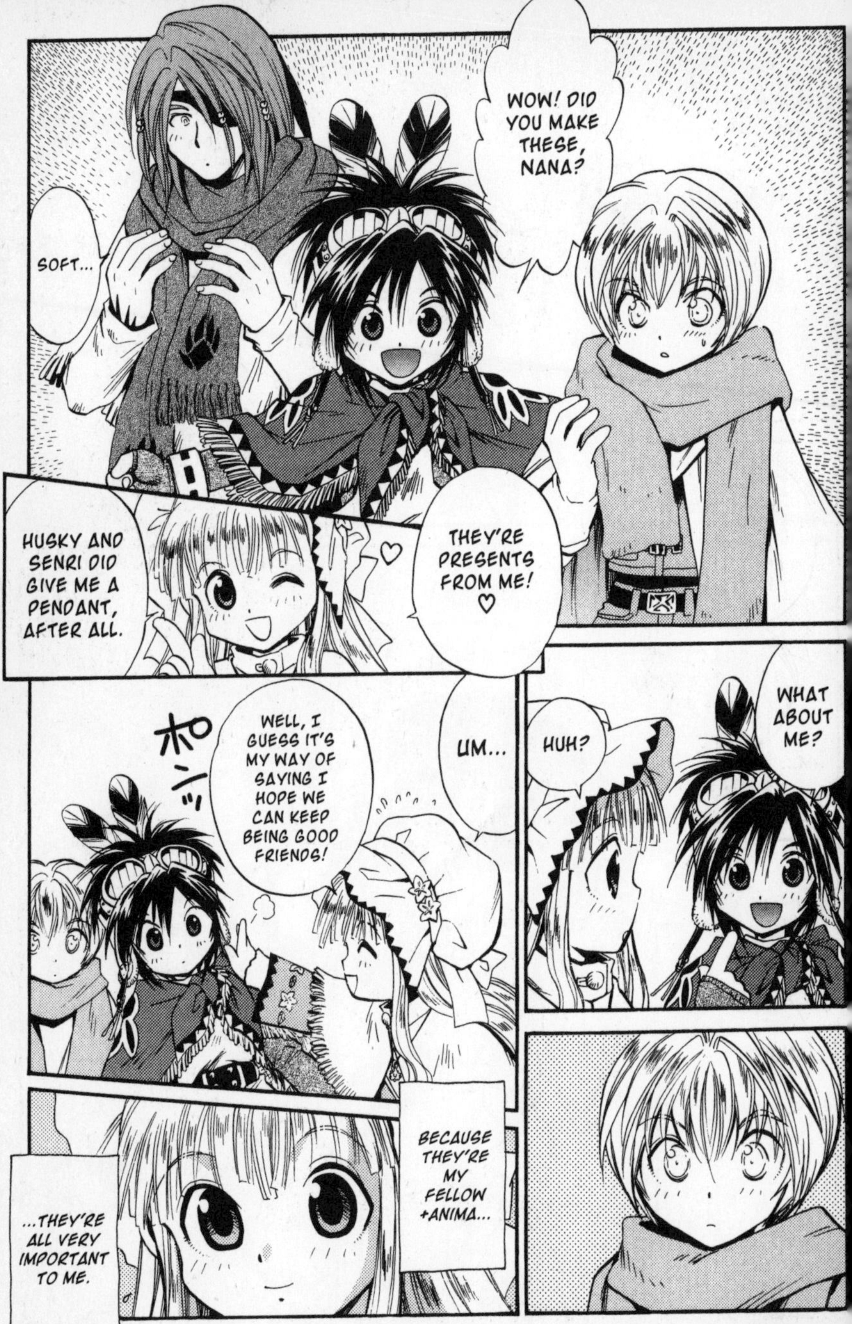
WOW! DID YOU MAKE THESE, NANA?
SOFT...
THEY'RE PRESENTS FROM ME! ♡
HUSKY AND SENRI DID GIVE ME A PENDANT, AFTER ALL.
WHAT ABOUT ME?
HUH?
UM...
WELL, I GUESS IT'S MY WAY OF SAYING I HOPE WE CAN KEEP BEING GOOD FRIENDS!
ポンッ
BECAUSE THEY'RE MY FELLOW +ANIMA...
...THEY'RE ALL VERY IMPORTANT TO ME.

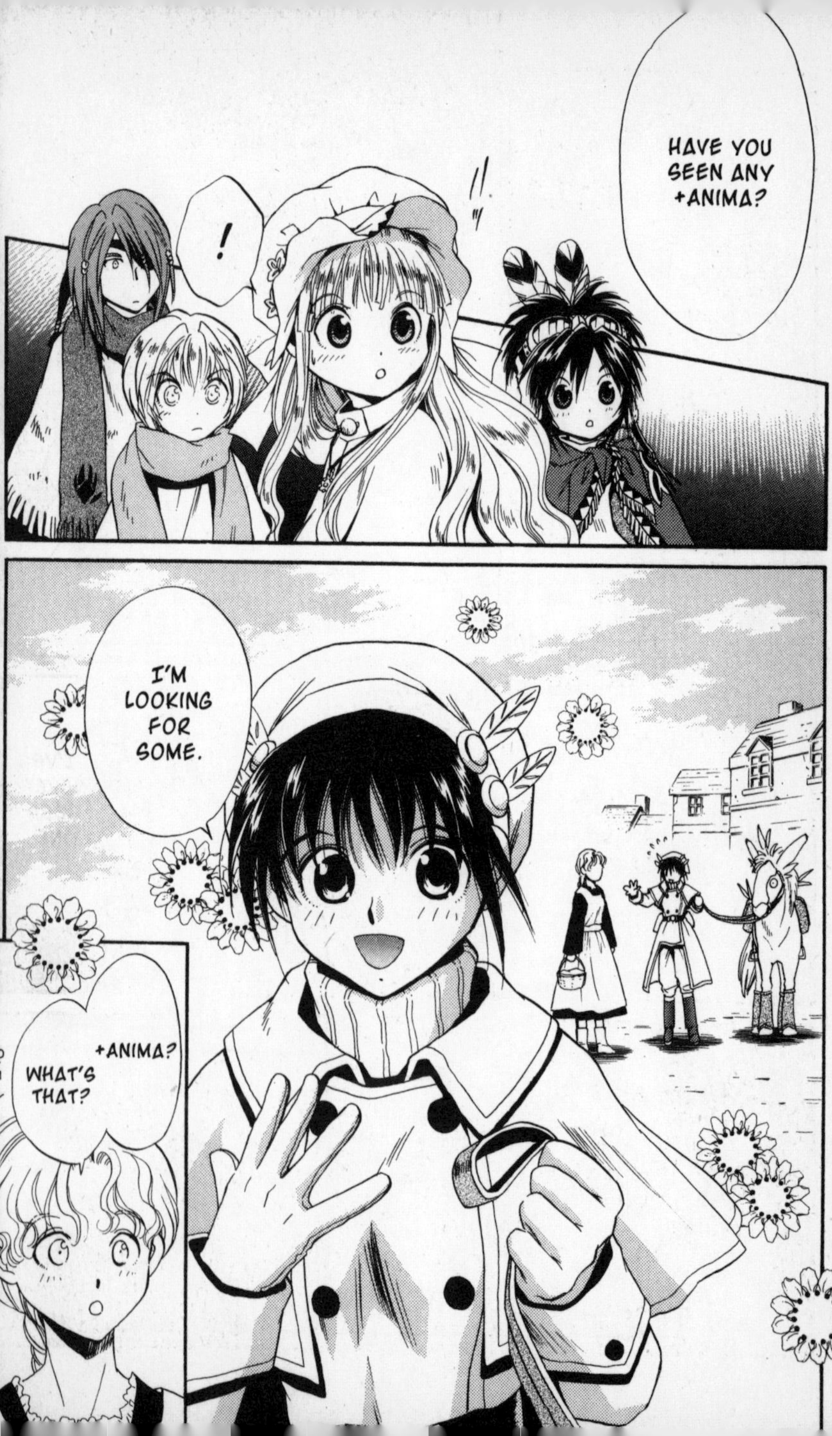
HAVE YOU SEEN ANY +ANIMA?
!!
!
I'M LOOKING FOR SOME.
+ANIMA? WHAT'S THAT?

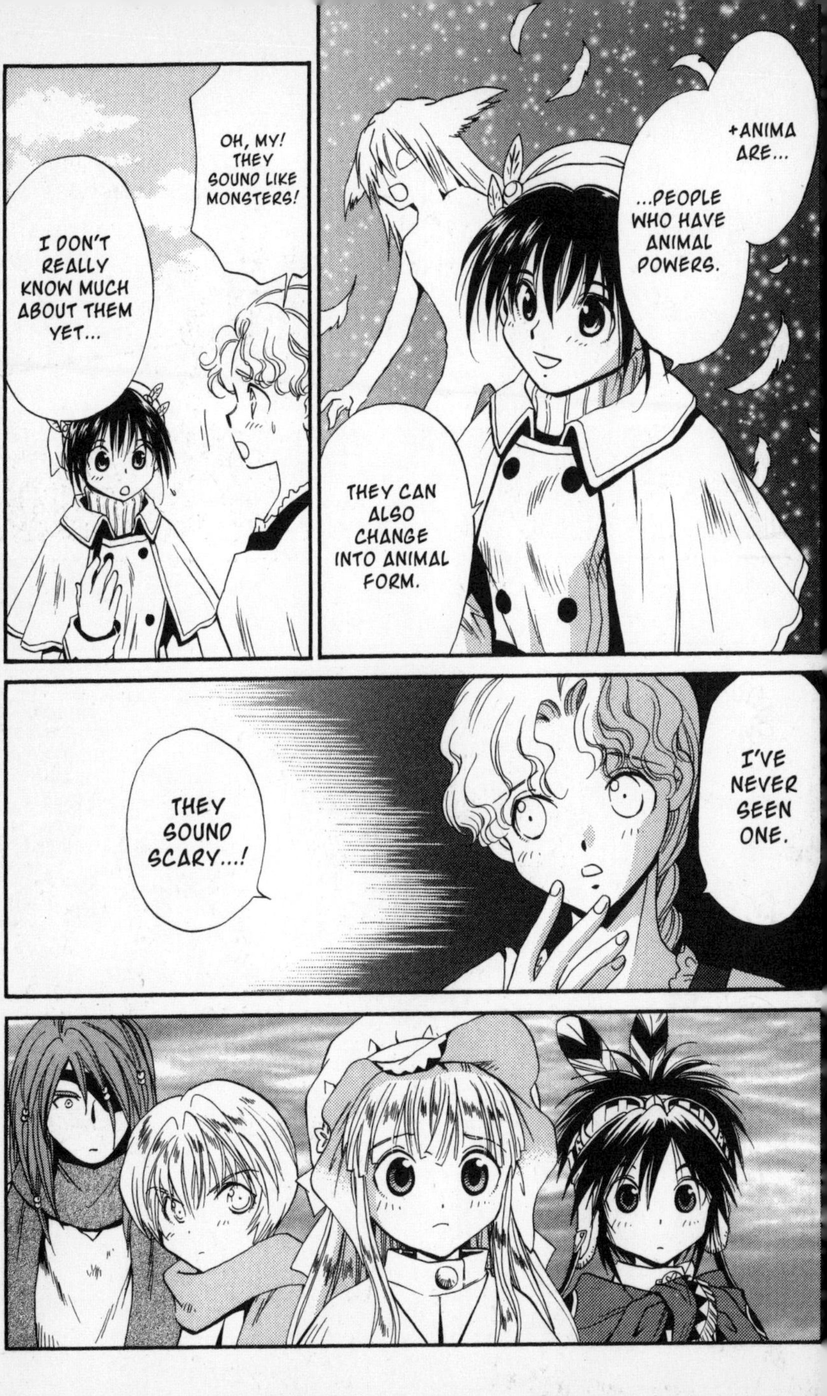
+ANIMA ARE...
...PEOPLE WHO HAVE ANIMAL POWERS.
THEY CAN ALSO CHANGE INTO ANIMAL FORM.
OH, MY! THEY SOUND LIKE MONSTERS!
I DON'T REALLY KNOW MUCH ABOUT THEM YET...
I'VE NEVER SEEN ONE.
THEY SOUND SCARY...!

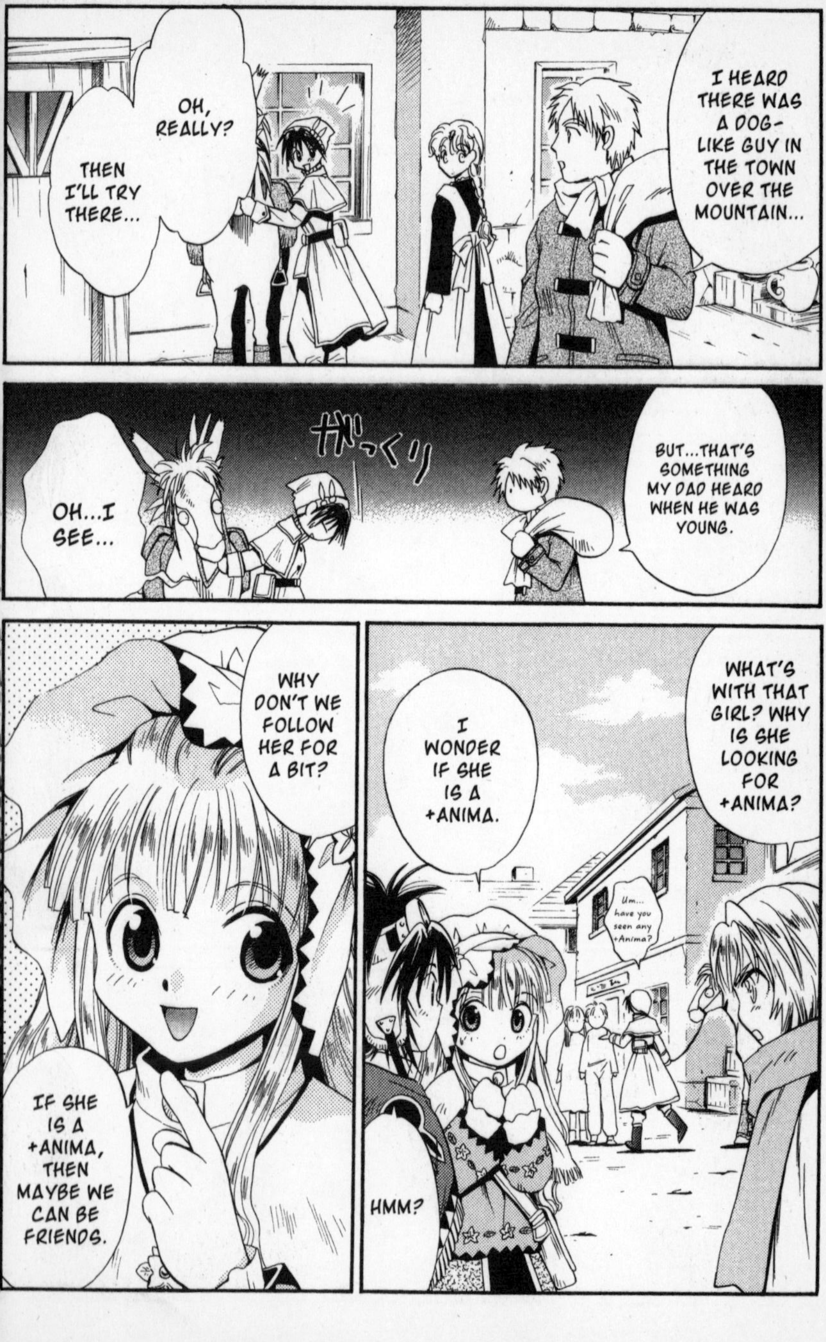

I HEARD THERE WAS A DOG-LIKE GUY IN THE TOWN OVER THE MOUNTAIN...
OH, REALLY?
THEN I'LL TRY THERE...
BUT...THAT'S SOMETHING MY DAD HEARD WHEN HE WAS YOUNG.
がっくり
OH...I SEE...
WHAT'S WITH THAT GIRL? WHY IS SHE LOOKING FOR +ANIMA?
I WONDER IF SHE IS A +ANIMA.
Um... have you seen any +Anima?
HMM?
WHY DON'T WE FOLLOW HER FOR A BIT?
IF SHE IS A +ANIMA, THEN MAYBE WE CAN BE FRIENDS.

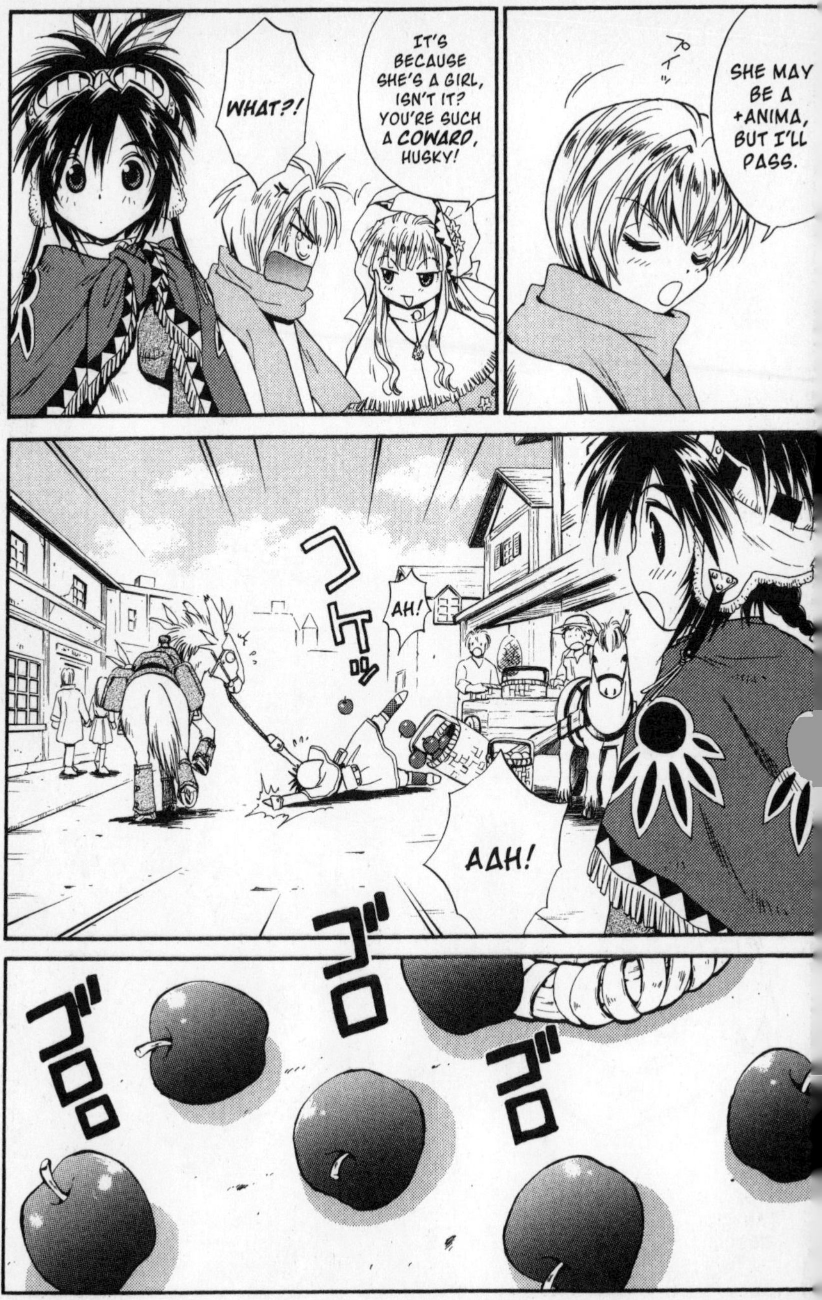
プイッ
SHE MAY BE A +ANIMA, BUT I'LL PASS.
IT'S BECAUSE SHE'S A GIRL, ISN'T IT? YOU'RE SUCH A COWARD, HUSKY!
WHAT?!
AH!
AAH!
ゴロ
ゴロ
ゴロロ

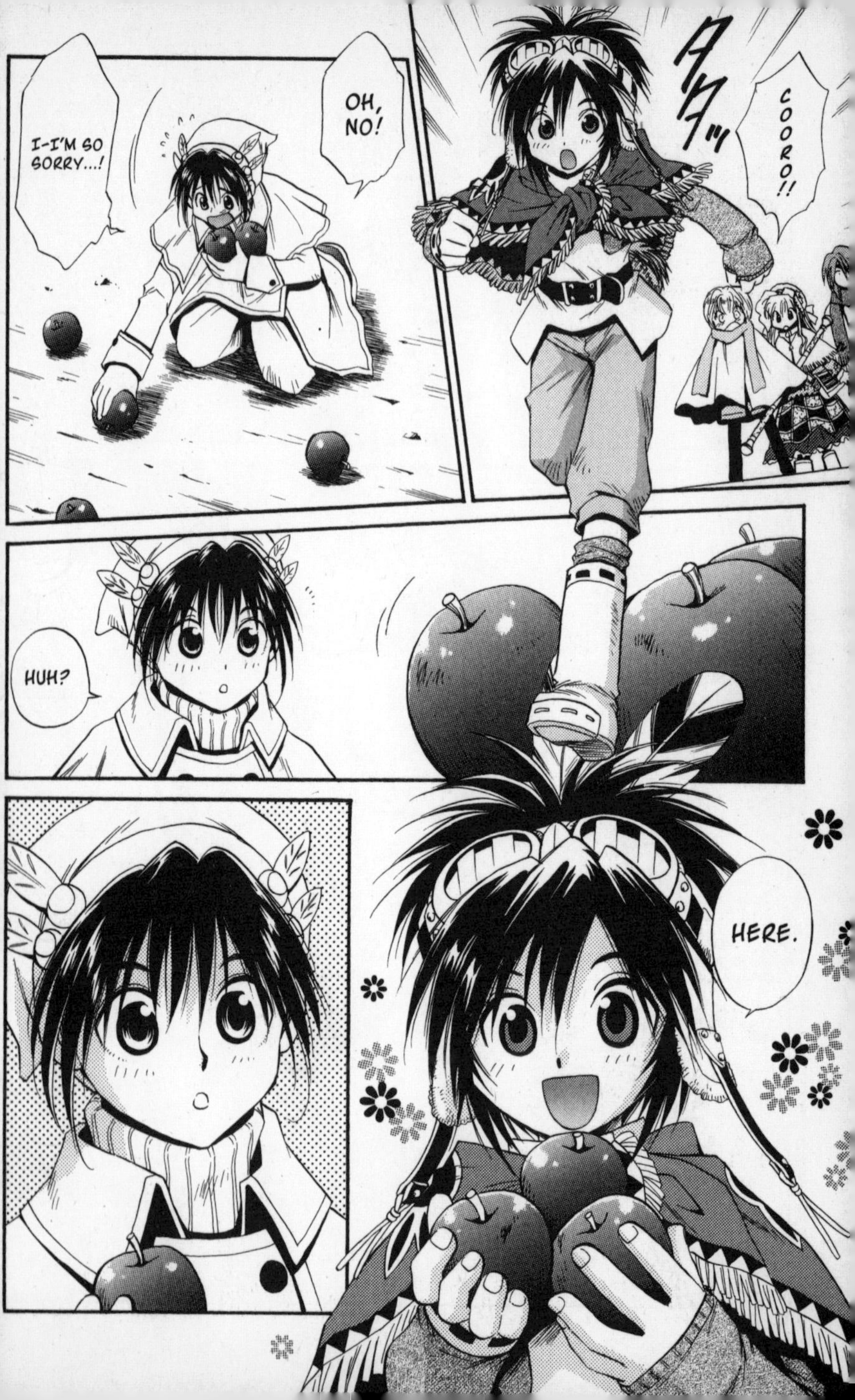
COORO!!
OH, NO!
I-I'M SO SORRY...!
HUH?
HERE.

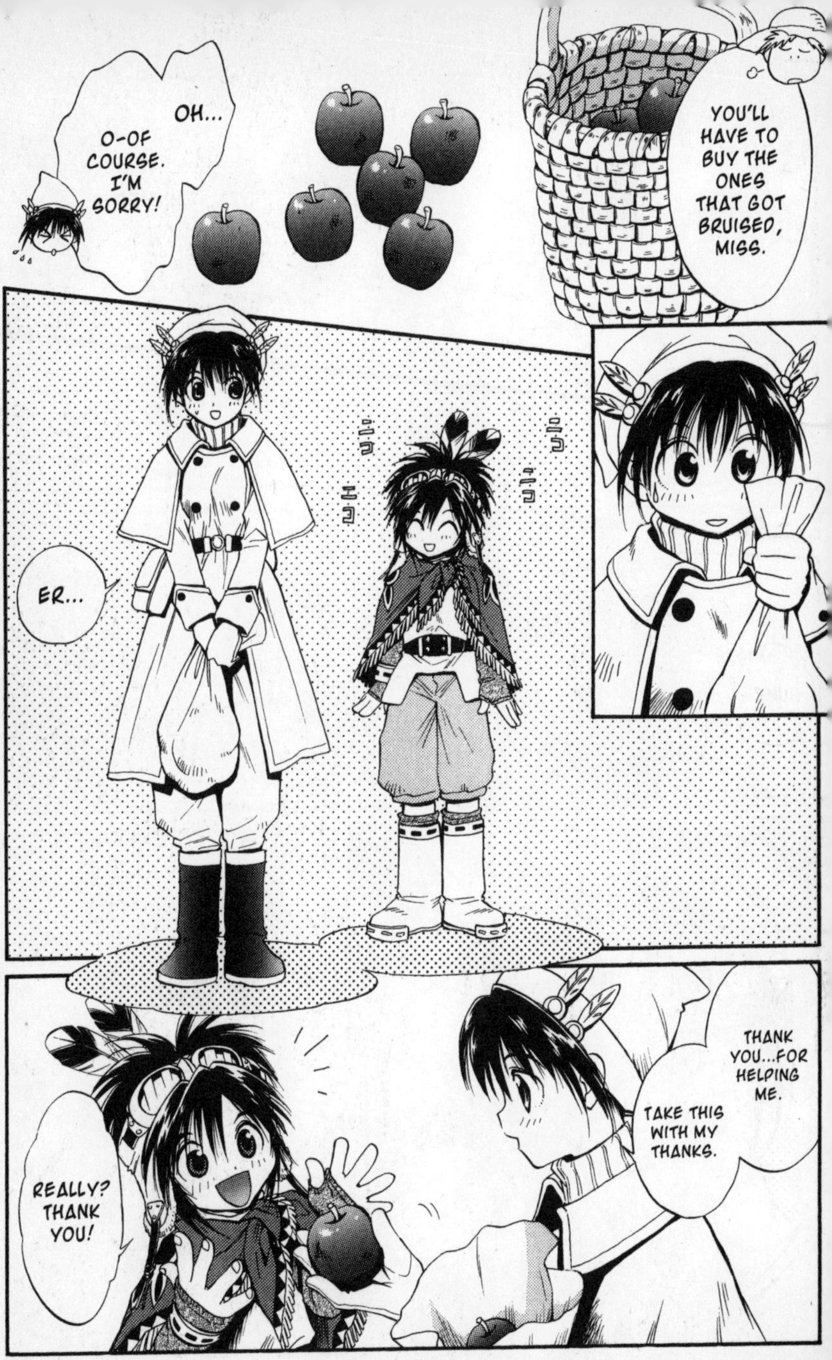
YOU'LL HAVE TO BUY THE ONES THAT GOT BRUISED, MISS.
OH...
O-OF COURSE. I'M SORRY!
ニコ ニコ
ニコ ニコ
ER...
THANK YOU...FOR HELPING ME.
TAKE THIS WITH MY THANKS.
REALLY? THANK YOU!

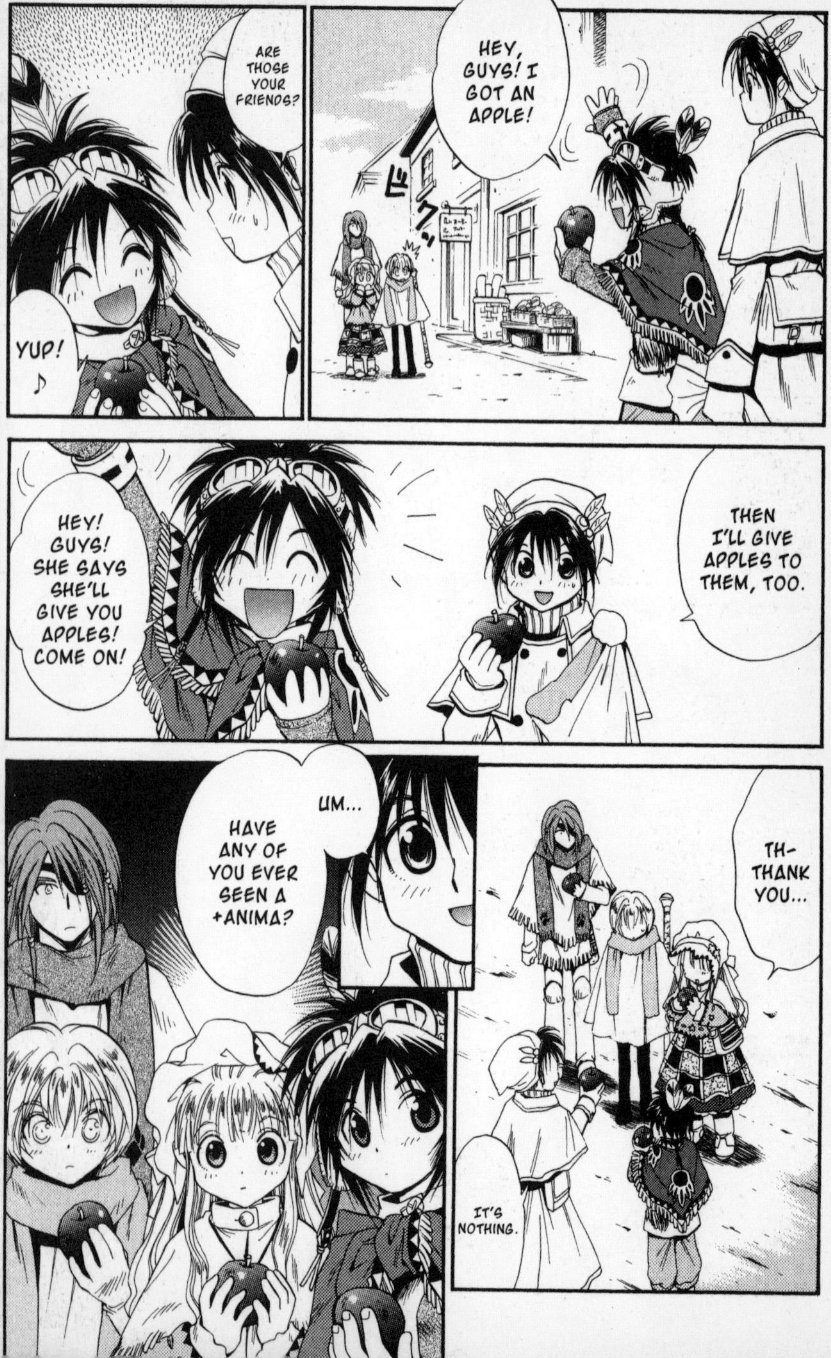
HEY, GUYS! I GOT AN APPLE!
ビクッ
ARE THOSE YOUR FRIENDS?
YUP! ♪
THEN I'LL GIVE APPLES TO THEM, TOO.
HEY! GUYS! SHE SAYS SHE'LL GIVE YOU APPLES! COME ON!
TH-THANK YOU...
IT'S NOTHING.
UM...
HAVE ANY OF YOU EVER SEEN A +ANIMA?

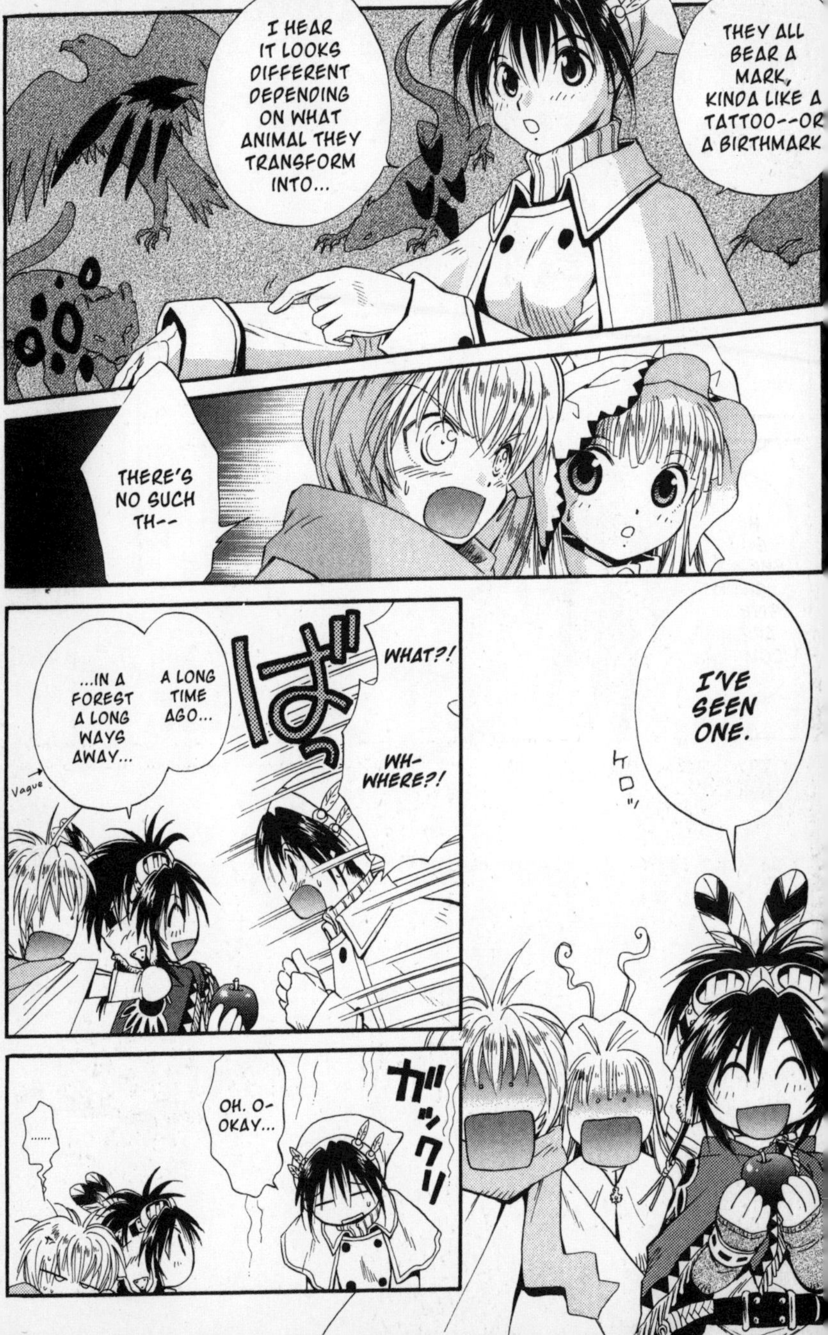
THEY ALL BEAR A MARK, KINDA LIKE A TATTOO--OR A BIRTHMARK
I HEAR IT LOOKS DIFFERENT DEPENDING ON WHAT ANIMAL THEY TRANSFORM INTO...
THERE'S NO SUCH TH--
I'VE SEEN ONE.
ケロッ
WHAT?!
ばっ
WH-WHERE?!
A LONG TIME AGO...
...IN A FOREST A LONG WAYS AWAY...
Vague
ガックリ
OH. O-OKAY...
......

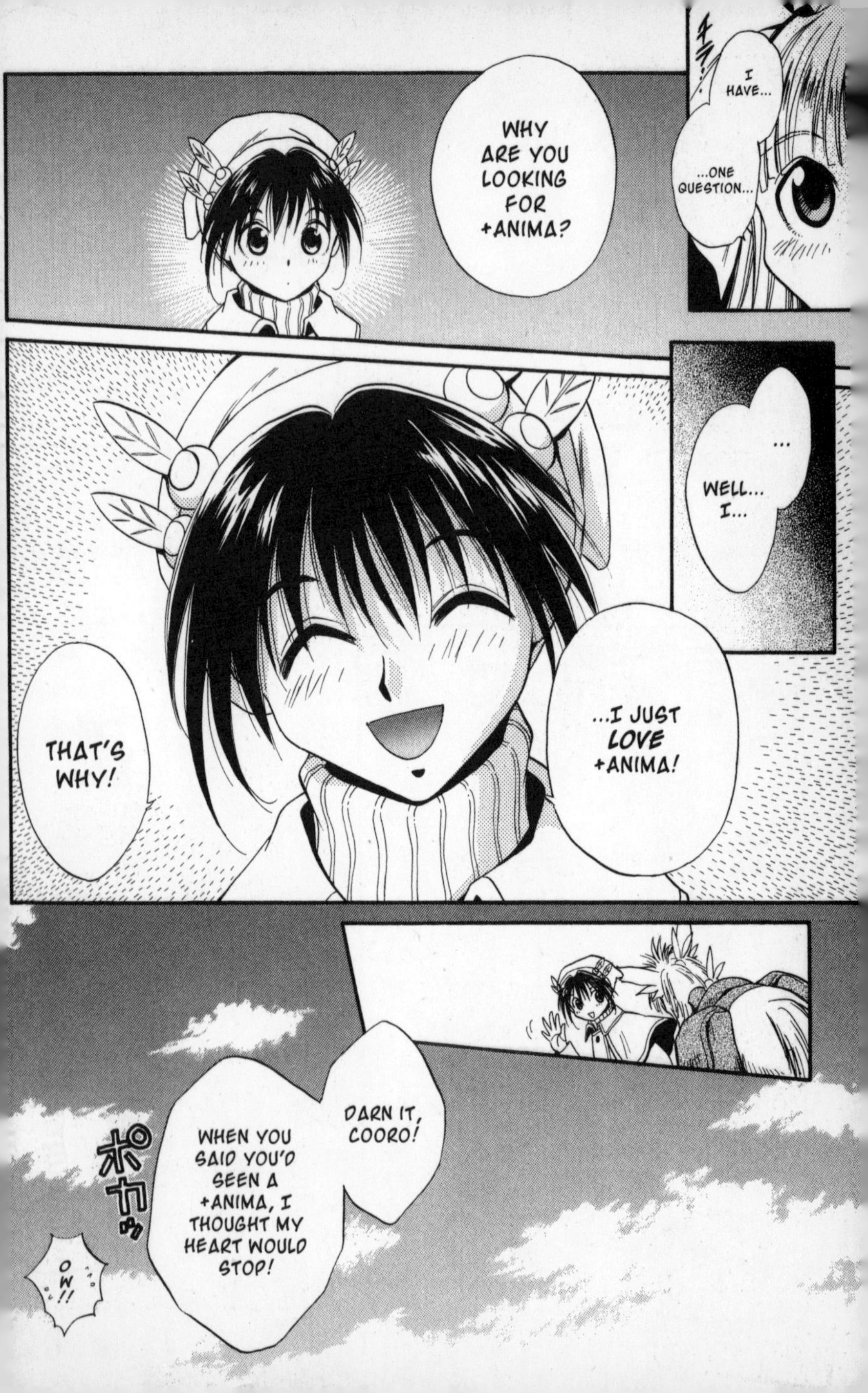
I HAVE...
...ONE QUESTION...
WHY ARE YOU LOOKING FOR +ANIMA?
...
WELL... I...
...I JUST *LOVE* +ANIMA!
THAT'S WHY!
DARN IT, COORO!
WHEN YOU SAID YOU'D SEEN A +ANIMA, I THOUGHT MY HEART WOULD STOP!
ポカッ
OW!!

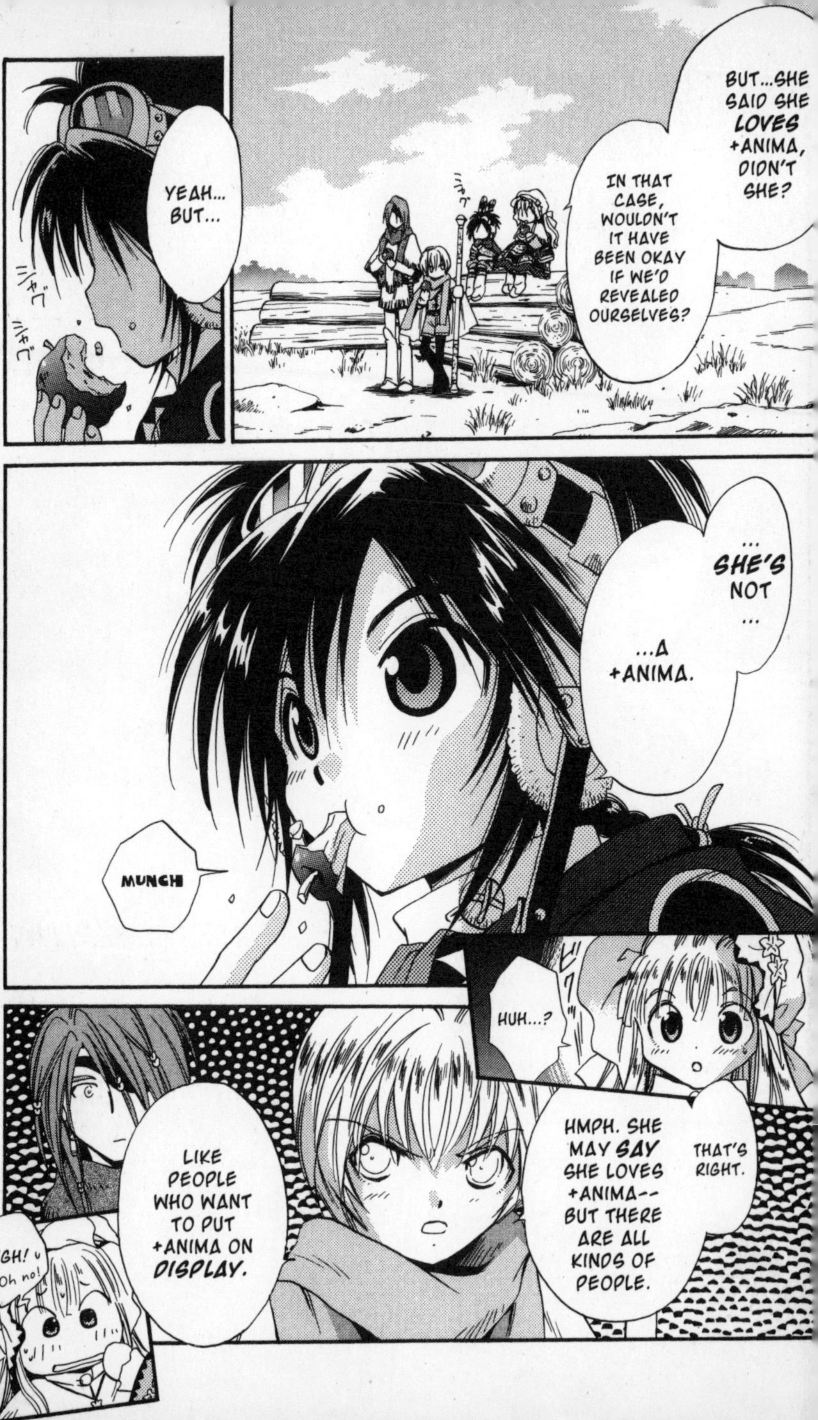
BUT...SHE SAID SHE *LOVES* +ANIMA, DIDN'T SHE?
IN THAT CASE, WOULDN'T IT HAVE BEEN OKAY IF WE'D REVEALED OURSELVES?
YEAH... BUT...
... *SHE'S* NOT ...
...A +ANIMA.
MUNCH
HUH...?
THAT'S RIGHT.
HMPH. SHE MAY *SAY* SHE LOVES +ANIMA-- BUT THERE ARE ALL KINDS OF PEOPLE.
LIKE PEOPLE WHO WANT TO PUT +ANIMA ON *DISPLAY*.
UGH! Oh no!

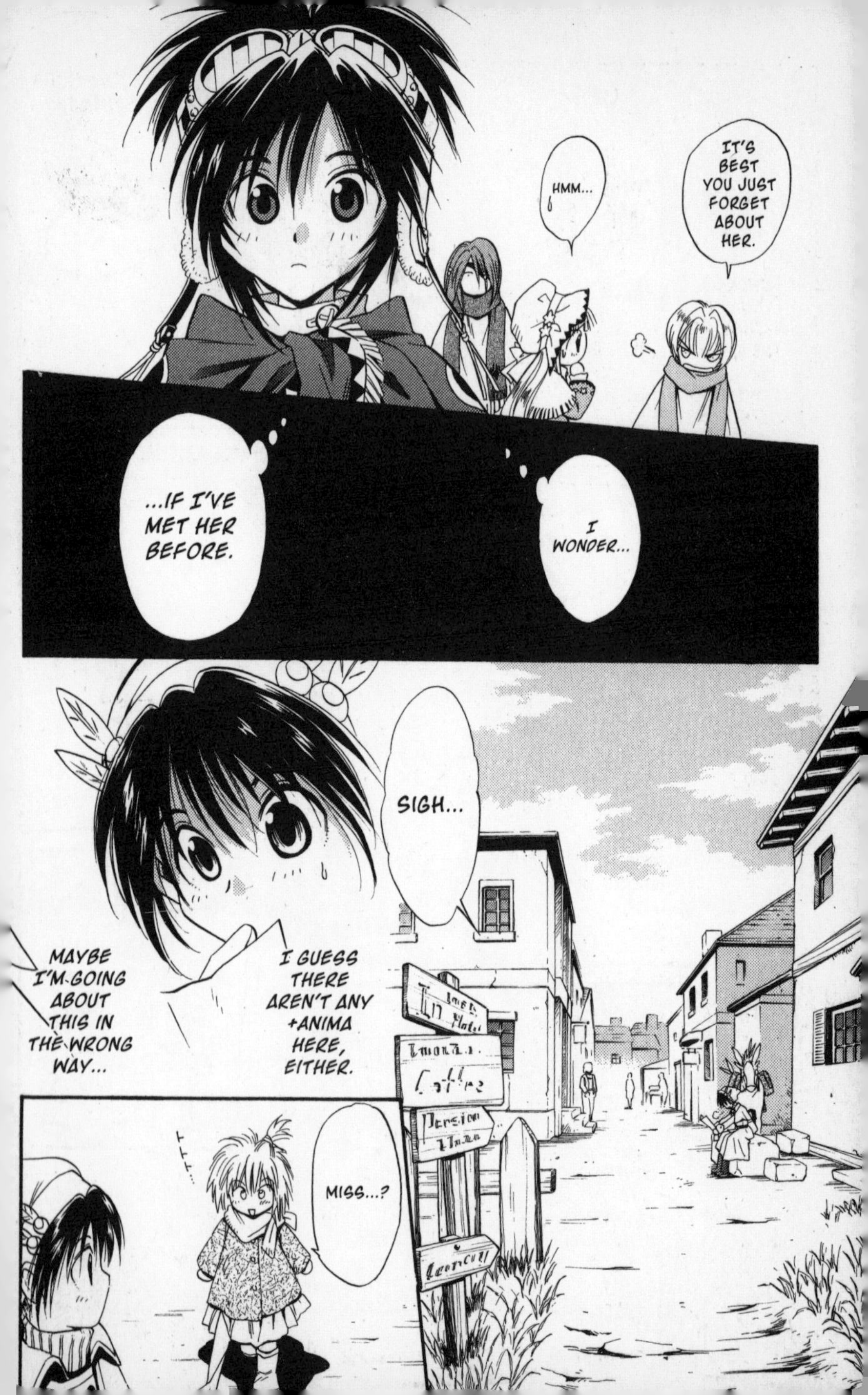
IT'S BEST YOU JUST FORGET ABOUT HER.
HMM...
I WONDER...
...IF I'VE MET HER BEFORE.
SIGH...
I GUESS THERE AREN'T ANY +ANIMA HERE, EITHER.
MAYBE I'M GOING ABOUT THIS IN THE WRONG WAY...
MISS...?

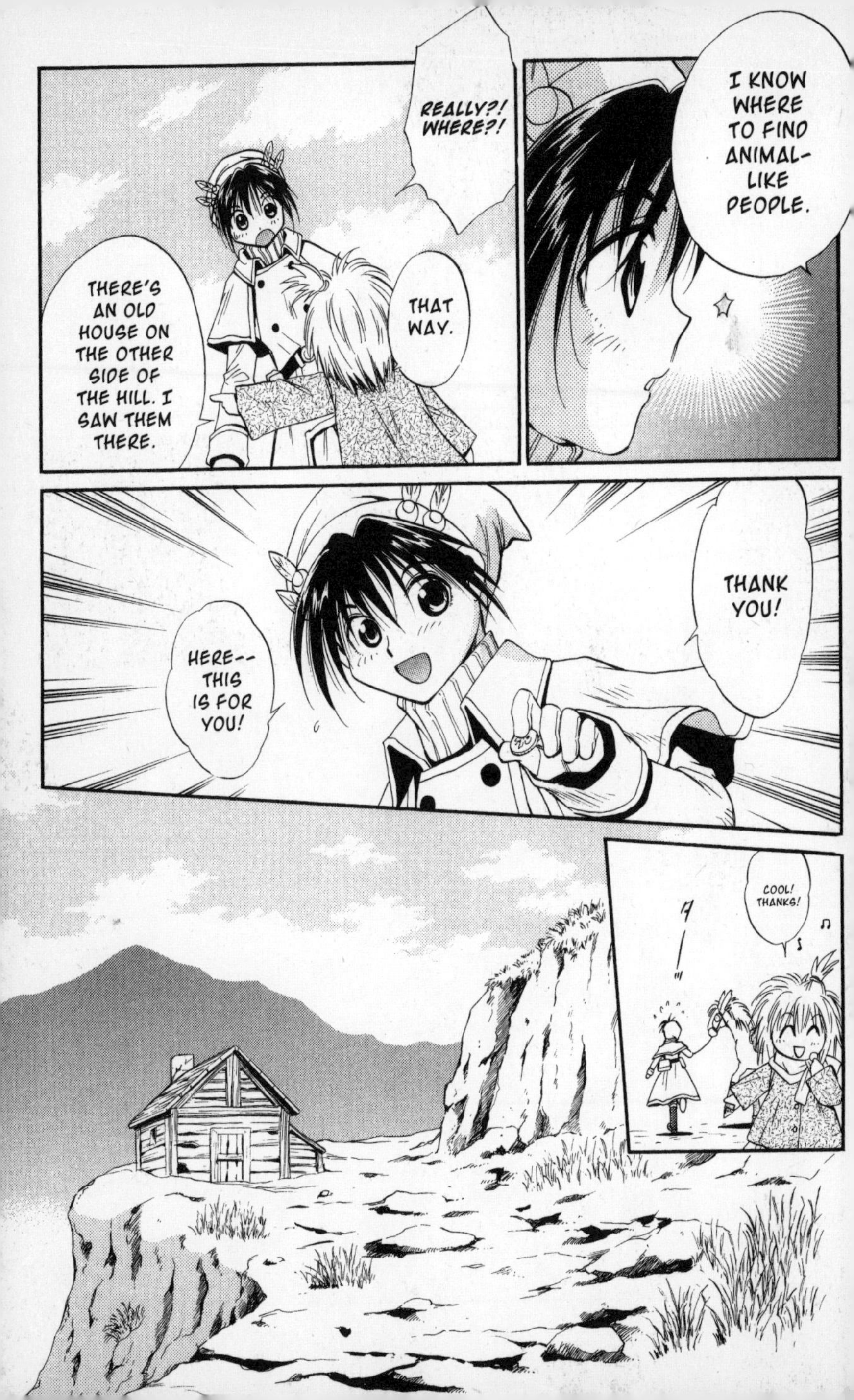
I KNOW WHERE TO FIND ANIMAL-LIKE PEOPLE.
REALLY?! WHERE?!
THAT WAY.
THERE'S AN OLD HOUSE ON THE OTHER SIDE OF THE HILL. I SAW THEM THERE.
THANK YOU!
HERE--THIS IS FOR YOU!
COOL! THANKS!

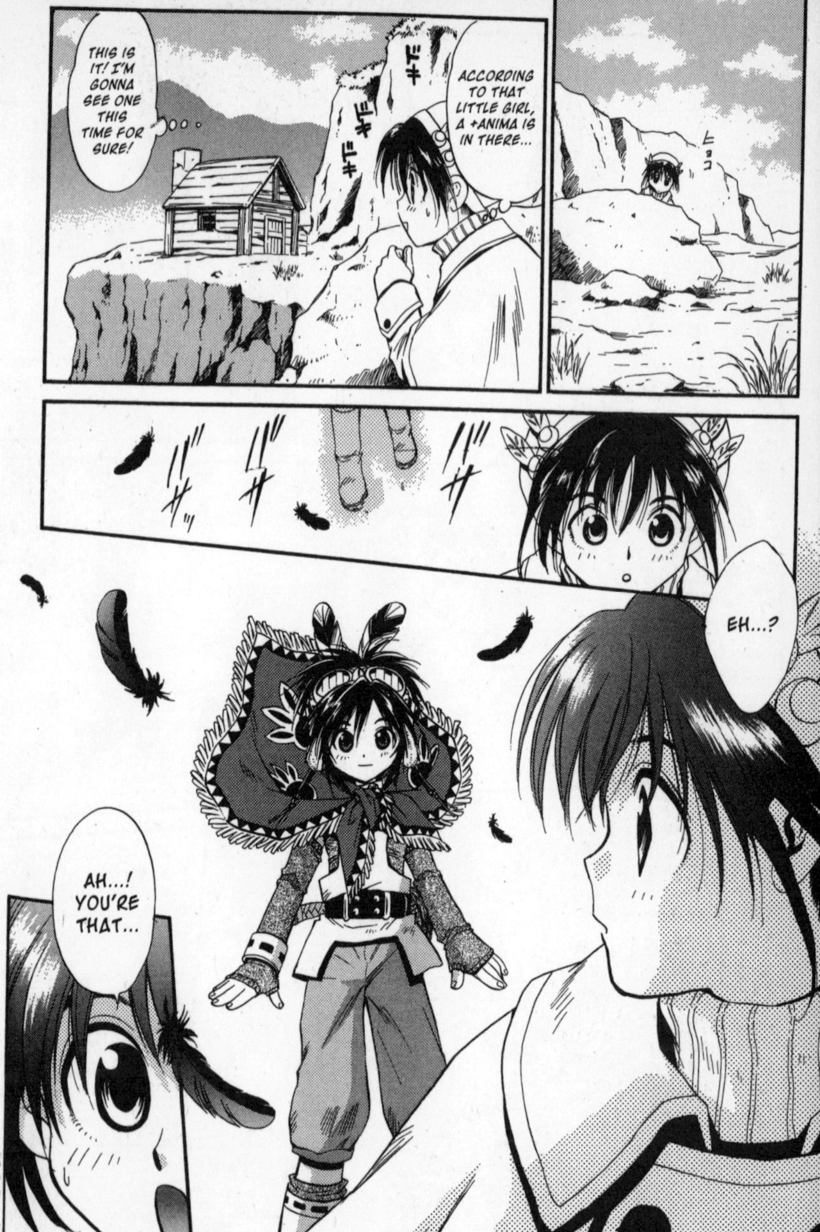
ヒョコ
ACCORDING TO THAT LITTLE GIRL, A +ANIMA IS IN THERE...
ドキ
ドキ
ドキ
THIS IS IT! I'M GONNA SEE ONE THIS TIME FOR SURE!
ザ
ザ
ザッ
EH...?
AH...! YOU'RE THAT...

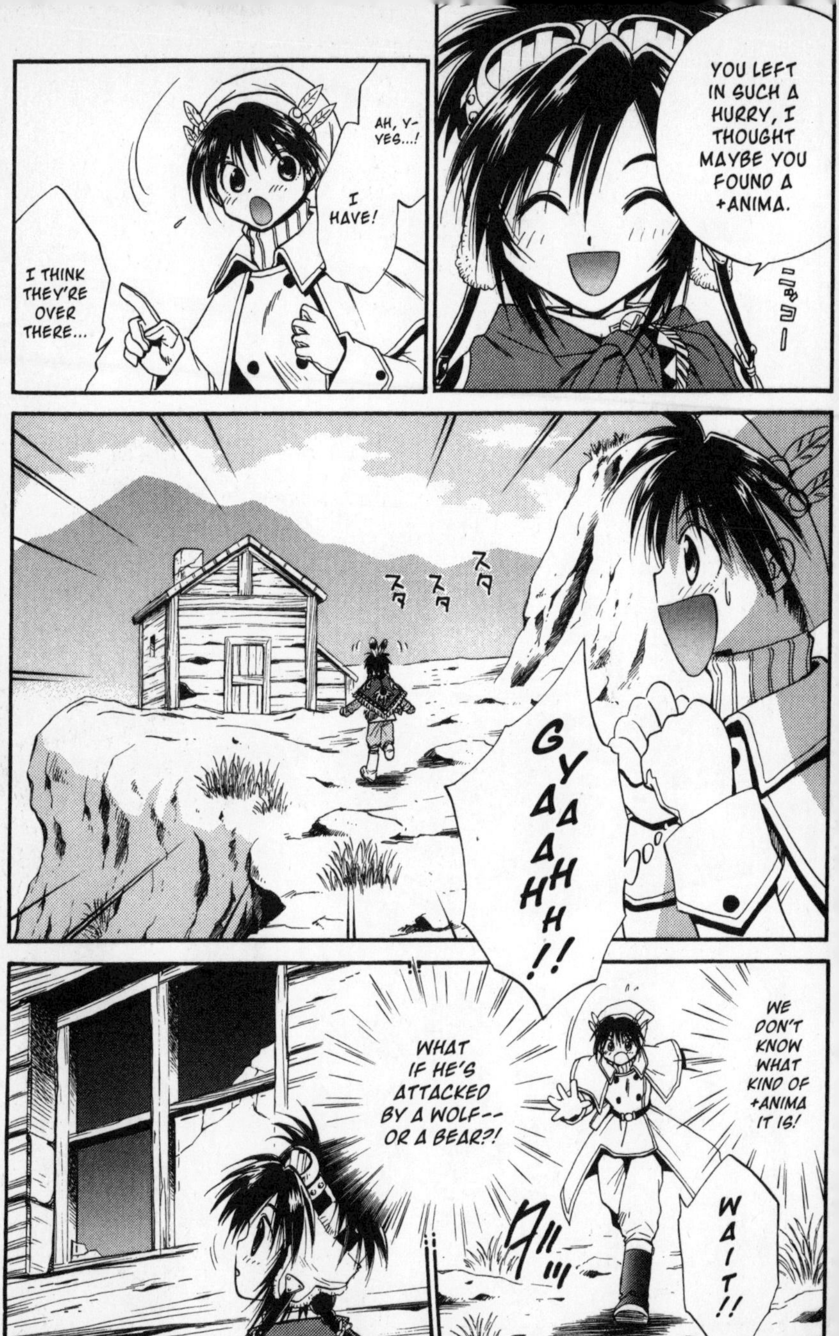
YOU LEFT IN SUCH A HURRY, I THOUGHT MAYBE YOU FOUND A +ANIMA.
AH, Y-YES...!
I HAVE!
I THINK THEY'RE OVER THERE...
GYAAAHHH!!
スタ スタ スタ
WE DON'T KNOW WHAT KIND OF +ANIMA IT IS!
WHAT IF HE'S ATTACKED BY A WOLF-- OR A BEAR?!
WAIT!!

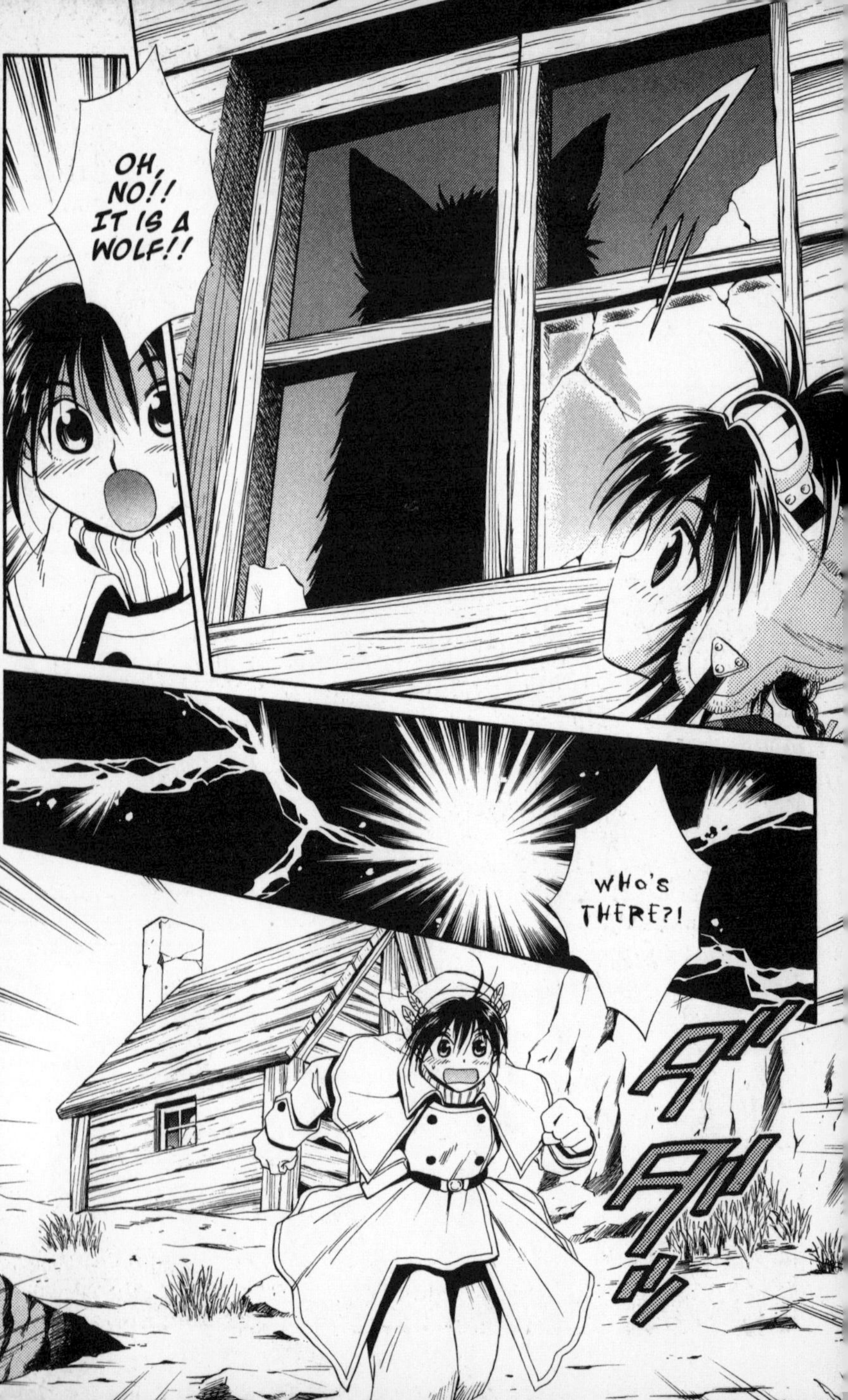
OH, NO!! IT IS A WOLF!!
WHO'S THERE?!
ダダダッ

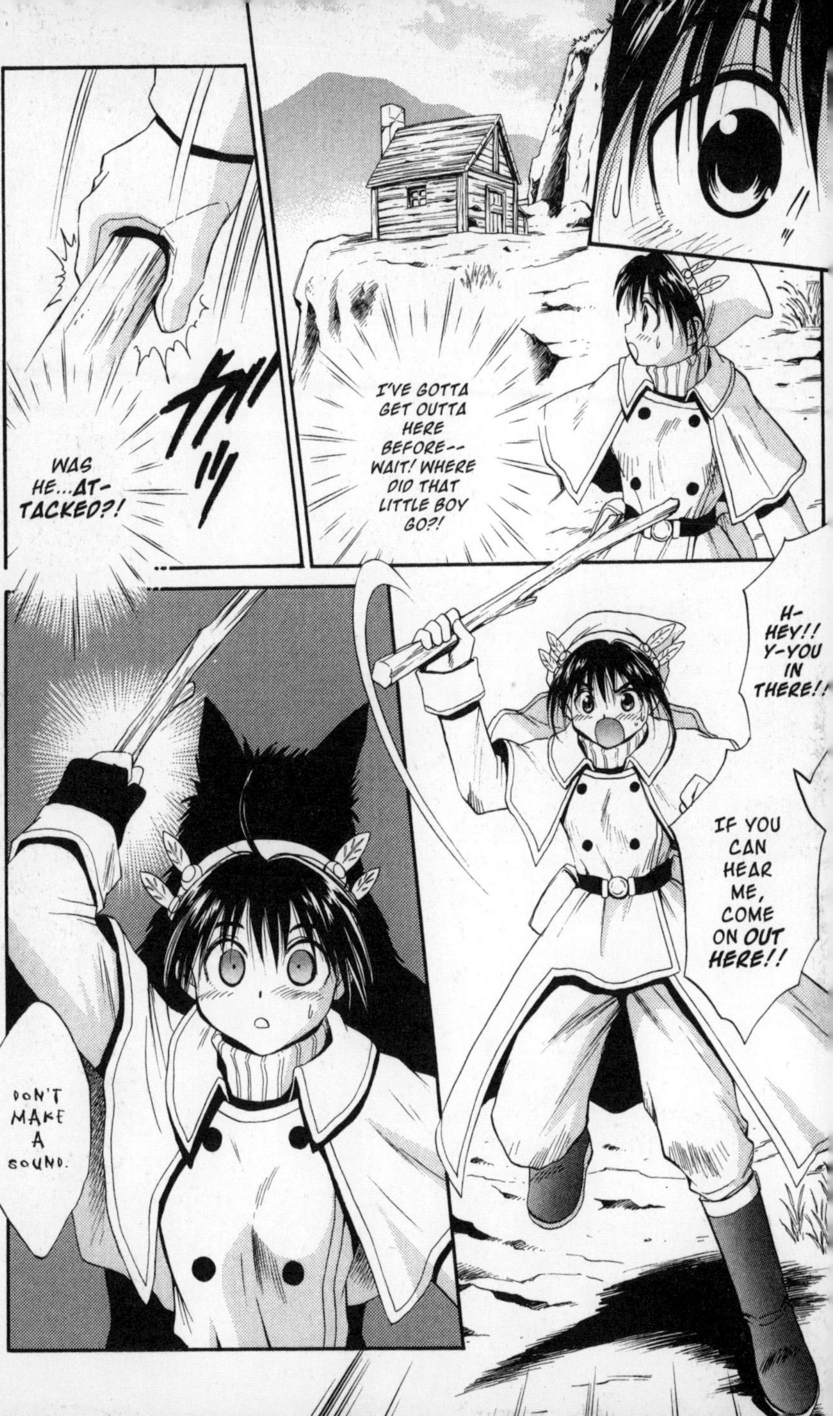
I'VE GOTTA GET OUTTA HERE BEFORE--WAIT! WHERE DID THAT LITTLE BOY GO?!
WAS HE...AT-TACKED?!
H-HEY!! Y-YOU IN THERE!!
IF YOU CAN HEAR ME, COME ON OUT HERE!!
DON'T MAKE A SOUND.

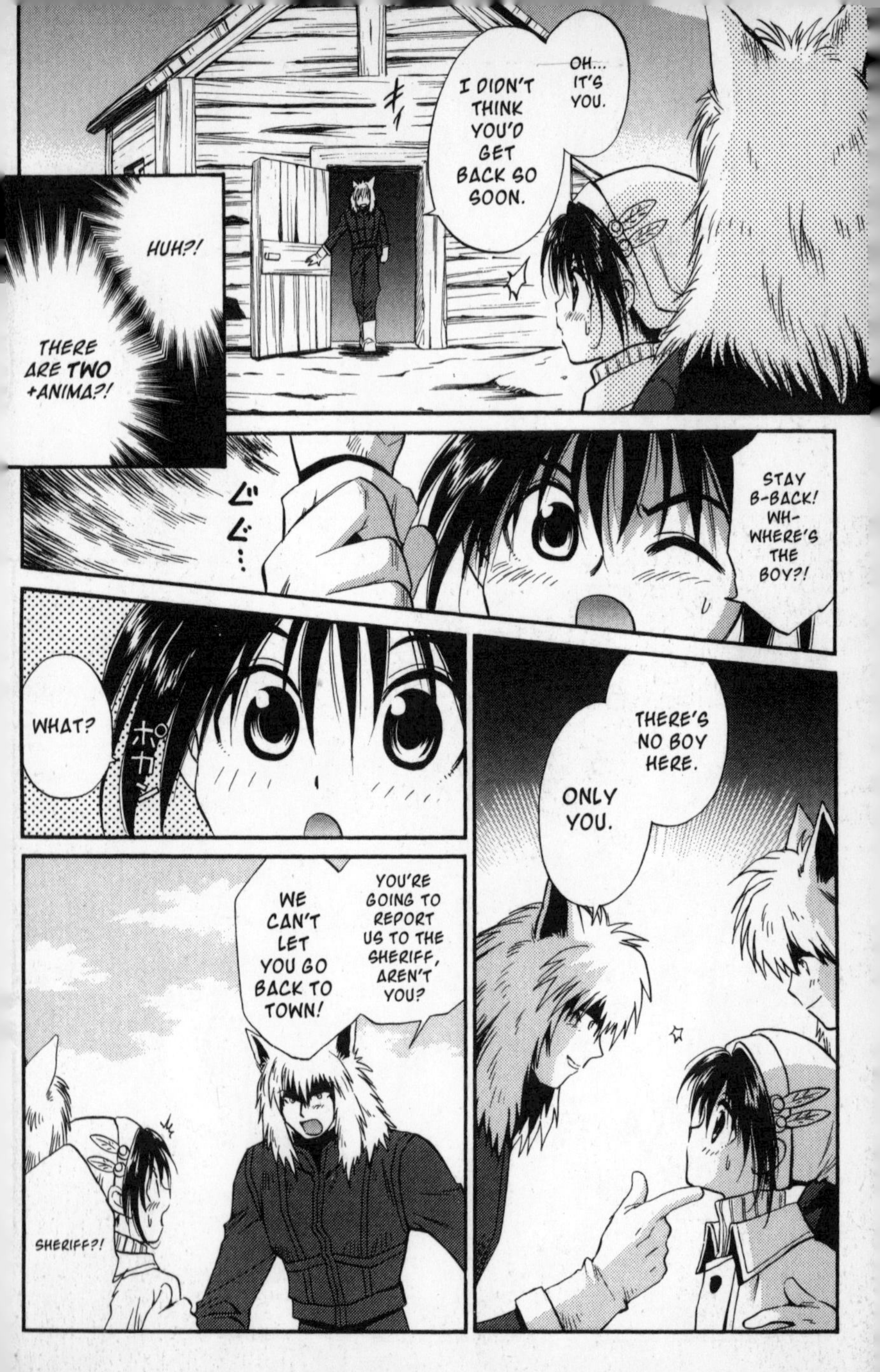
OH... IT'S YOU.
I DIDN'T THINK YOU'D GET BACK SO SOON.
キィ
HUH?!
THERE ARE TWO +ANIMA?!
STAY B-BACK! WH-WHERE'S THE BOY?!
ムグ…
THERE'S NO BOY HERE.
ONLY YOU.
WHAT?
ポカン
YOU'RE GOING TO REPORT US TO THE SHERIFF, AREN'T YOU?
WE CAN'T LET YOU GO BACK TO TOWN!
SHERIFF?!

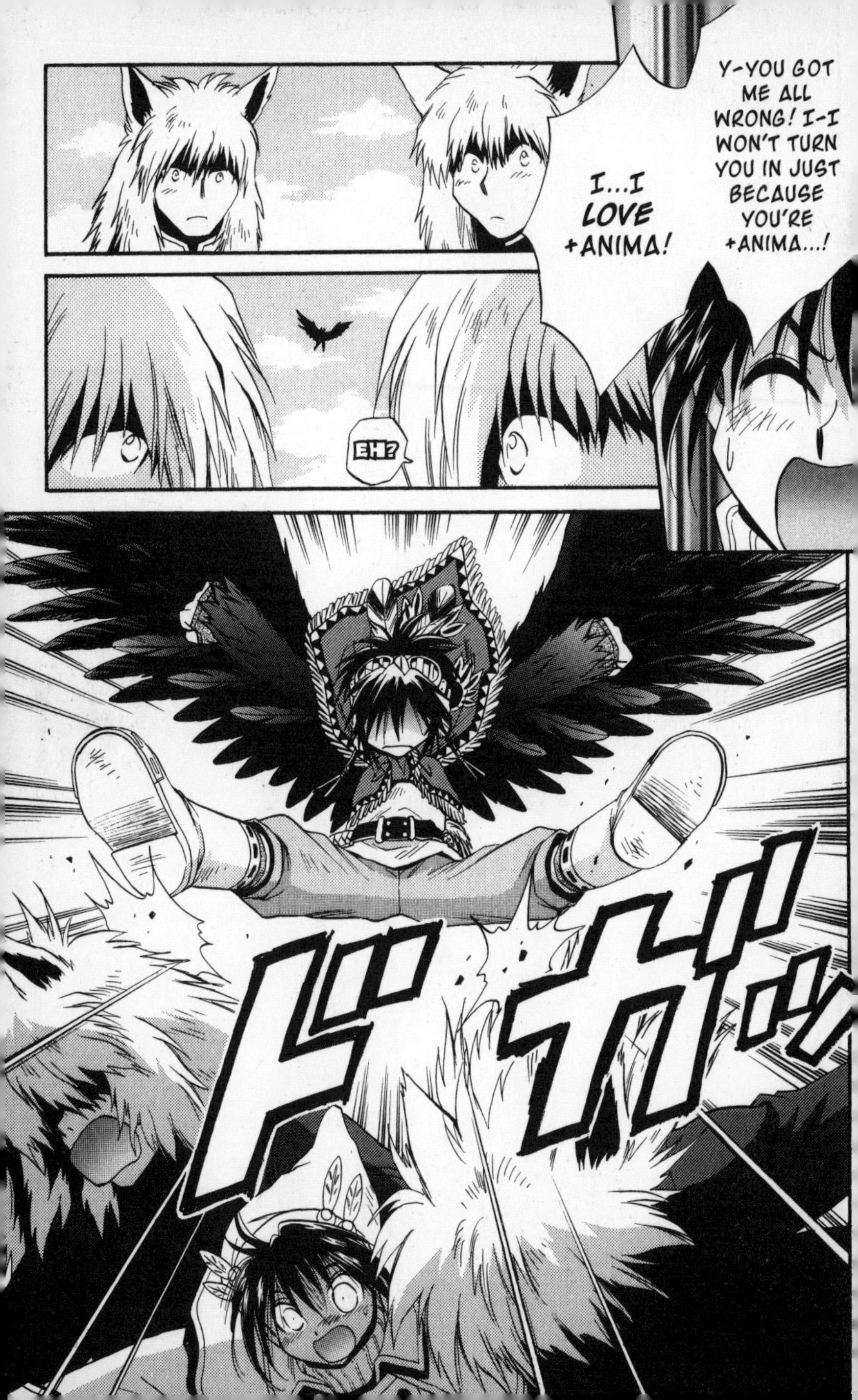
Y-YOU GOT ME ALL WRONG! I-I WON'T TURN YOU IN JUST BECAUSE YOU'RE +ANIMA...!
I...I LOVE +ANIMA!
EH?
ドカッ

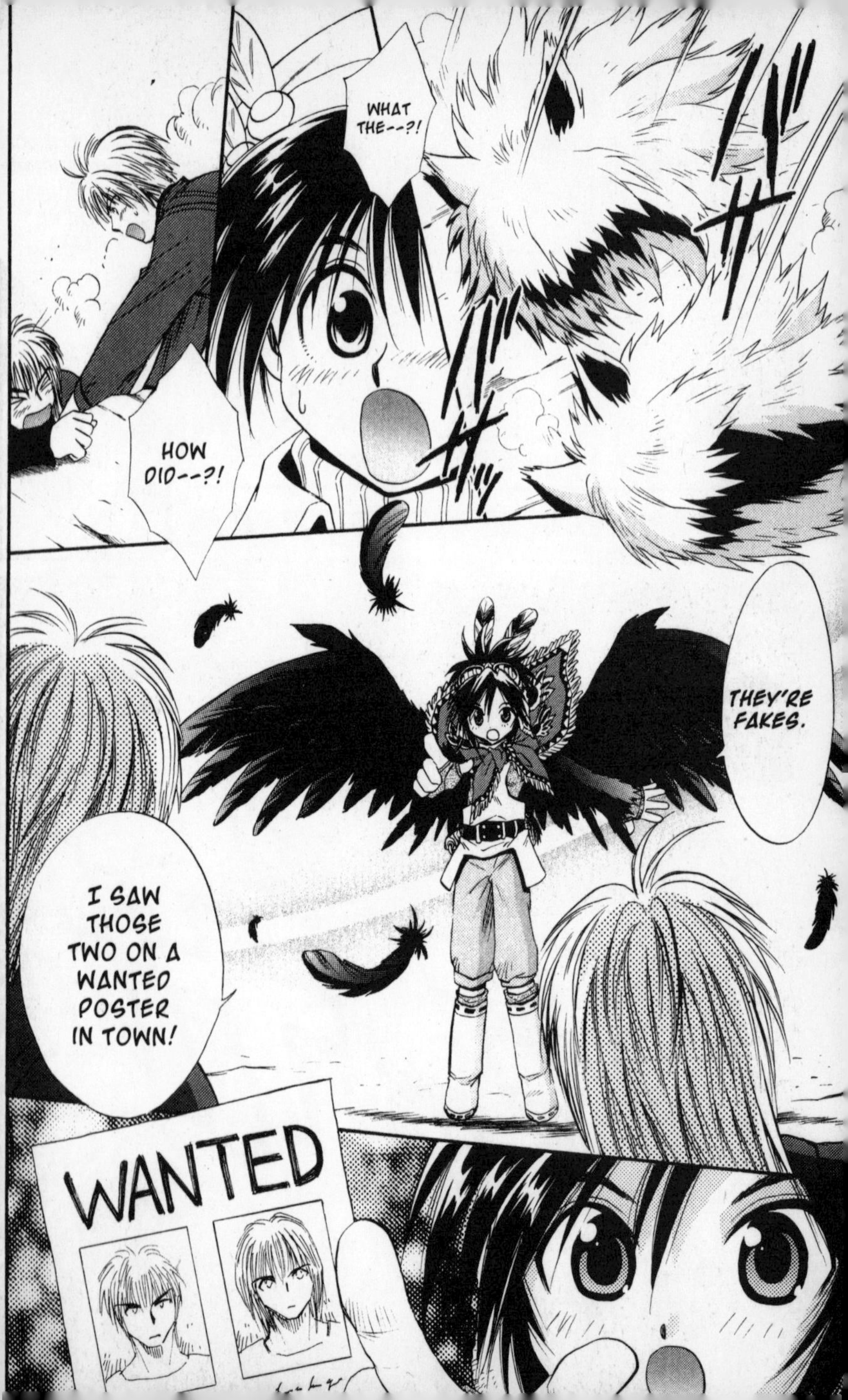
WHAT THE--?!
HOW DID--?!
THEY'RE FAKES.
I SAW THOSE TWO ON A WANTED POSTER IN TOWN!
WANTED

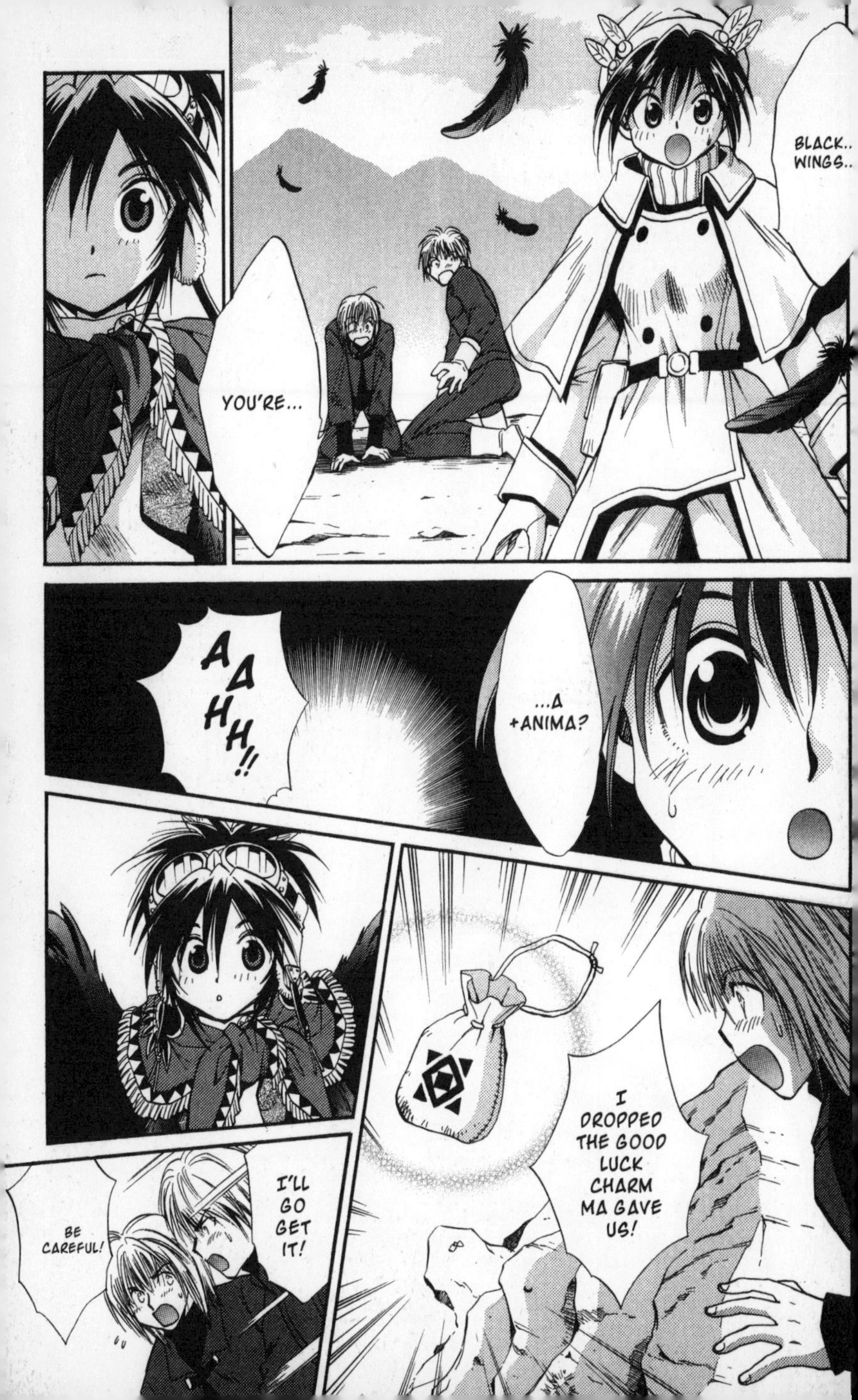
BLACK.. WINGS..
YOU'RE...
...A +ANIMA?
AAHH!!
I DROPPED THE GOOD LUCK CHARM MA GAVE US!
I'LL GO GET IT!
BE CAREFUL!

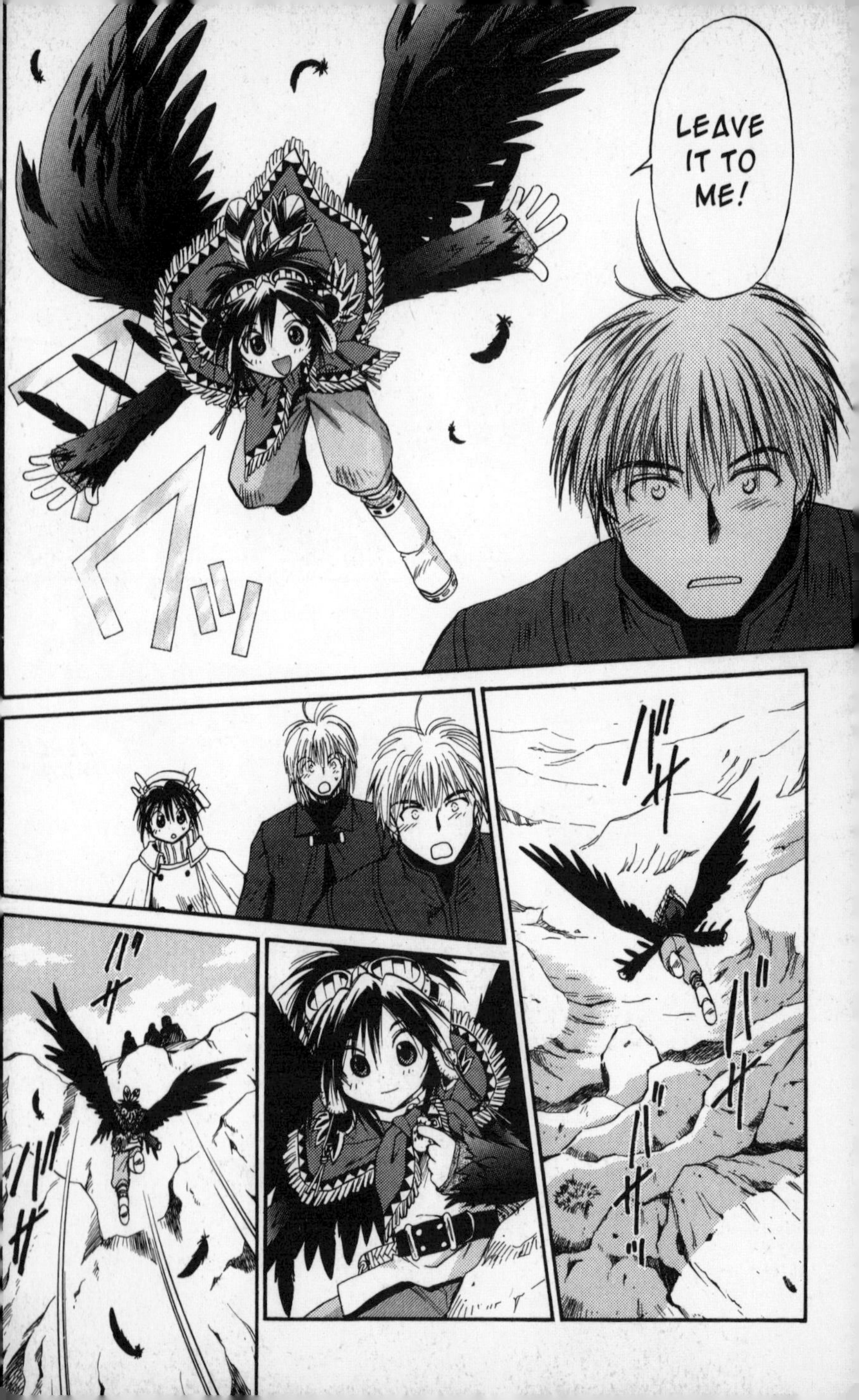
LEAVE IT TO ME!

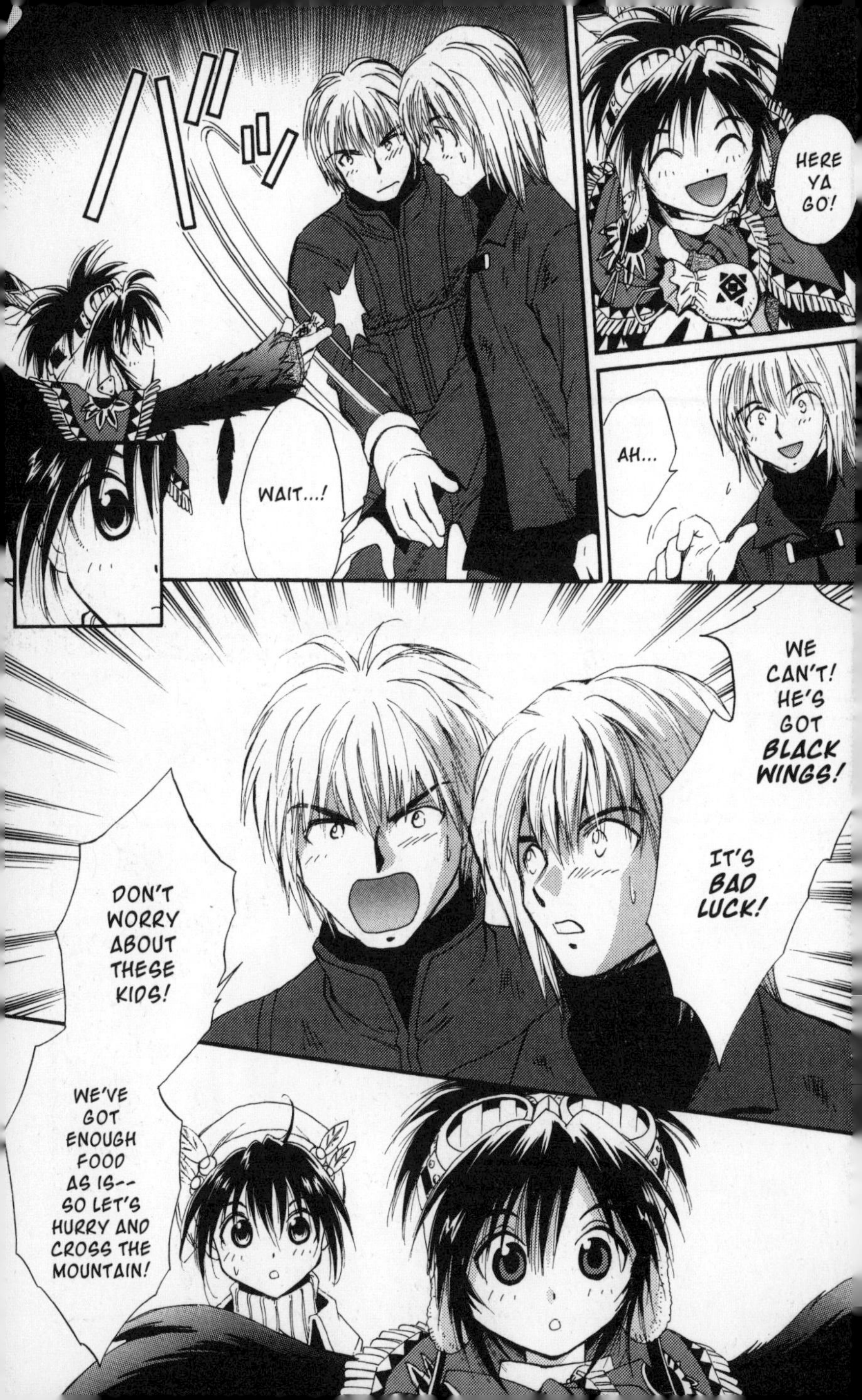
HERE YA GO!
AH...
WAIT...!
WE CAN'T! HE'S GOT BLACK WINGS!
IT'S BAD LUCK!
DON'T WORRY ABOUT THESE KIDS!
WE'VE GOT ENOUGH FOOD AS IS-- SO LET'S HURRY AND CROSS THE MOUNTAIN!

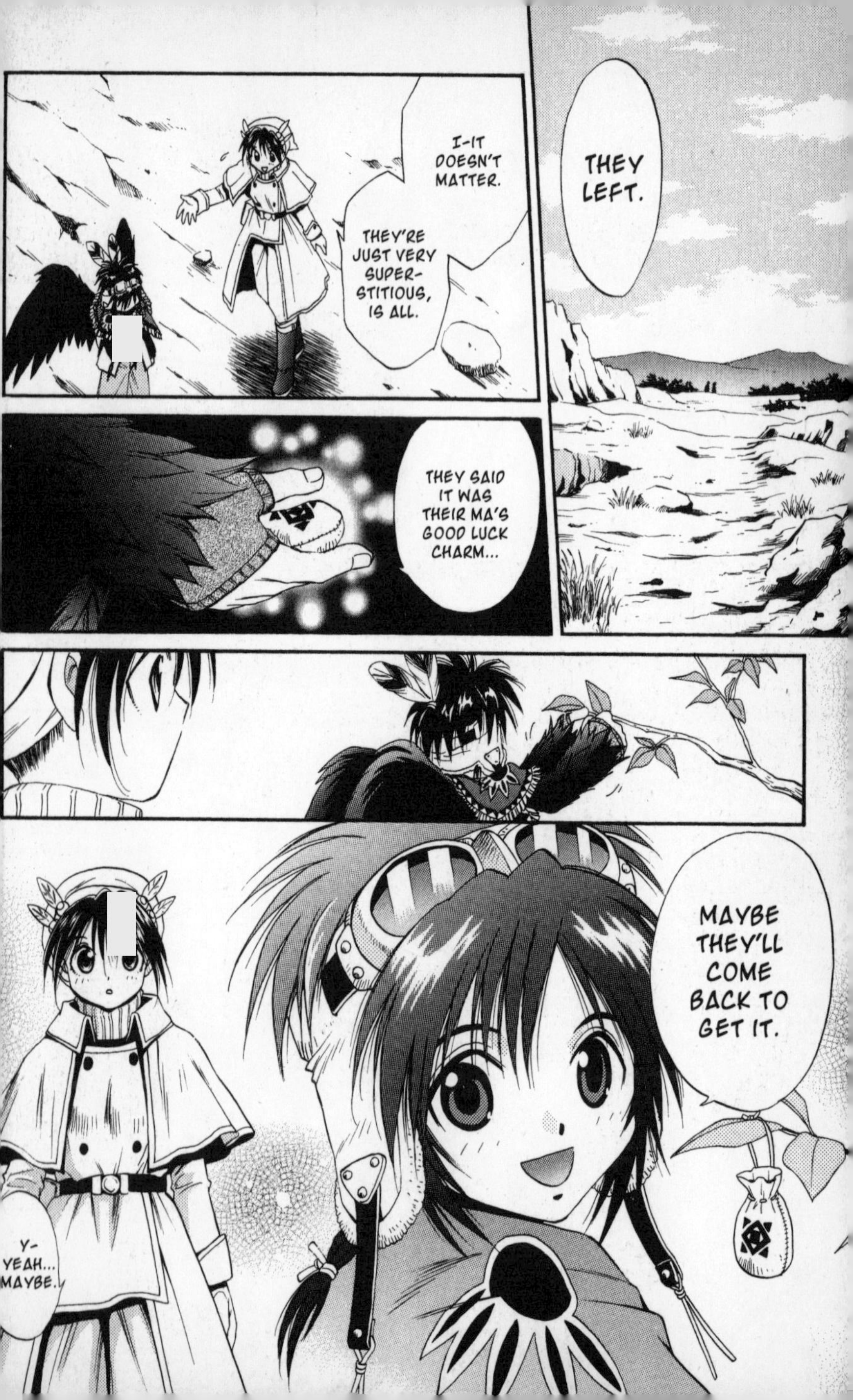
THEY LEFT.
I-IT DOESN'T MATTER.
THEY'RE JUST VERY SUPER-STITIOUS, IS ALL.
THEY SAID IT WAS THEIR MA'S GOOD LUCK CHARM...
MAYBE THEY'LL COME BACK TO GET IT.
Y-YEAH... MAYBE.

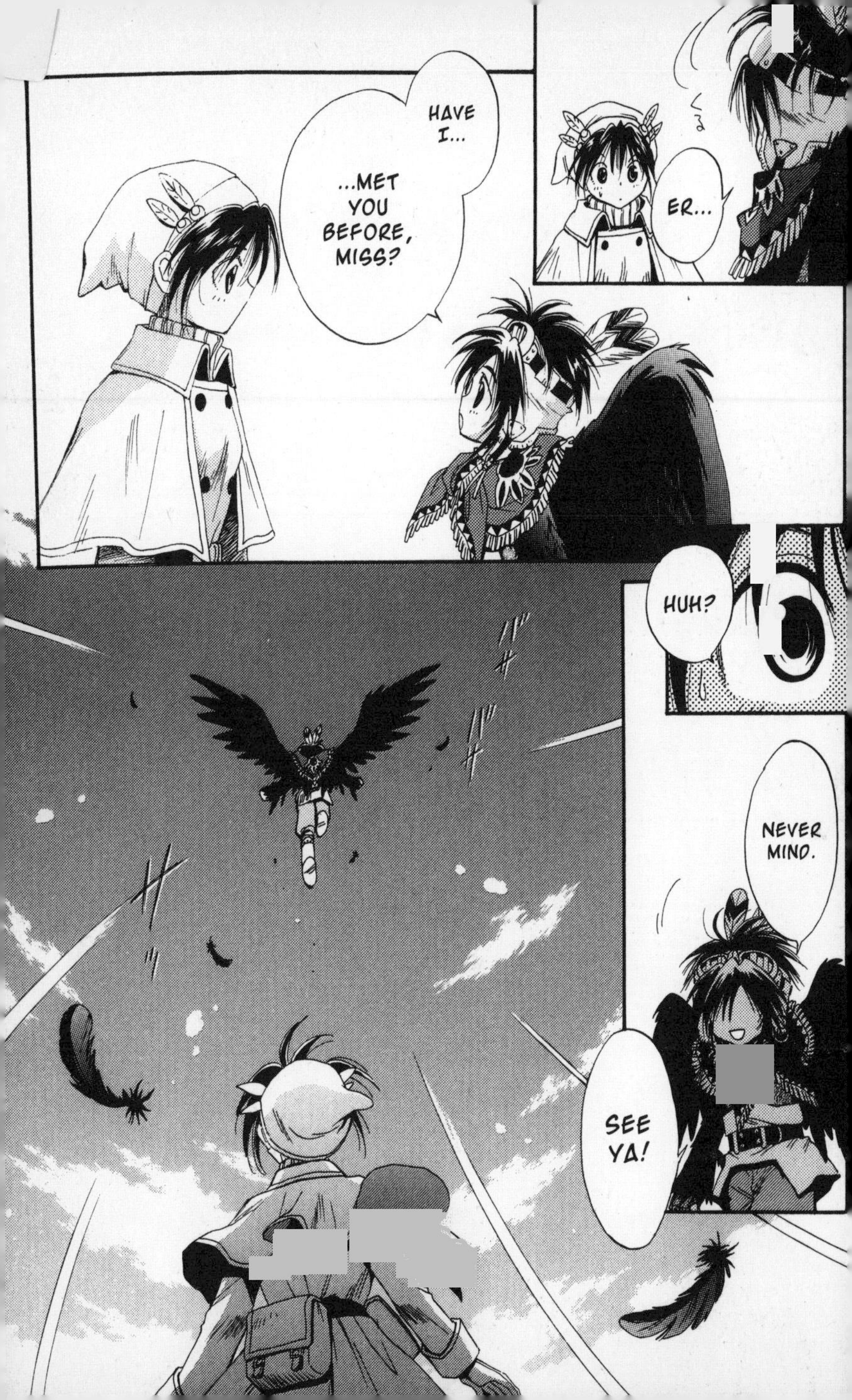
くる
ER...
HAVE I...
...MET YOU BEFORE, MISS?
HUH?
NEVER MIND.
SEE YA!

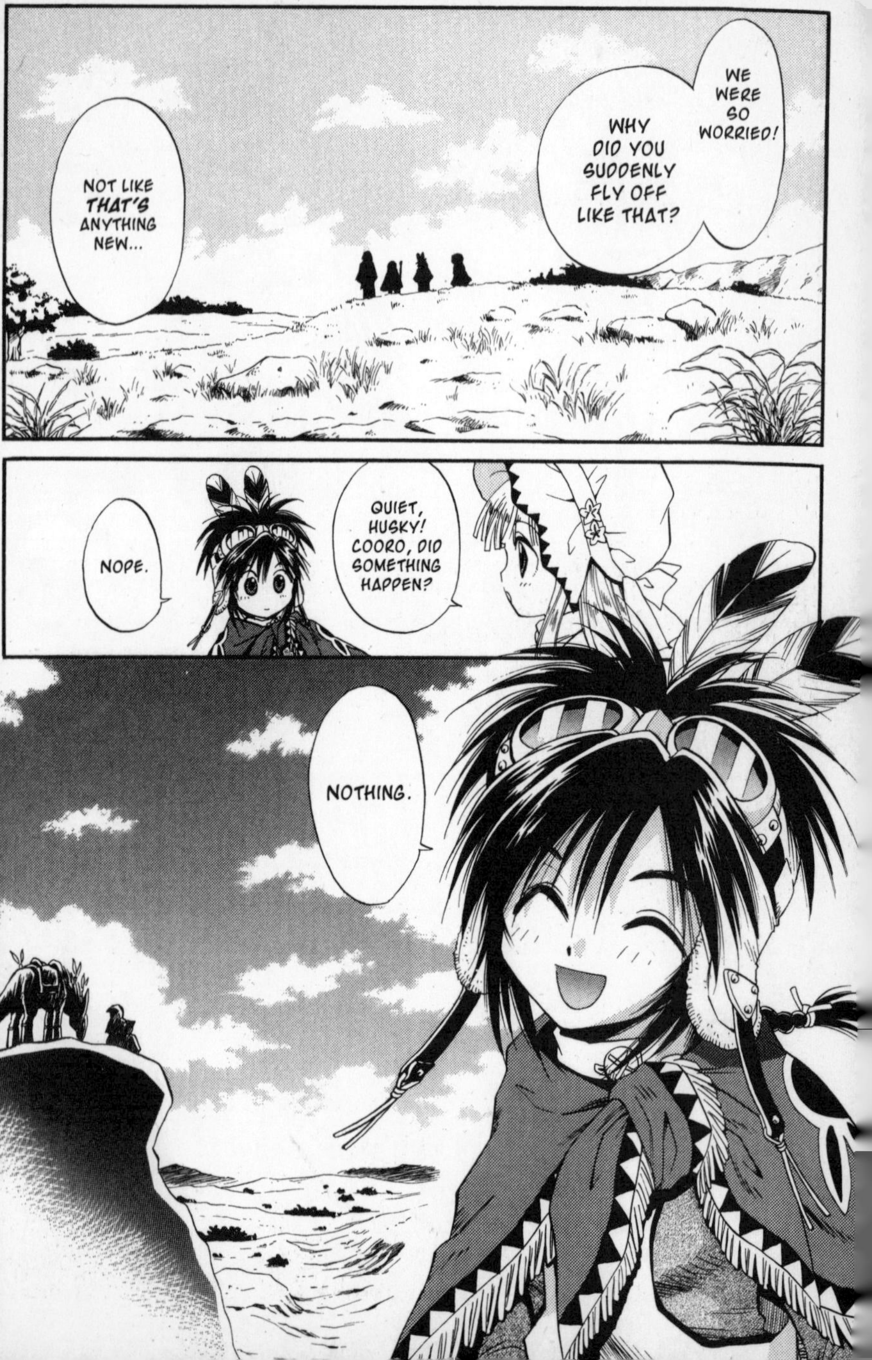
WE WERE SO WORRIED!
WHY DID YOU SUDDENLY FLY OFF LIKE THAT?
NOT LIKE THAT'S ANYTHING NEW...
QUIET, HUSKY! COORO, DID SOMETHING HAPPEN?
NOPE.
NOTHING.

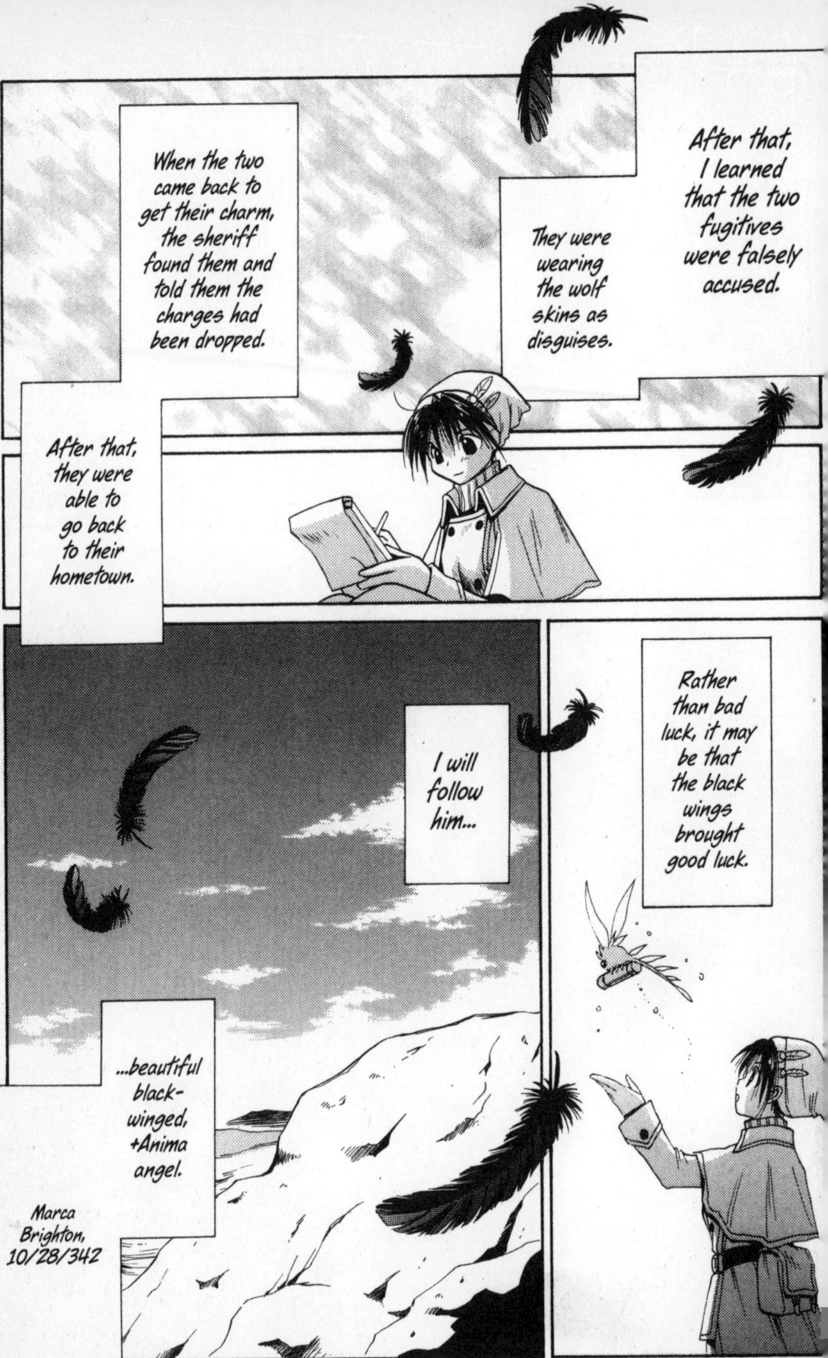
After that, I learned that the two fugitives were falsely accused.
They were wearing the wolf skins as disguises.
When the two came back to get their charm, the sheriff found them and told them the charges had been dropped.
After that, they were able to go back to their hometown.
Rather than bad luck, it may be that the black wings brought good luck.
I will follow him...
...beautiful black-winged, +Anima angel.
Marca Brighton, 10/28/342

Who is she?

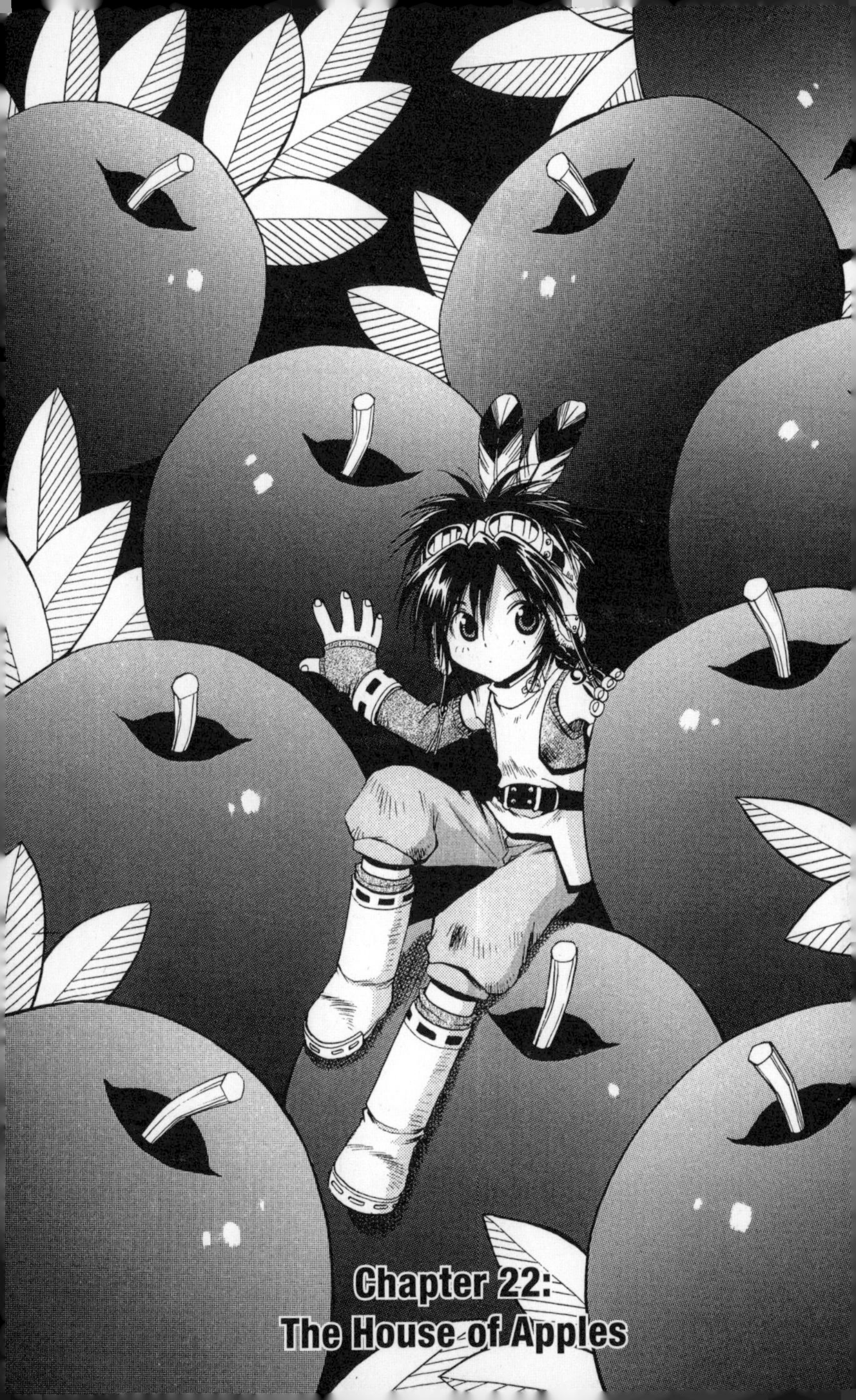

Chapter 22: The House of Apples

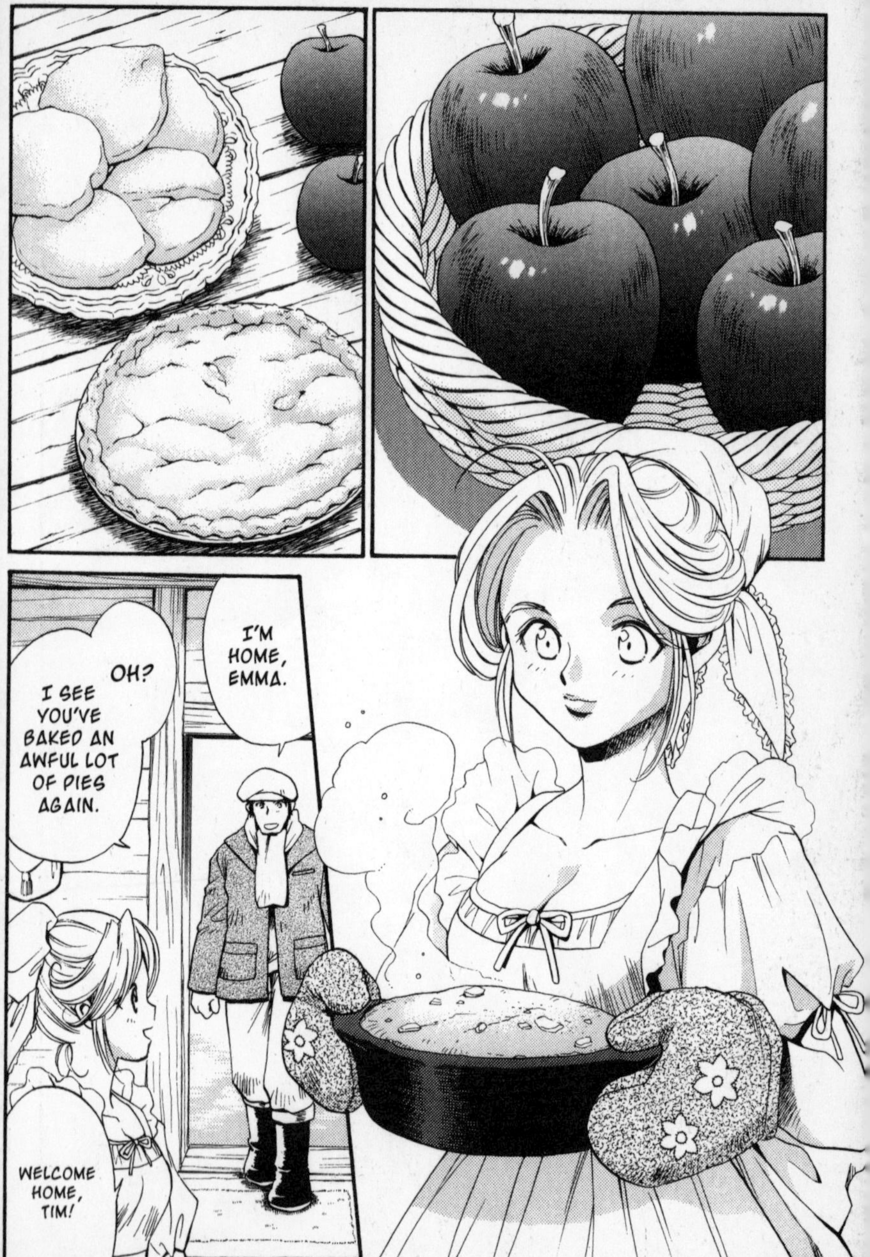
I'M HOME, EMMA.
OH? I SEE YOU'VE BAKED AN AWFUL LOT OF PIES AGAIN.
WELCOME HOME, TIM!

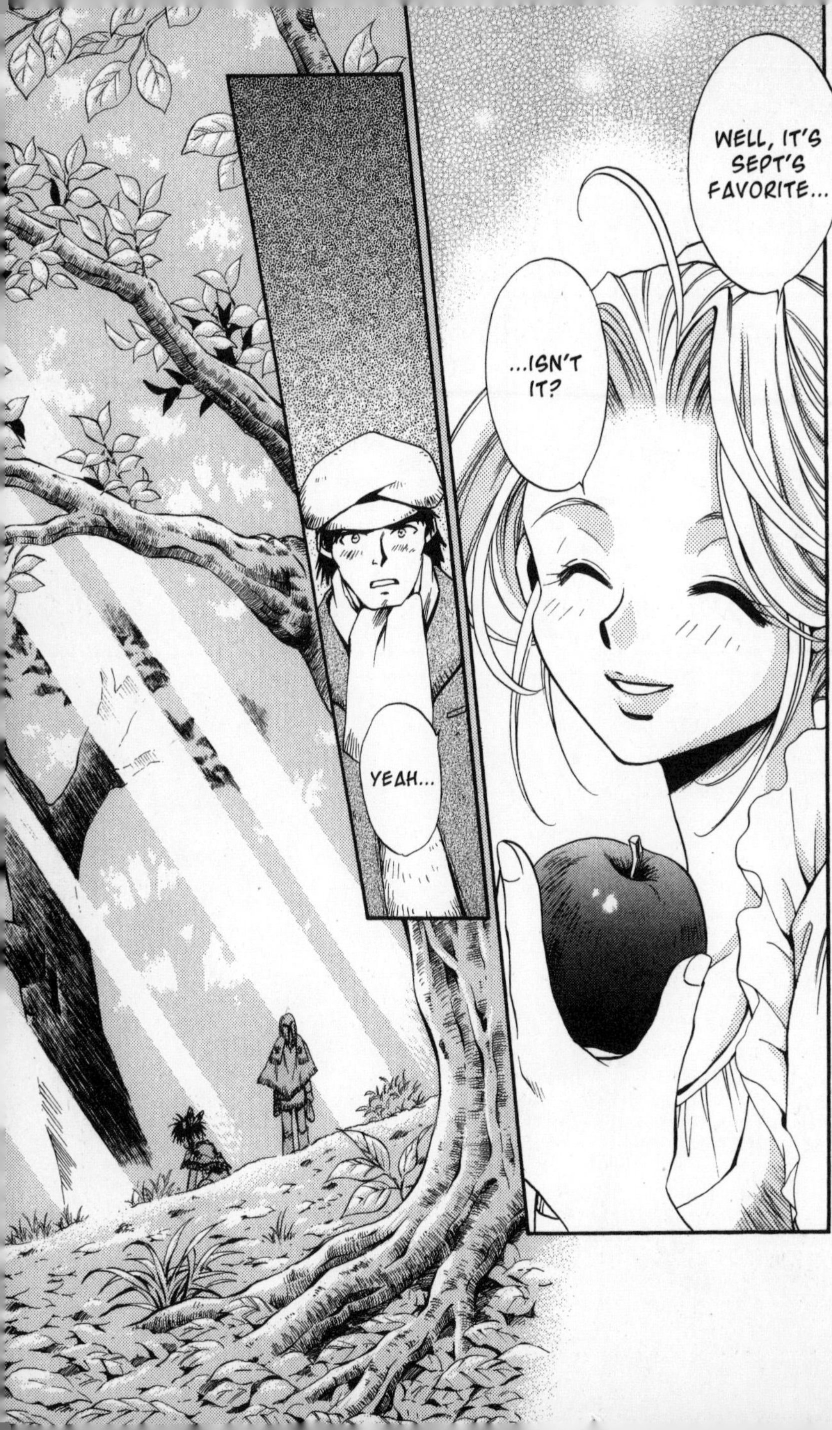
WELL, IT'S SEPT'S FAVORITE...
...ISN'T IT?
YEAH...

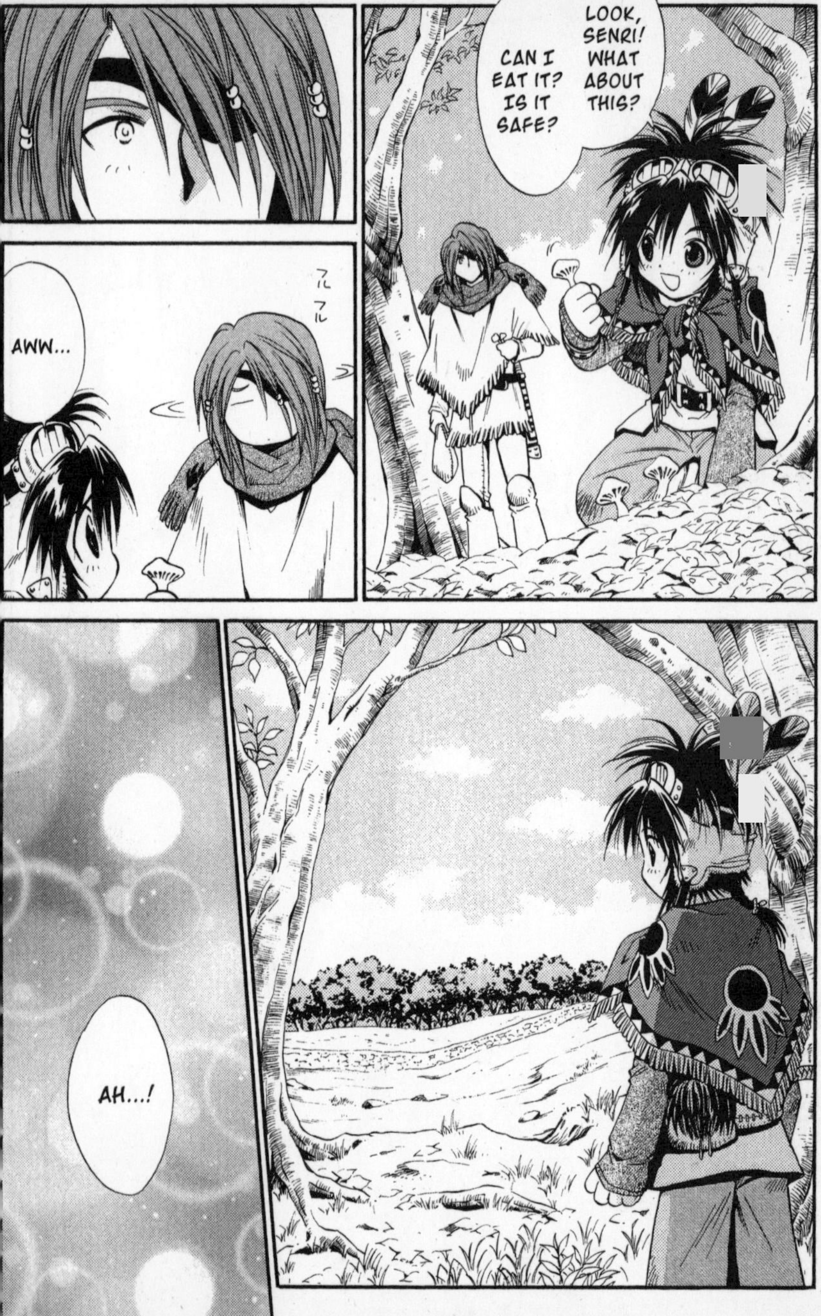
LOOK, SENRI! WHAT ABOUT THIS?
CAN I EAT IT? IS IT SAFE?
フル フル
AWW...
AH...!

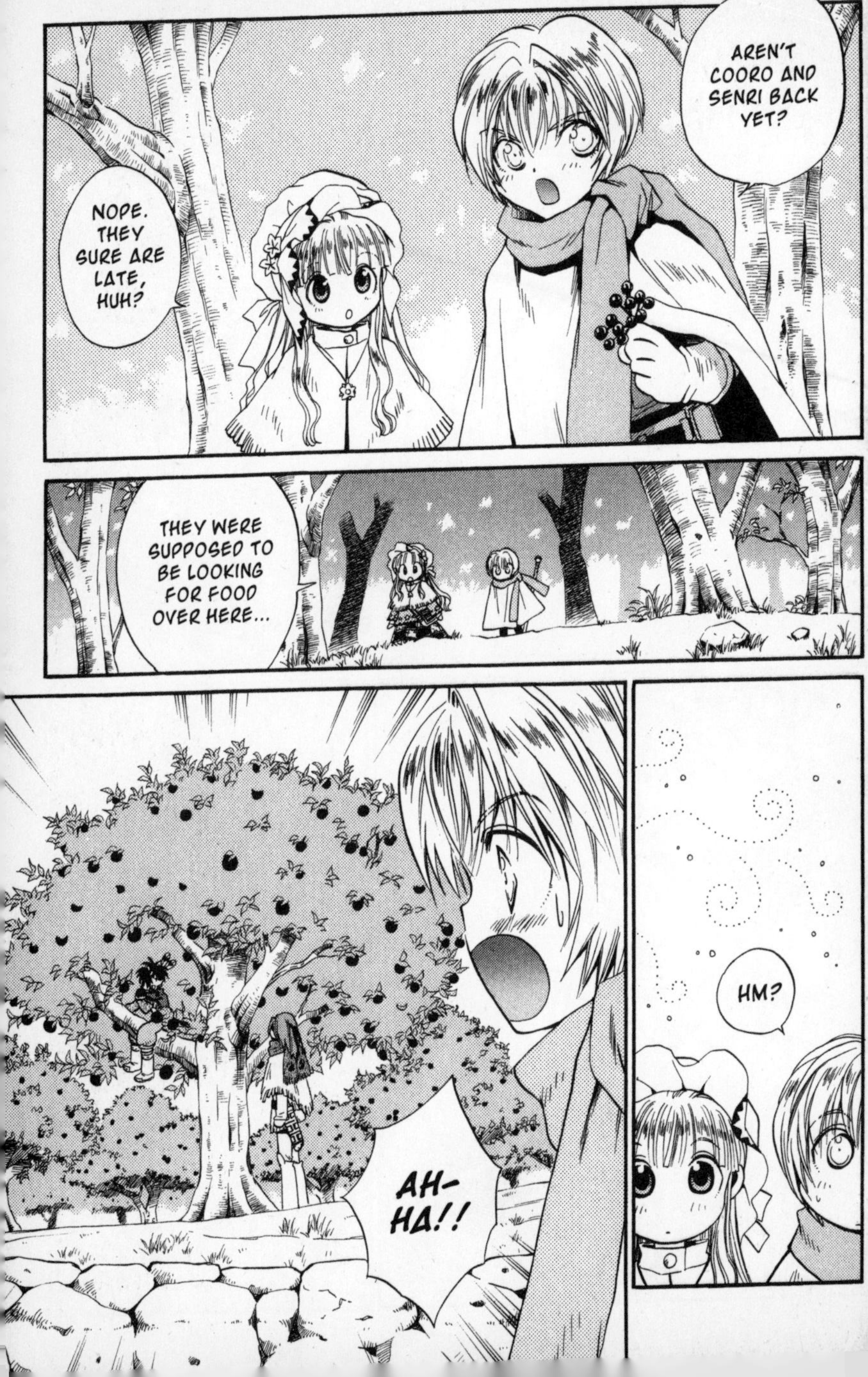
AREN'T COORO AND SENRI BACK YET?
NOPE. THEY SURE ARE LATE, HUH?
THEY WERE SUPPOSED TO BE LOOKING FOR FOOD OVER HERE...
HM?
AH-HA!!

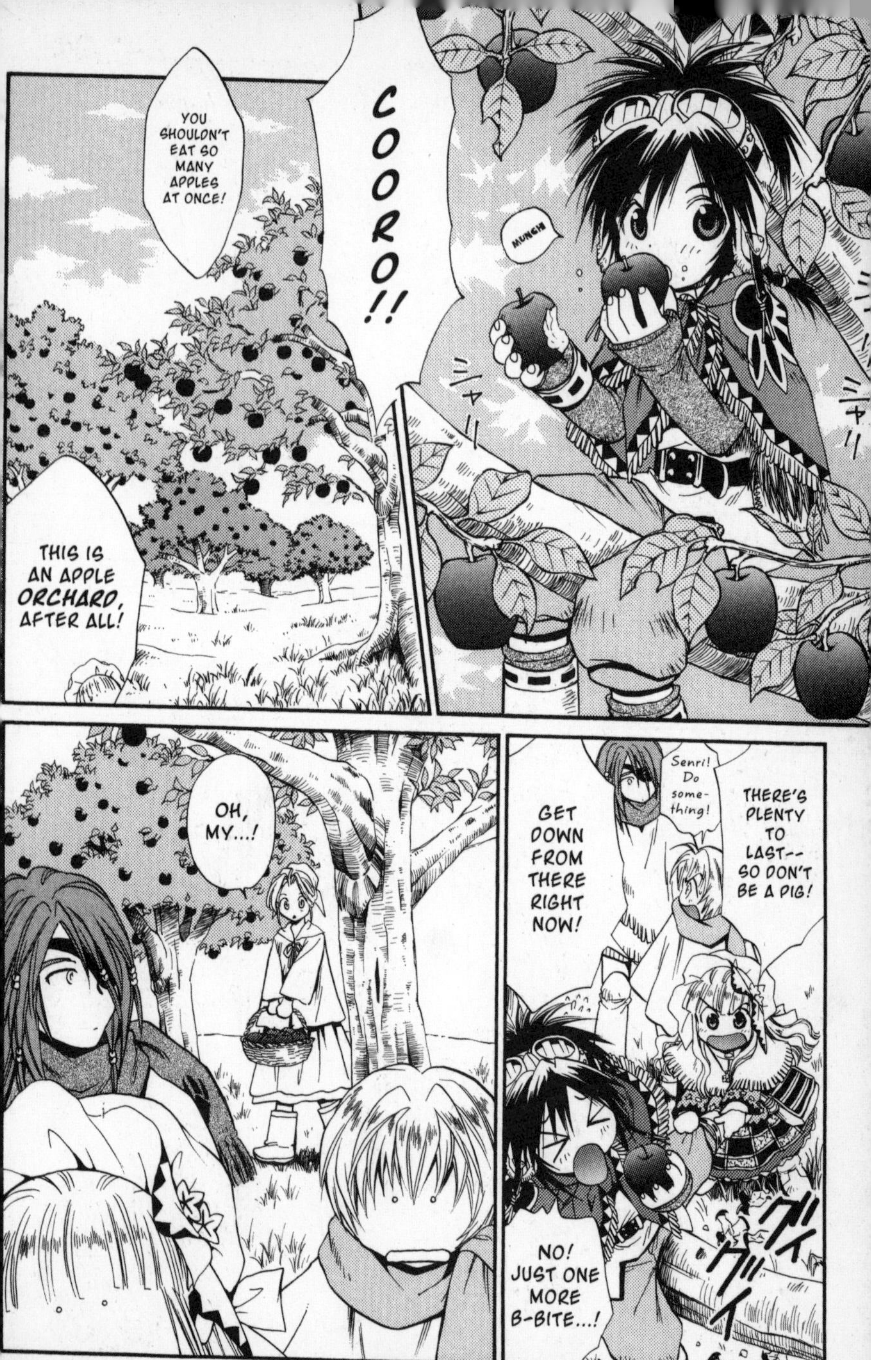
COOORO!!
MUNCH
YOU SHOULDN'T EAT SO MANY APPLES AT ONCE!
THIS IS AN APPLE ORCHARD, AFTER ALL!
THERE'S PLENTY TO LAST-- SO DON'T BE A PIG!
Senri! Do some-thing!
GET DOWN FROM THERE RIGHT NOW!
NO! JUST ONE MORE B-BITE...!
OH, MY...!

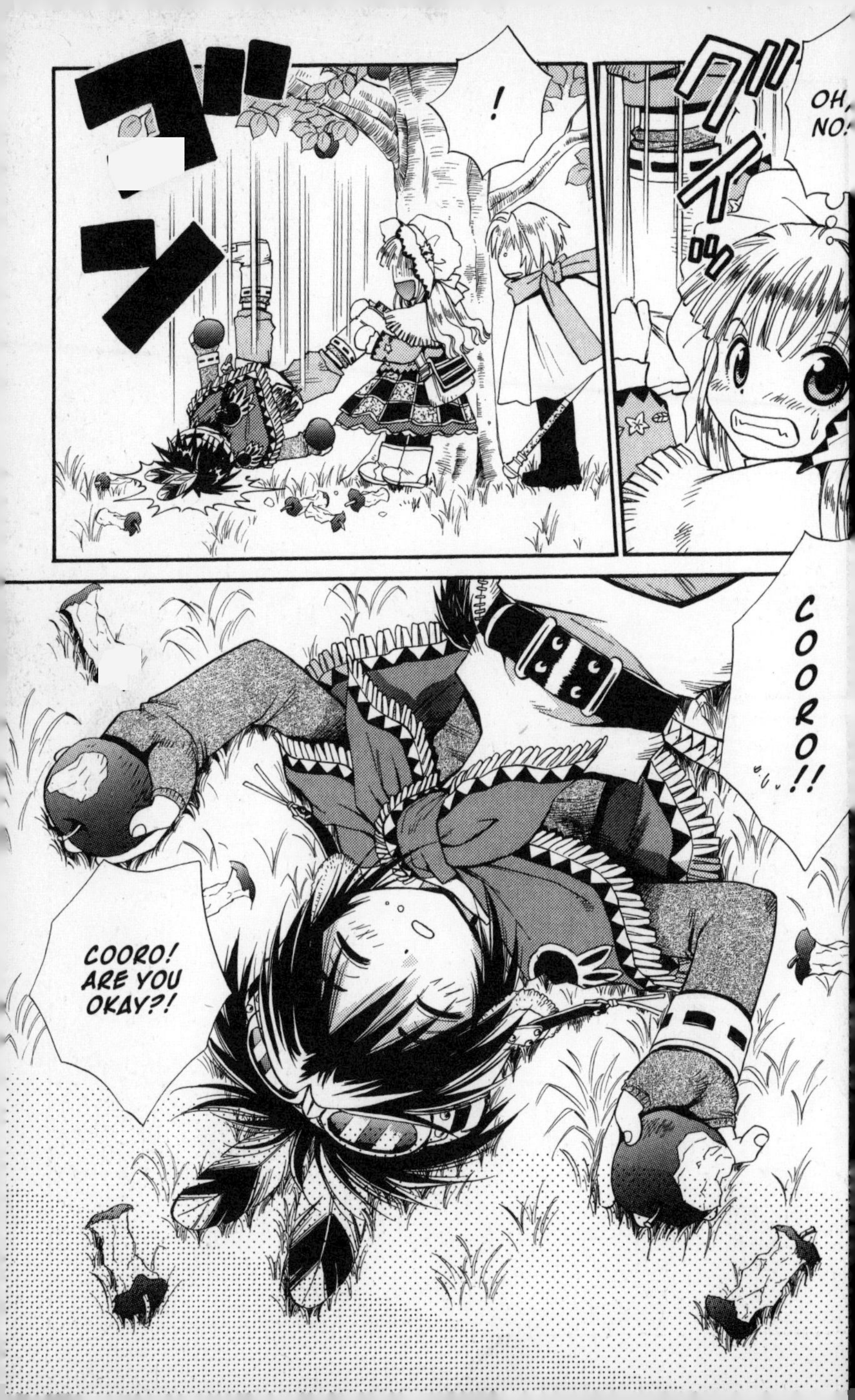
OH, NO!
!
COORO!!
COORO! ARE YOU OKAY?!

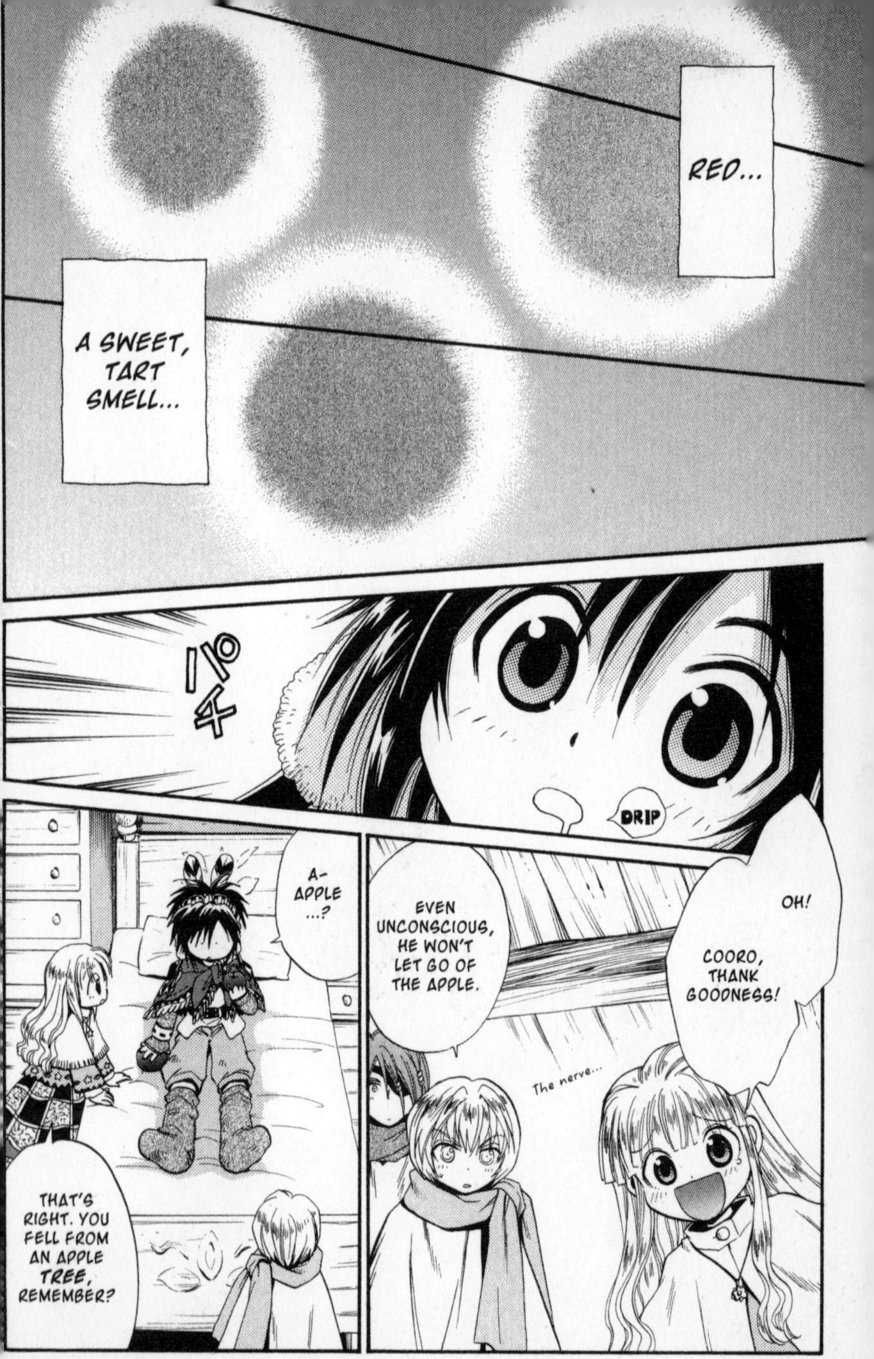
RED...
A SWEET, TART SMELL...
DRIP
OH!
COORO, THANK GOODNESS!
The nerve...
EVEN UNCONSCIOUS, HE WON'T LET GO OF THE APPLE.
A- APPLE ...?
THAT'S RIGHT. YOU FELL FROM AN APPLE TREE, REMEMBER?

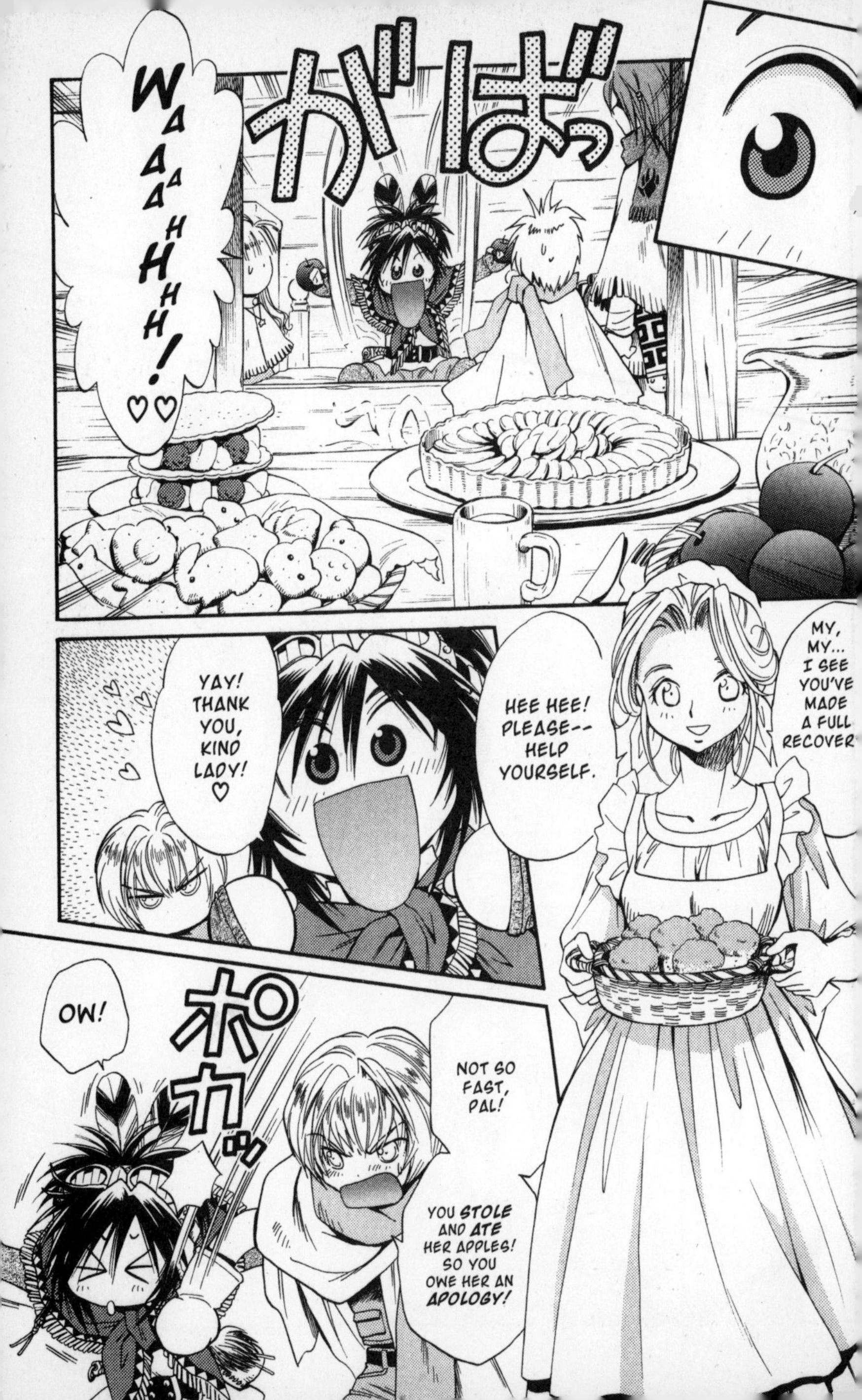
がばっ
WAAAAHHHHH! ♡♡
MY, MY... I SEE YOU'VE MADE A FULL RECOVER
HEE HEE! PLEASE-- HELP YOURSELF.
YAY! THANK YOU, KIND LADY! ♡
ポカッ
OW!
NOT SO FAST, PAL!
YOU STOLE AND ATE HER APPLES! SO YOU OWE HER AN APOLOGY!

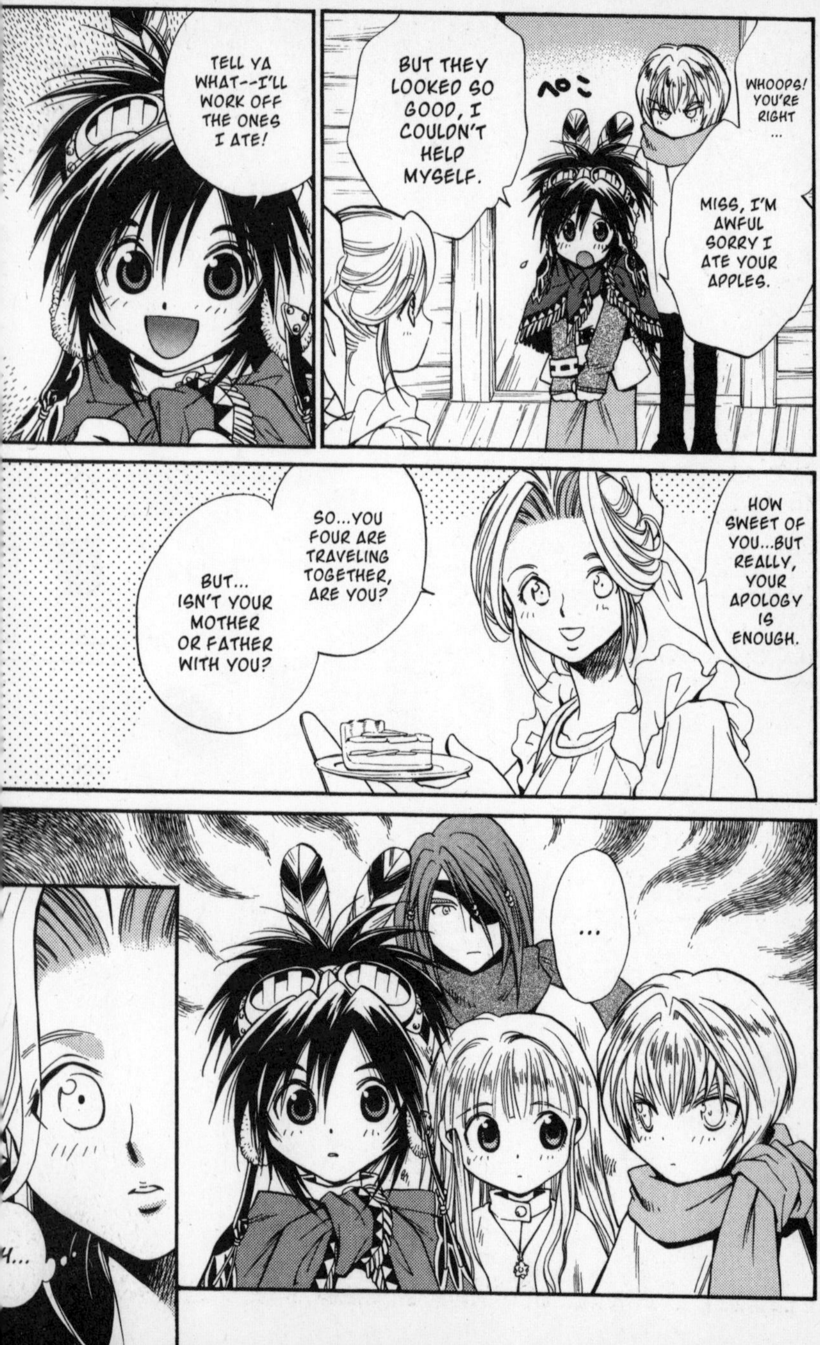
WHOOPS! YOU'RE RIGHT ...
MISS, I'M AWFUL SORRY I ATE YOUR APPLES.
へこ
BUT THEY LOOKED SO GOOD, I COULDN'T HELP MYSELF.
TELL YA WHAT--I'LL WORK OFF THE ONES I ATE!
HOW SWEET OF YOU...BUT REALLY, YOUR APOLOGY IS ENOUGH.
SO...YOU FOUR ARE TRAVELING TOGETHER, ARE YOU?
BUT... ISN'T YOUR MOTHER OR FATHER WITH YOU?
...

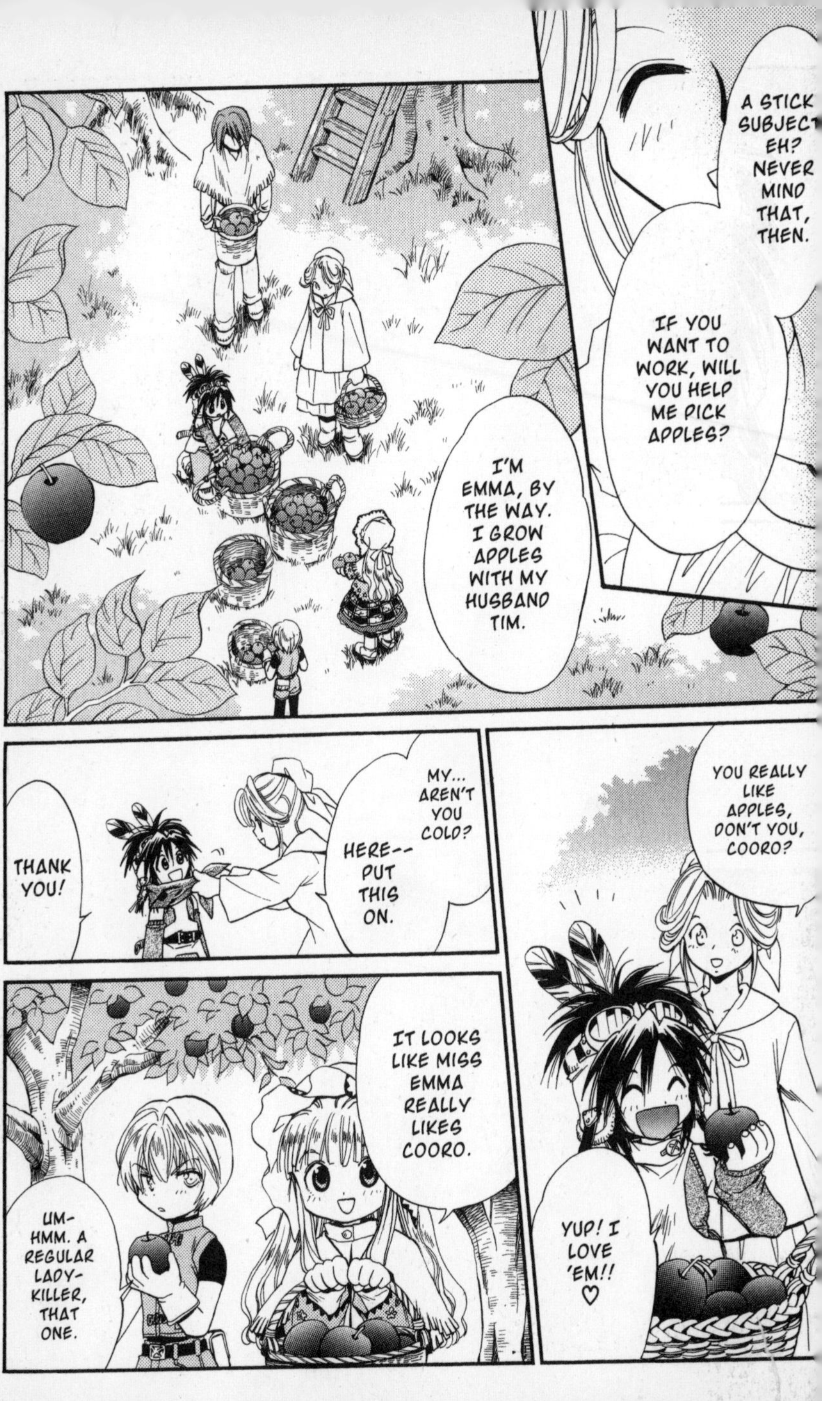
A STICK SUBJECT EH? NEVER MIND THAT, THEN.
IF YOU WANT TO WORK, WILL YOU HELP ME PICK APPLES?
I'M EMMA, BY THE WAY. I GROW APPLES WITH MY HUSBAND TIM.
YOU REALLY LIKE APPLES, DON'T YOU, COORO?
YUP! I LOVE 'EM!! ♡
MY... AREN'T YOU COLD?
HERE--PUT THIS ON.
THANK YOU!
IT LOOKS LIKE MISS EMMA REALLY LIKES COORO.
UM-HMM. A REGULAR LADY-KILLER, THAT ONE.

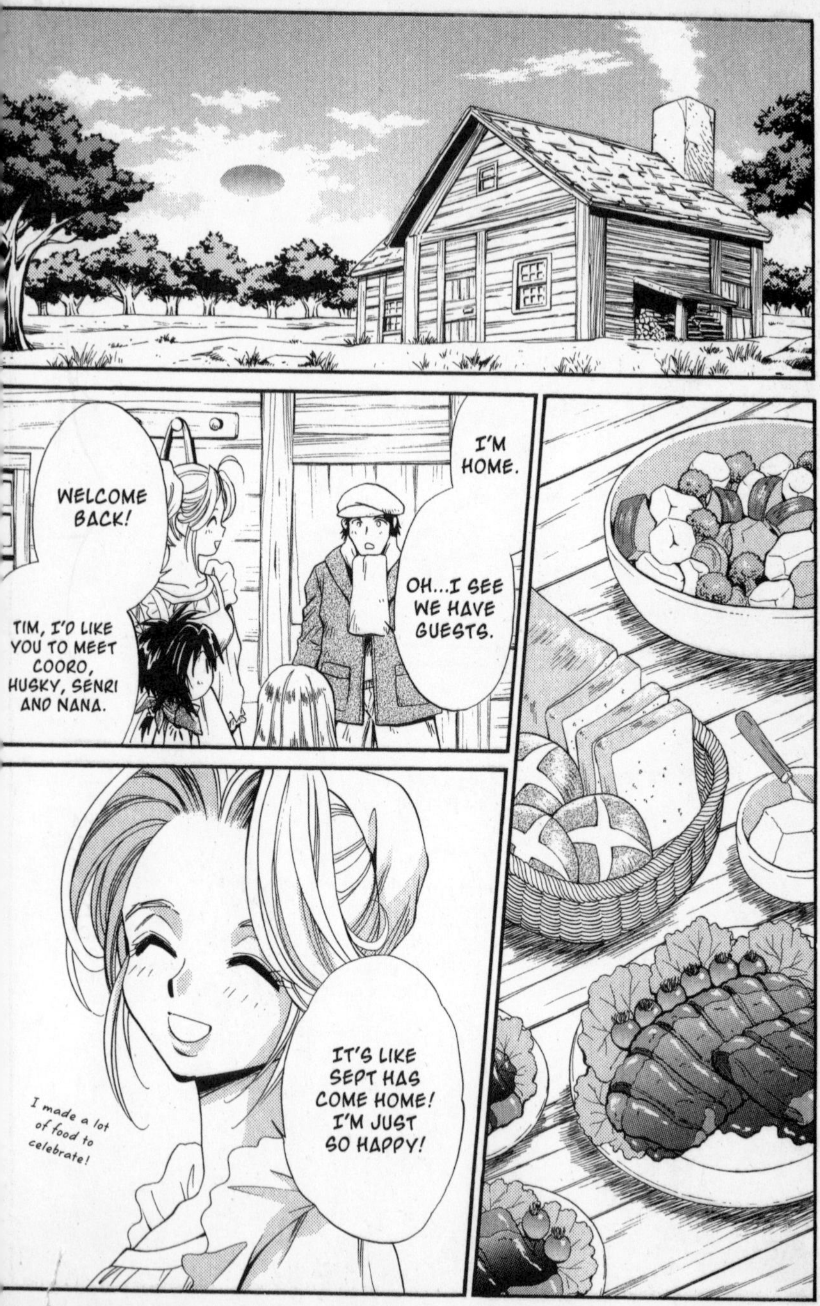
I'M HOME.
WELCOME BACK!
OH...I SEE WE HAVE GUESTS.
TIM, I'D LIKE YOU TO MEET COORO, HUSKY, SENRI AND NANA.
IT'S LIKE SEPT HAS COME HOME! I'M JUST SO HAPPY!
I made a lot of food to celebrate!

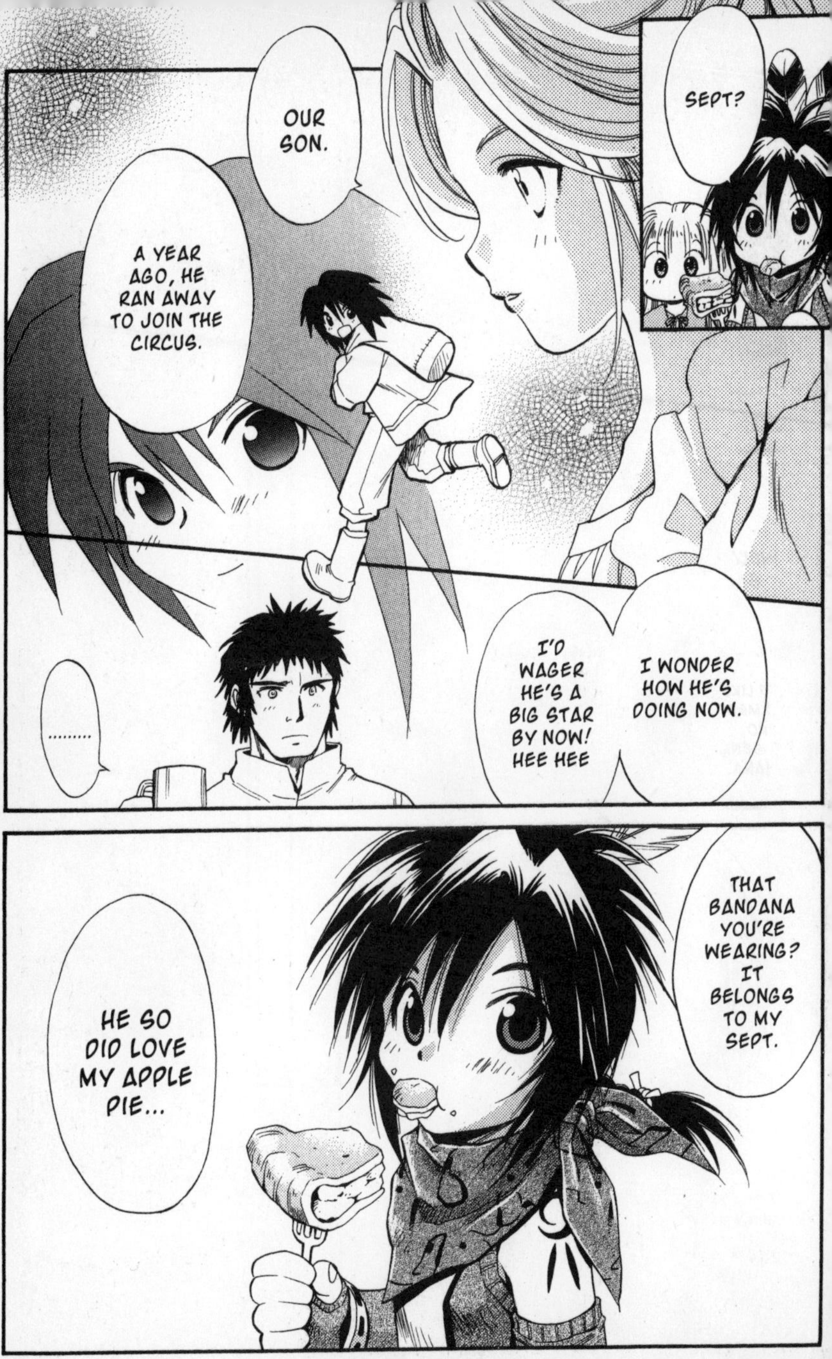
SEPT?
OUR SON.
A YEAR AGO, HE RAN AWAY TO JOIN THE CIRCUS.
I WONDER HOW HE'S DOING NOW.
I'D WAGER HE'S A BIG STAR BY NOW! HEE HEE
....
THAT BANDANA YOU'RE WEARING? IT BELONGS TO MY SEPT.
HE SO DID LOVE MY APPLE PIE...

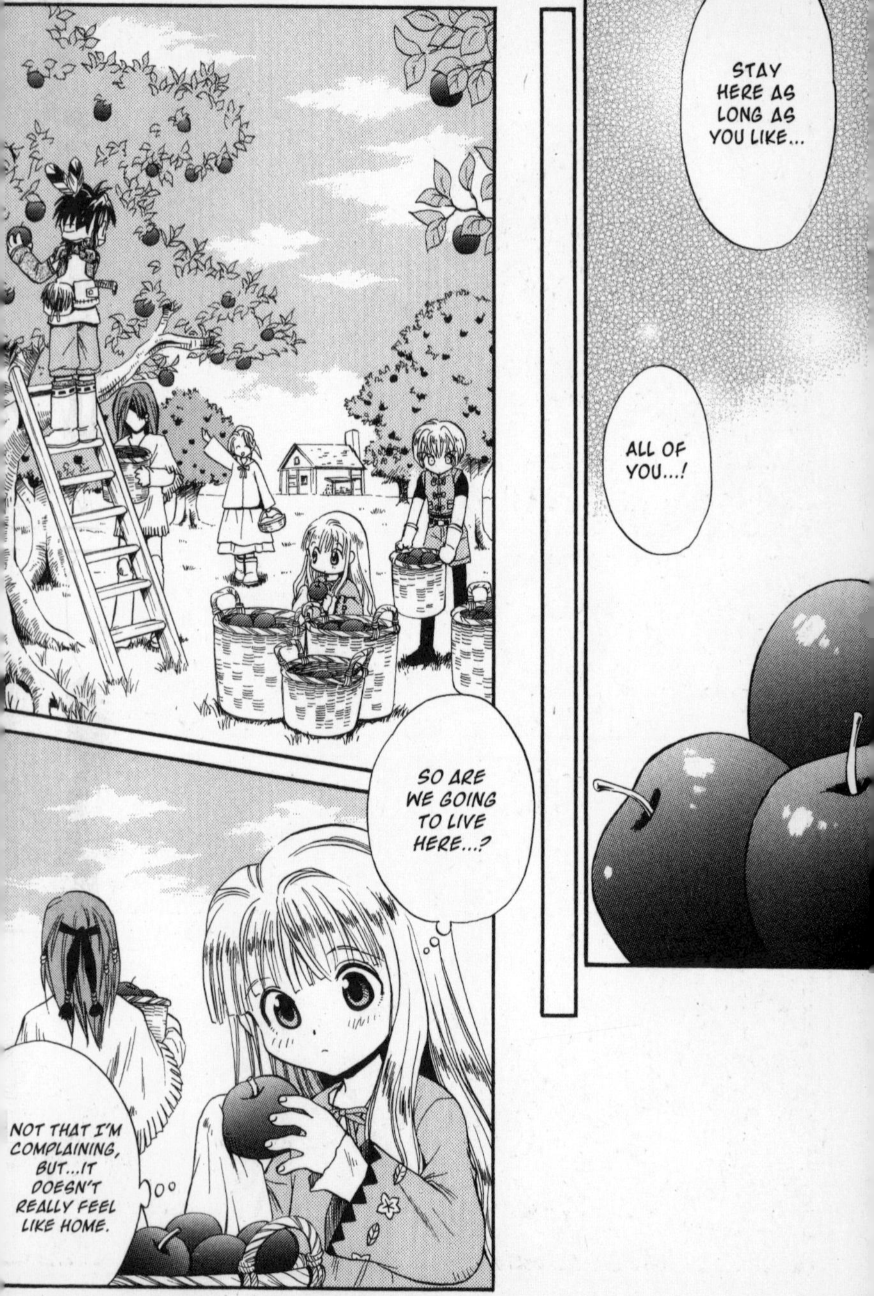
STAY HERE AS LONG AS YOU LIKE...
ALL OF YOU...!
SO ARE WE GOING TO LIVE HERE...?
NOT THAT I'M COMPLAINING, BUT...IT DOESN'T REALLY FEEL LIKE HOME.

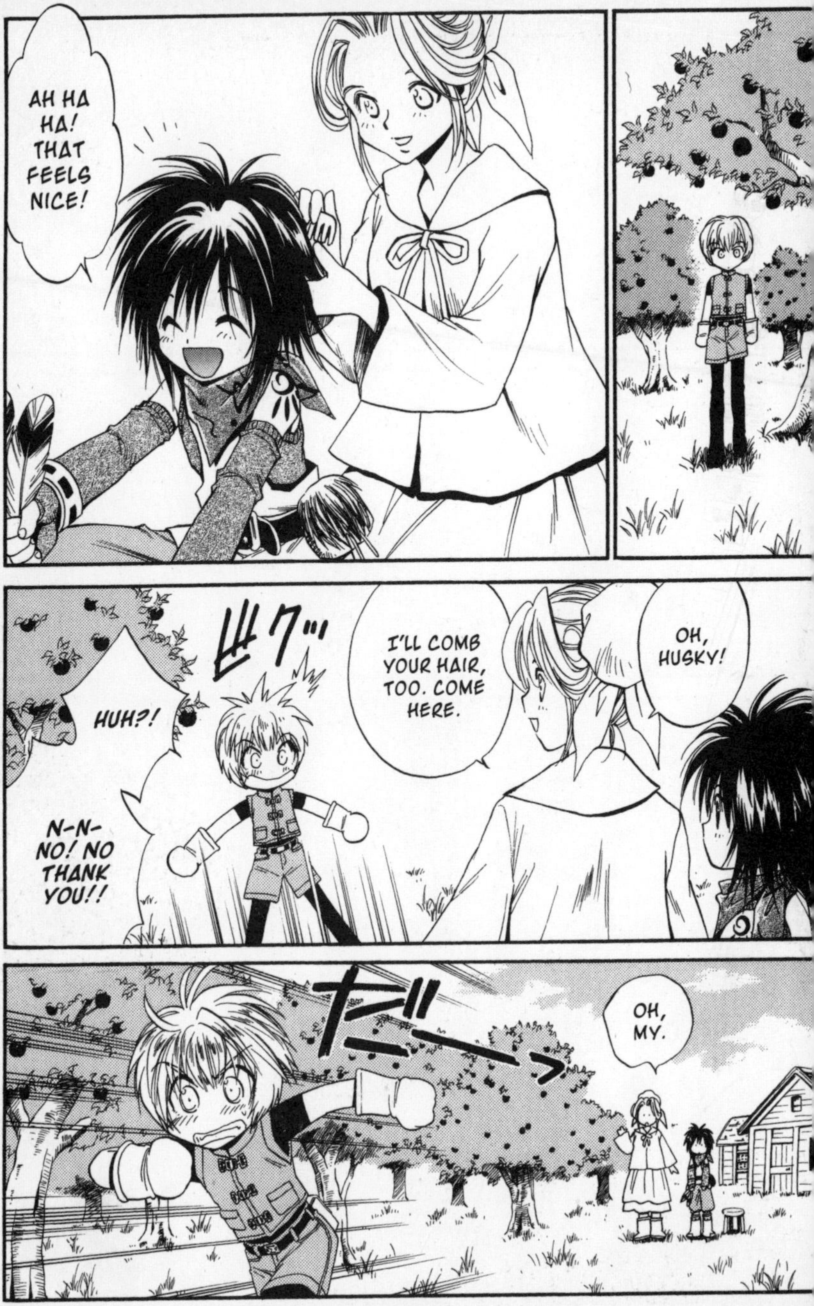
AH HA HA! THAT FEELS NICE!
OH, HUSKY!
I'LL COMB YOUR HAIR, TOO. COME HERE.
HUH?!
N-N-NO! NO THANK YOU!!
OH, MY.

HUSKY? WHAT'S WRONG?
HAVEN'T WE DONE ENOUGH YET?!
I MEAN, WE'VE MORE THAN MADE UP FOR THE APPLES COORO STOLE, HAVEN'T WE?!
WHAT ARE YOU SAYING?
I'M SAYING LET'S GET OUT OF HERE!
I KNOW SHE SAID WE CAN STAY AS LONG AS WE WANT, BUT...
...I JUST CAN'T STAND WOMEN LIKE HER!
SHE'S KIND OF... WELL, DEPRESS-ING.
BUT...WE FINALLY HAVE A PLACE WHERE WE CAN STAY.
AND MISS EMMA IS SO NICE...

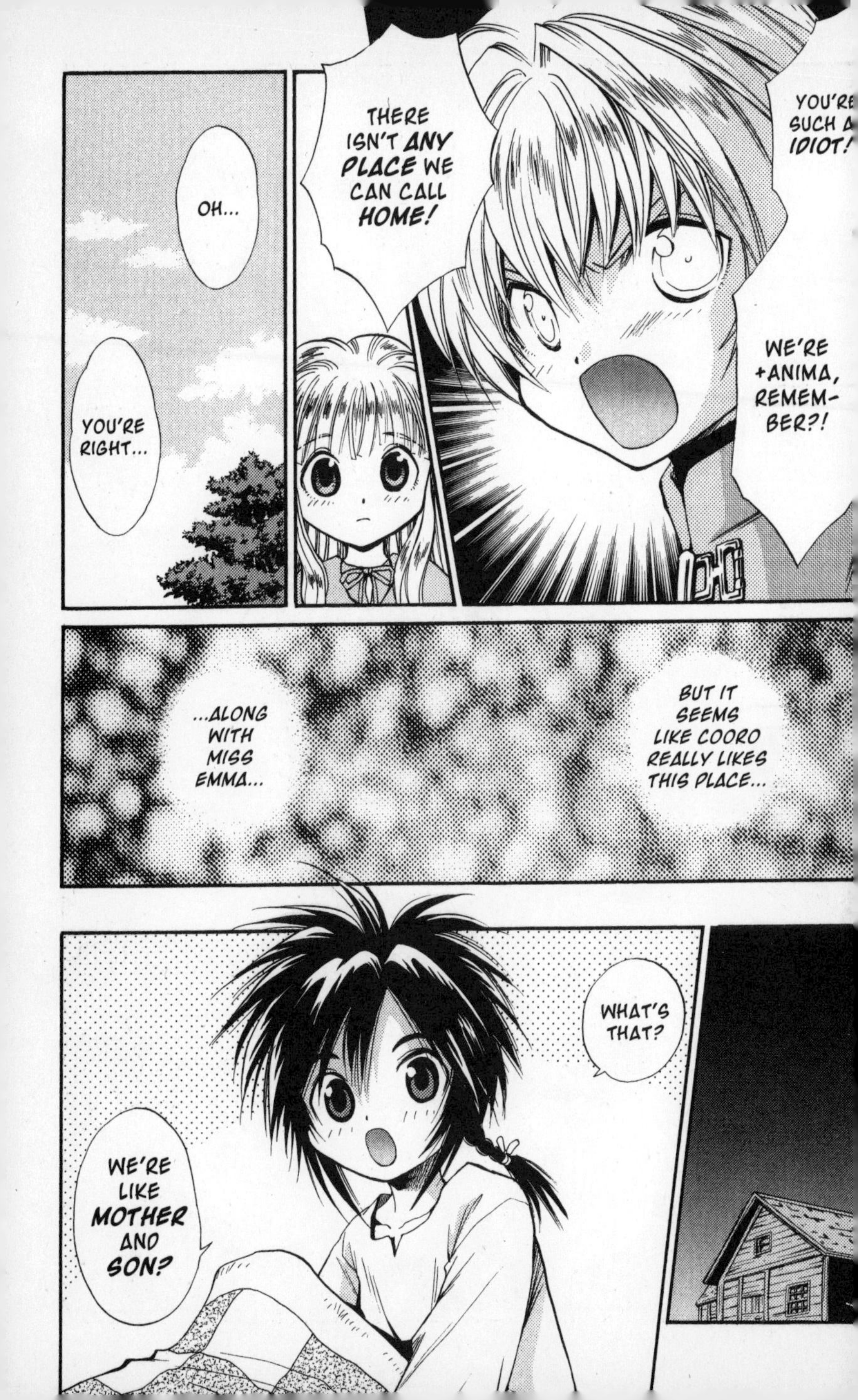
YOU'RE SUCH A IDIOT!
THERE ISN'T ANY PLACE WE CAN CALL HOME!
WE'RE +ANIMA, REMEMBER?!
OH...
YOU'RE RIGHT...
BUT IT SEEMS LIKE COORO REALLY LIKES THIS PLACE...
...ALONG WITH MISS EMMA...
WHAT'S THAT?
WE'RE LIKE MOTHER AND SON?

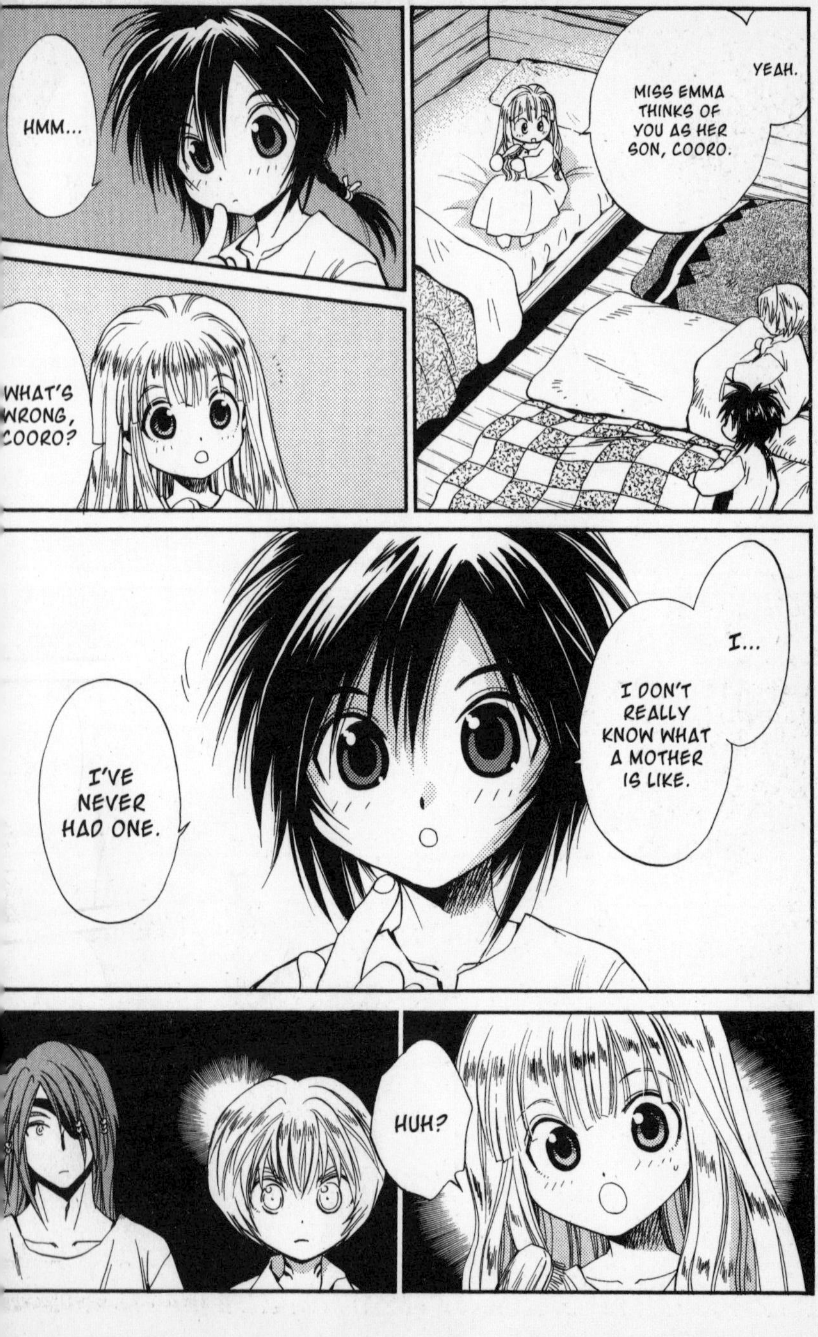
YEAH. MISS EMMA THINKS OF YOU AS HER SON, COORO.
HMM...
WHAT'S WRONG, COORO?
I... I DON'T REALLY KNOW WHAT A MOTHER IS LIKE.
I'VE NEVER HAD ONE.
HUH?

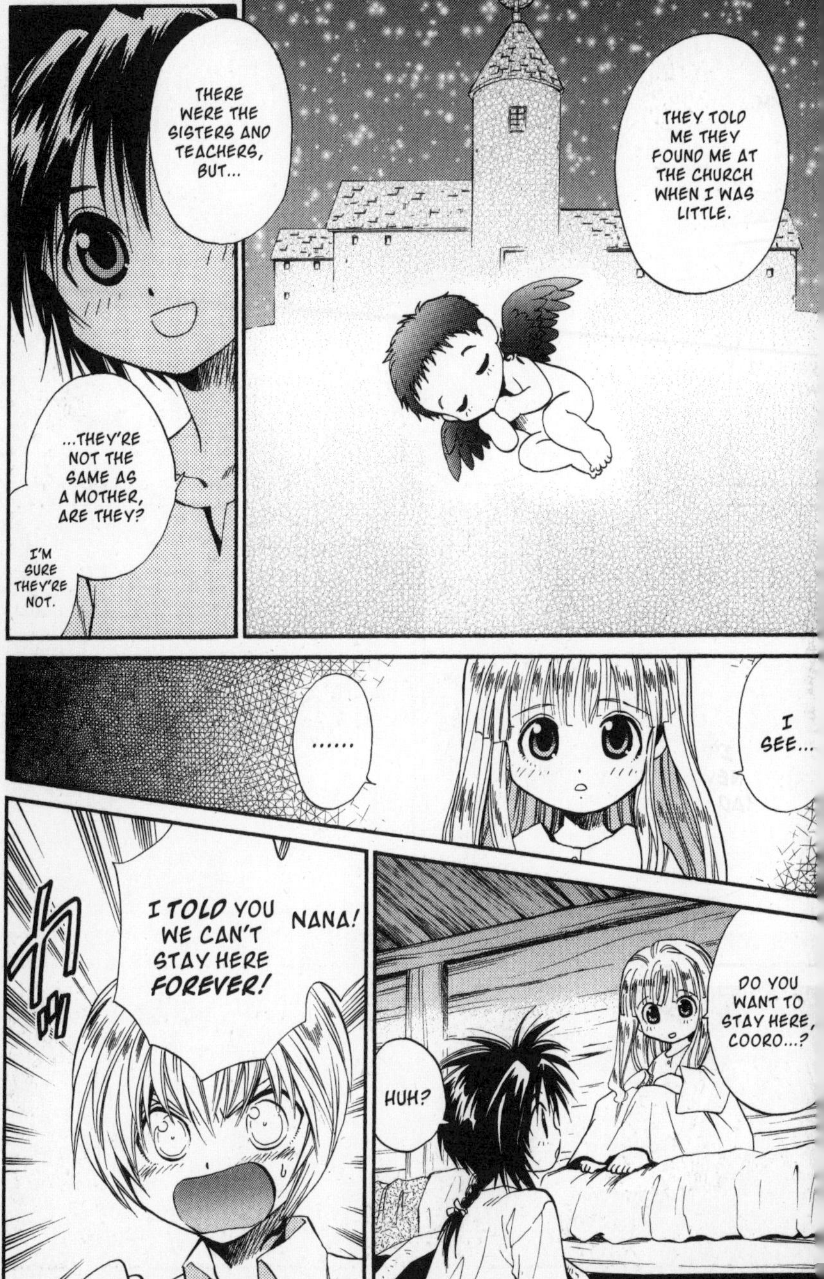
THEY TOLD ME THEY FOUND ME AT THE CHURCH WHEN I WAS LITTLE.
THERE WERE THE SISTERS AND TEACHERS, BUT...
...THEY'RE NOT THE SAME AS A MOTHER, ARE THEY?
I'M SURE THEY'RE NOT.
I SEE...
......
DO YOU WANT TO STAY HERE, COORO...?
HUH?
NANA!
I *TOLD* YOU WE CAN'T STAY HERE **FOREVER!**

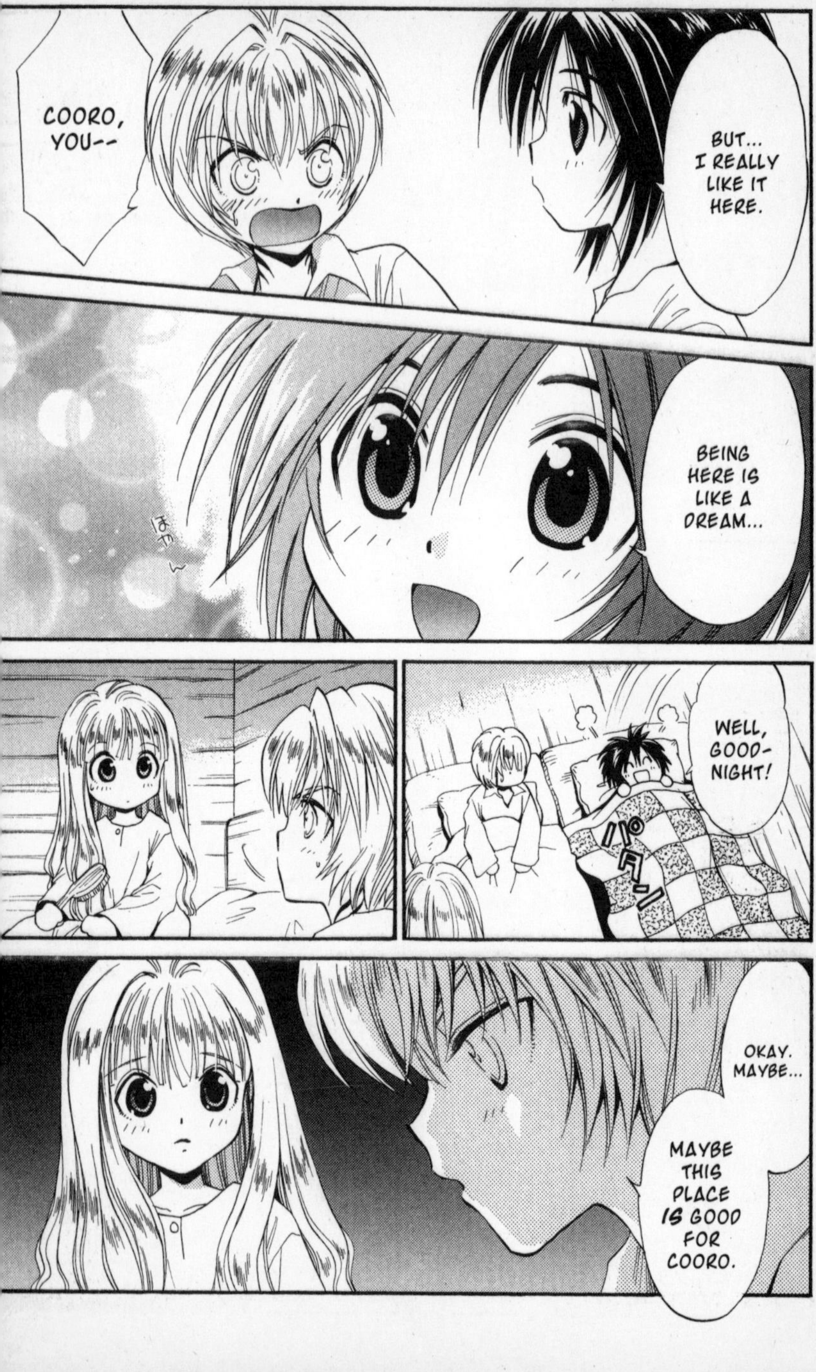
BUT... I REALLY LIKE IT HERE.
COORO, YOU--
BEING HERE IS LIKE A DREAM...
ほや〜
WELL, GOOD-NIGHT!
OKAY. MAYBE...
MAYBE THIS PLACE IS GOOD FOR COORO.

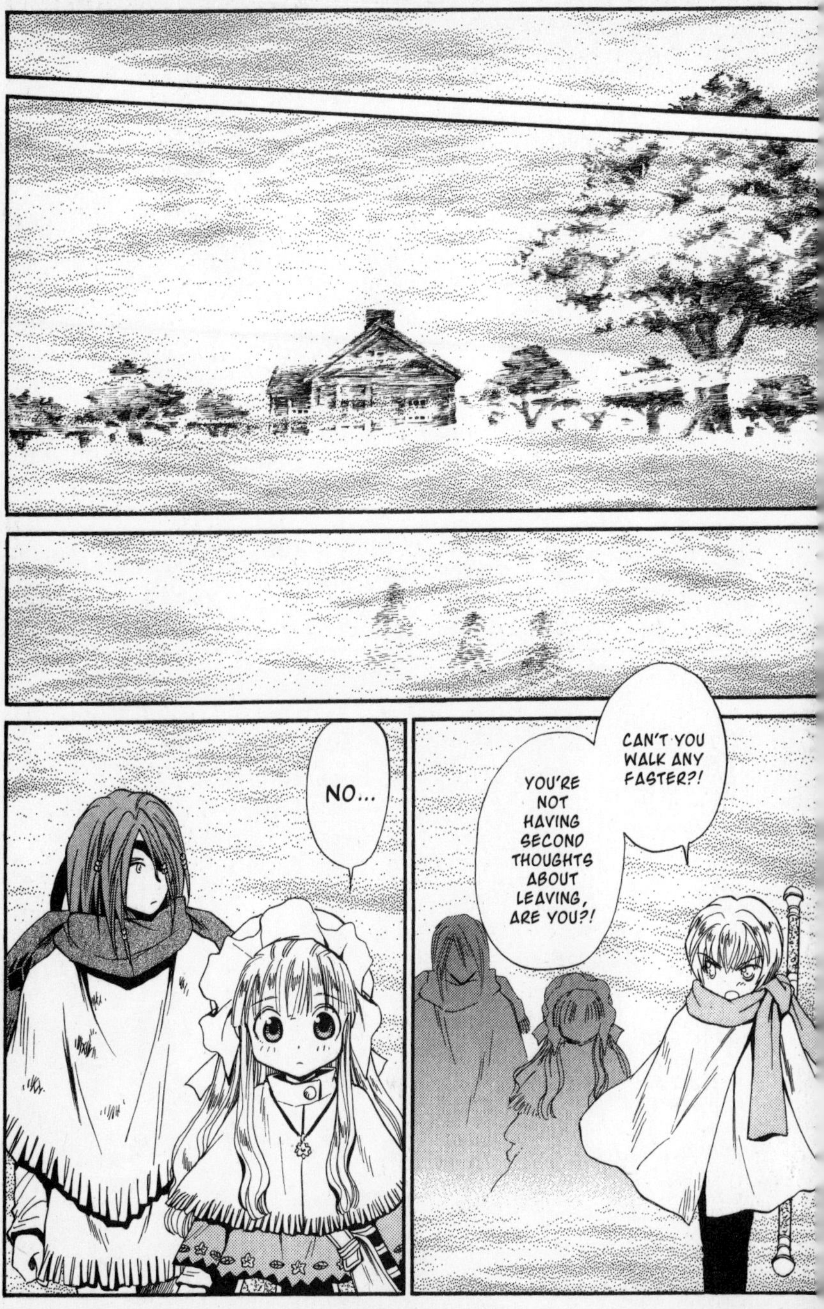
CAN'T YOU WALK ANY FASTER?!
YOU'RE NOT HAVING SECOND THOUGHTS ABOUT LEAVING, ARE YOU?!
NO...

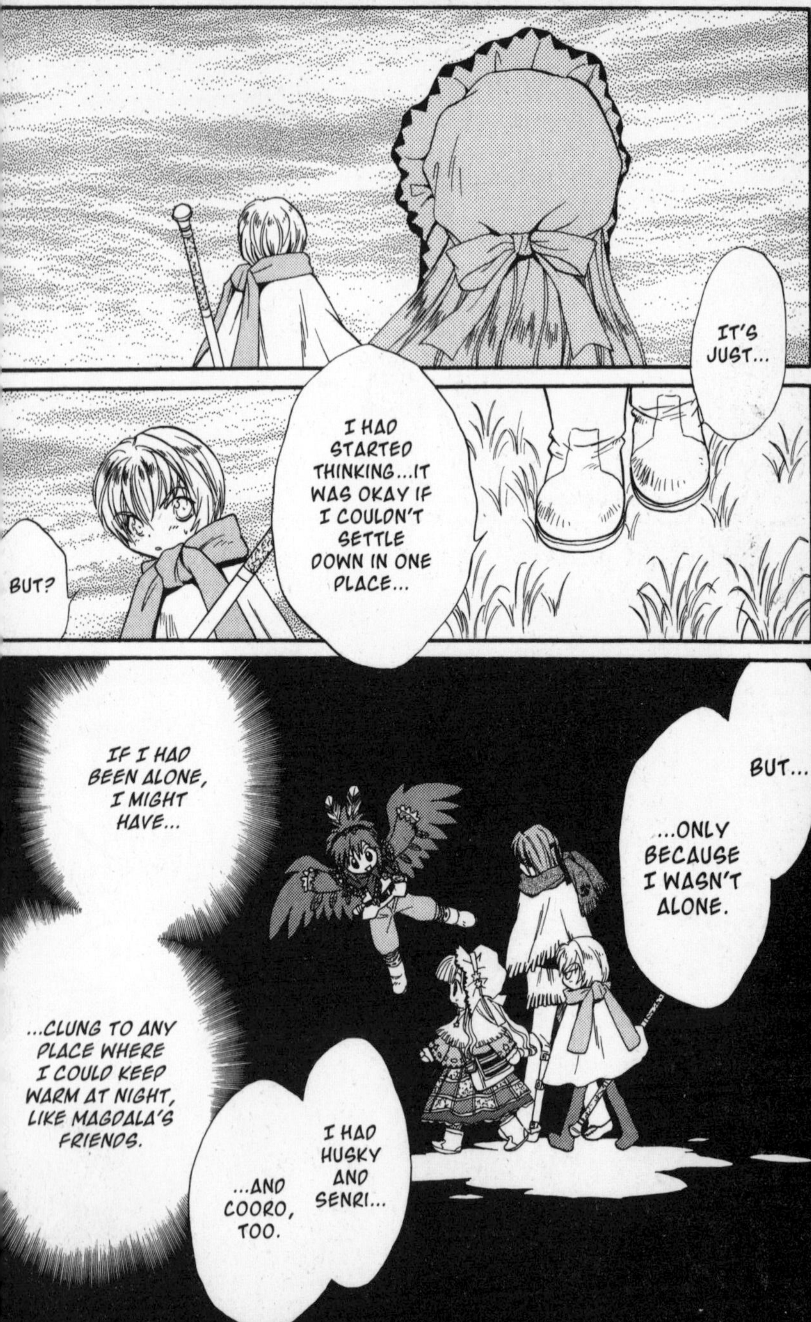
IT'S JUST...
I HAD STARTED THINKING...IT WAS OKAY IF I COULDN'T SETTLE DOWN IN ONE PLACE...
BUT?
BUT...
...ONLY BECAUSE I WASN'T ALONE.
IF I HAD BEEN ALONE, I MIGHT HAVE...
...CLUNG TO ANY PLACE WHERE I COULD KEEP WARM AT NIGHT, LIKE MAGDALA'S FRIENDS.
I HAD HUSKY AND SENRI...
...AND COORO, TOO.

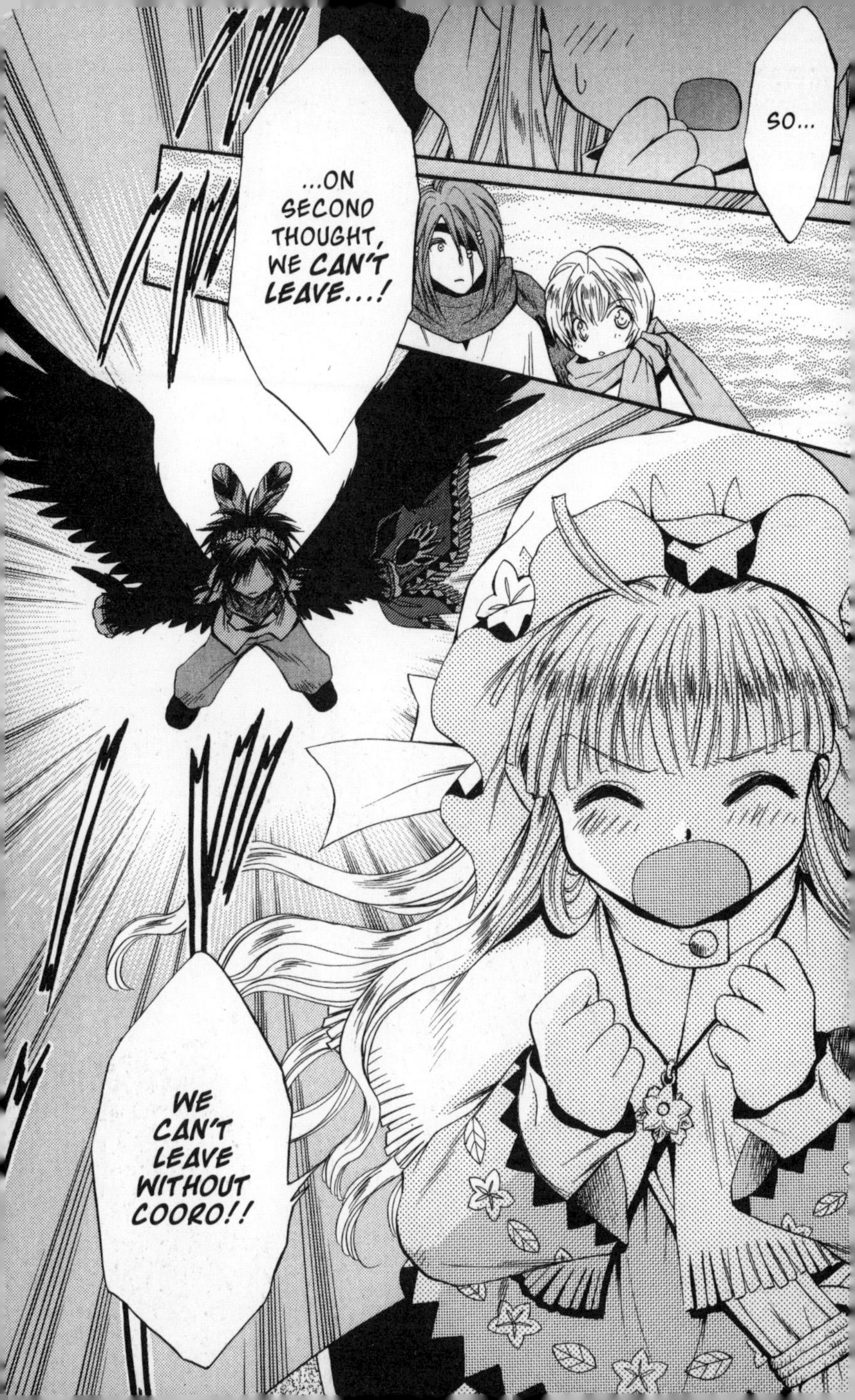
SO...
...ON SECOND THOUGHT, WE CAN'T LEAVE...!
WE CAN'T LEAVE WITHOUT COORO!!

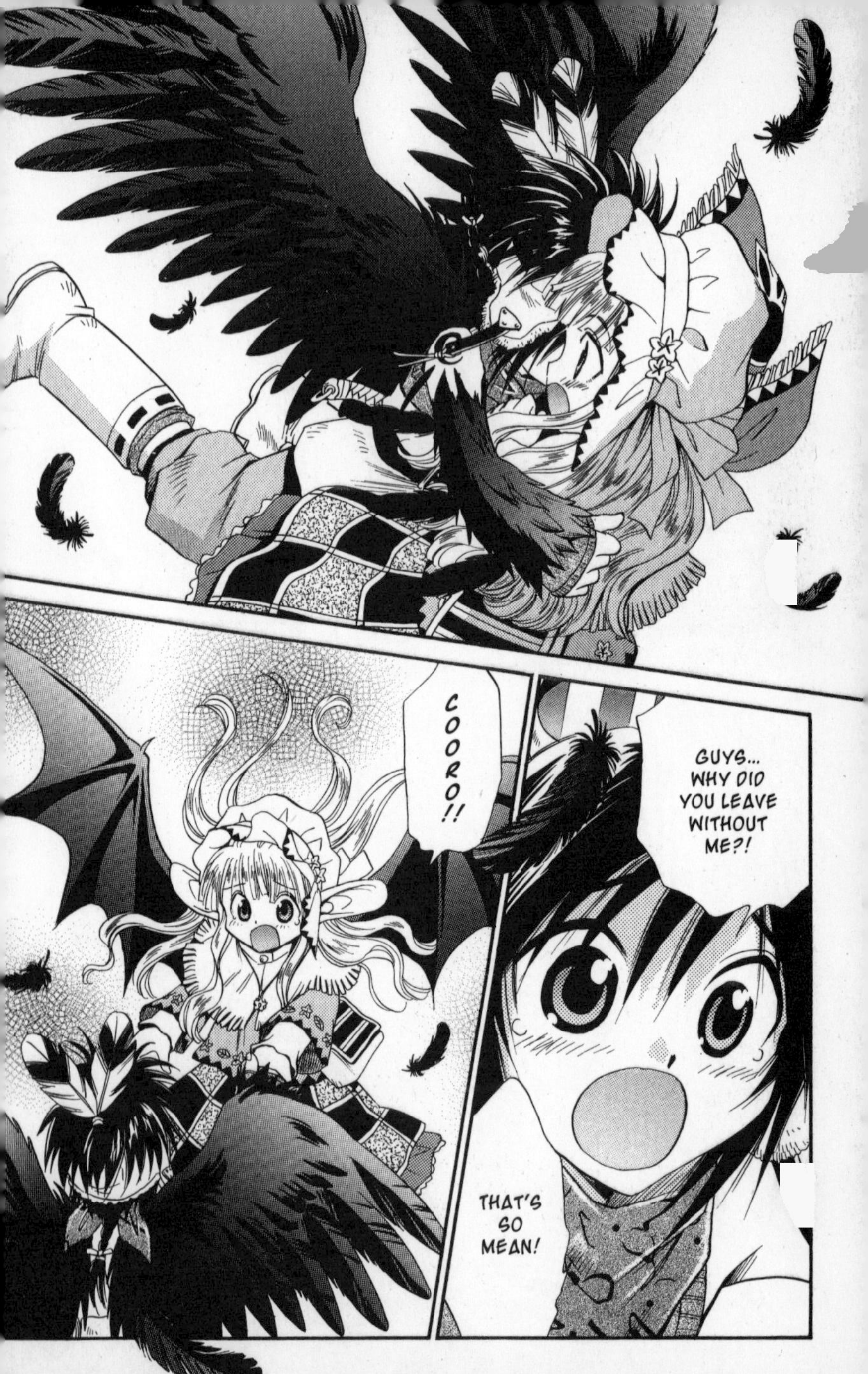
GUYS... WHY DID YOU LEAVE WITHOUT ME?!
THAT'S SO MEAN!
COORO!!

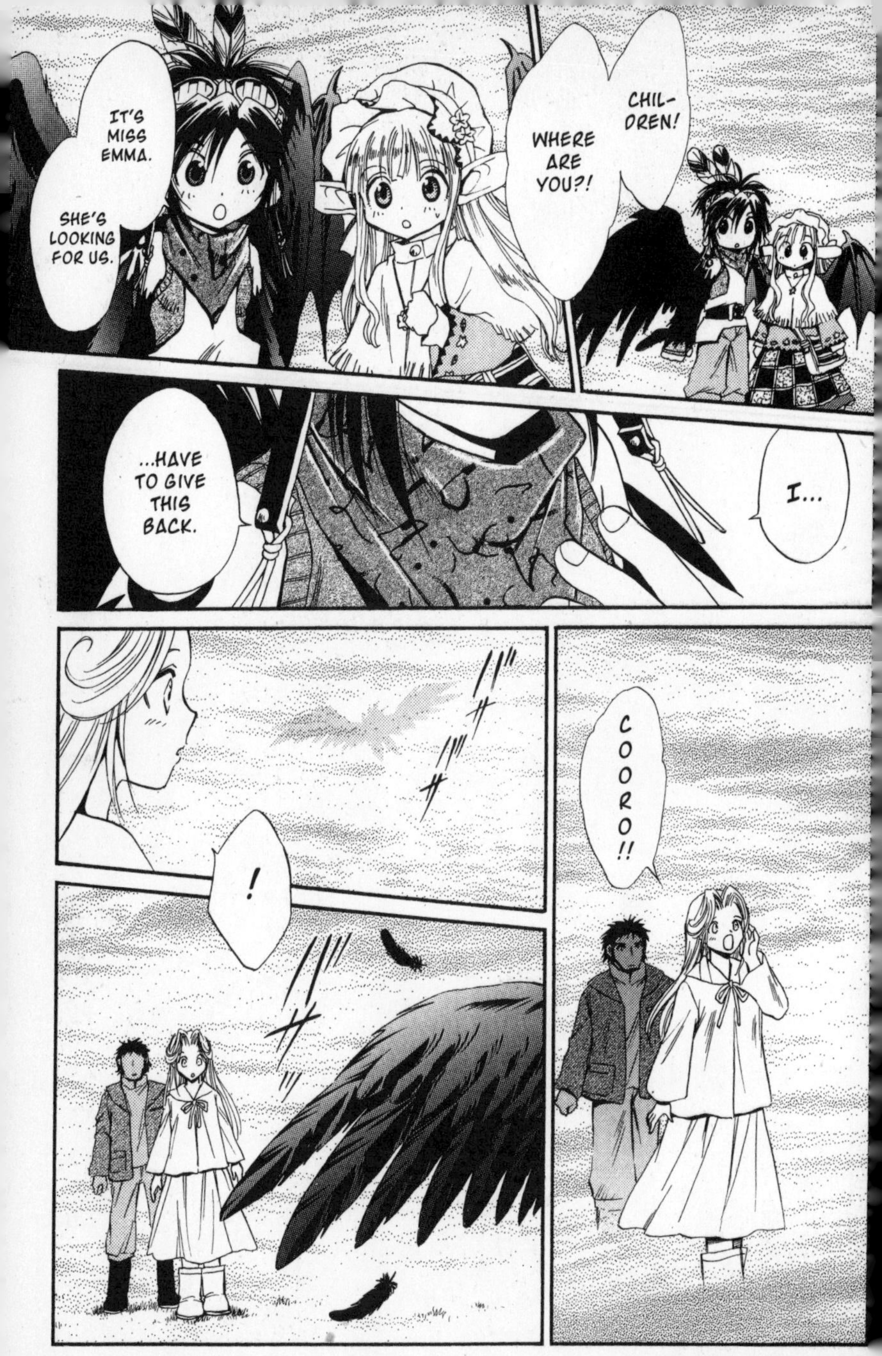
CHIL-DREN!
WHERE ARE YOU?!
IT'S MISS EMMA.
SHE'S LOOKING FOR US.
I...
...HAVE TO GIVE THIS BACK.
COORO!!
!

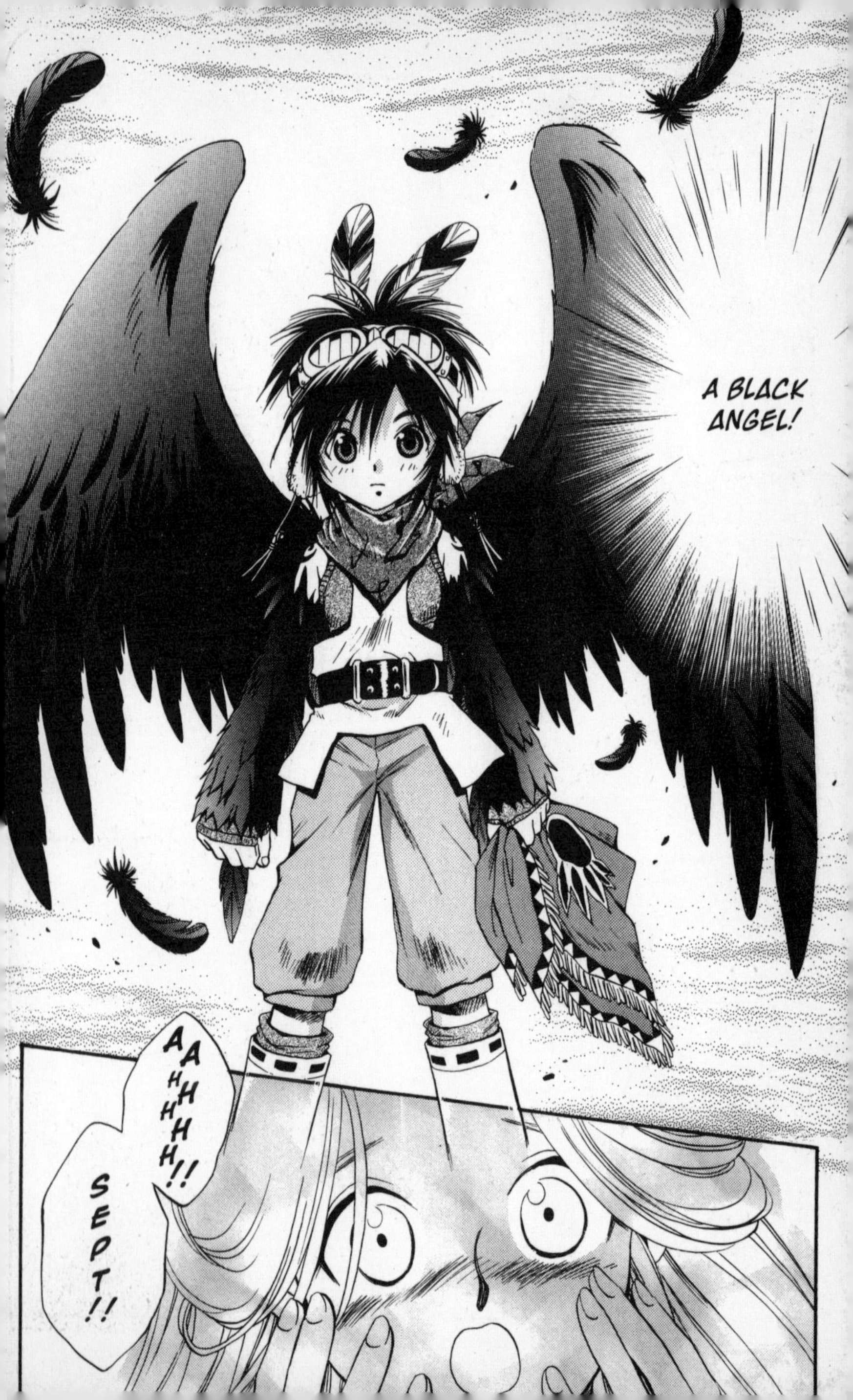
A BLACK ANGEL!
AAHHHHH!!
SEPT!!

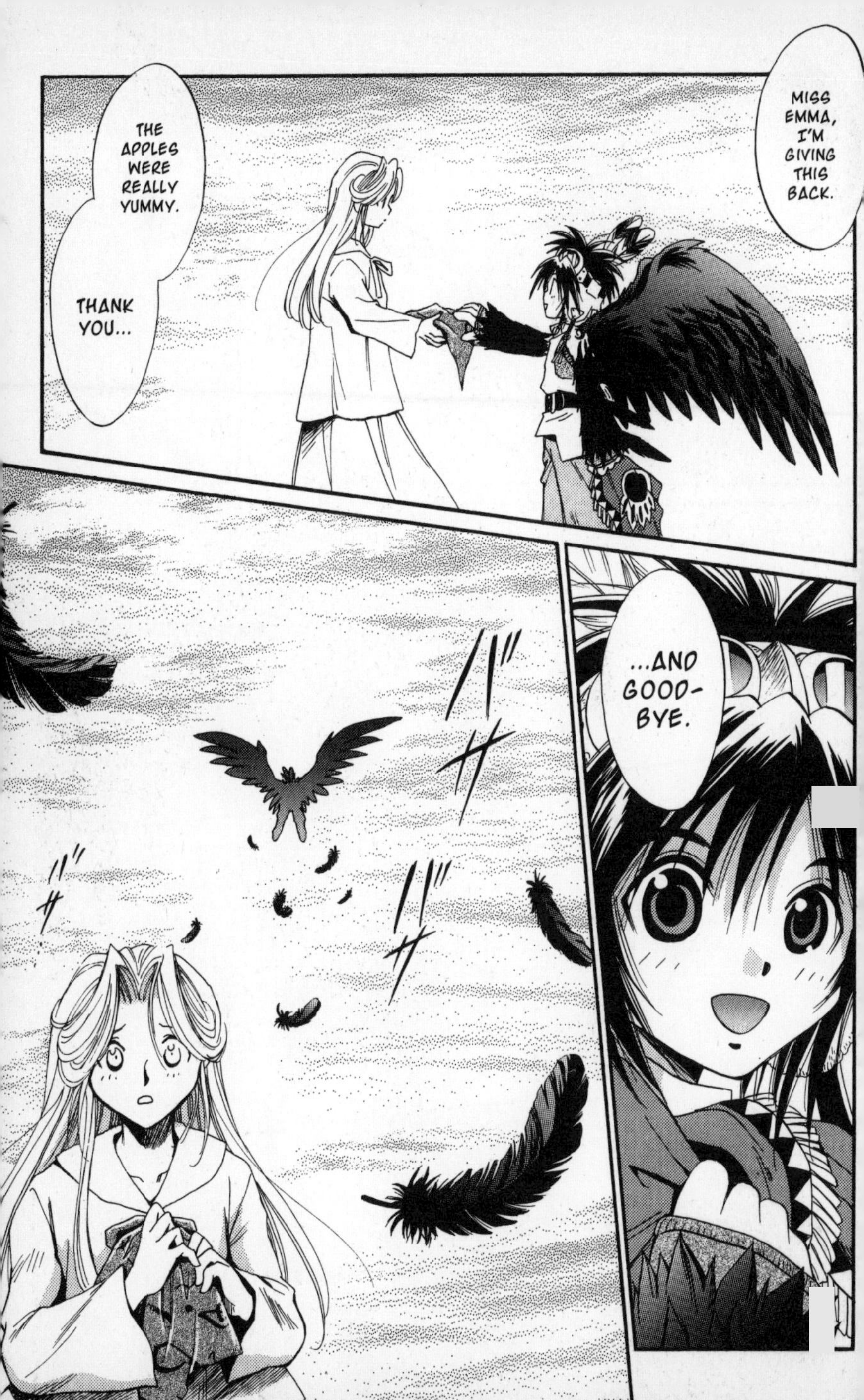
MISS EMMA, I'M GIVING THIS BACK.
THE APPLES WERE REALLY YUMMY.
THANK YOU...
...AND GOOD-BYE.

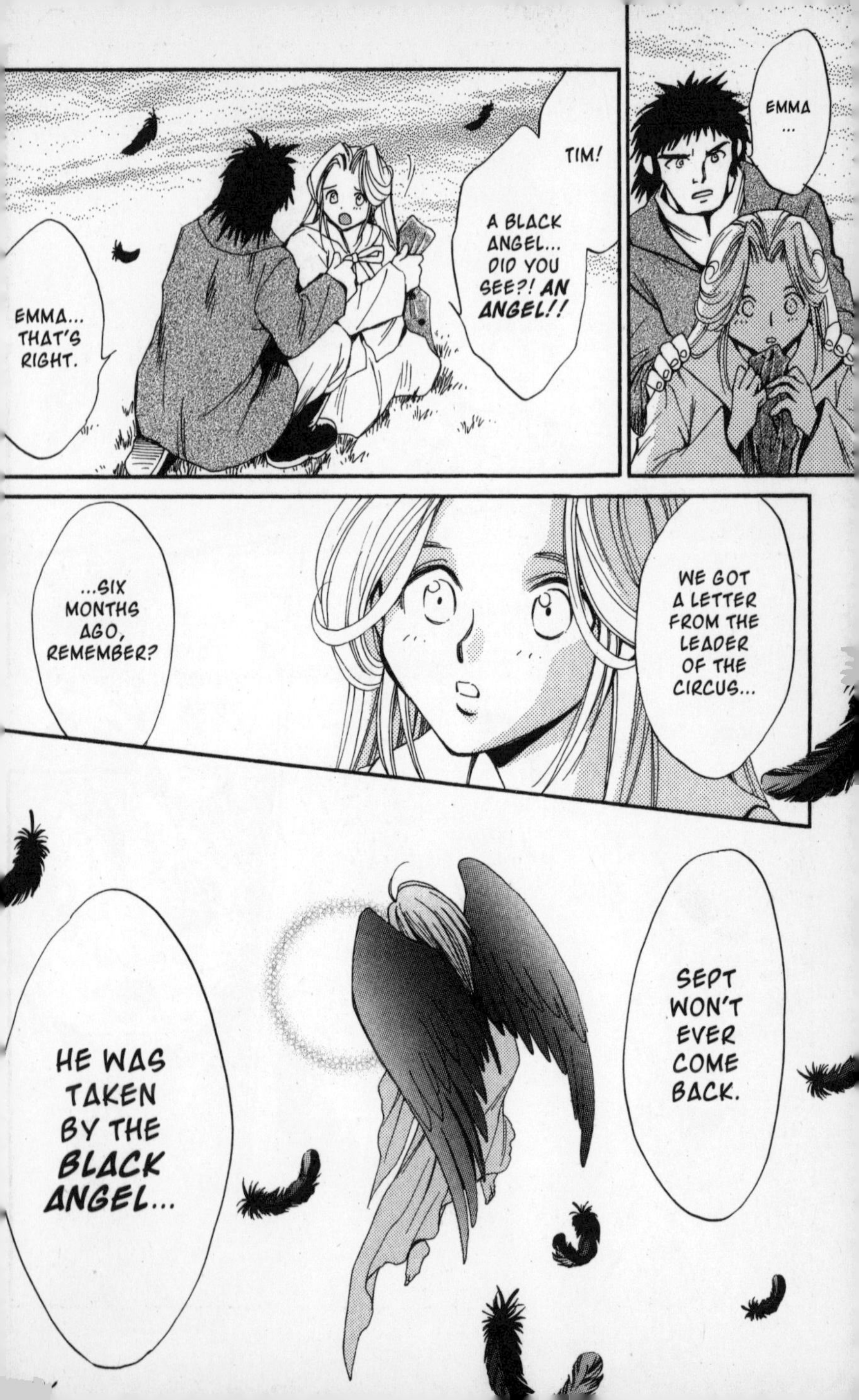
EMMA ...
TIM! A BLACK ANGEL... DID YOU SEE?! AN ANGEL!!
EMMA... THAT'S RIGHT.
WE GOT A LETTER FROM THE LEADER OF THE CIRCUS...
...SIX MONTHS AGO, REMEMBER?
SEPT WON'T EVER COME BACK.
HE WAS TAKEN BY THE BLACK ANGEL...

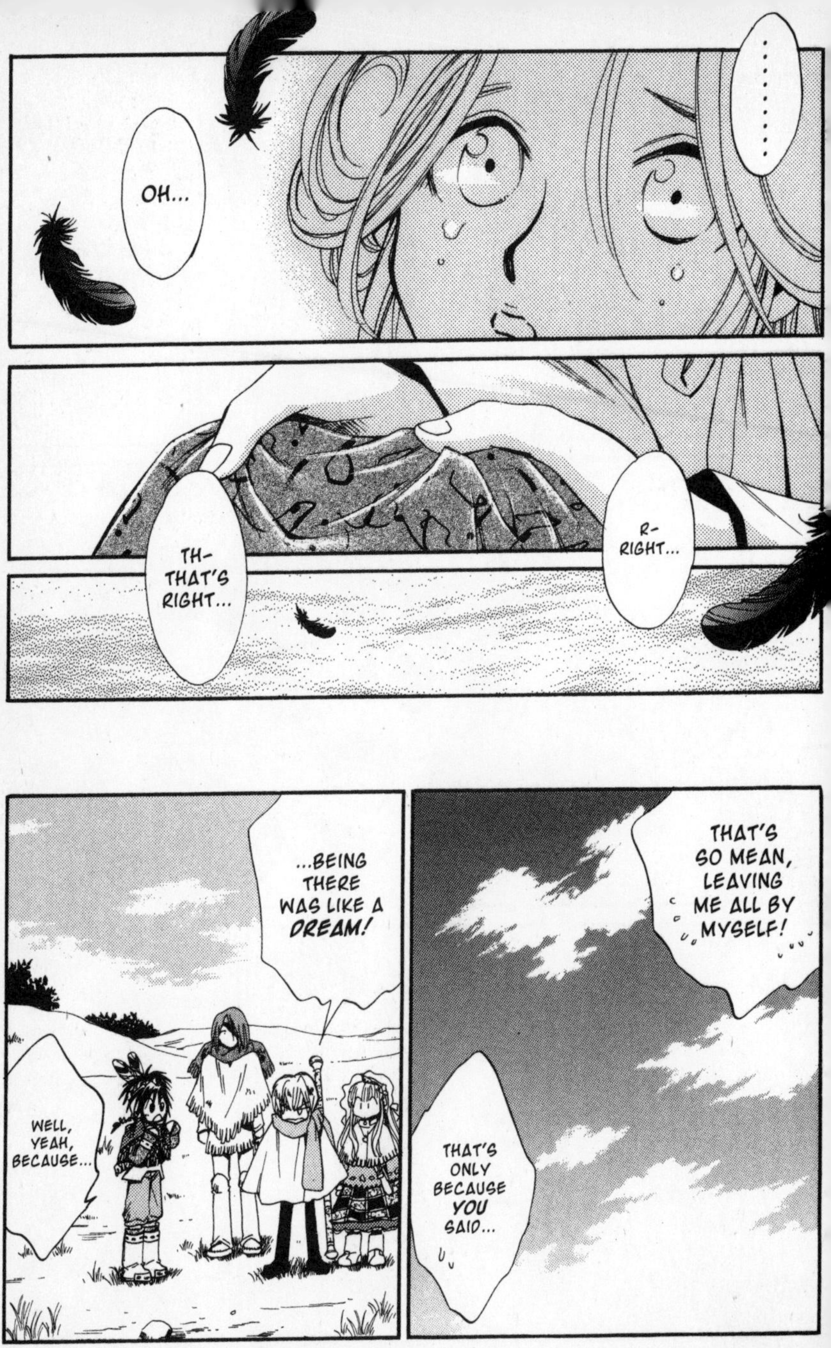
......
OH...
R- RIGHT...
TH- THAT'S RIGHT...
THAT'S SO MEAN, LEAVING ME ALL BY MYSELF!
THAT'S ONLY BECAUSE *YOU* SAID...
...BEING THERE WAS LIKE A *DREAM!*
WELL, YEAH, BECAUSE...

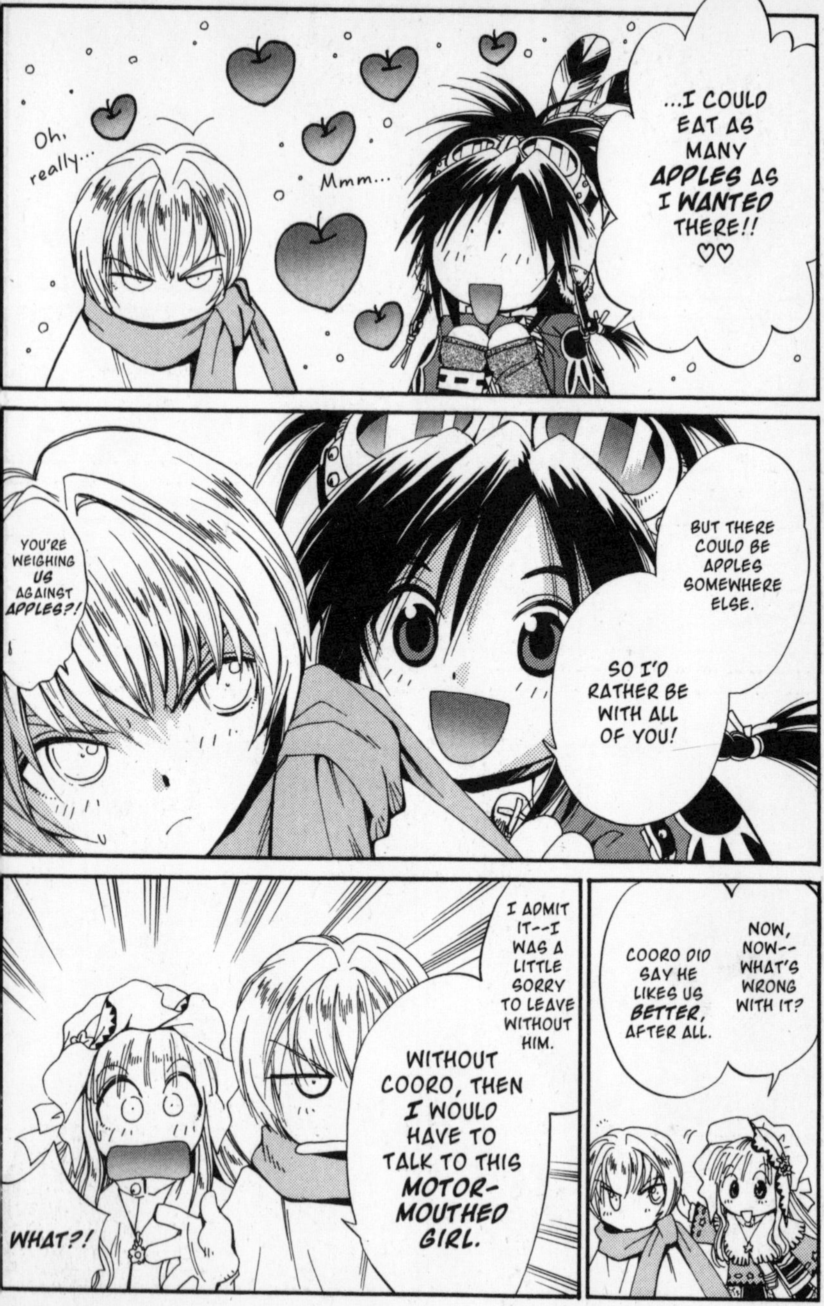
...I COULD EAT AS MANY APPLES AS I WANTED THERE!! ♡♡
Mmm...
Oh, really...
BUT THERE COULD BE APPLES SOMEWHERE ELSE.
SO I'D RATHER BE WITH ALL OF YOU!
YOU'RE WEIGHING US AGAINST APPLES?!
NOW, NOW--WHAT'S WRONG WITH IT?
COORO DID SAY HE LIKES US BETTER, AFTER ALL.
I ADMIT IT--I WAS A LITTLE SORRY TO LEAVE WITHOUT HIM.
WITHOUT COORO, THEN I WOULD HAVE TO TALK TO THIS MOTOR-MOUTHED GIRL.
WHAT?!

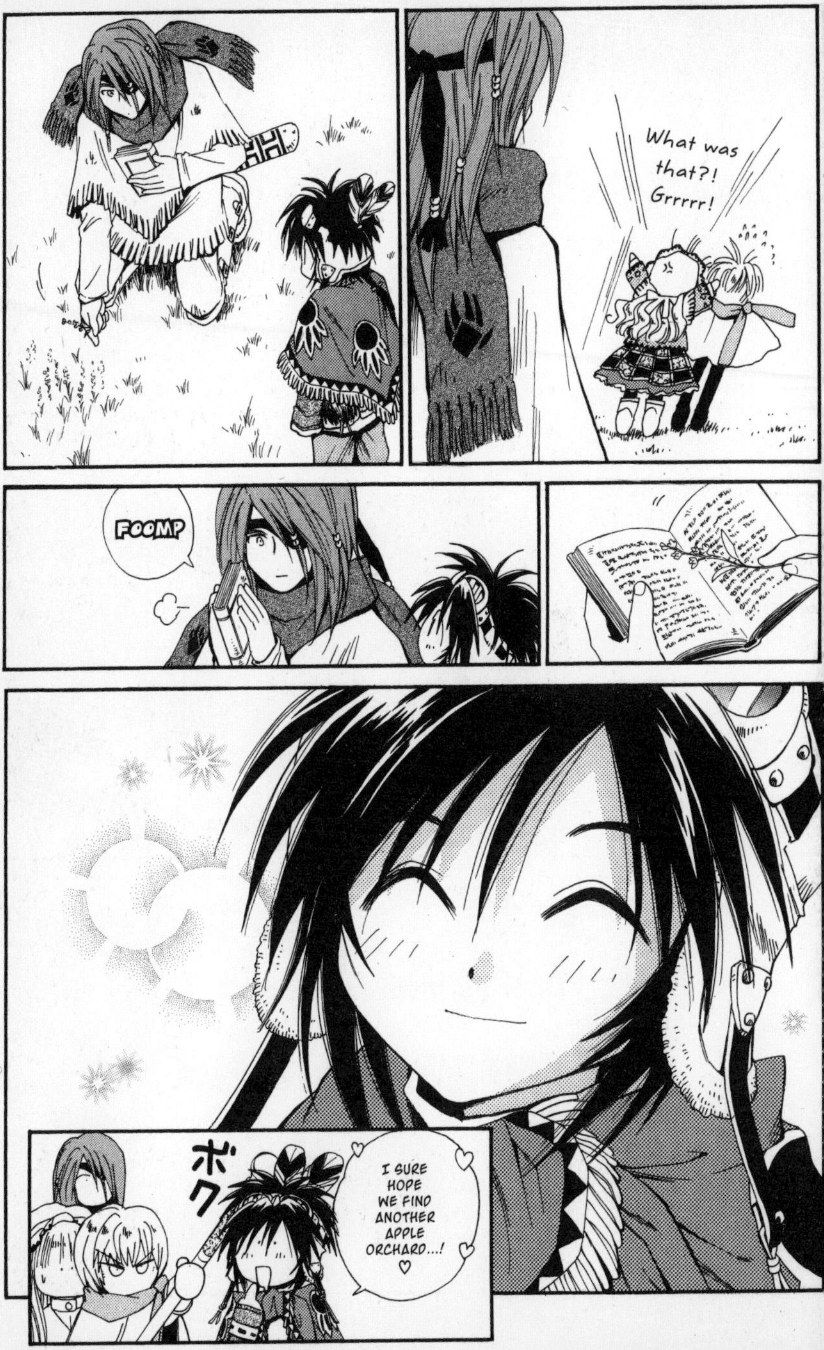
What was that?! Grrrrr!
FOOMP
I SURE HOPE WE FIND ANOTHER APPLE ORCHARD...! ♡
ボク

Cooro's favorite dream.

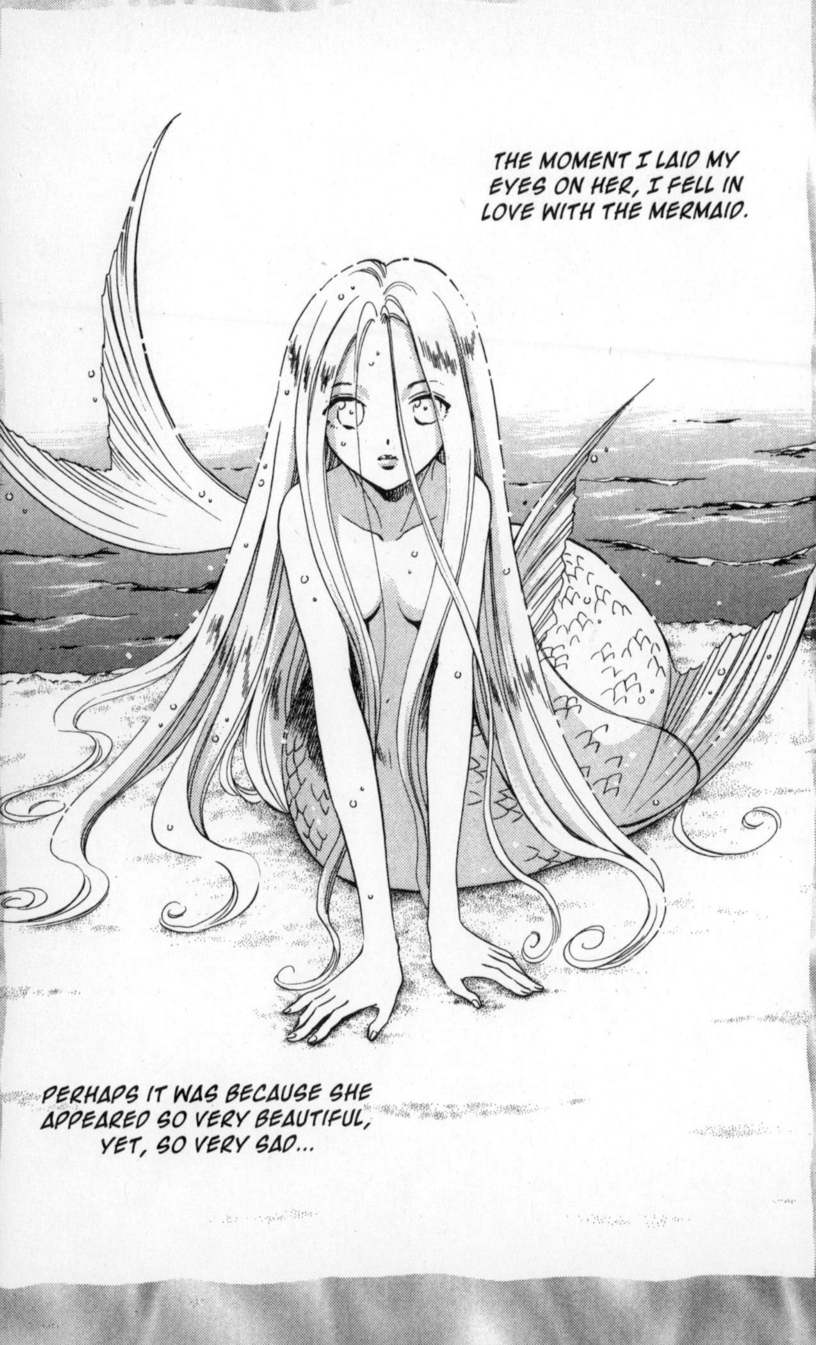
THE MOMENT I LAID MY EYES ON HER, I FELL IN LOVE WITH THE MERMAID.
PERHAPS IT WAS BECAUSE SHE APPEARED SO VERY BEAUTIFUL, YET, SO VERY SAD...

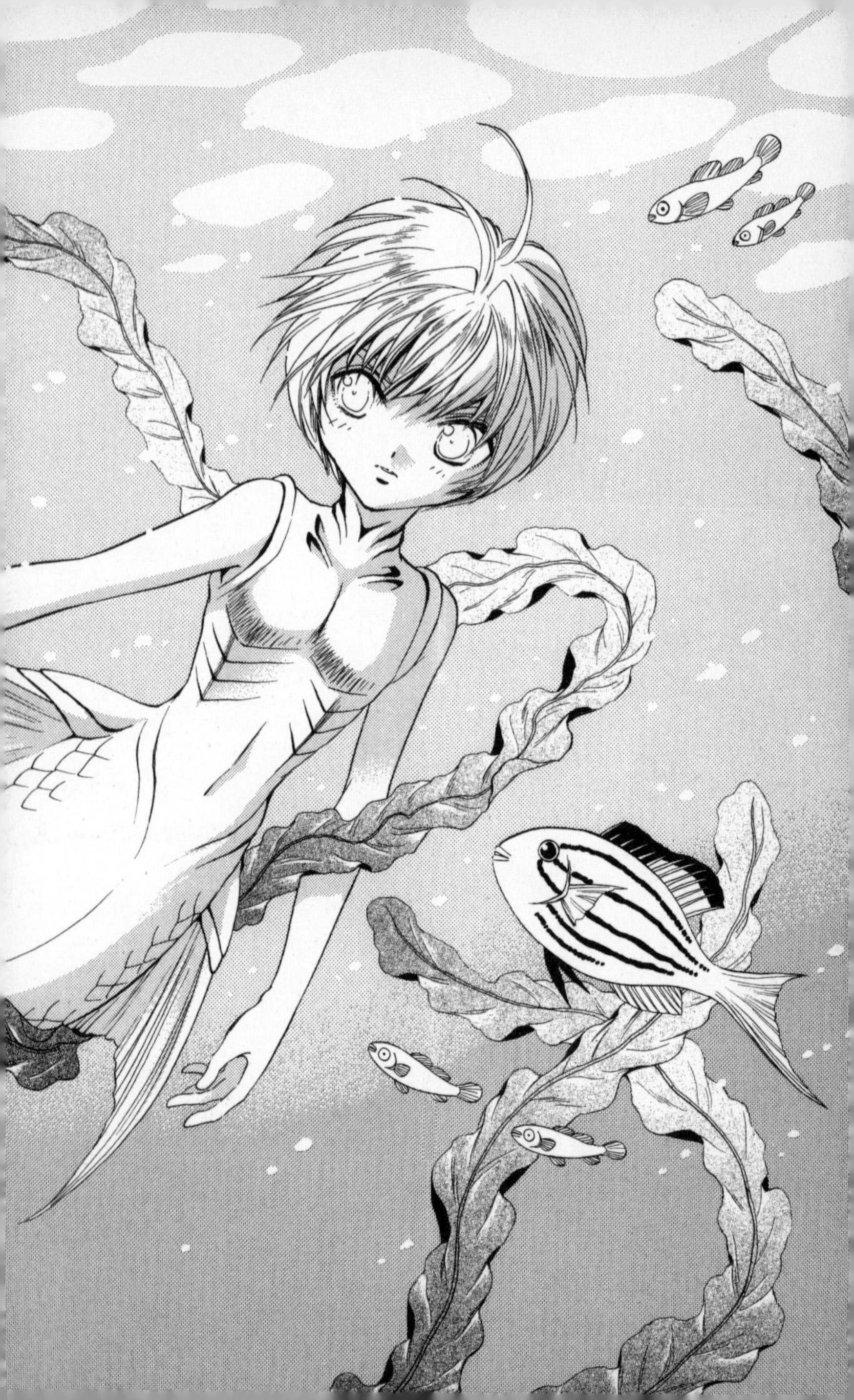

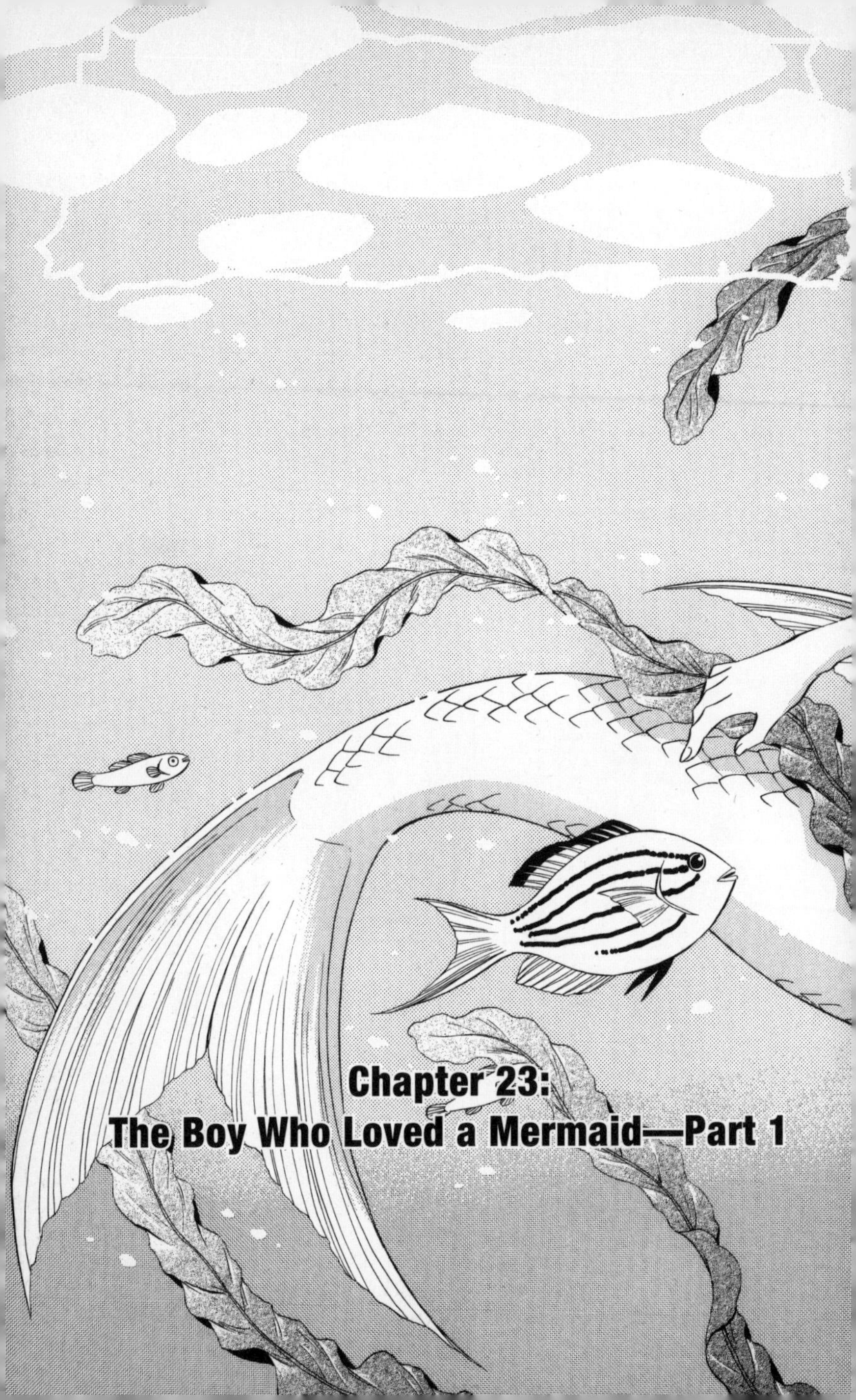

Chapter 23: The Boy Who Loved a Mermaid—Part 1

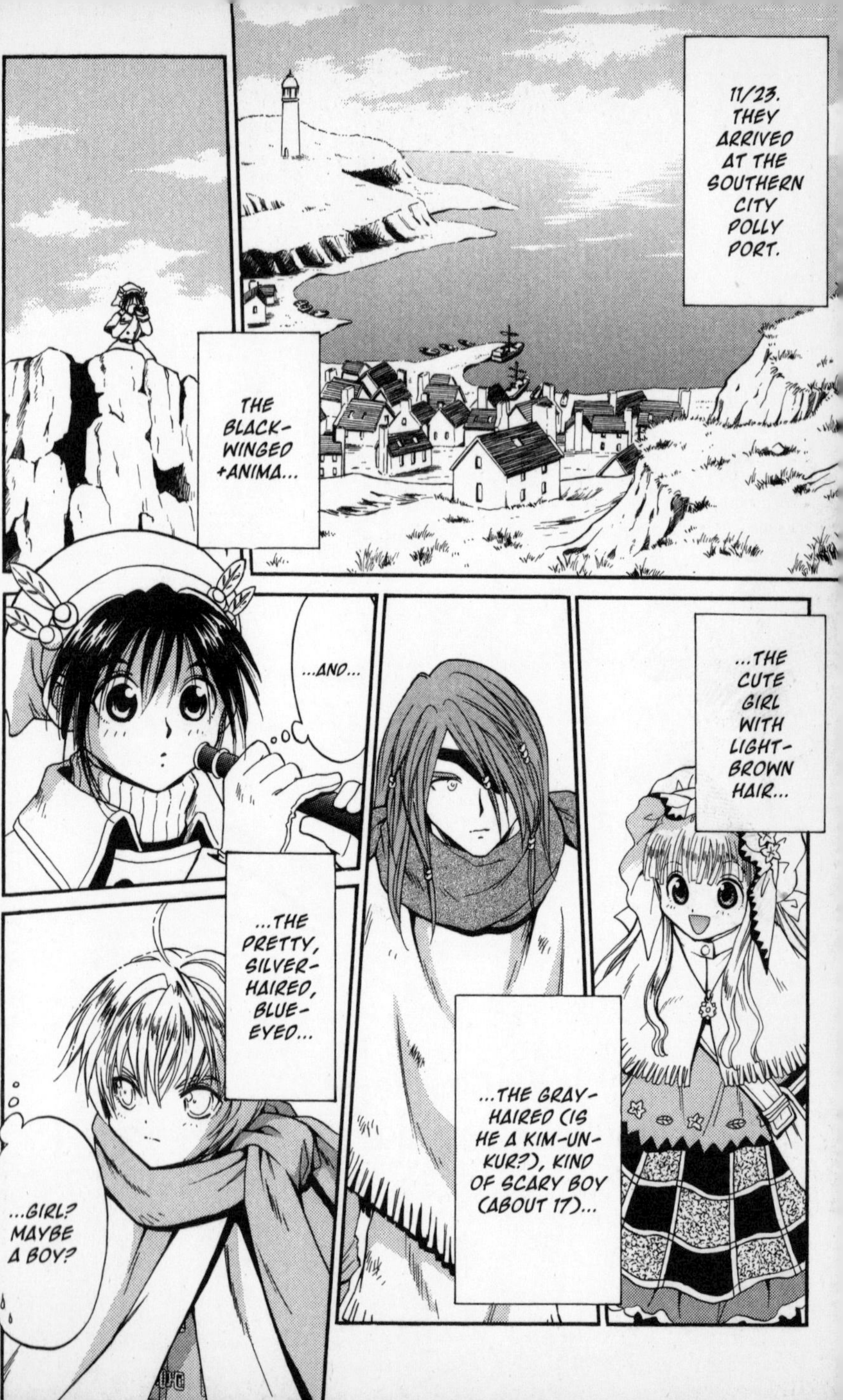
11/23. THEY ARRIVED AT THE SOUTHERN CITY POLLY PORT.
THE BLACK-WINGED +ANIMA...
...THE CUTE GIRL WITH LIGHT-BROWN HAIR...
...THE GRAY-HAIRED (IS HE A KIM-UN-KUR?), KIND OF SCARY BOY (ABOUT 17)...
...AND...
...THE PRETTY, SILVER-HAIRED, BLUE-EYED...
...GIRL? MAYBE A BOY?

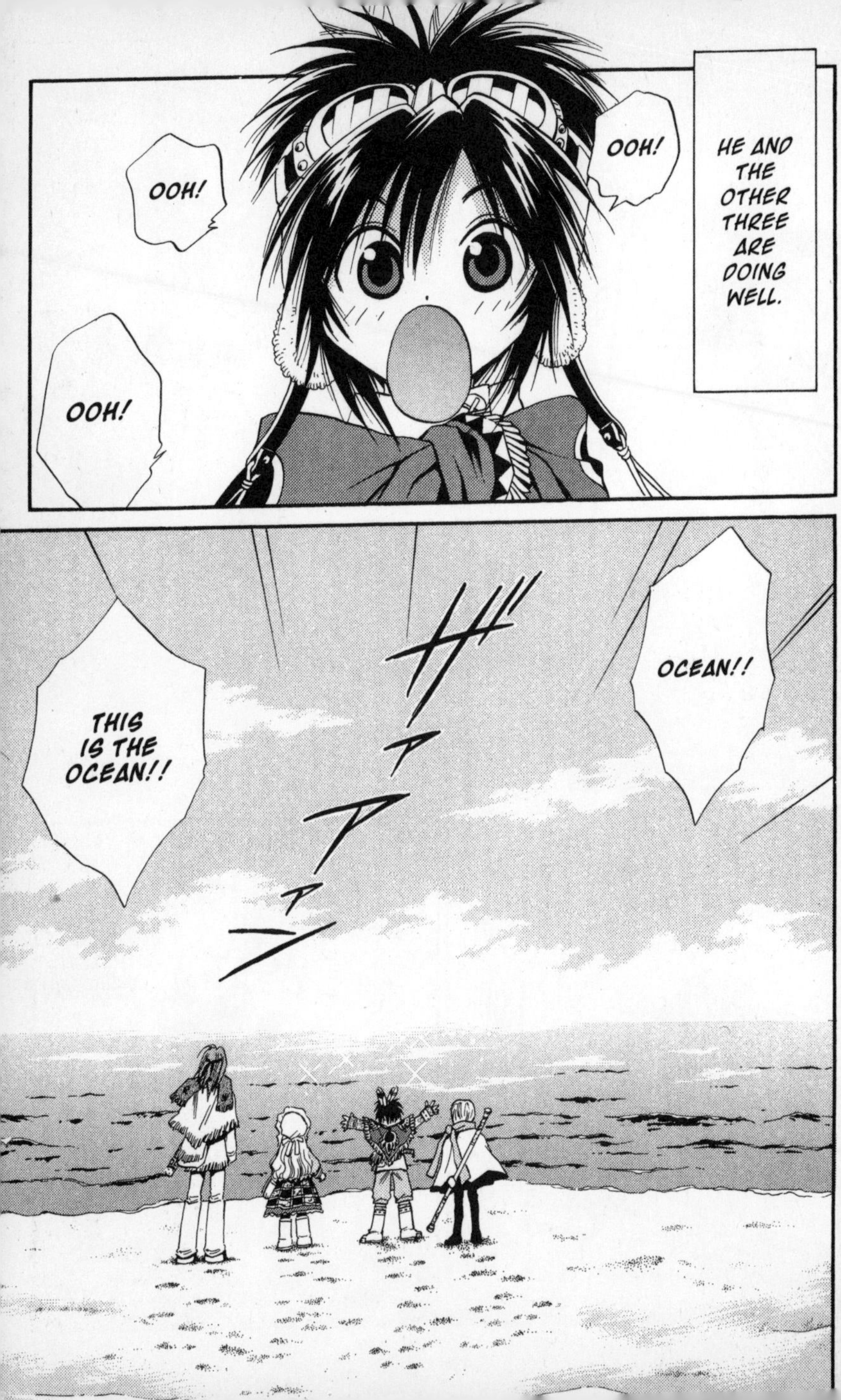
HE AND THE OTHER THREE ARE DOING WELL.
OOH!
OOH!
OOH!
OCEAN!!
THIS IS THE OCEAN!!

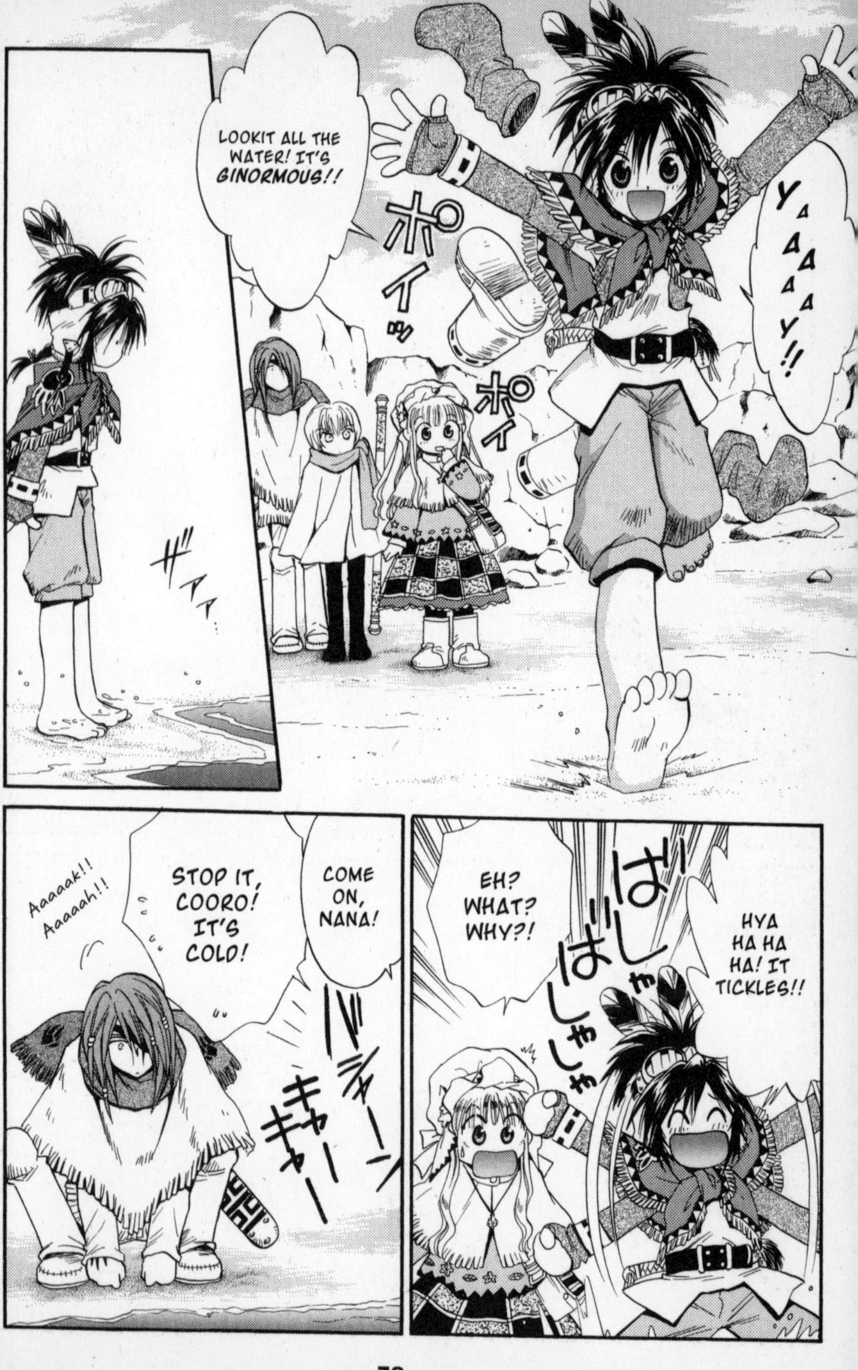
YAAAAAY!!
LOOKIT ALL THE WATER! IT'S GINORMOUS!!
ポイッ
ポイ
ザァァ…
HYA HA HA HA! IT TICKLES!!
ぱしゃ
ぱしゃしゃしゃ
EH? WHAT? WHY?!
COME ON, NANA!
STOP IT, COORO! IT'S COLD!
Aaaaak!! Aaaaah!!
ジャーー
キャーキャー

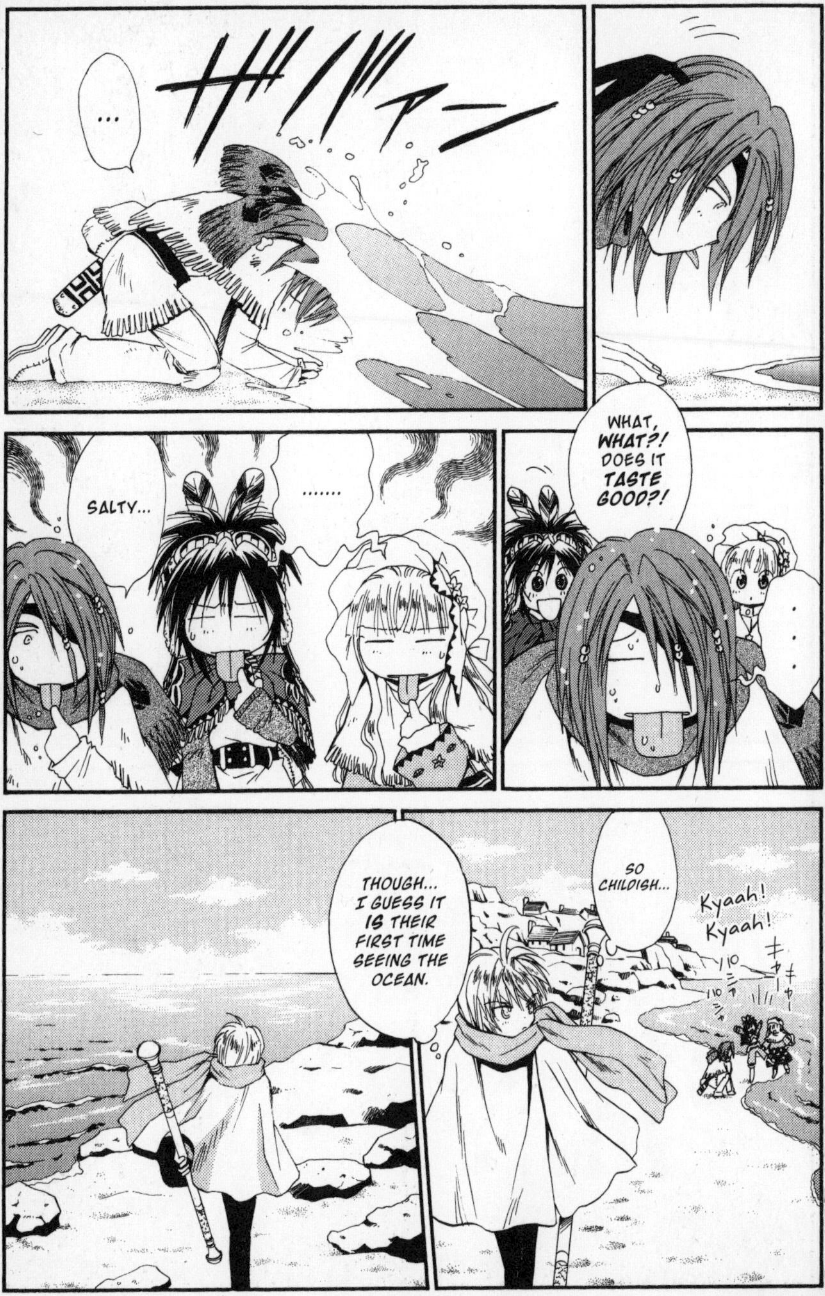
...
WHAT, WHAT?! DOES IT TASTE GOOD?!
...
....
SALTY...
Kyaah! Kyaah!
キャー キャー
SO CHILDISH...
THOUGH... I GUESS IT IS THEIR FIRST TIME SEEING THE OCEAN.

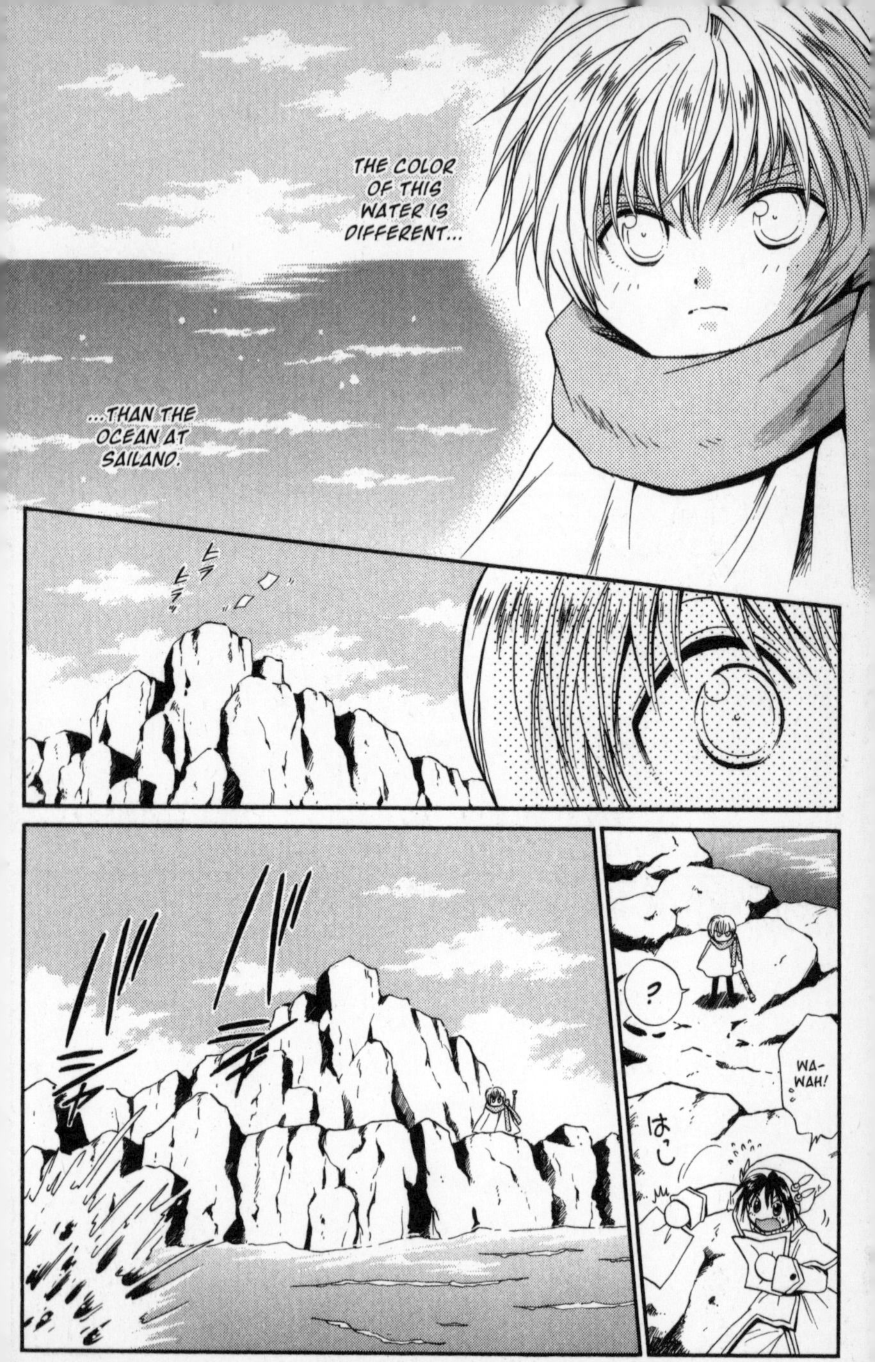
THE COLOR OF THIS WATER IS DIFFERENT...
...THAN THE OCEAN AT SAILAND.
?
WA-WAH!

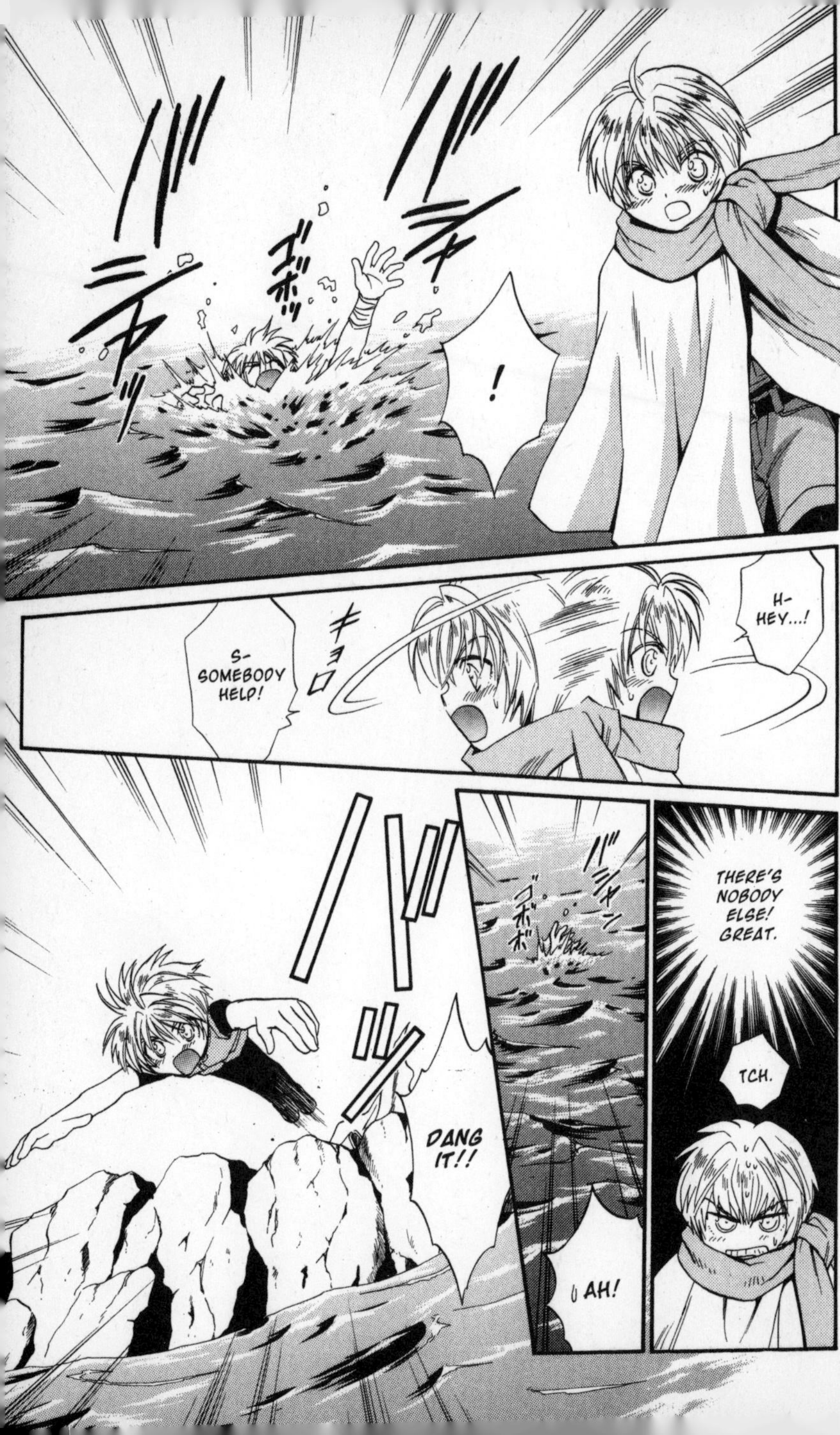
!
H-HEY...!
S-SOMEBODY HELP!
THERE'S NOBODY ELSE! GREAT.
TCH.
AH!
DANG IT!!

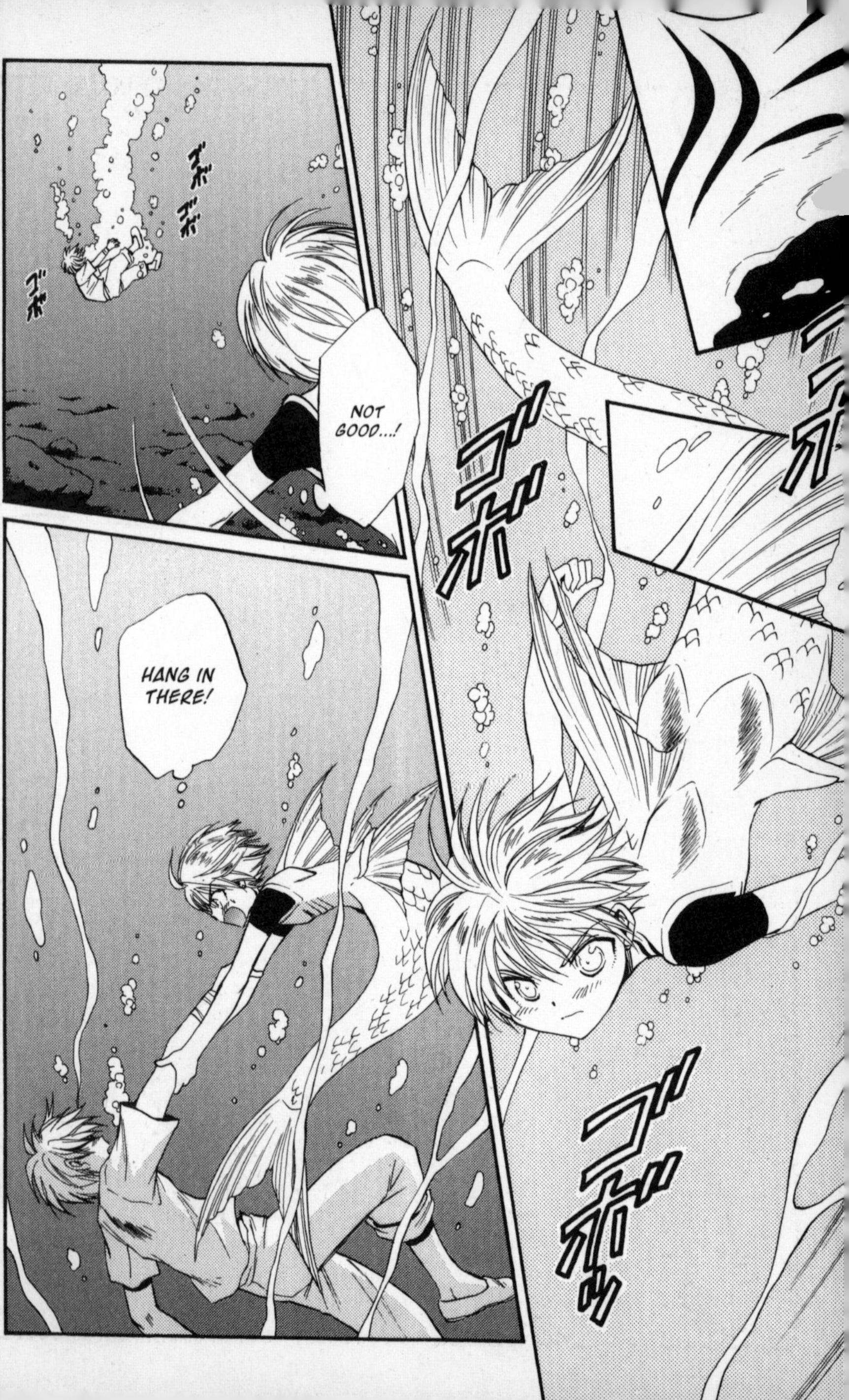
NOT GOOD...!
HANG IN THERE!

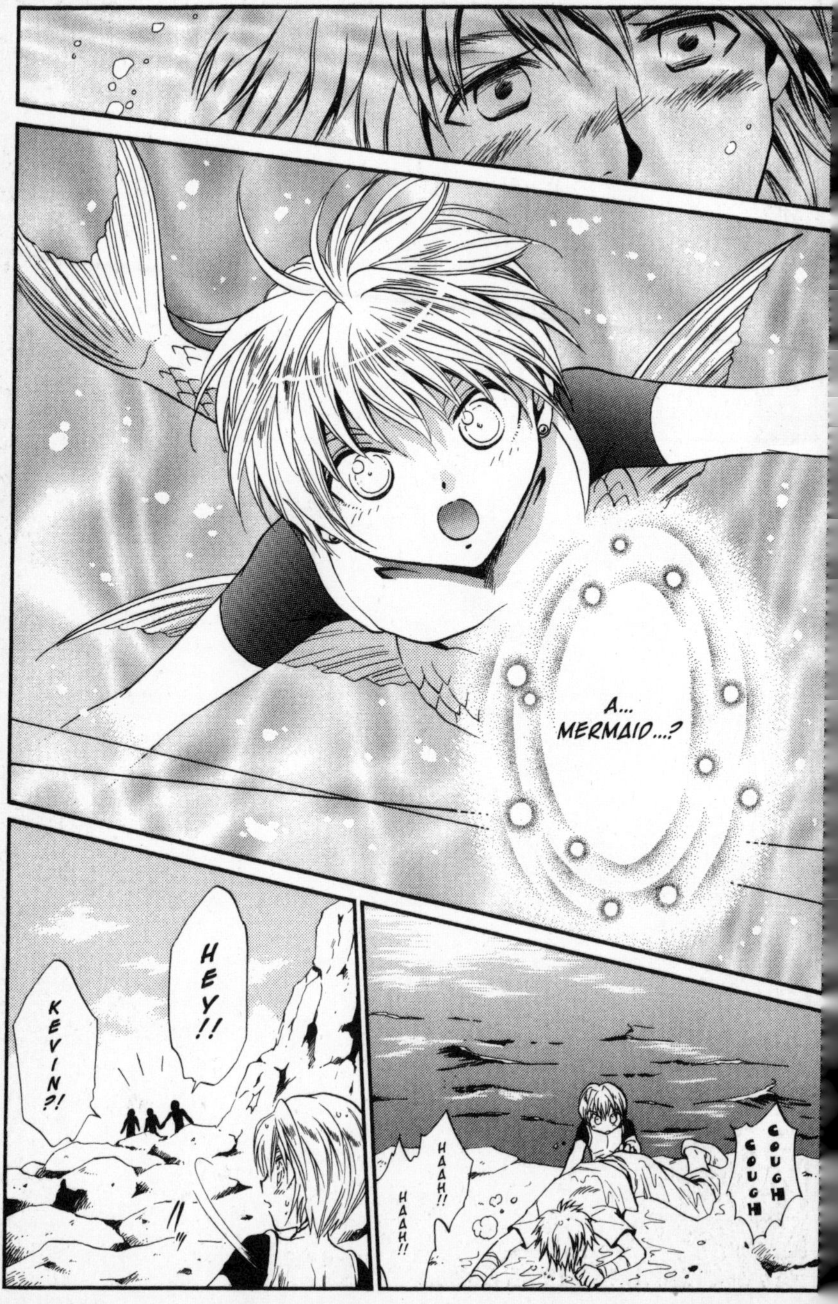
A... MERMAID...?
COUGH COUGH
HAAH!! HAAH!!
HEY!!
KEVIN?!

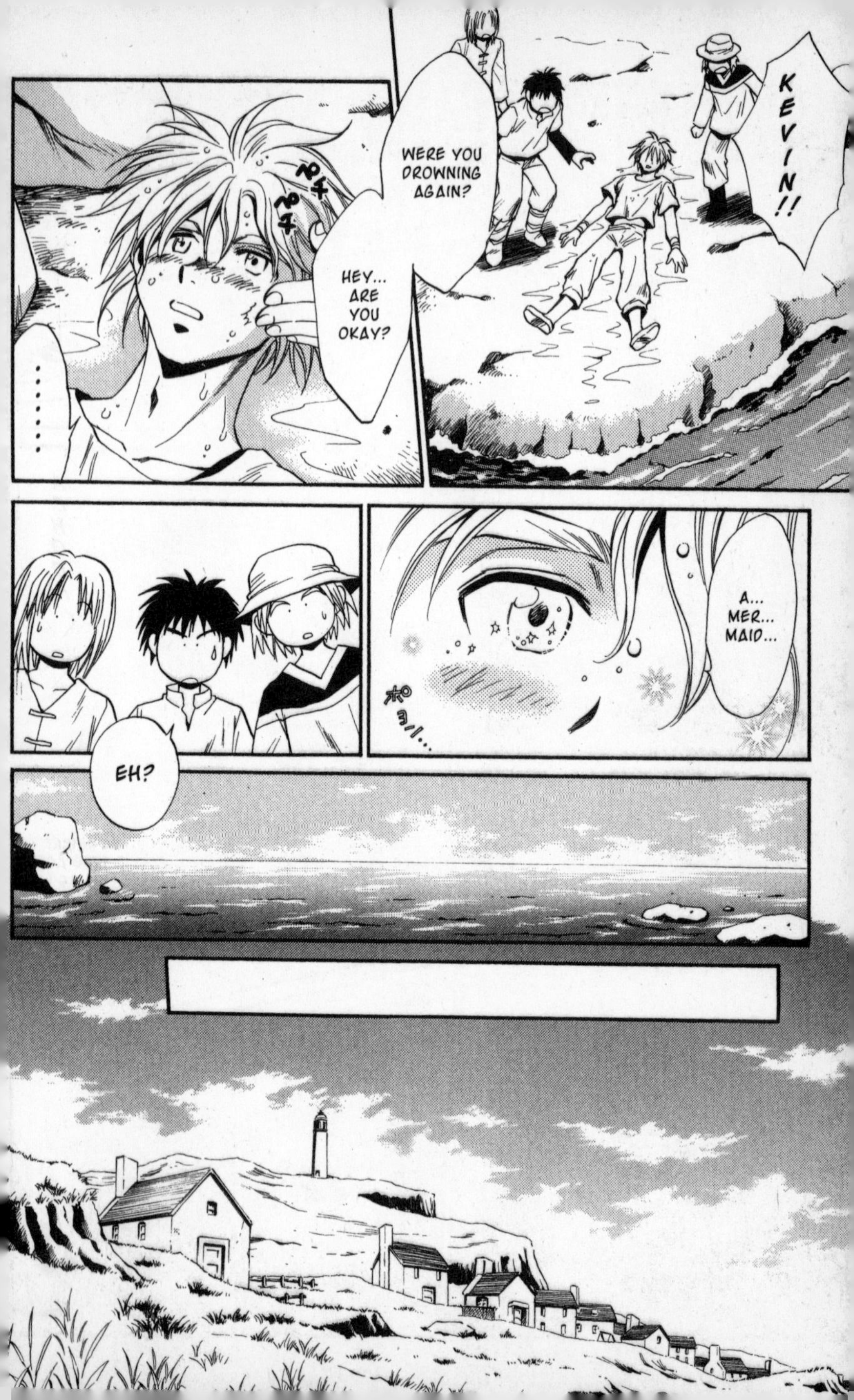
KEVIN!!
WERE YOU DROWNING AGAIN?
HEY... ARE YOU OKAY?
......
A... MER... MAID...
EH?

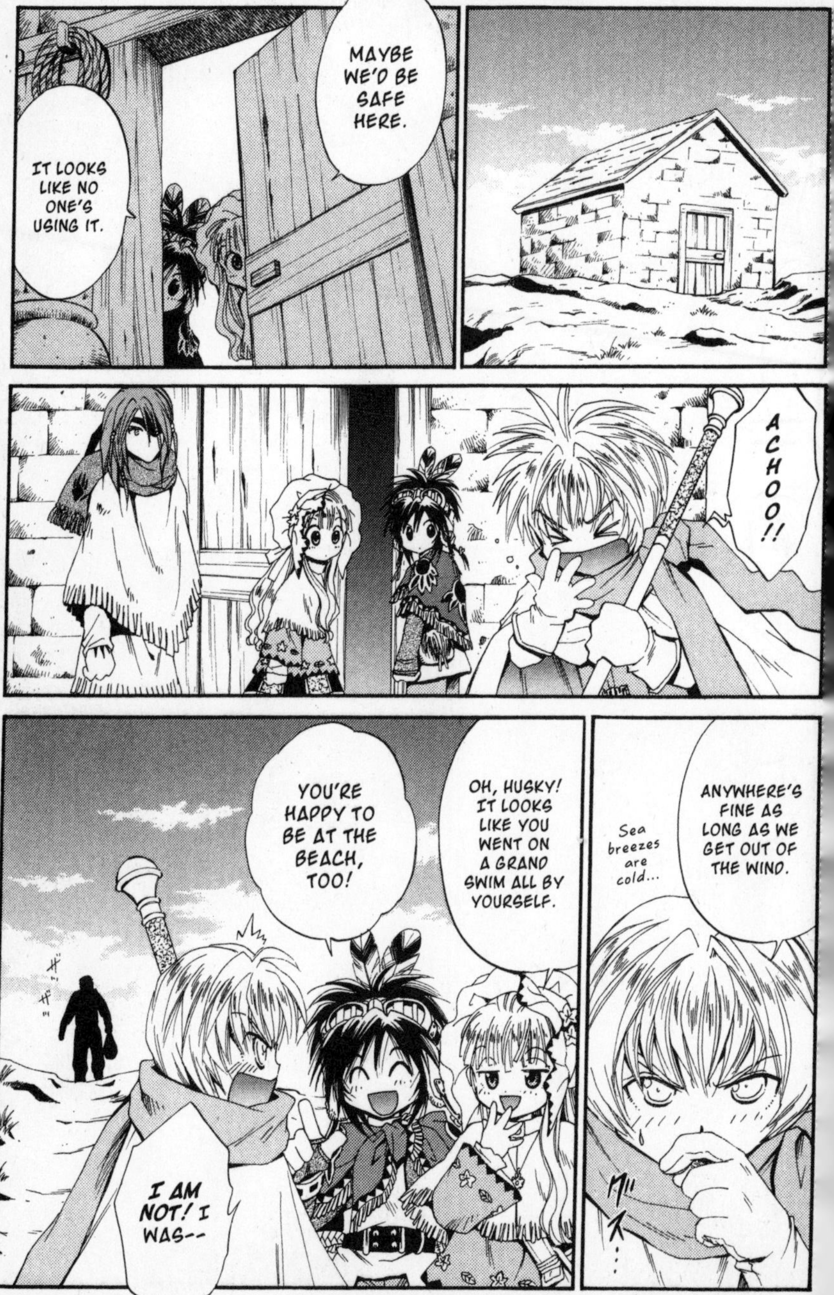
MAYBE WE'D BE SAFE HERE.
IT LOOKS LIKE NO ONE'S USING IT.
ACHOO!!
ANYWHERE'S FINE AS LONG AS WE GET OUT OF THE WIND.
Sea breezes are cold...
OH, HUSKY! IT LOOKS LIKE YOU WENT ON A GRAND SWIM ALL BY YOURSELF.
YOU'RE HAPPY TO BE AT THE BEACH, TOO!
I AM NOT! I WAS--

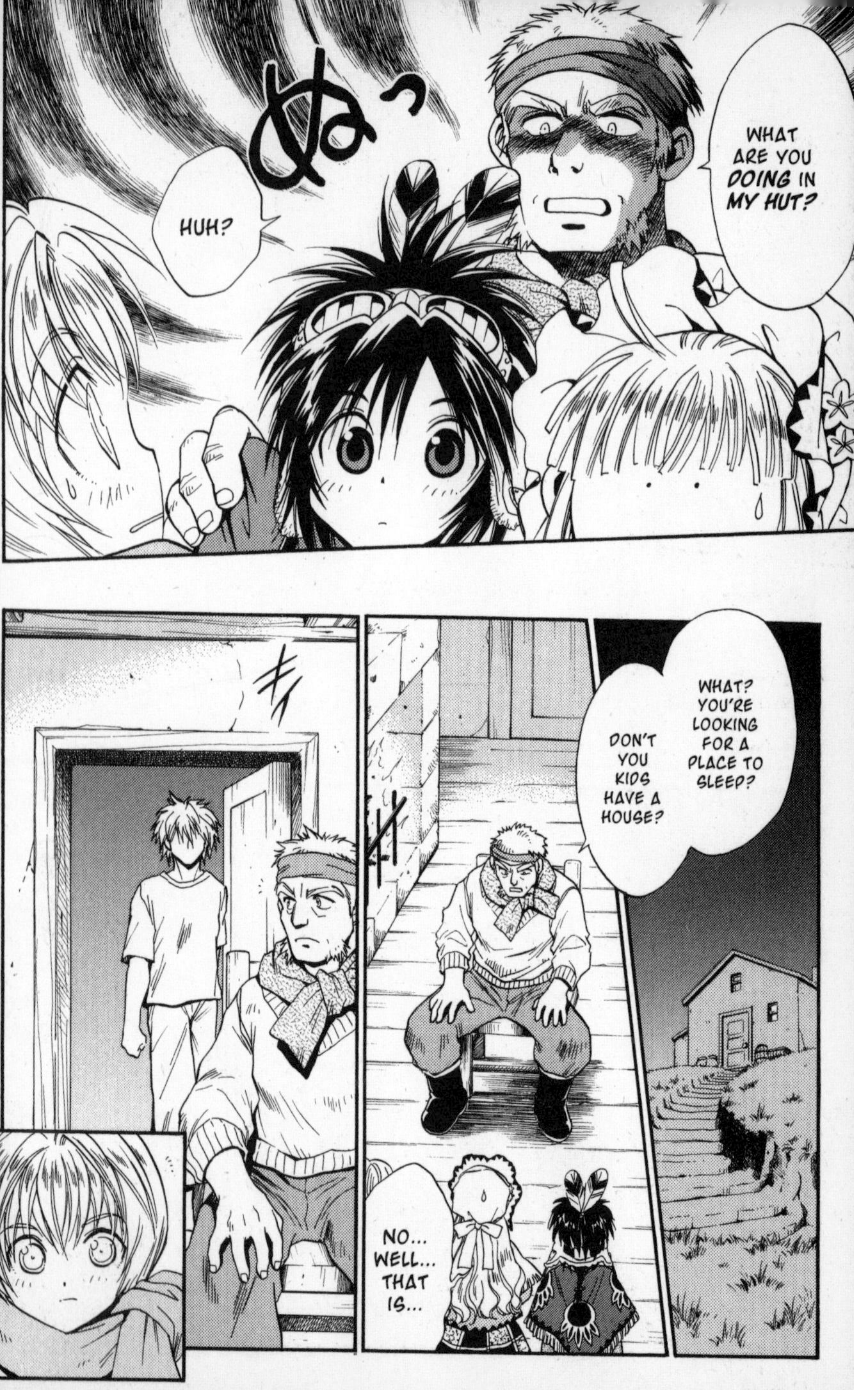
WHAT ARE YOU DOING IN MY HUT?
ぬっ
HUH?
WHAT? YOU'RE LOOKING FOR A PLACE TO SLEEP?
DON'T YOU KIDS HAVE A HOUSE?
NO... WELL... THAT IS...

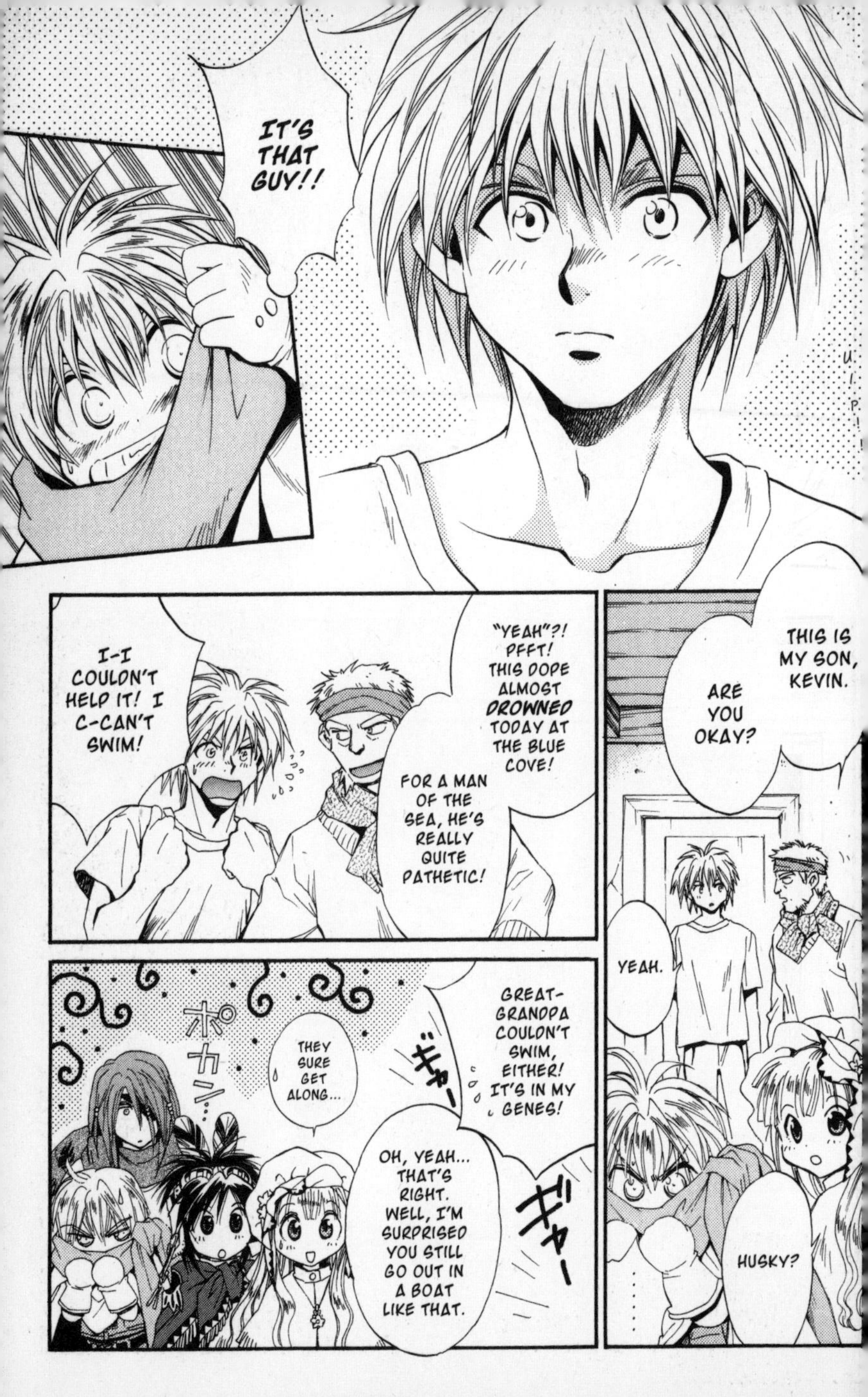
ULP!!
IT'S THAT GUY!!
THIS IS MY SON, KEVIN.
ARE YOU OKAY?
YEAH.
HUSKY?
...
"YEAH"?! PFFT! THIS DOPE ALMOST DROWNED TODAY AT THE BLUE COVE!
FOR A MAN OF THE SEA, HE'S REALLY QUITE PATHETIC!
I-I COULDN'T HELP IT! I C-CAN'T SWIM!
GREAT-GRANDPA COULDN'T SWIM, EITHER! IT'S IN MY GENES!
ギャー
ギャー
OH, YEAH... THAT'S RIGHT. WELL, I'M SURPRISED YOU STILL GO OUT IN A BOAT LIKE THAT.
THEY SURE GET ALONG...
ポカン…

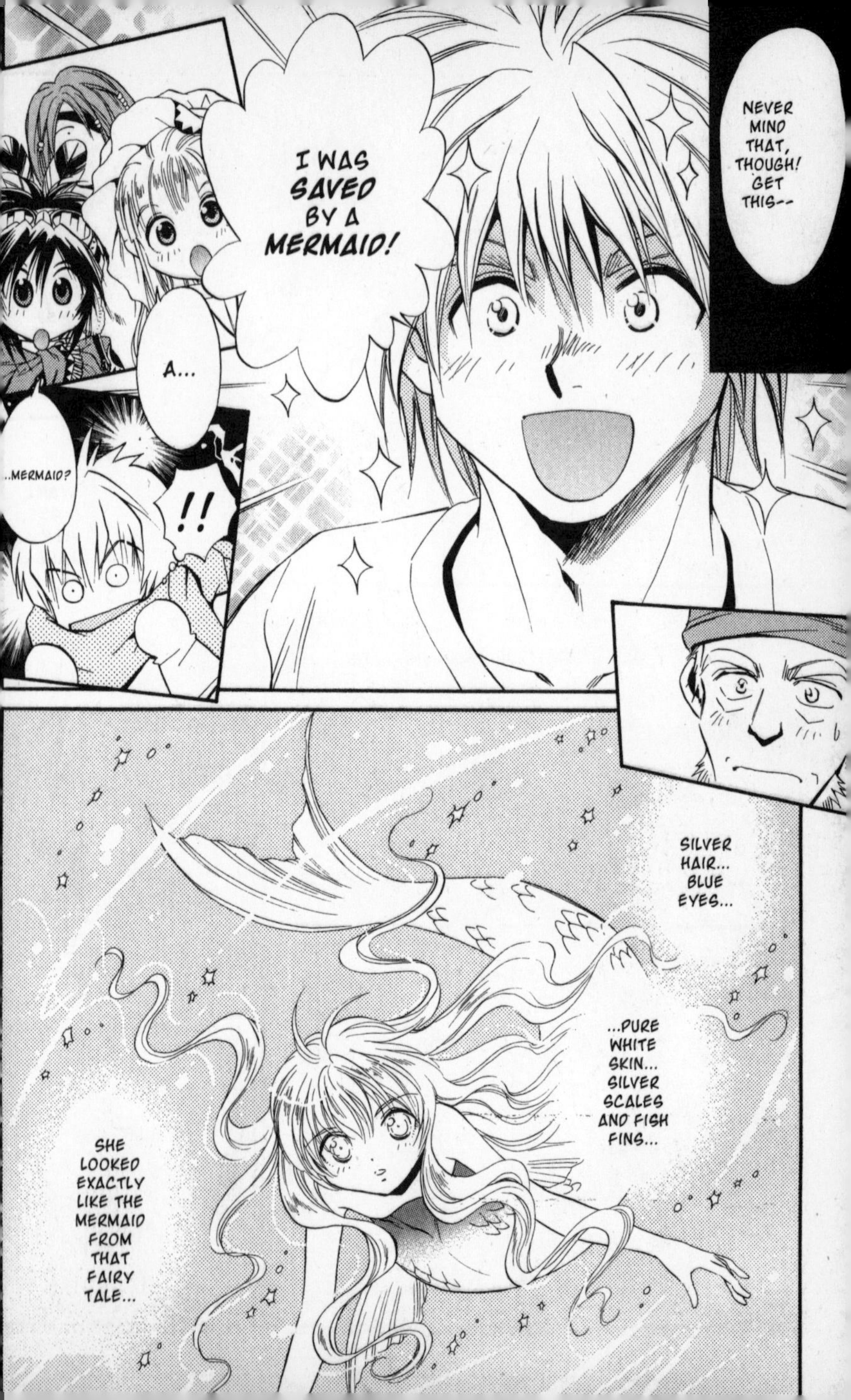
NEVER MIND THAT, THOUGH! GET THIS--
I WAS SAVED BY A MERMAID!
A...
...MERMAID?
!!
SILVER HAIR... BLUE EYES...
...PURE WHITE SKIN... SILVER SCALES AND FISH FINS...
SHE LOOKED EXACTLY LIKE THE MERMAID FROM THAT FAIRY TALE...

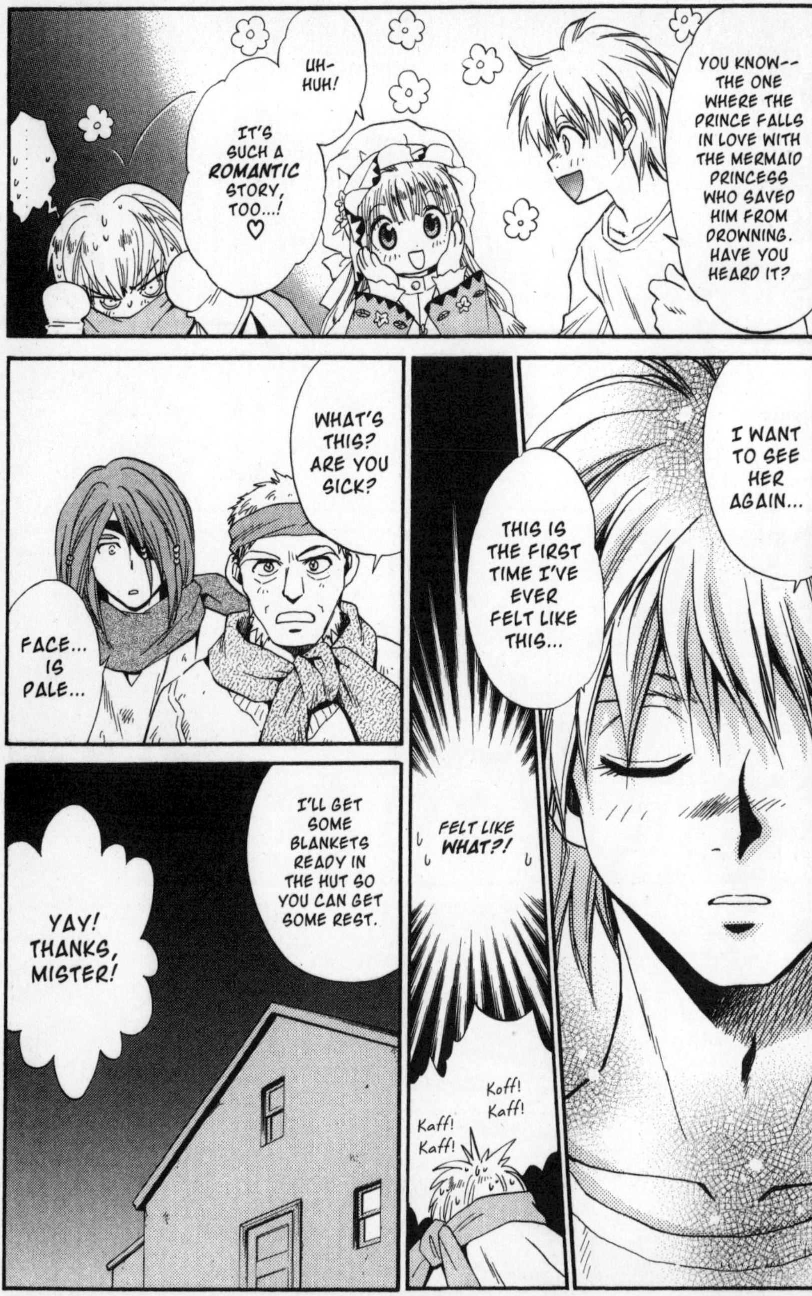
YOU KNOW-- THE ONE WHERE THE PRINCE FALLS IN LOVE WITH THE MERMAID PRINCESS WHO SAVED HIM FROM DROWNING. HAVE YOU HEARD IT?
UH-HUH!
IT'S SUCH A ROMANTIC STORY, TOO...! ♡
...
I WANT TO SEE HER AGAIN...
THIS IS THE FIRST TIME I'VE EVER FELT LIKE THIS...
FELT LIKE WHAT?!
Koff! Kaff!
Kaff! Kaff!
WHAT'S THIS? ARE YOU SICK?
FACE... IS PALE...
I'LL GET SOME BLANKETS READY IN THE HUT SO YOU CAN GET SOME REST.
YAY! THANKS, MISTER!

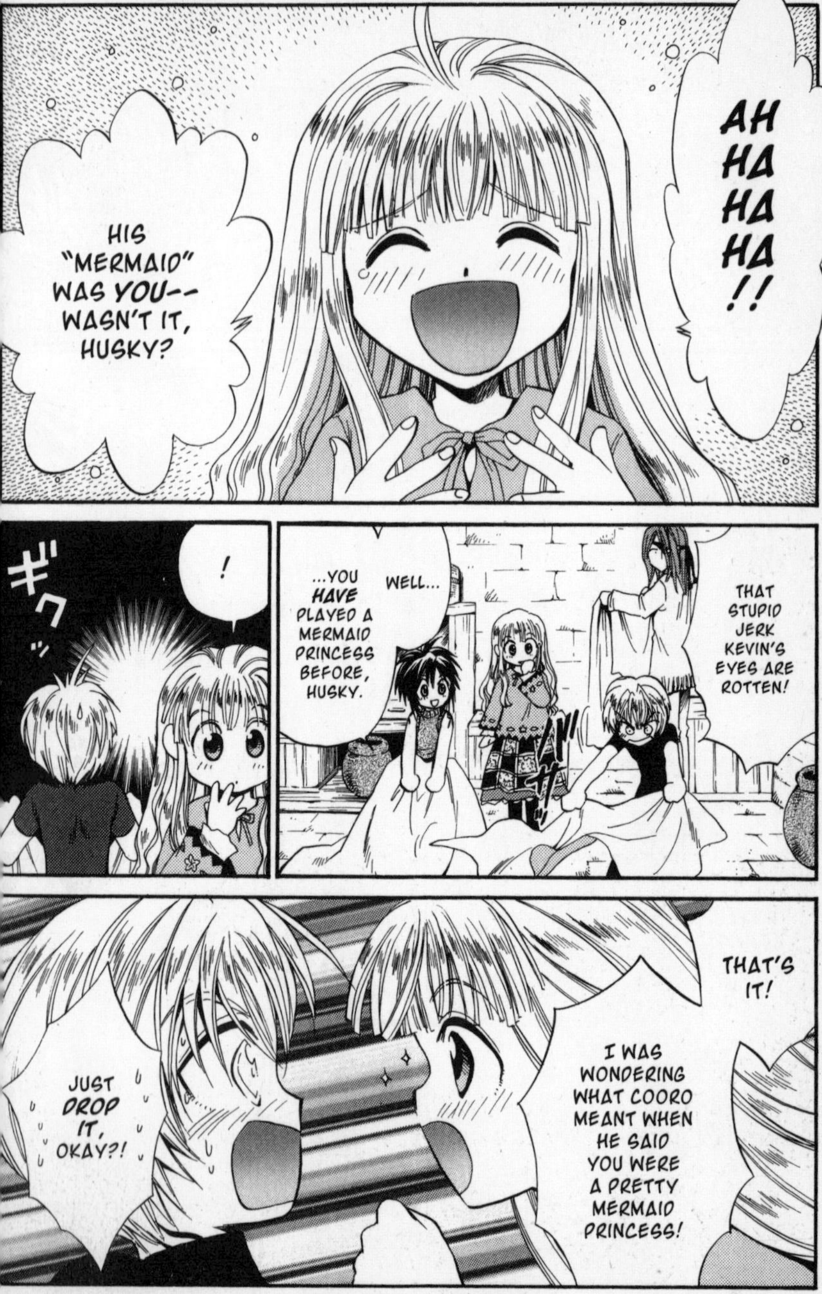
AH HA HA HA!!
HIS "MERMAID" WAS *YOU*-- WASN'T IT, HUSKY?
THAT STUPID JERK KEVIN'S EYES ARE ROTTEN!
WELL...
...YOU *HAVE* PLAYED A MERMAID PRINCESS BEFORE, HUSKY.
!
ギクッ
THAT'S IT!
I WAS WONDERING WHAT COORO MEANT WHEN HE SAID YOU WERE A PRETTY MERMAID PRINCESS!
JUST *DROP* IT, OKAY?!

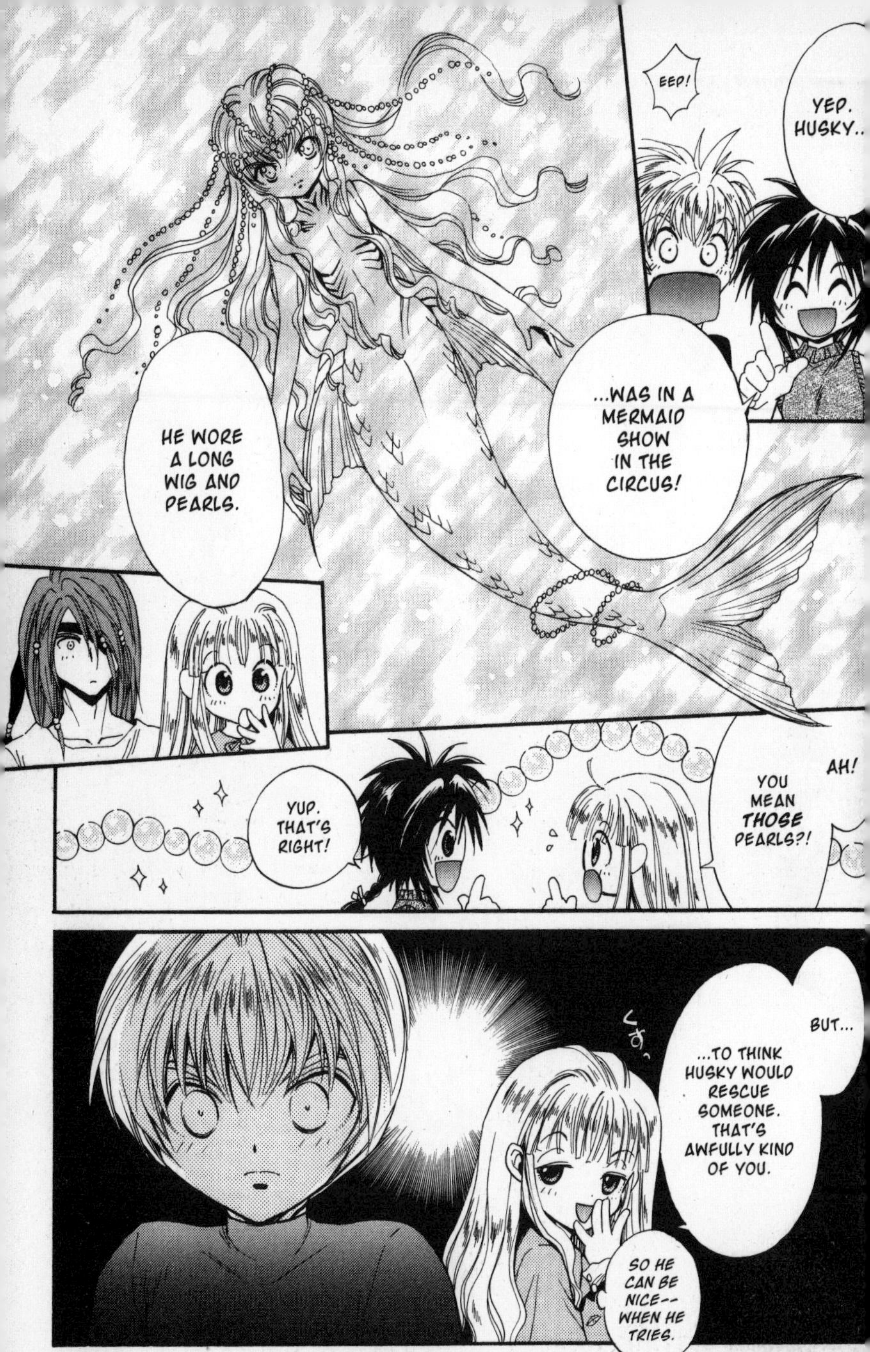
YEP. HUSKY..
EEP!
...WAS IN A MERMAID SHOW IN THE CIRCUS!
HE WORE A LONG WIG AND PEARLS.
AH!
YOU MEAN *THOSE* PEARLS?!
YUP. THAT'S RIGHT!
BUT...
...TO THINK HUSKY WOULD RESCUE SOMEONE. THAT'S AWFULLY KIND OF YOU.
SO HE CAN BE NICE--WHEN HE TRIES.

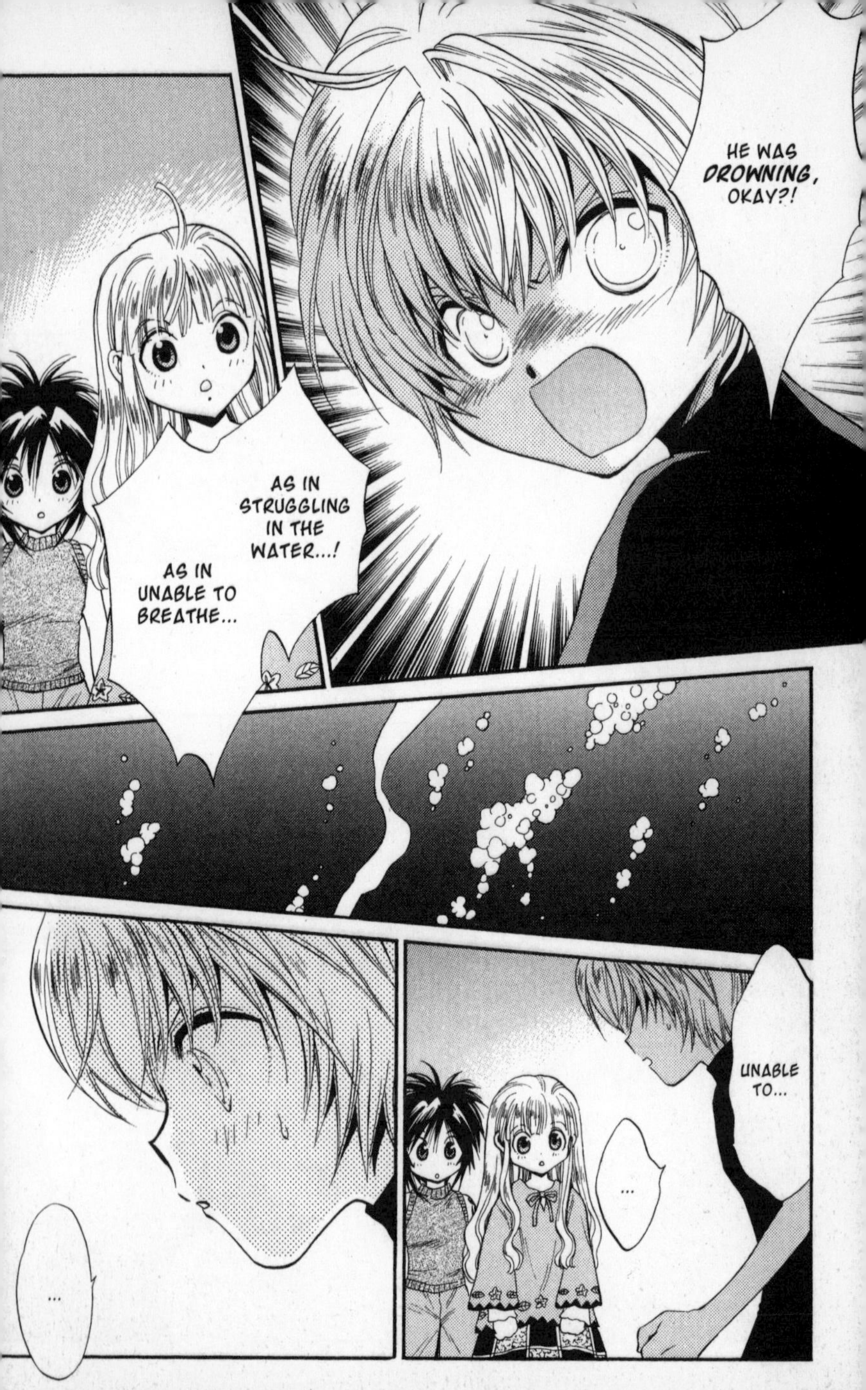
HE WAS DROWNING, OKAY?!
AS IN STRUGGLING IN THE WATER...!
AS IN UNABLE TO BREATHE...
UNABLE TO...
...
...

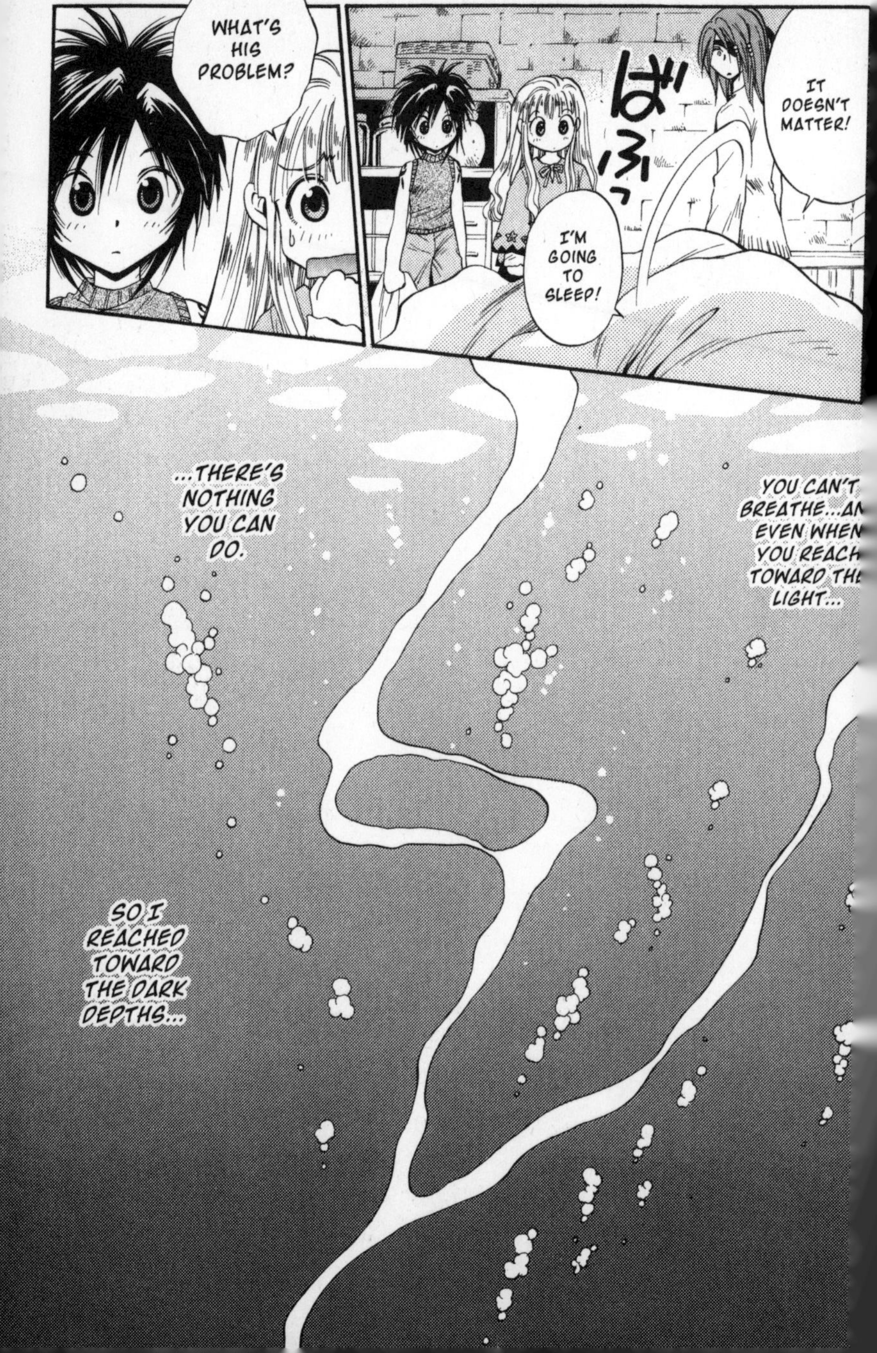
IT DOESN'T MATTER!
ばふっ
I'M GOING TO SLEEP!
WHAT'S HIS PROBLEM?
YOU CAN'T BREATHE...AN
EVEN WHEN
YOU REACH
TOWARD TH
LIGHT...
...THERE'S NOTHING YOU CAN DO.
SO I REACHED TOWARD THE DARK DEPTHS...

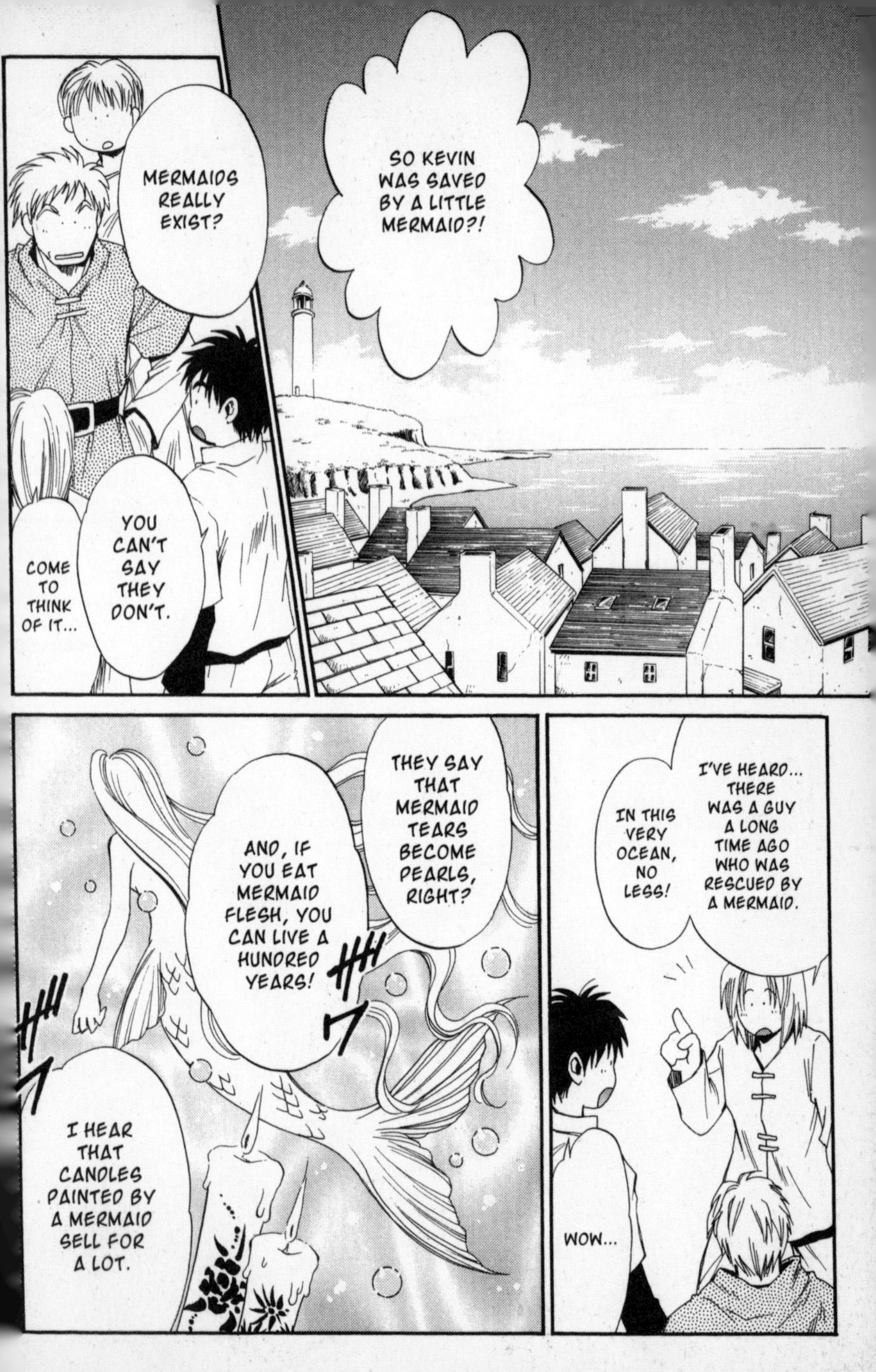
SO KEVIN WAS SAVED BY A LITTLE MERMAID?!
MERMAIDS REALLY EXIST?
YOU CAN'T SAY THEY DON'T.
COME TO THINK OF IT...
I'VE HEARD... THERE WAS A GUY A LONG TIME AGO WHO WAS RESCUED BY A MERMAID.
IN THIS VERY OCEAN, NO LESS!
WOW...
THEY SAY THAT MERMAID TEARS BECOME PEARLS, RIGHT?
AND, IF YOU EAT MERMAID FLESH, YOU CAN LIVE A HUNDRED YEARS!
I HEAR THAT CANDLES PAINTED BY A MERMAID SELL FOR A LOT.

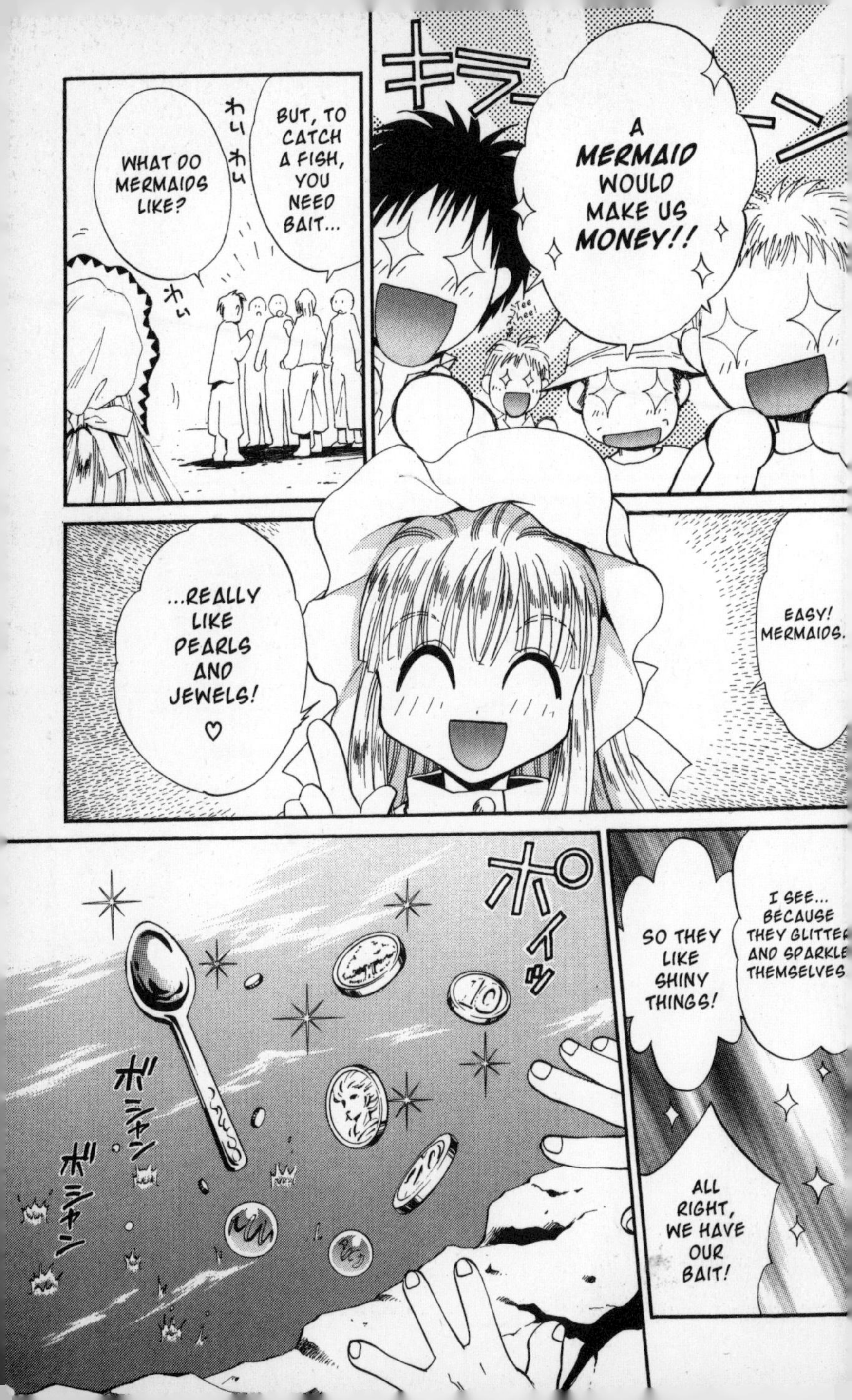

キラーン
A MERMAID WOULD MAKE US MONEY!!
Tee hee!
BUT, TO CATCH A FISH, YOU NEED BAIT...
わい わい
WHAT DO MERMAIDS LIKE?
わい
EASY! MERMAIDS.
...REALLY LIKE PEARLS AND JEWELS! ♡
I SEE... BECAUSE THEY GLITTER AND SPARKLE THEMSELVES
SO THEY LIKE SHINY THINGS!
ALL RIGHT, WE HAVE OUR BAIT!
ポイッ
ボシャン
ボシャン

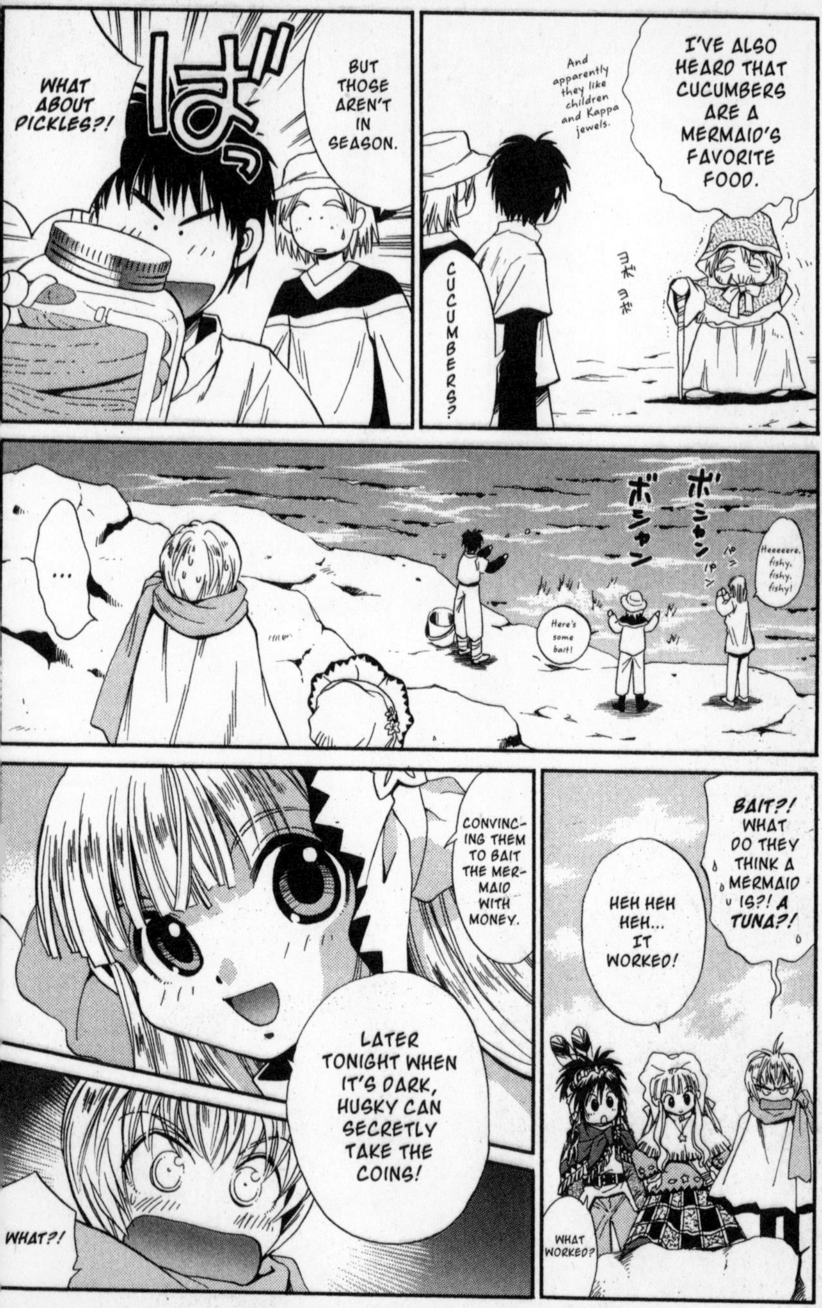
I'VE ALSO HEARD THAT CUCUMBERS ARE A MERMAID'S FAVORITE FOOD.
And apparently they like children and Kappa jewels.
ヨボ ヨボ
CUCUMBERS?
BUT THOSE AREN'T IN SEASON.
ぱっ
WHAT ABOUT PICKLES?!
Heeeeere, fishy, fishy, fishy!
ボシャン
ボシャン
Here's some bait!
...
BAIT?! WHAT DO THEY THINK A MERMAID IS?! A TUNA?!
HEH HEH HEH... IT WORKED!
WHAT WORKED?
CONVINCING THEM TO BAIT THE MERMAID WITH MONEY.
LATER TONIGHT WHEN IT'S DARK, HUSKY CAN SECRETLY TAKE THE COINS!
WHAT?!

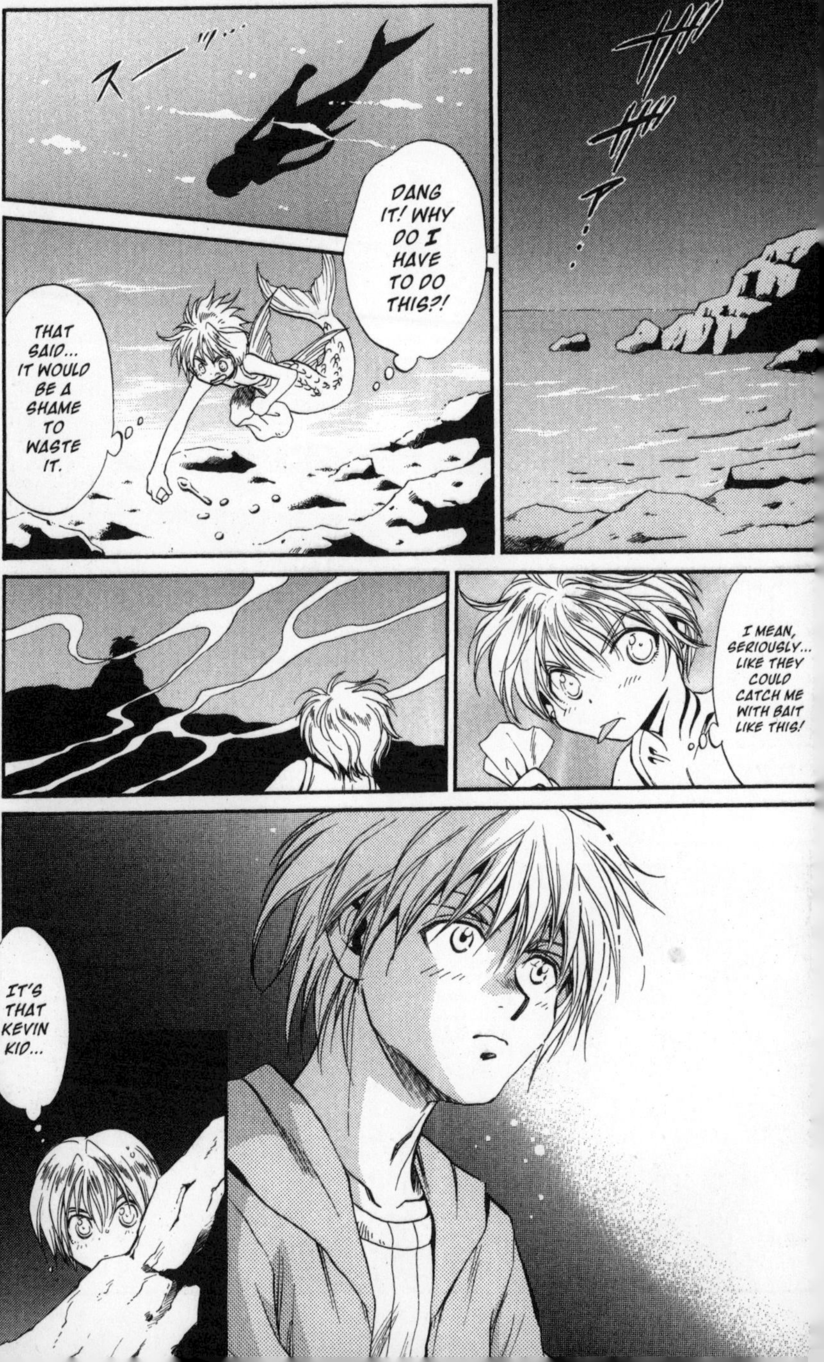
ザザ ザァ...
スーッ...
DANG IT! WHY DO I HAVE TO DO THIS?!
THAT SAID... IT WOULD BE A SHAME TO WASTE IT.
I MEAN, SERIOUSLY... LIKE THEY COULD CATCH ME WITH BAIT LIKE THIS!
IT'S THAT KEVIN KID...

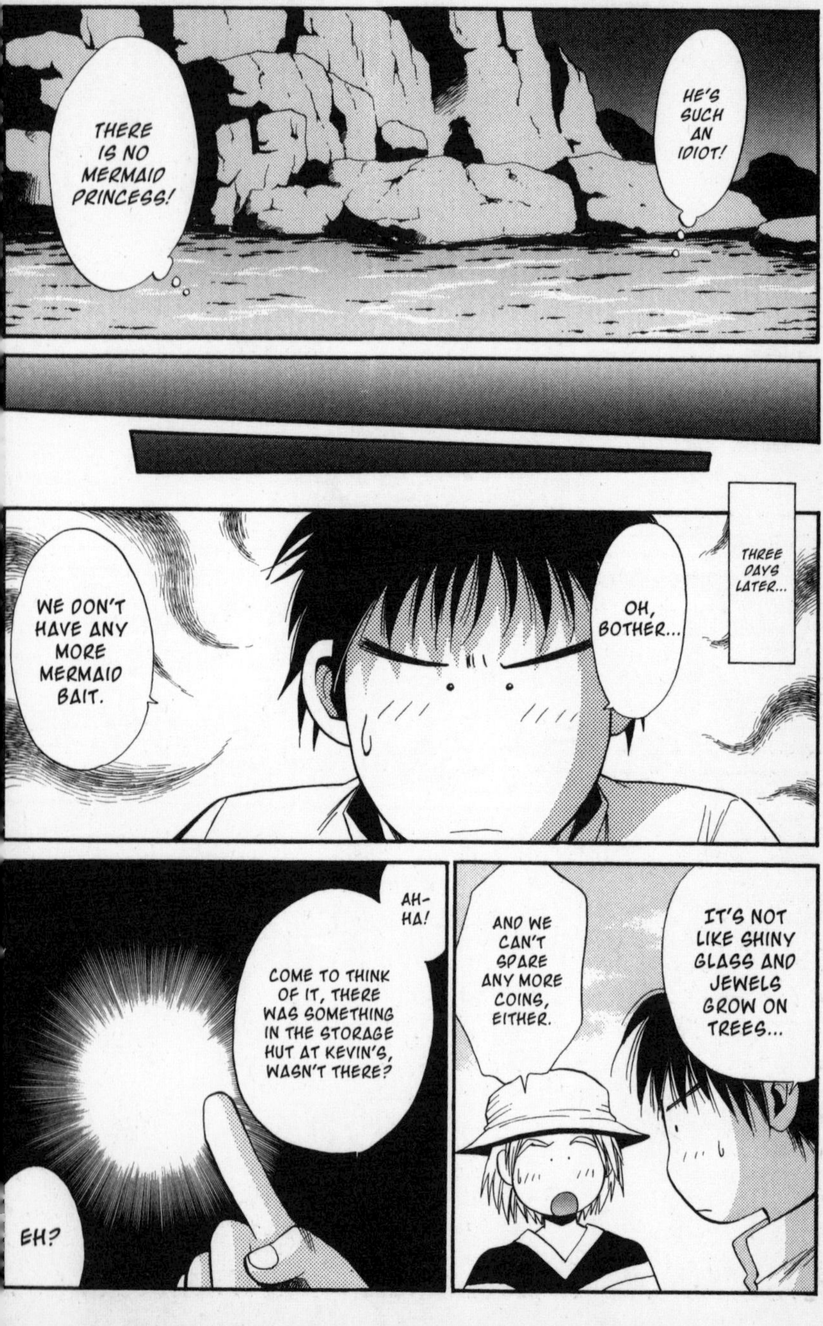
HE'S SUCH AN IDIOT!
THERE IS NO MERMAID PRINCESS!
THREE DAYS LATER...
OH, BOTHER...
WE DON'T HAVE ANY MORE MERMAID BAIT.
IT'S NOT LIKE SHINY GLASS AND JEWELS GROW ON TREES...
AND WE CAN'T SPARE ANY MORE COINS, EITHER.
AH-HA!
COME TO THINK OF IT, THERE WAS SOMETHING IN THE STORAGE HUT AT KEVIN'S, WASN'T THERE?
EH?

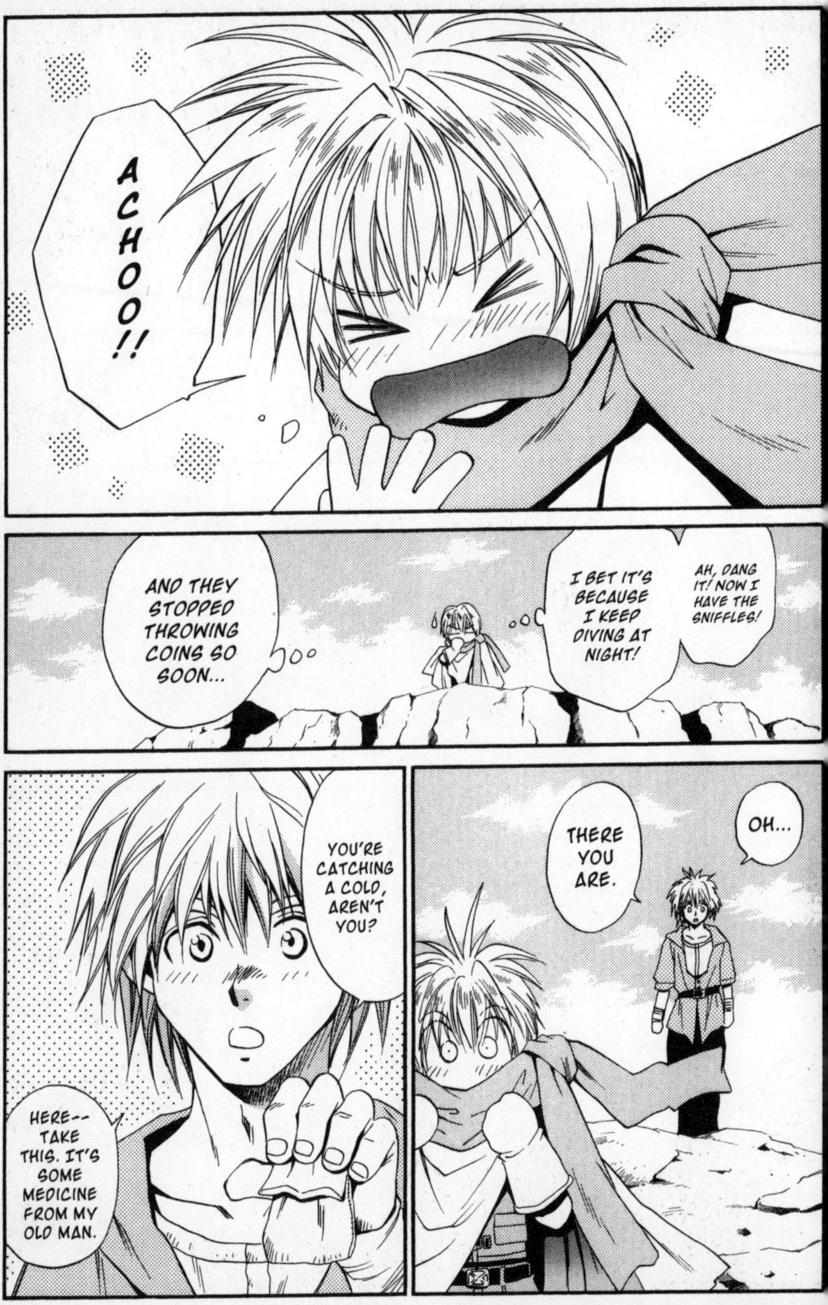
ACHOO!!
AH, DANG IT! NOW I HAVE THE SNIFFLES!
I BET IT'S BECAUSE I KEEP DIVING AT NIGHT!
AND THEY STOPPED THROWING COINS SO SOON...
OH...
THERE YOU ARE.
YOU'RE CATCHING A COLD, AREN'T YOU?
HERE--TAKE THIS. IT'S SOME MEDICINE FROM MY OLD MAN.

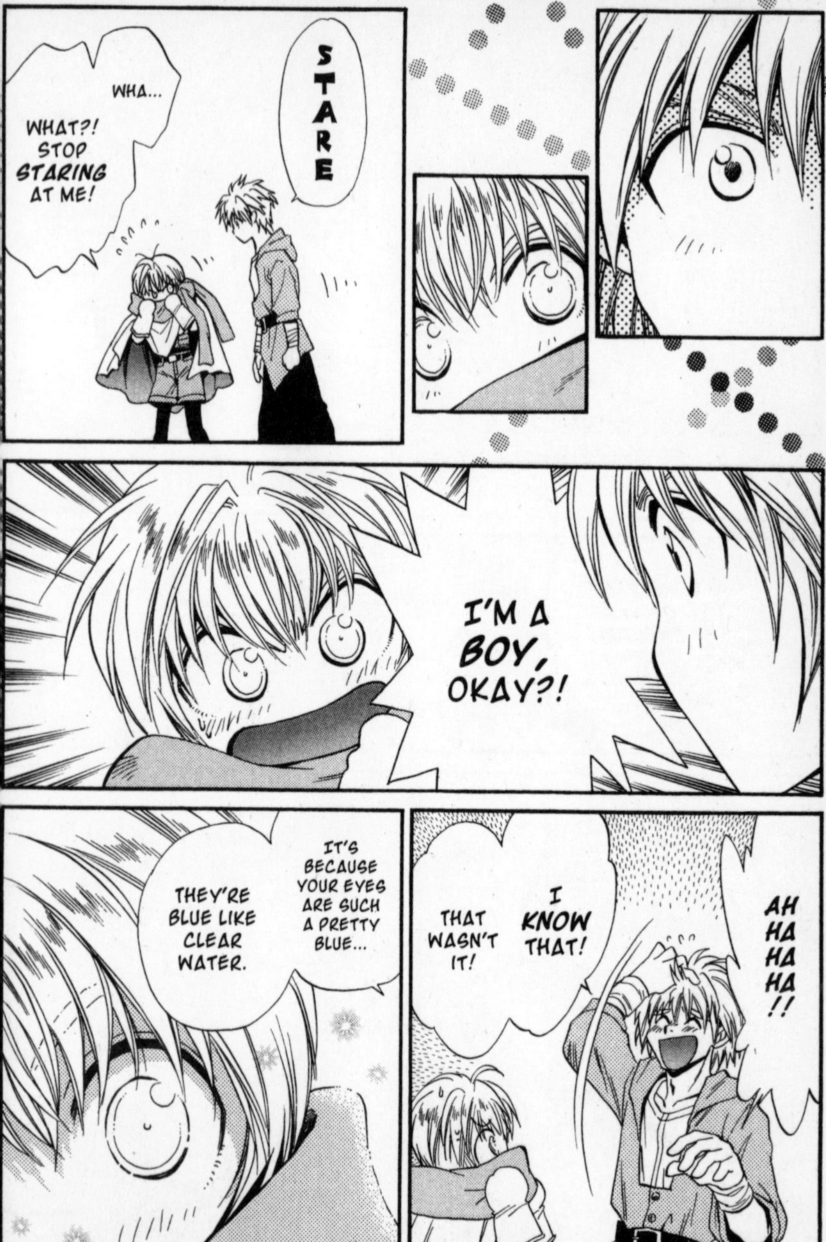
STARE
WHA... WHAT?! STOP STARING AT ME!
I'M A BOY, OKAY?!
AH HA HA HA!!
I KNOW THAT!
THAT WASN'T IT!
IT'S BECAUSE YOUR EYES ARE SUCH A PRETTY BLUE...
THEY'RE BLUE LIKE CLEAR WATER.

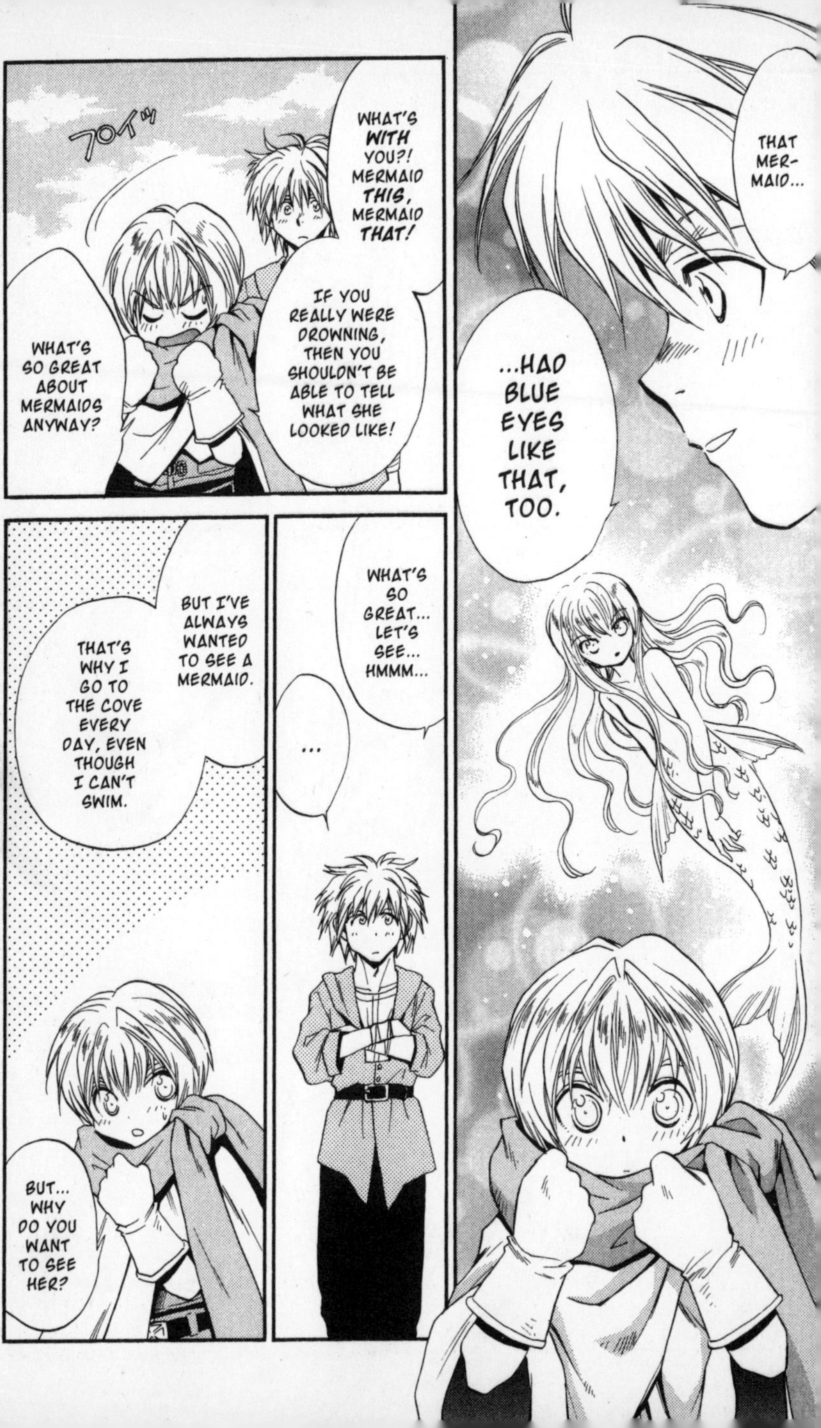
THAT MERMAID...
...HAD BLUE EYES LIKE THAT, TOO.
フイッ
WHAT'S WITH YOU?! MERMAID THIS, MERMAID THAT!
IF YOU REALLY WERE DROWNING, THEN YOU SHOULDN'T BE ABLE TO TELL WHAT SHE LOOKED LIKE!
WHAT'S SO GREAT ABOUT MERMAIDS ANYWAY?
WHAT'S SO GREAT... LET'S SEE... HMMM...
...
BUT I'VE ALWAYS WANTED TO SEE A MERMAID.
THAT'S WHY I GO TO THE COVE EVERY DAY, EVEN THOUGH I CAN'T SWIM.
BUT... WHY DO YOU WANT TO SEE HER?

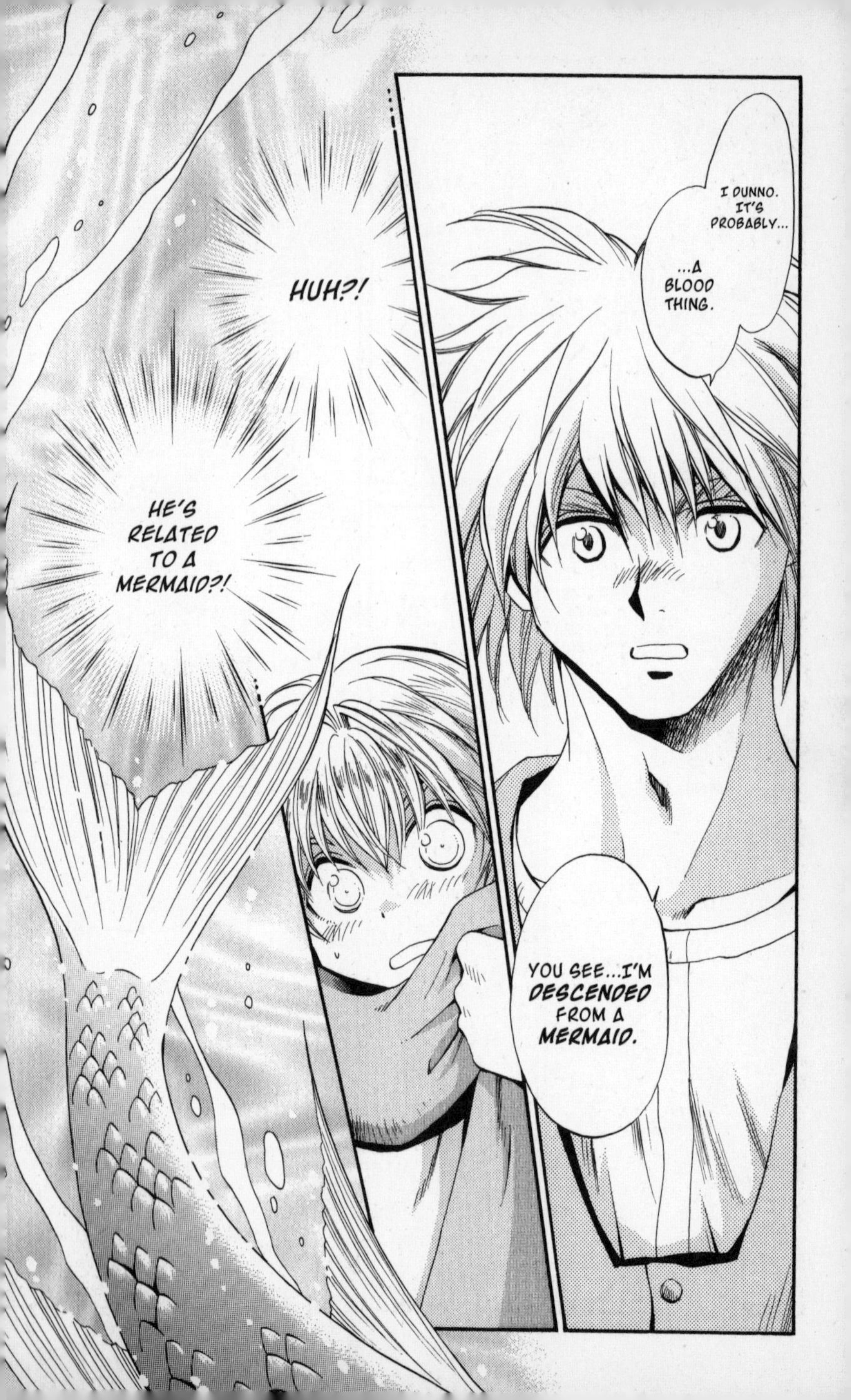
I DUNNO. IT'S PROBABLY...
...A BLOOD THING.
YOU SEE...I'M DESCENDED FROM A MERMAID.
HUH?!
HE'S RELATED TO A MERMAID?!

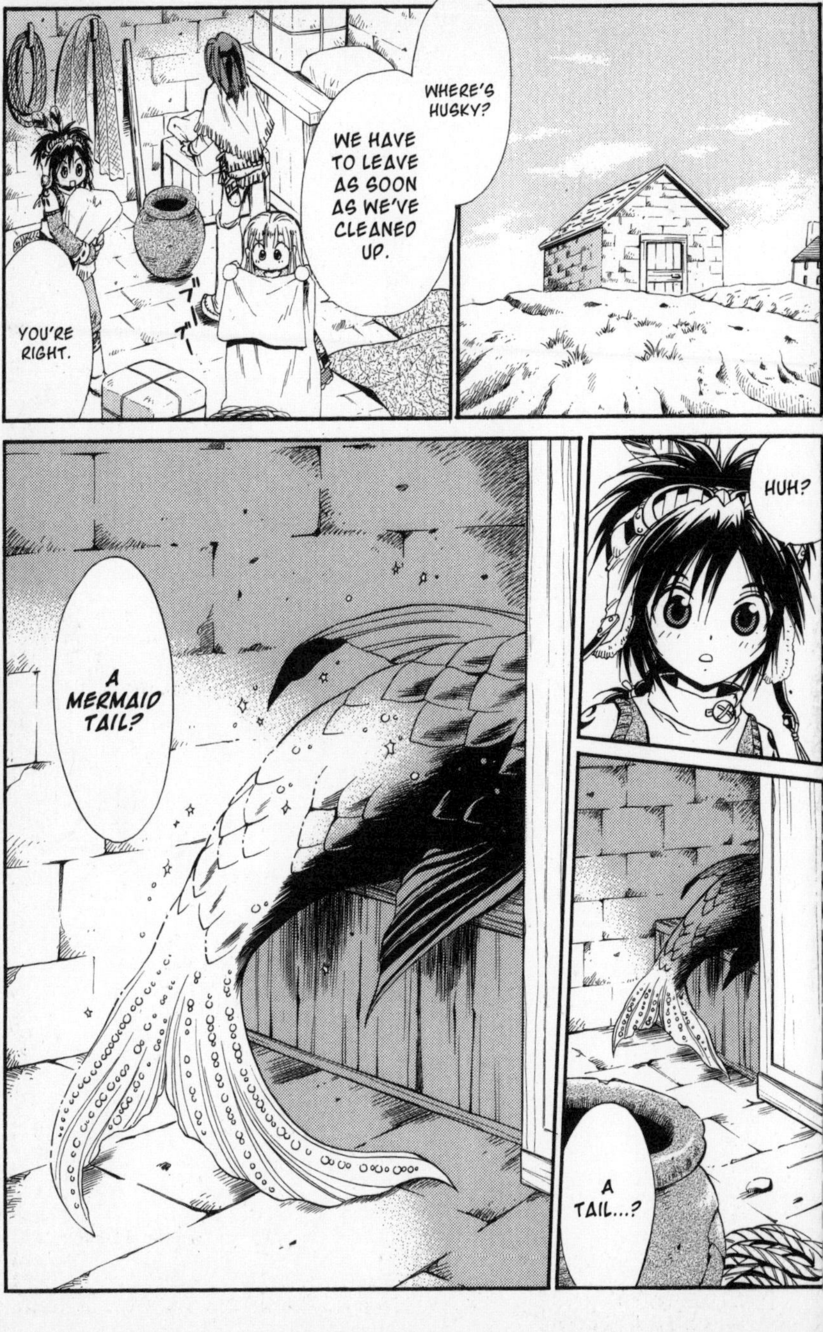
WHERE'S HUSKY?
WE HAVE TO LEAVE AS SOON AS WE'VE CLEANED UP.
YOU'RE RIGHT.
HUH?
A TAIL...?
A MERMAID TAIL?

Clean the sea!

Chapter 24:
The Boy Who Loved a Mermaid—Part 2

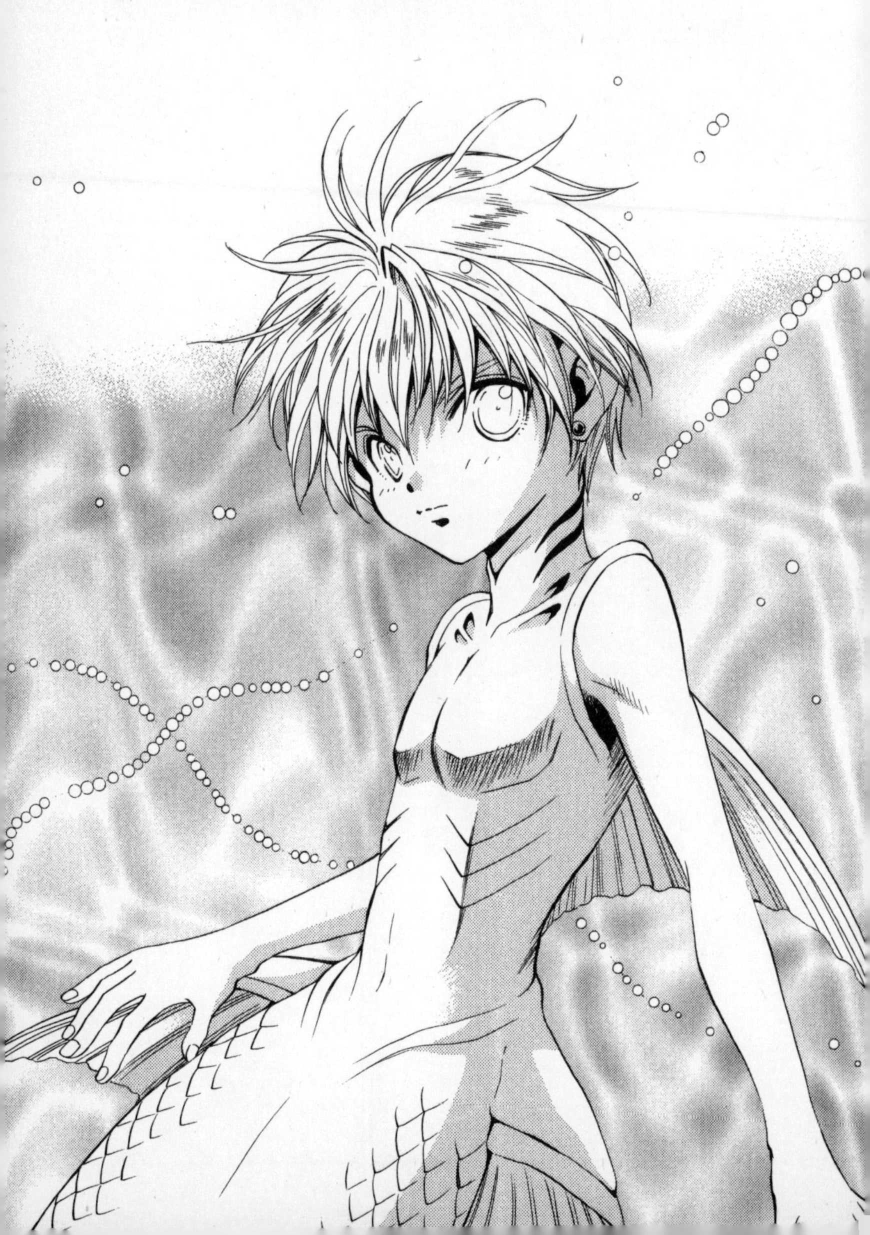

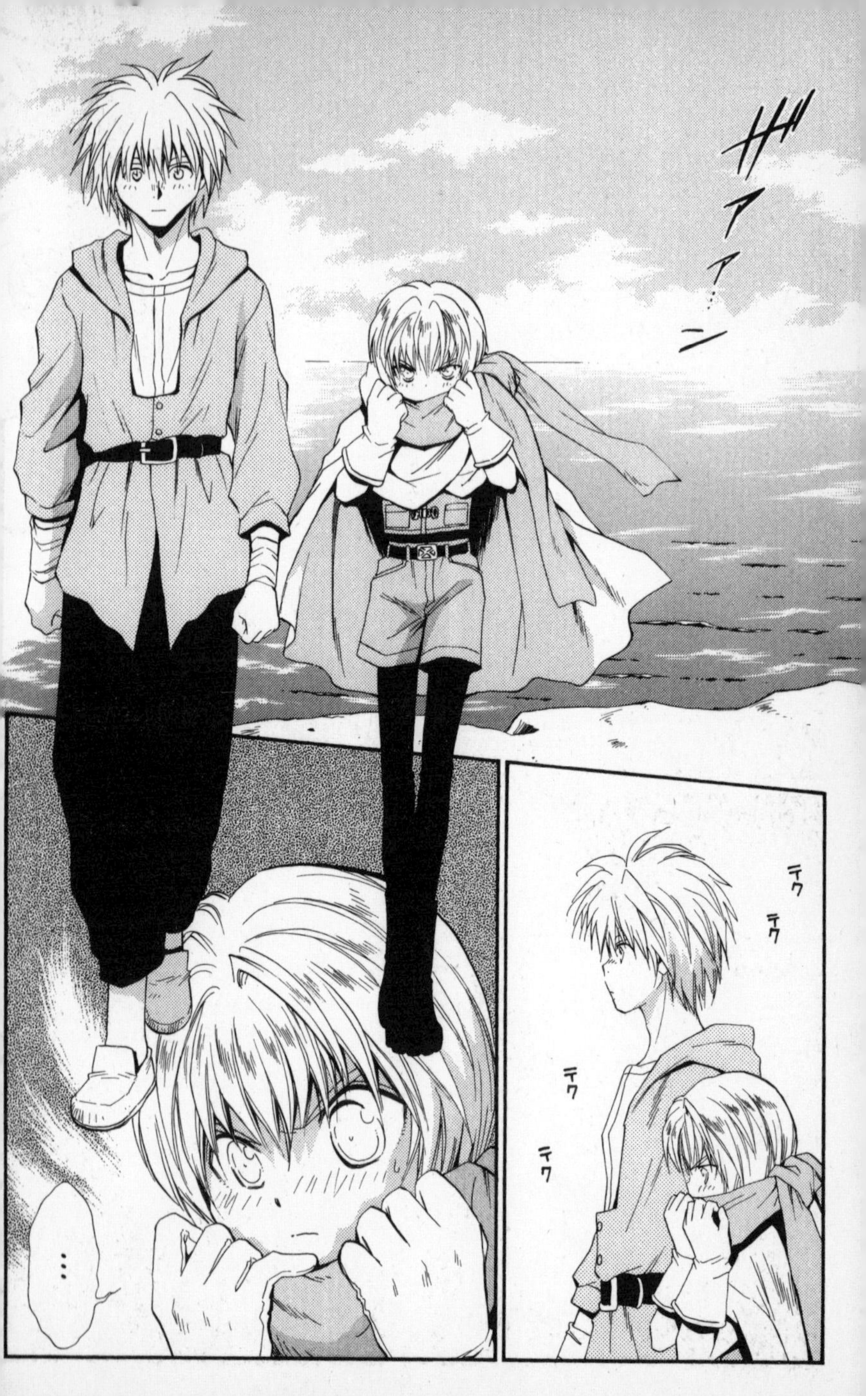
ザアア…ン
テク
テク
テク
テク
…

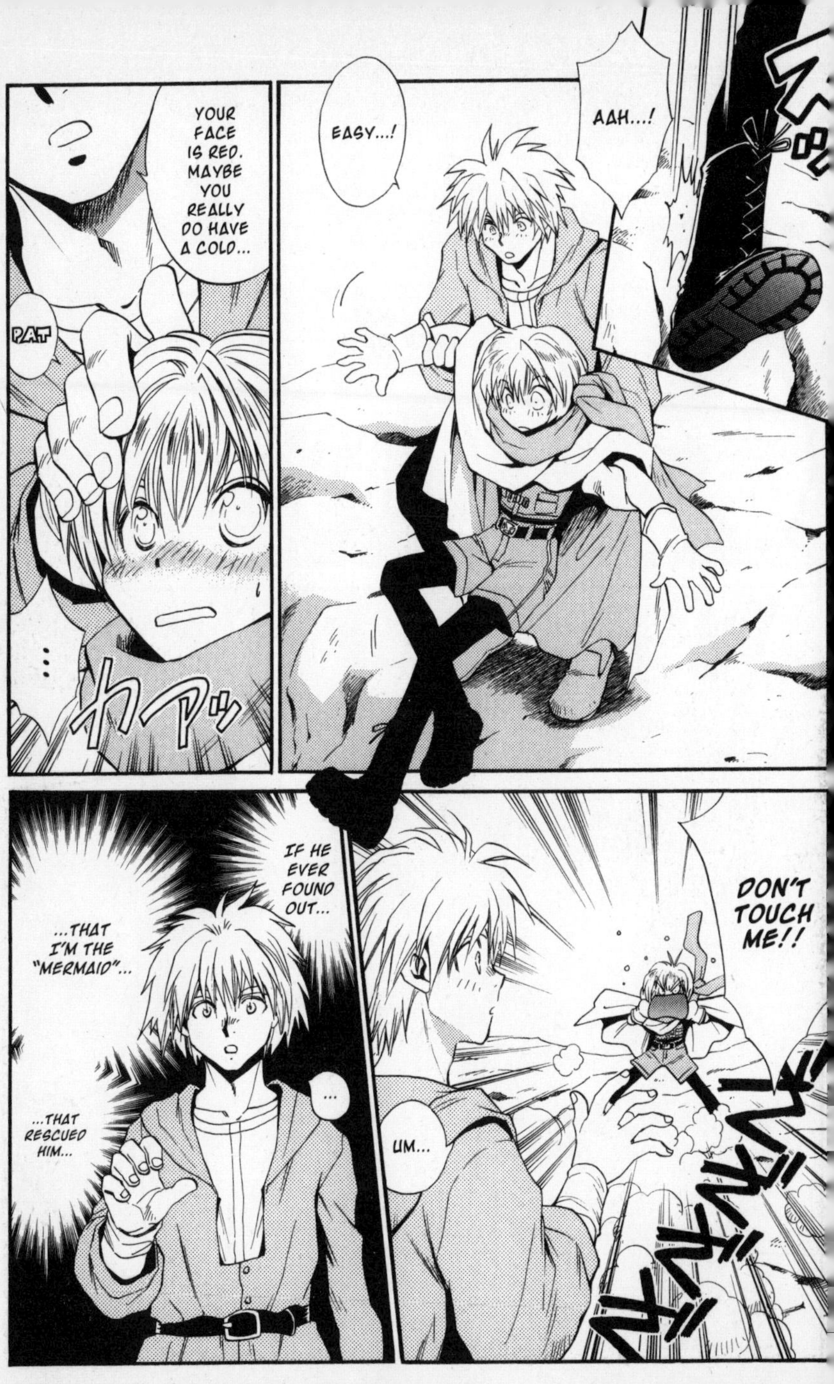
AAH...!
EASY...!
YOUR FACE IS RED. MAYBE YOU REALLY DO HAVE A COLD...
PAT
...
DON'T TOUCH ME!!
UM...
IF HE EVER FOUND OUT...
...
...THAT I'M THE "MERMAID"...
...THAT RESCUED HIM...

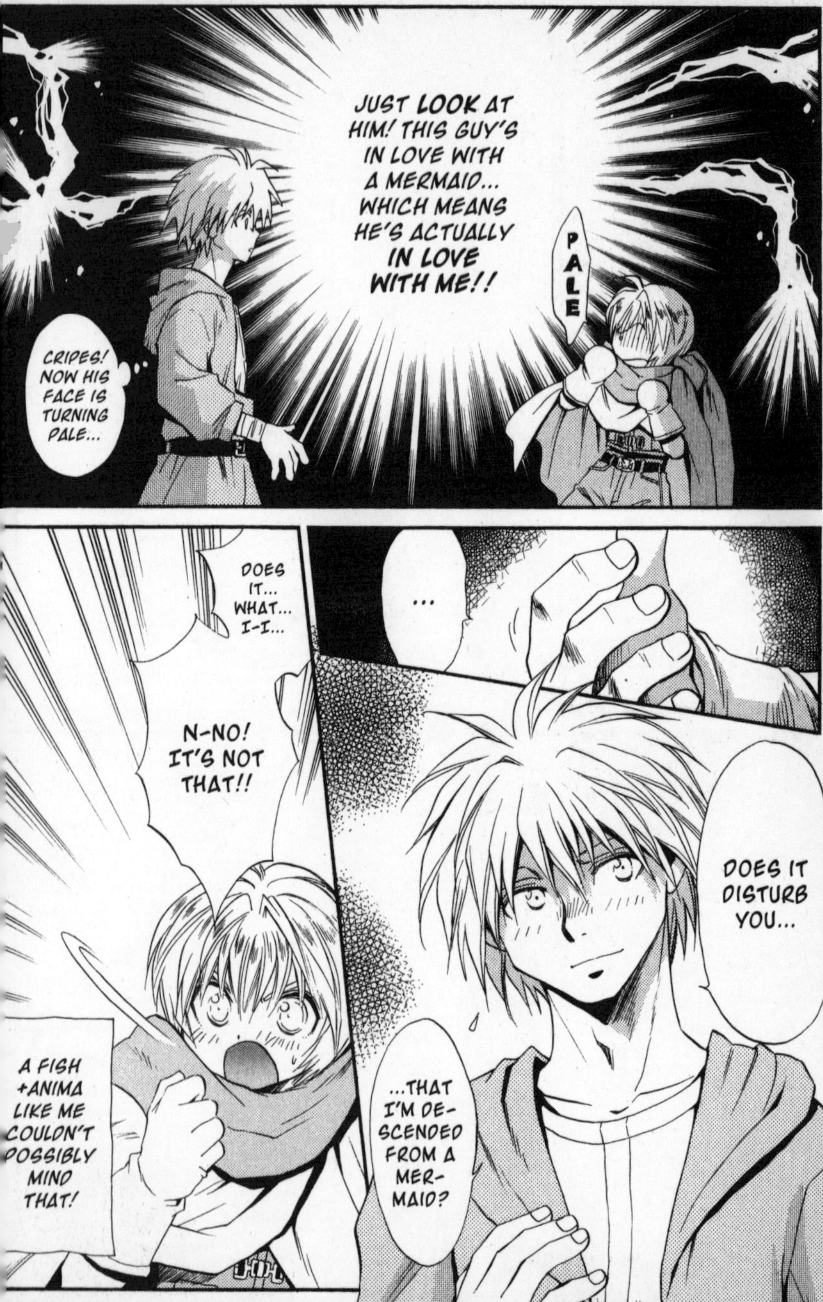
JUST LOOK AT HIM! THIS GUY'S IN LOVE WITH A MERMAID... WHICH MEANS HE'S ACTUALLY IN LOVE WITH ME!!
PALE
CRIPES! NOW HIS FACE IS TURNING PALE...
...
DOES IT DISTURB YOU...
...THAT I'M DE-SCENDED FROM A MER-MAID?
DOES IT... WHAT... I-I...
N-NO! IT'S NOT THAT!!
A FISH +ANIMA LIKE ME COULDN'T POSSIBLY MIND THAT!

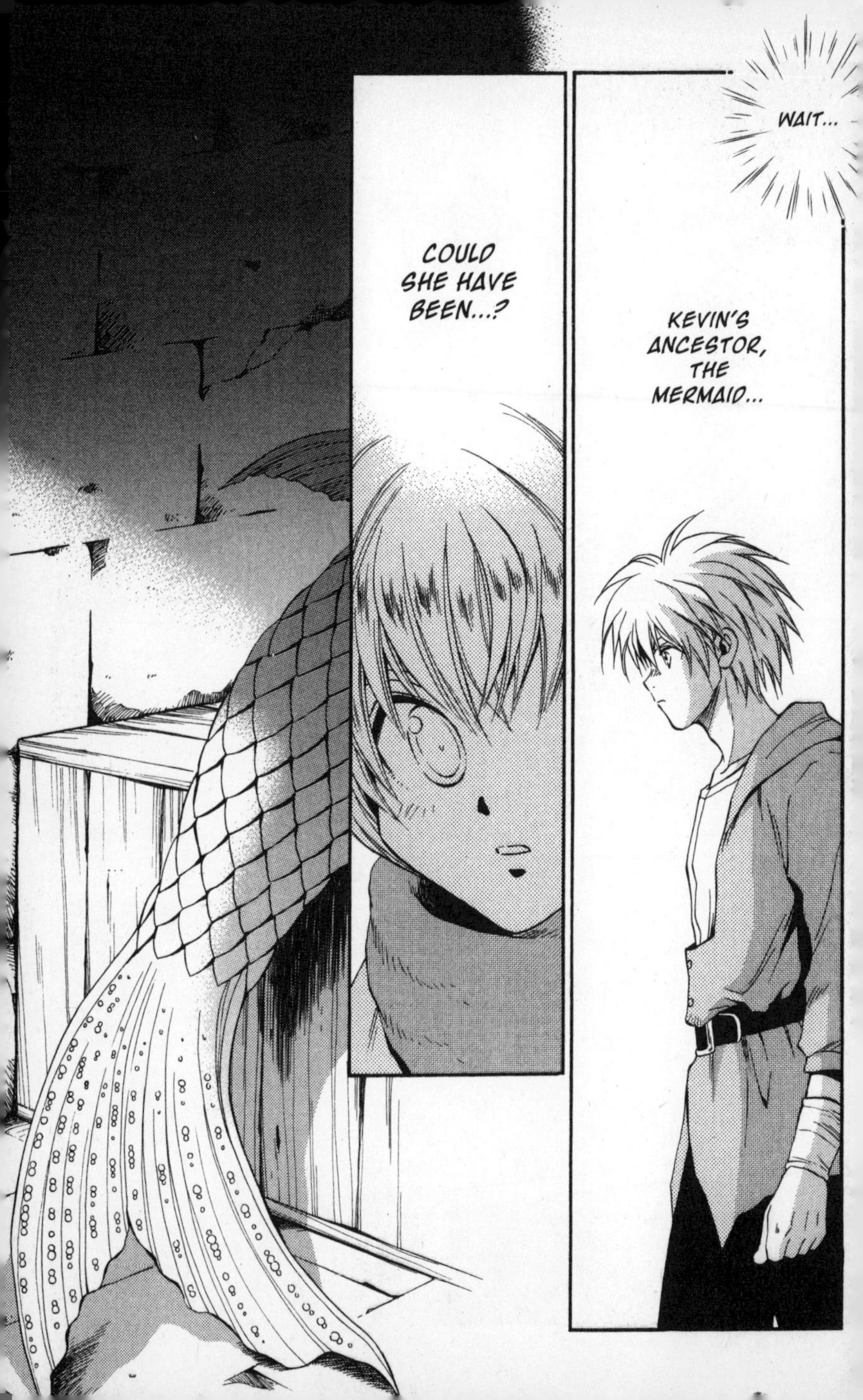
WAIT...
KEVIN'S ANCESTOR, THE MERMAID...
COULD SHE HAVE BEEN...?

IS IT, LIKE... FOR REAL?

EW...

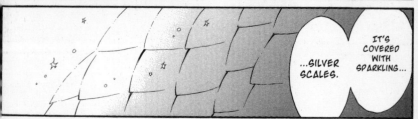

IT'S COVERED WITH SPARKLING...

...SILVER SCALES.

THE PEOPLE IN TOWN WERE SAYING...

...THAT A MERMAID CAME TO THIS OCEAN ONCE BEFORE.

COULD IT BE... THAT THIS IS HER?

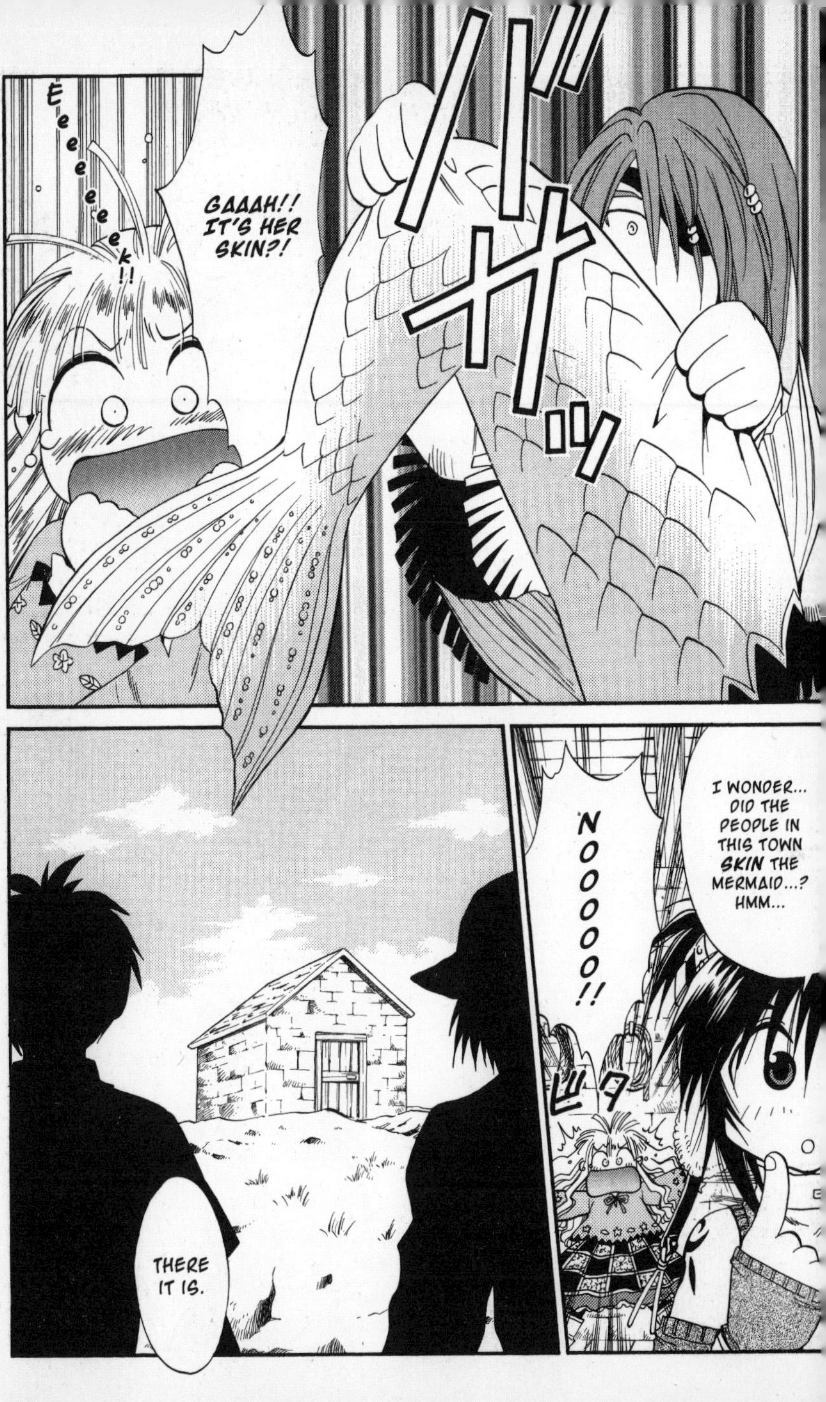
Eeeeeeeek!!
GAAAH!! IT'S HER SKIN?!
I WONDER... DID THE PEOPLE IN THIS TOWN SKIN THE MERMAID...? HMM...
NOOOOOOO!!
THERE IT IS.

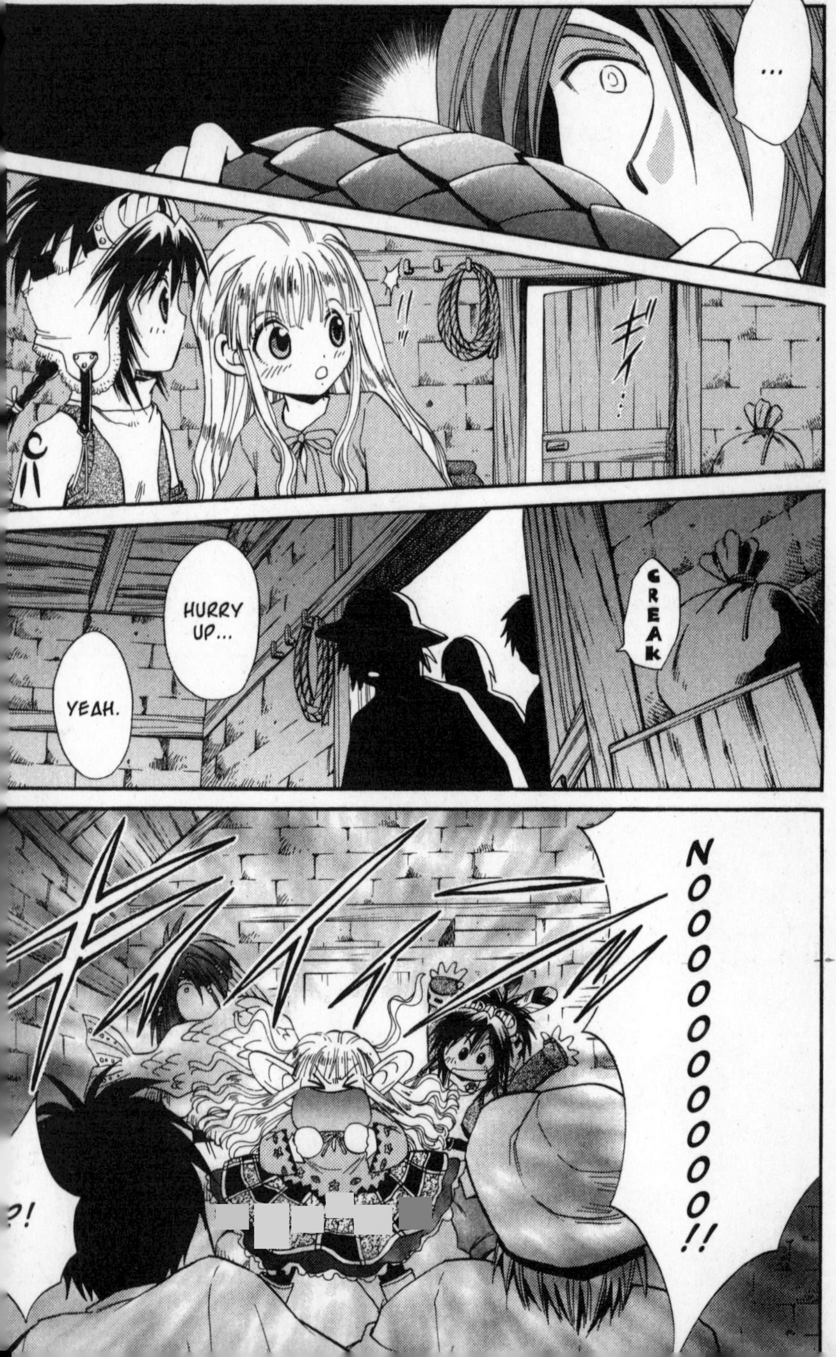
...
HURRY UP...
YEAH.
CREAK
NOOOOOOOOOOOOO!!
?!

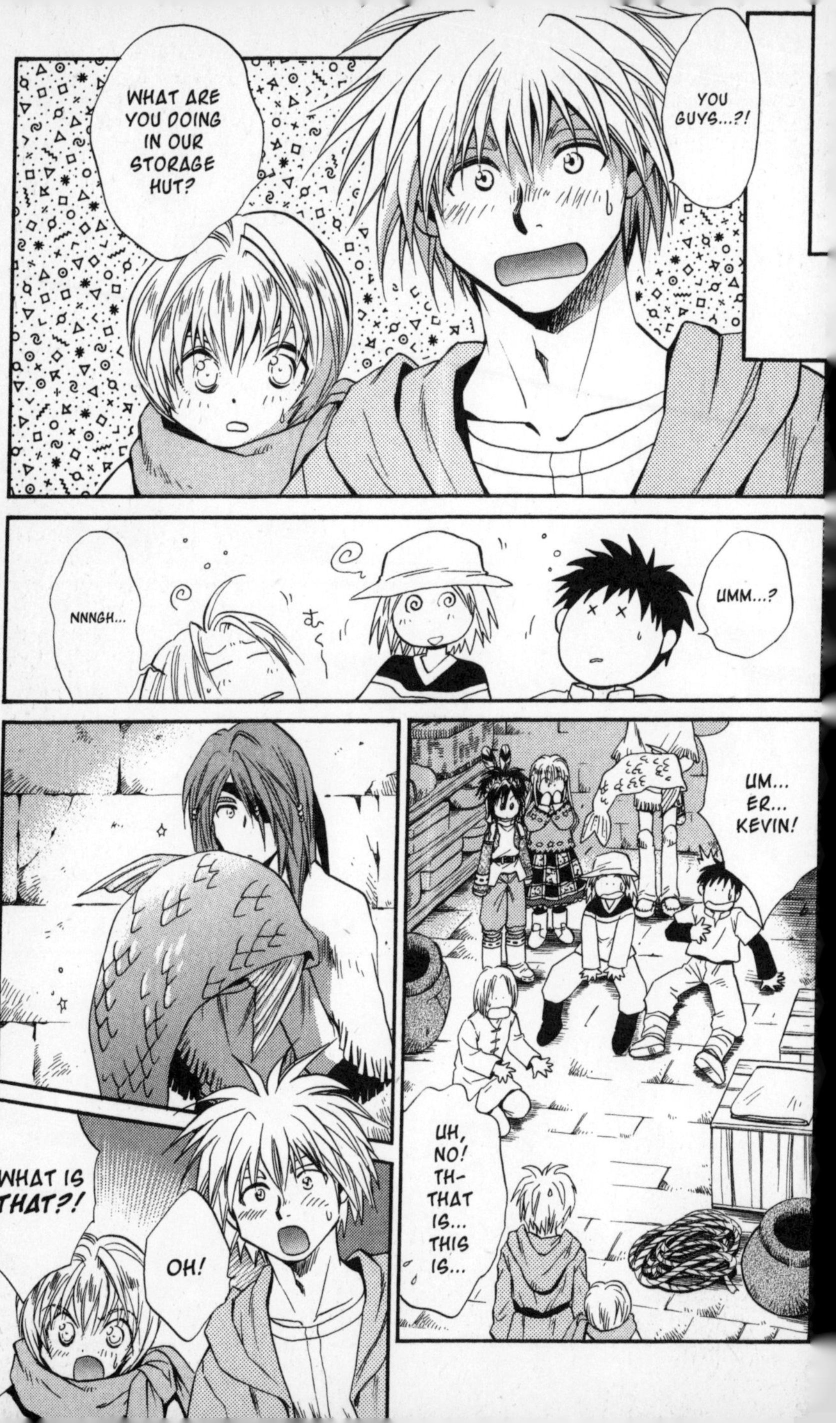
YOU GUYS...?!
WHAT ARE YOU DOING IN OUR STORAGE HUT?
UMM...?
NNNGH...
UM... ER... KEVIN!
UH, NO! TH-THAT IS... THIS IS...
WHAT IS THAT?!
OH!

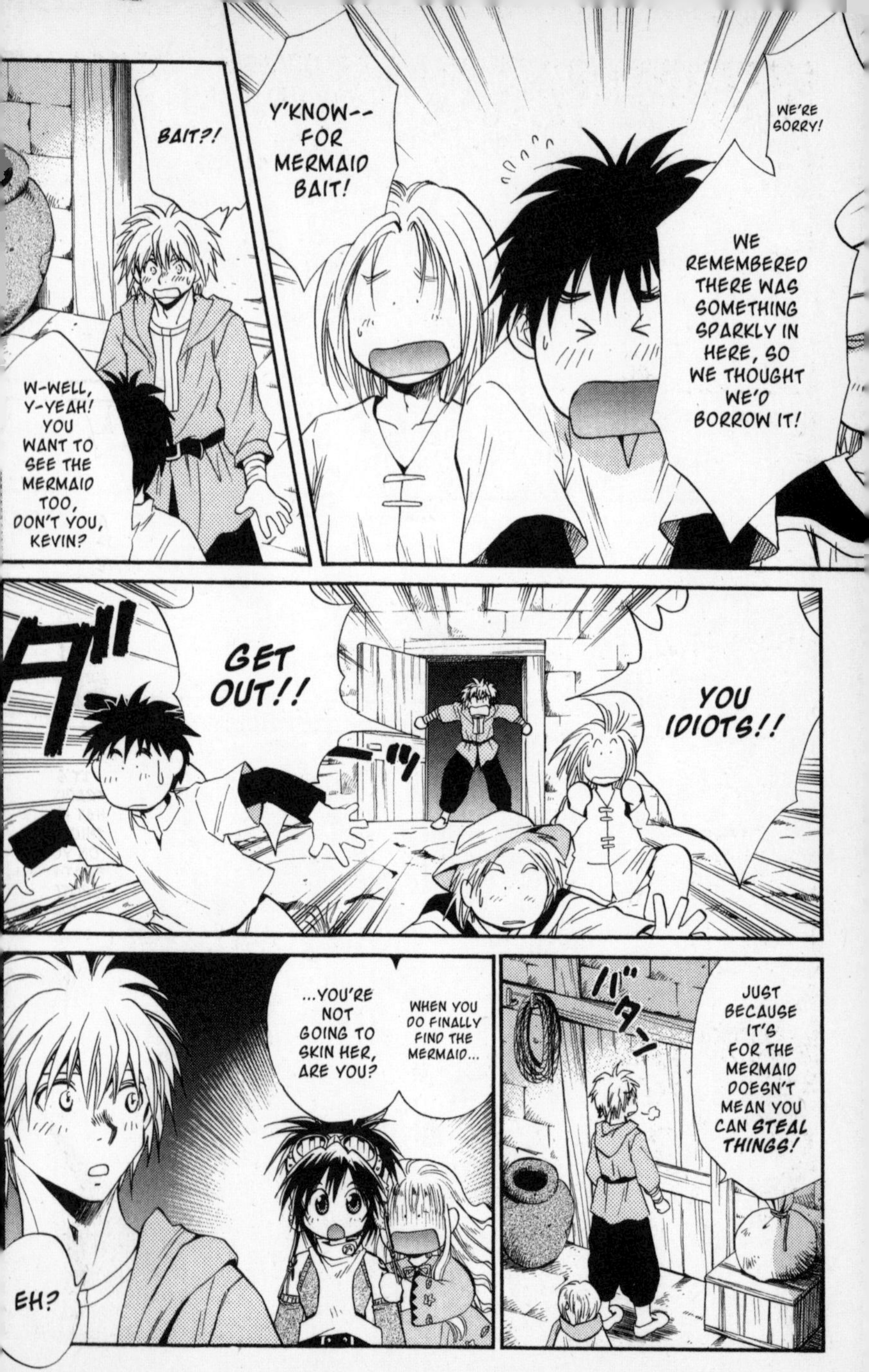
WE'RE SORRY!
WE REMEMBERED THERE WAS SOMETHING SPARKLY IN HERE, SO WE THOUGHT WE'D BORROW IT!
Y'KNOW-- FOR MERMAID BAIT!
BAIT?!
W-WELL, Y-YEAH! YOU WANT TO SEE THE MERMAID TOO, DON'T YOU, KEVIN?
YOU IDIOTS!!
GET OUT!!
ダ
ッ
バタン
JUST BECAUSE IT'S FOR THE MERMAID DOESN'T MEAN YOU CAN STEAL THINGS!
WHEN YOU DO FINALLY FIND THE MERMAID...
...YOU'RE NOT GOING TO SKIN HER, ARE YOU?
EH?

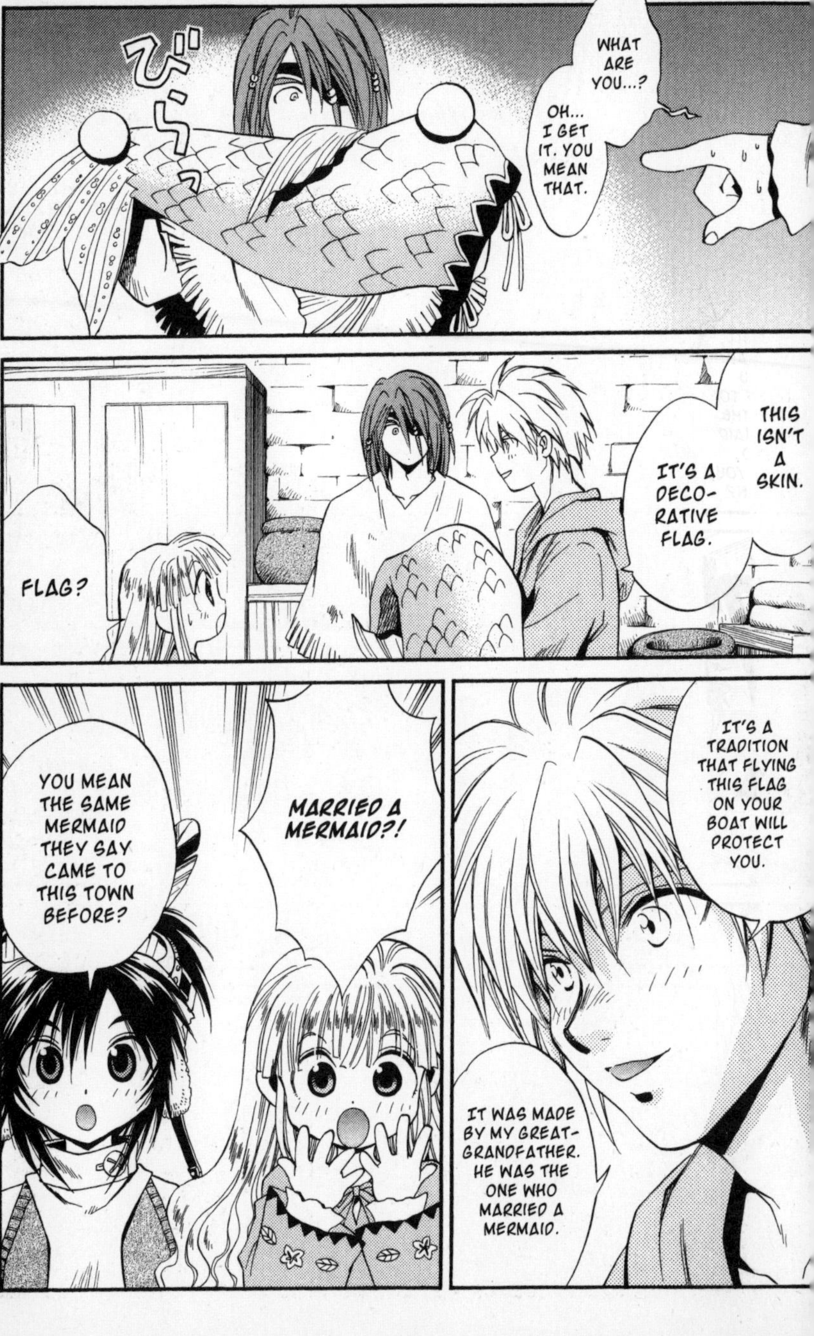
WHAT ARE YOU...?
OH... I GET IT. YOU MEAN THAT.
びらっ
THIS ISN'T A SKIN.
IT'S A DECO-RATIVE FLAG.
FLAG?
IT'S A TRADITION THAT FLYING THIS FLAG ON YOUR BOAT WILL PROTECT YOU.
IT WAS MADE BY MY GREAT-GRANDFATHER. HE WAS THE ONE WHO MARRIED A MERMAID.
MARRIED A MERMAID?!
YOU MEAN THE SAME MERMAID THEY SAY CAME TO THIS TOWN BEFORE?

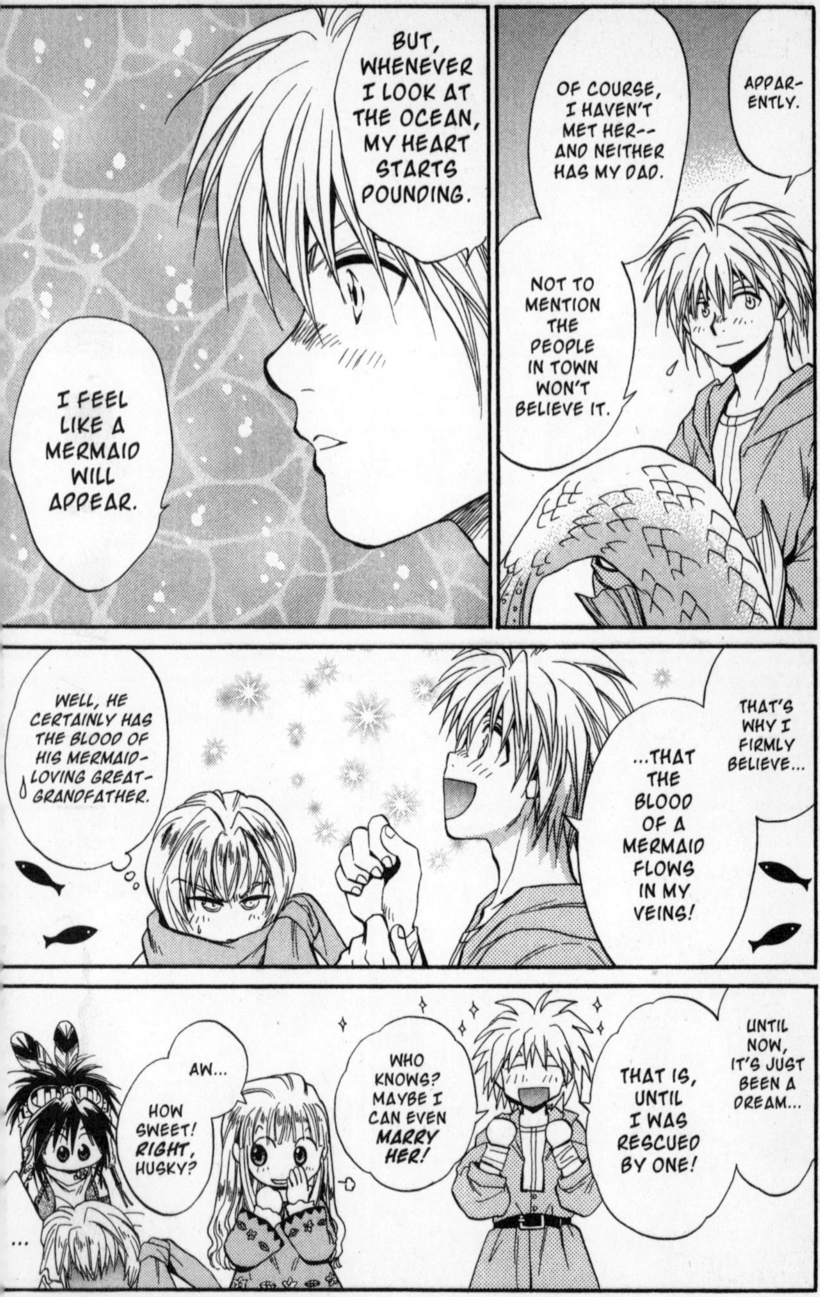
APPAR-ENTLY.
OF COURSE, I HAVEN'T MET HER--AND NEITHER HAS MY DAD.
NOT TO MENTION THE PEOPLE IN TOWN WON'T BELIEVE IT.
BUT, WHENEVER I LOOK AT THE OCEAN, MY HEART STARTS POUNDING.
I FEEL LIKE A MERMAID WILL APPEAR.
THAT'S WHY I FIRMLY BELIEVE...
...THAT THE BLOOD OF A MERMAID FLOWS IN MY VEINS!
WELL, HE CERTAINLY HAS THE BLOOD OF HIS MERMAID-LOVING GREAT-GRANDFATHER.
UNTIL NOW, IT'S JUST BEEN A DREAM...
THAT IS, UNTIL I WAS RESCUED BY ONE!
WHO KNOWS? MAYBE I CAN EVEN MARRY HER!
AW...
HOW SWEET! RIGHT, HUSKY?
...

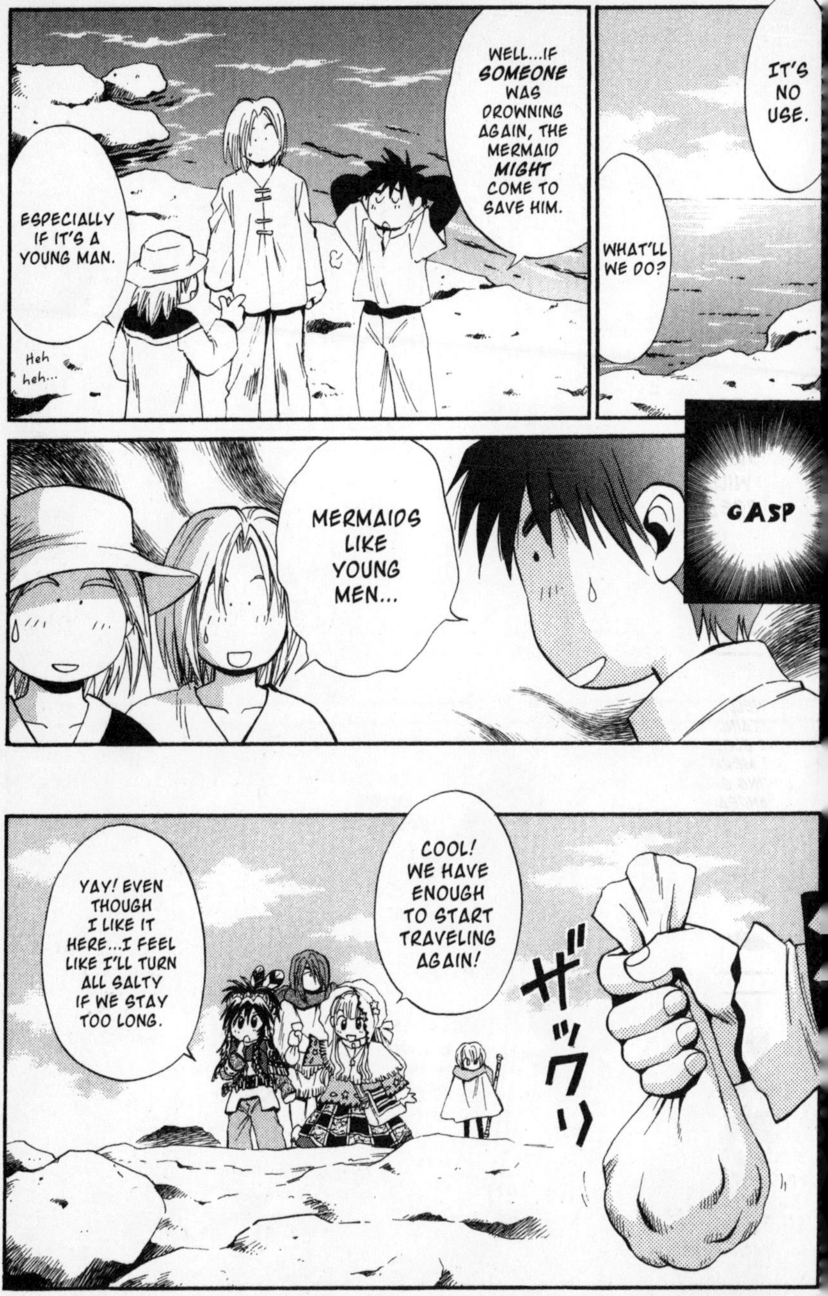
IT'S NO USE.
WHAT'LL WE DO?
WELL...IF SOMEONE WAS DROWNING AGAIN, THE MERMAID MIGHT COME TO SAVE HIM.
ESPECIALLY IF IT'S A YOUNG MAN.
Heh heh...
GASP
MERMAIDS LIKE YOUNG MEN...
ザックリ
COOL! WE HAVE ENOUGH TO START TRAVELING AGAIN!
YAY! EVEN THOUGH I LIKE IT HERE...I FEEL LIKE I'LL TURN ALL SALTY IF WE STAY TOO LONG.

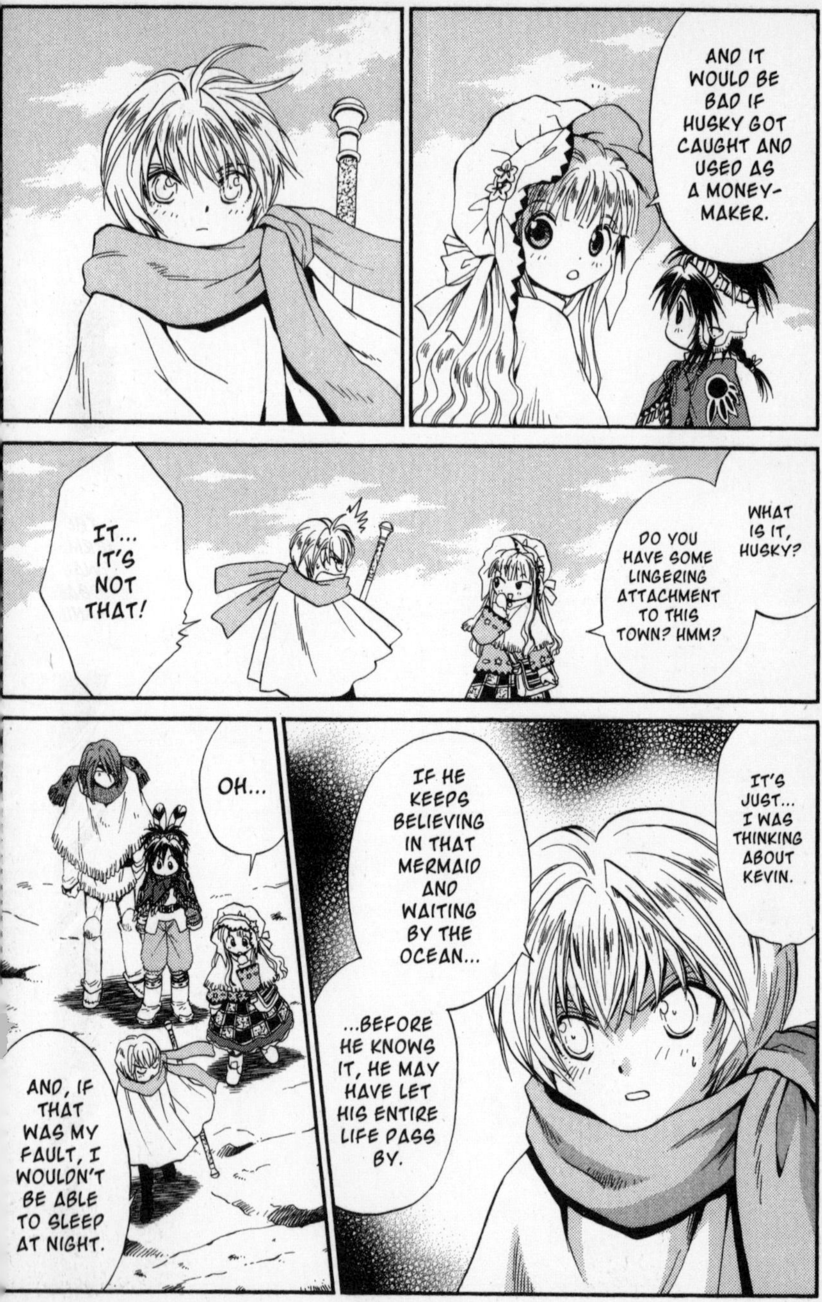
AND IT WOULD BE BAD IF HUSKY GOT CAUGHT AND USED AS A MONEY-MAKER.
WHAT IS IT, HUSKY?
DO YOU HAVE SOME LINGERING ATTACHMENT TO THIS TOWN? HMM?
IT... IT'S NOT THAT!
IT'S JUST... I WAS THINKING ABOUT KEVIN.
IF HE KEEPS BELIEVING IN THAT MERMAID AND WAITING BY THE OCEAN...
...BEFORE HE KNOWS IT, HE MAY HAVE LET HIS ENTIRE LIFE PASS BY.
OH...
AND, IF THAT WAS MY FAULT, I WOULDN'T BE ABLE TO SLEEP AT NIGHT.

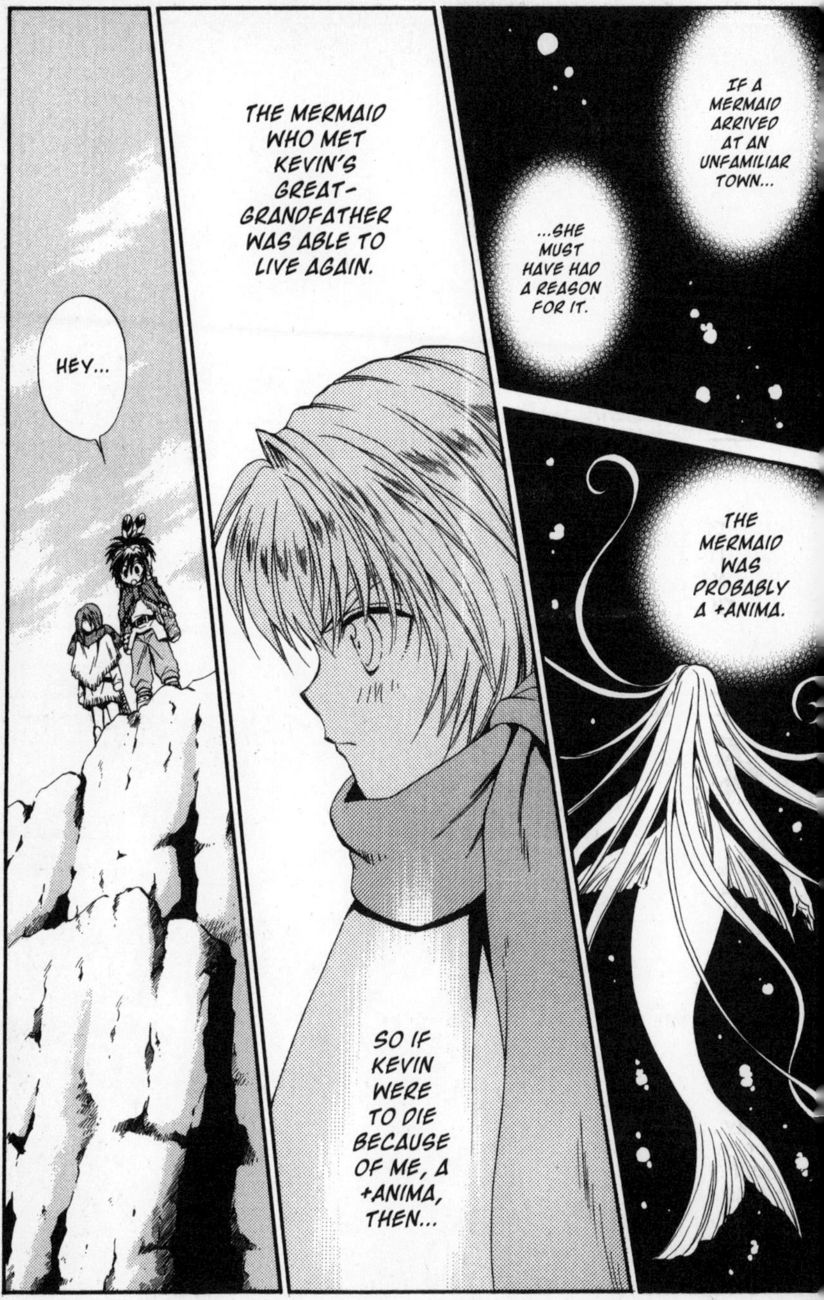
IF A MERMAID ARRIVED AT AN UNFAMILIAR TOWN...
...SHE MUST HAVE HAD A REASON FOR IT.
THE MERMAID WAS PROBABLY A +ANIMA.
THE MERMAID WHO MET KEVIN'S GREAT-GRANDFATHER WAS ABLE TO LIVE AGAIN.
SO IF KEVIN WERE TO DIE BECAUSE OF ME, A +ANIMA, THEN...
HEY...

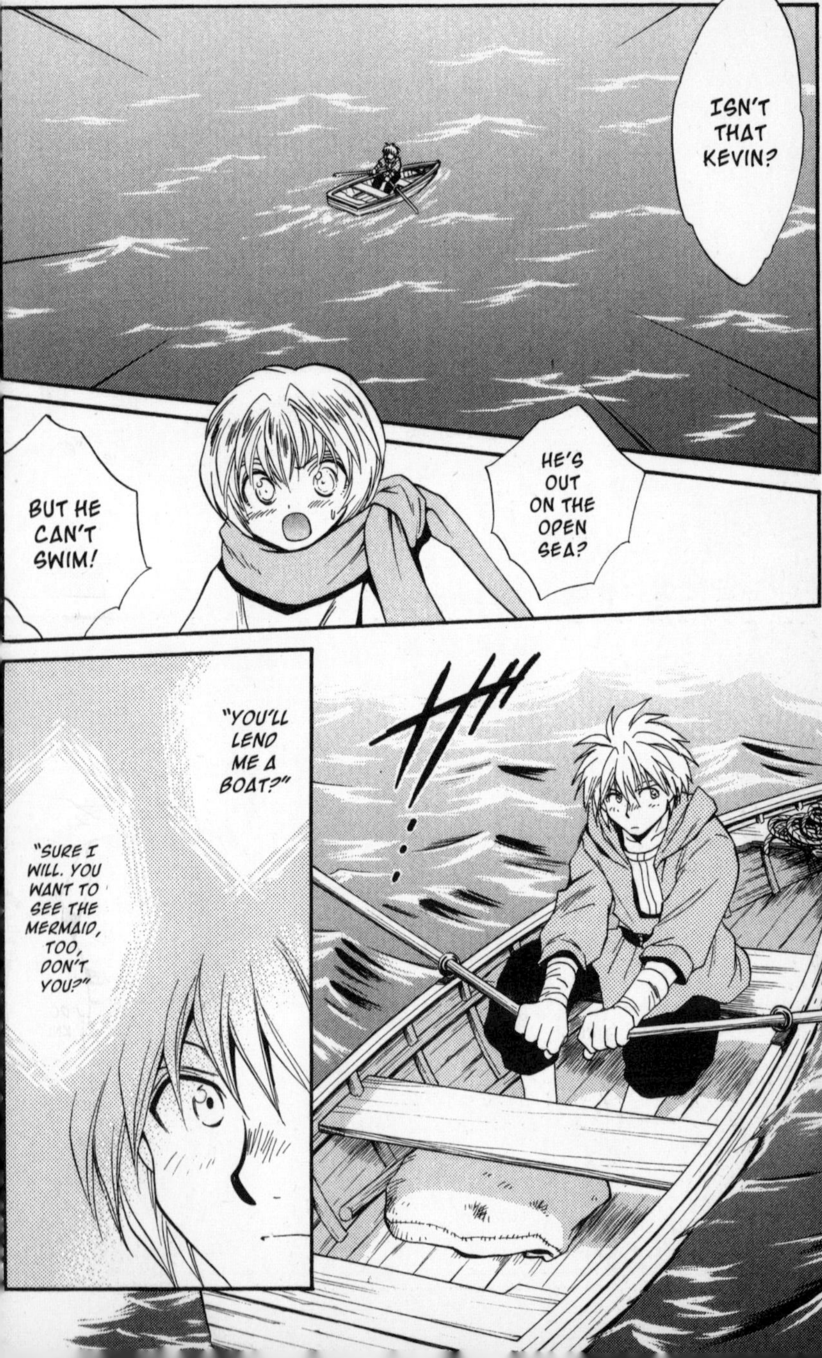
ISN'T THAT KEVIN?
HE'S OUT ON THE OPEN SEA?
BUT HE CAN'T SWIM!
"YOU'LL LEND ME A BOAT?"
"SURE I WILL. YOU WANT TO SEE THE MERMAID, TOO, DON'T YOU?"

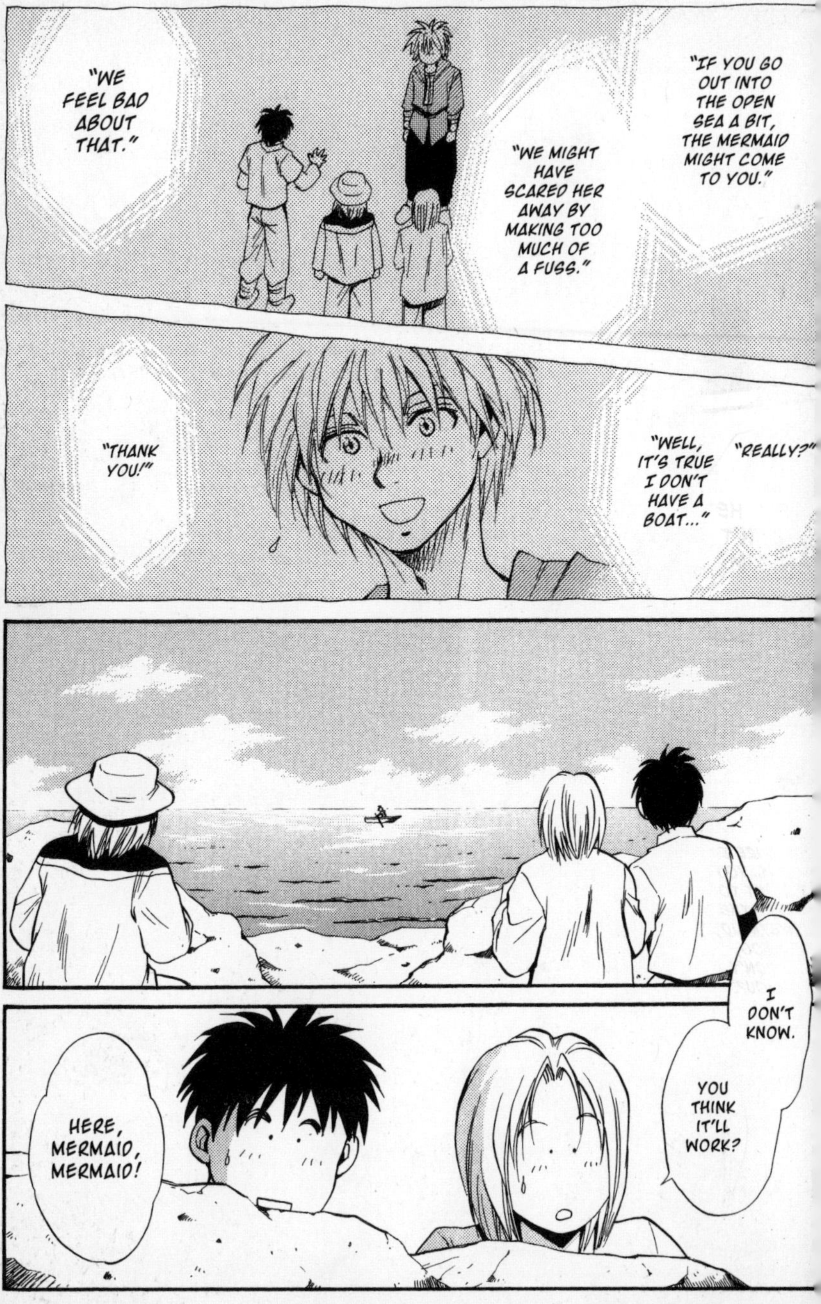
"IF YOU GO OUT INTO THE OPEN SEA A BIT, THE MERMAID MIGHT COME TO YOU."
"WE MIGHT HAVE SCARED HER AWAY BY MAKING TOO MUCH OF A FUSS."
"WE FEEL BAD ABOUT THAT."
"REALLY?"
"WELL, IT'S TRUE I DON'T HAVE A BOAT..."
"THANK YOU!"
I DON'T KNOW.
YOU THINK IT'LL WORK?
HERE, MERMAID, MERMAID!

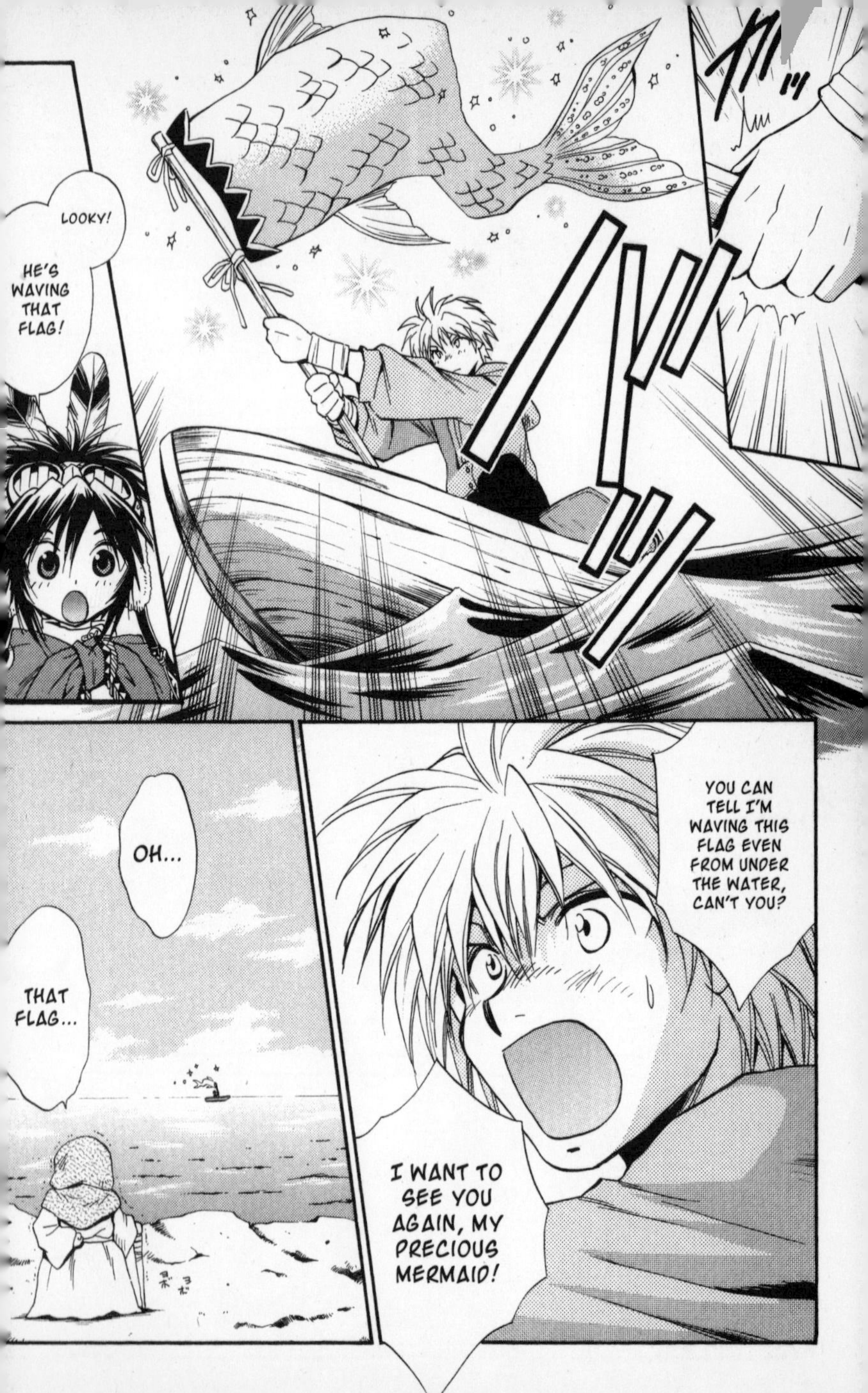
LOOKY!
HE'S WAVING THAT FLAG!
YOU CAN TELL I'M WAVING THIS FLAG EVEN FROM UNDER THE WATER, CAN'T YOU?
I WANT TO SEE YOU AGAIN, MY PRECIOUS MERMAID!
OH...
THAT FLAG...

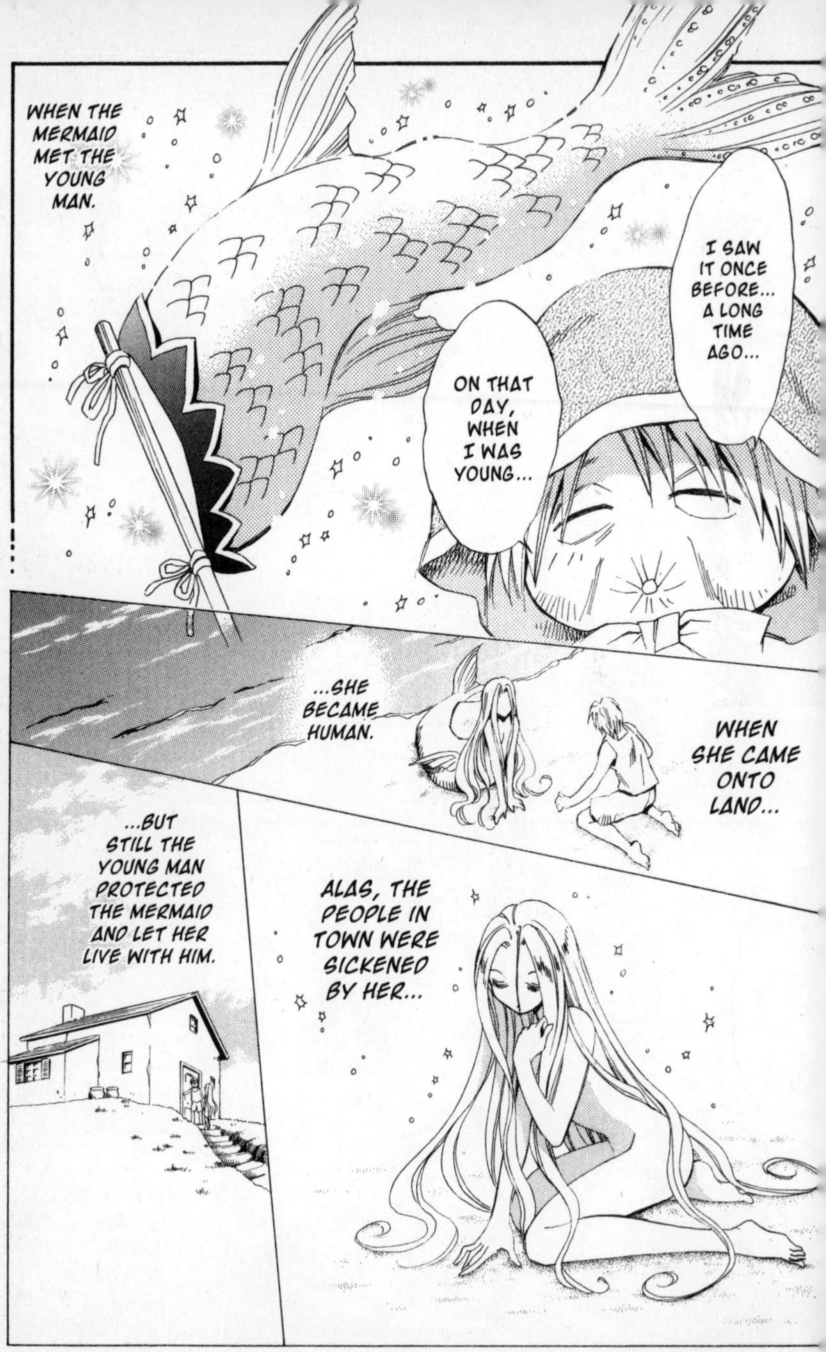
I SAW IT ONCE BEFORE... A LONG TIME AGO...
ON THAT DAY, WHEN I WAS YOUNG...
WHEN THE MERMAID MET THE YOUNG MAN.
WHEN SHE CAME ONTO LAND...
...SHE BECAME HUMAN.
ALAS, THE PEOPLE IN TOWN WERE SICKENED BY HER...
...BUT STILL THE YOUNG MAN PROTECTED THE MERMAID AND LET HER LIVE WITH HIM.

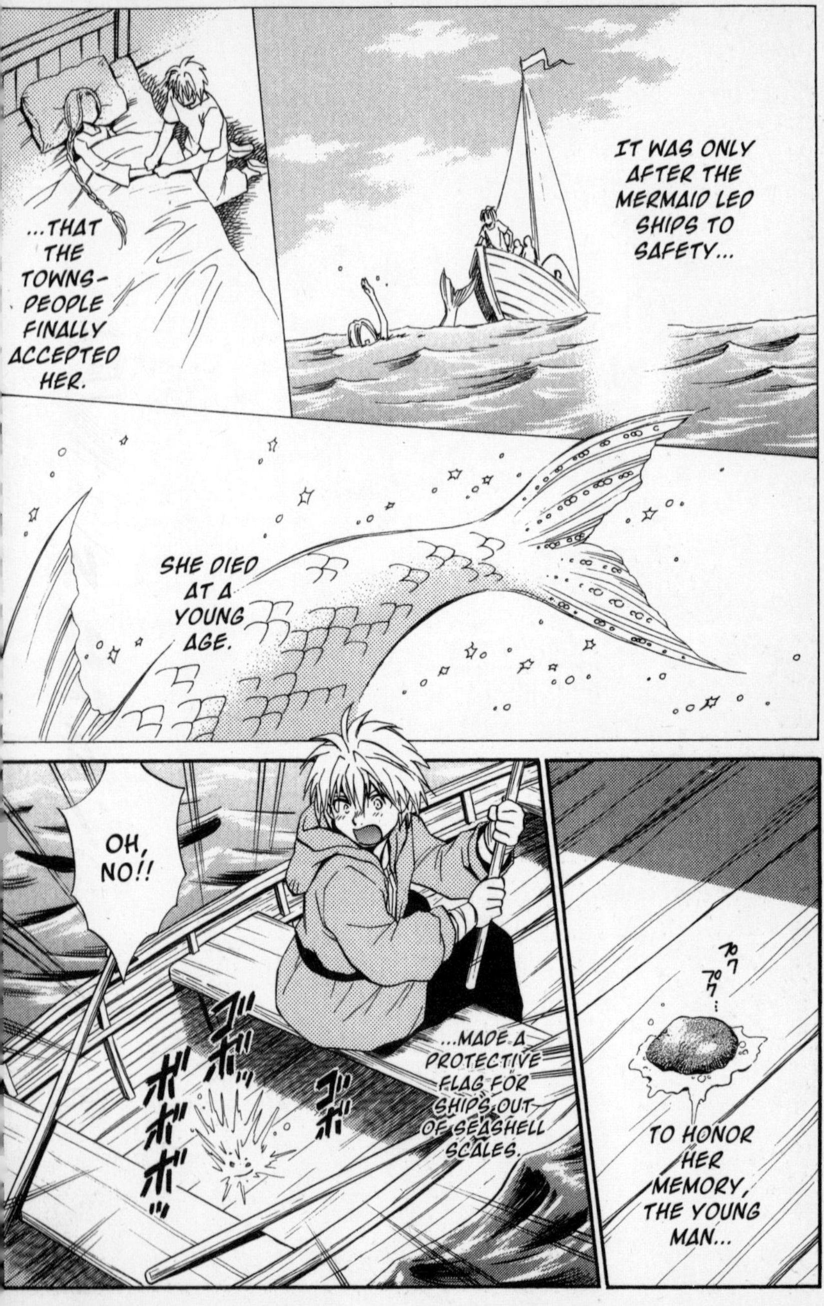
IT WAS ONLY AFTER THE MERMAID LED SHIPS TO SAFETY...
...THAT THE TOWNS-PEOPLE FINALLY ACCEPTED HER.
SHE DIED AT A YOUNG AGE.
TO HONOR HER MEMORY, THE YOUNG MAN...
...MADE A PROTECTIVE FLAG FOR SHIPS OUT OF SEASHELL SCALES.
OH, NO!!

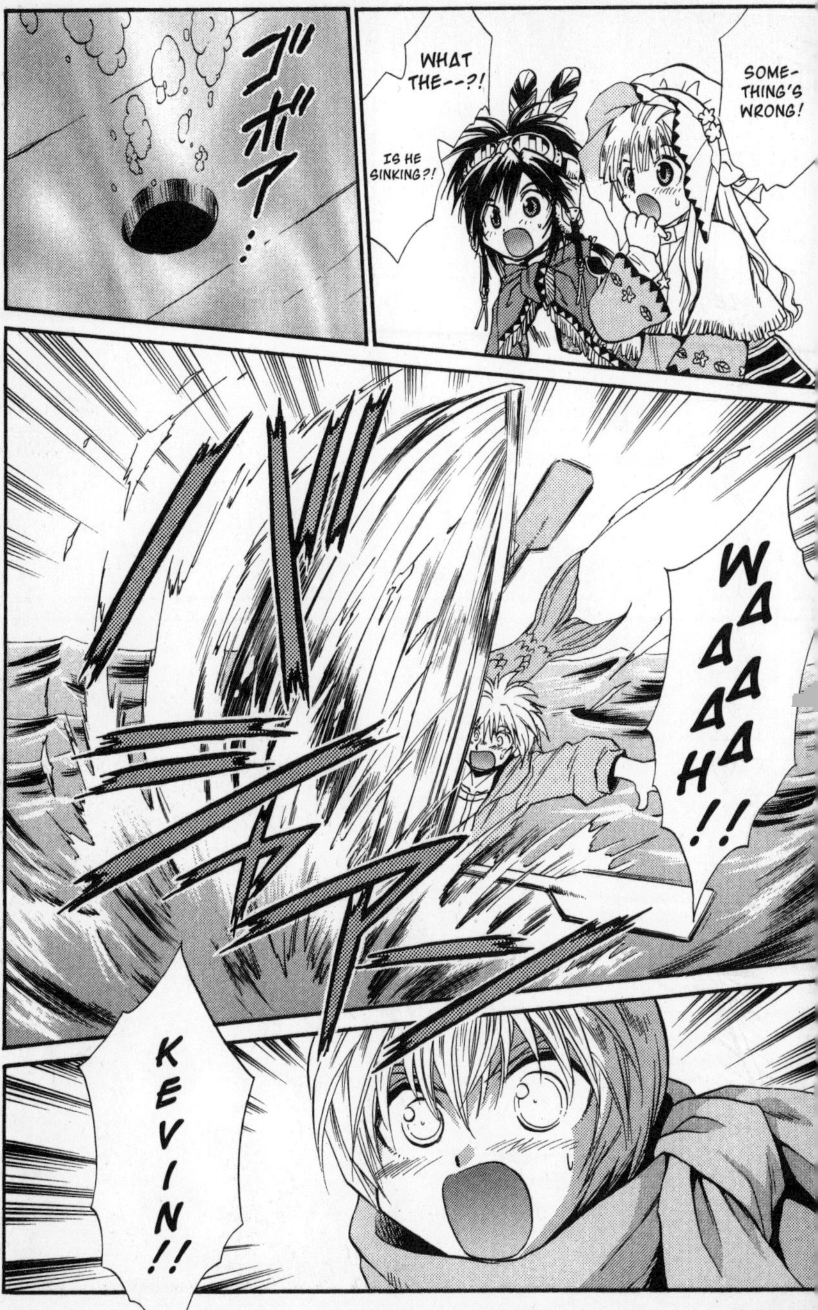
SOME-THING'S WRONG!
WHAT THE--?!
IS HE SINKING?!
ゴボア…
WAAAAAAH!!
KEVIN!!

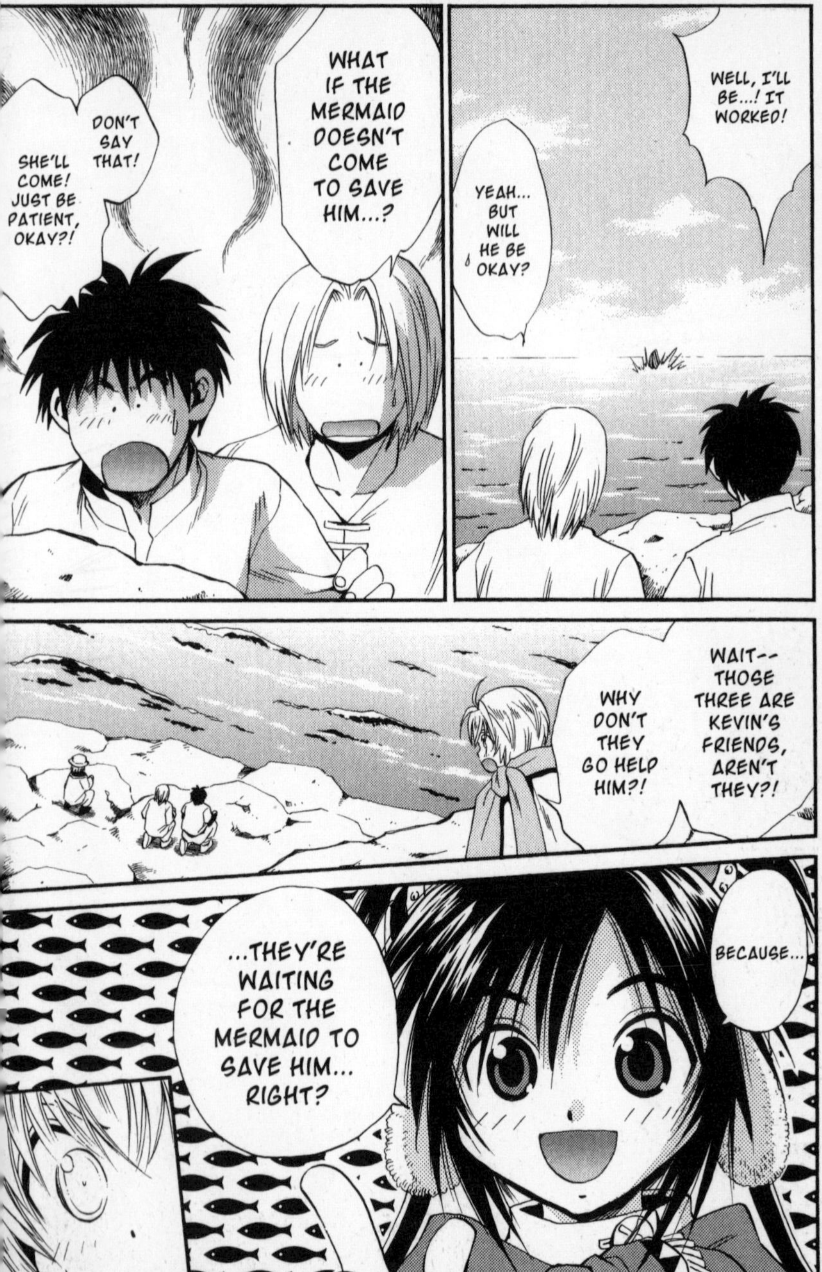
WELL, I'LL BE...! IT WORKED!
YEAH... BUT WILL HE BE OKAY?
WHAT IF THE MERMAID DOESN'T COME TO SAVE HIM...?
DON'T SAY THAT!
SHE'LL COME! JUST BE PATIENT, OKAY?!
WAIT-- THOSE THREE ARE KEVIN'S FRIENDS, AREN'T THEY?!
WHY DON'T THEY GO HELP HIM?!
BECAUSE...
...THEY'RE WAITING FOR THE MERMAID TO SAVE HIM... RIGHT?

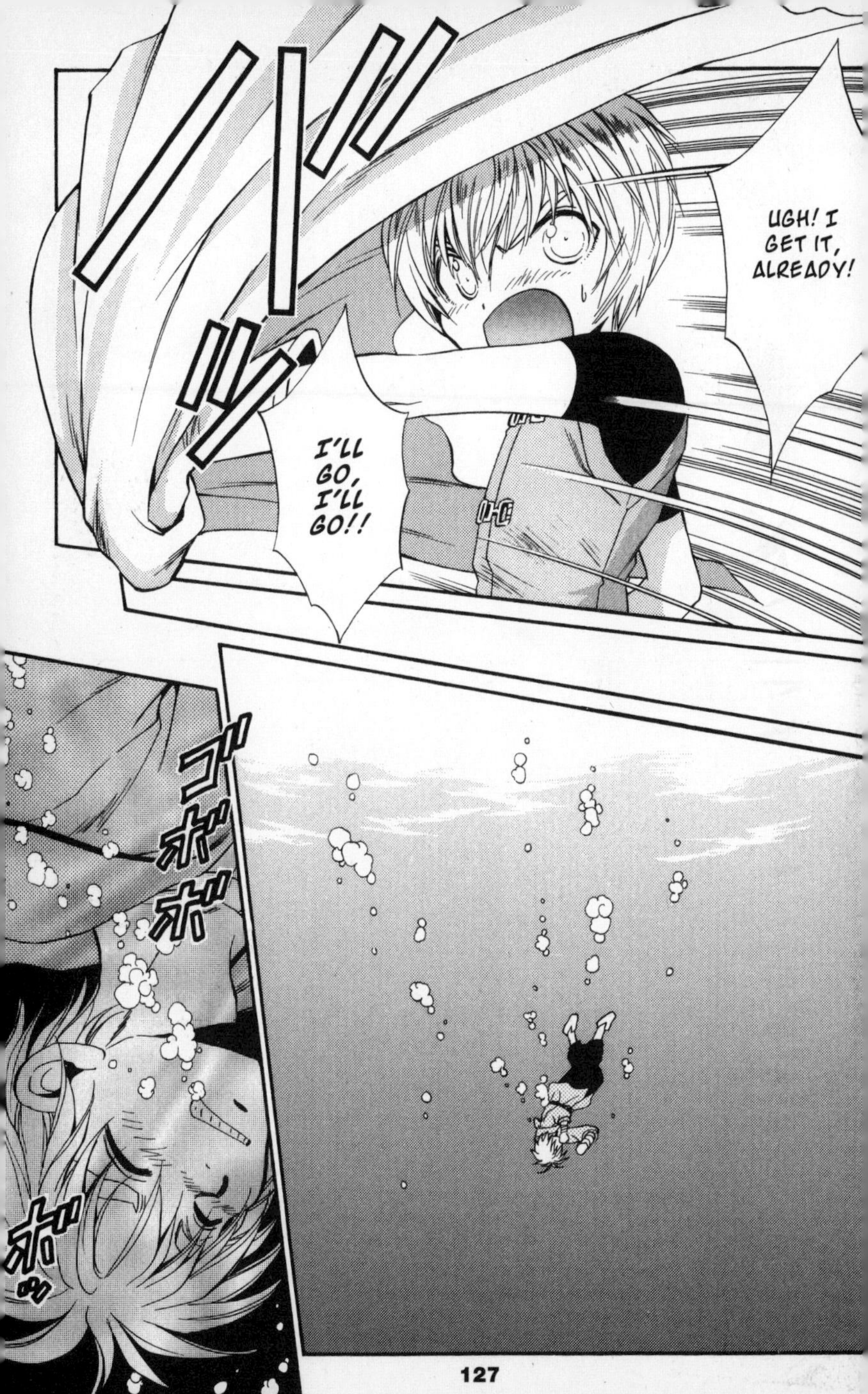
UGH! I GET IT, ALREADY!
I'LL GO, I'LL GO!!

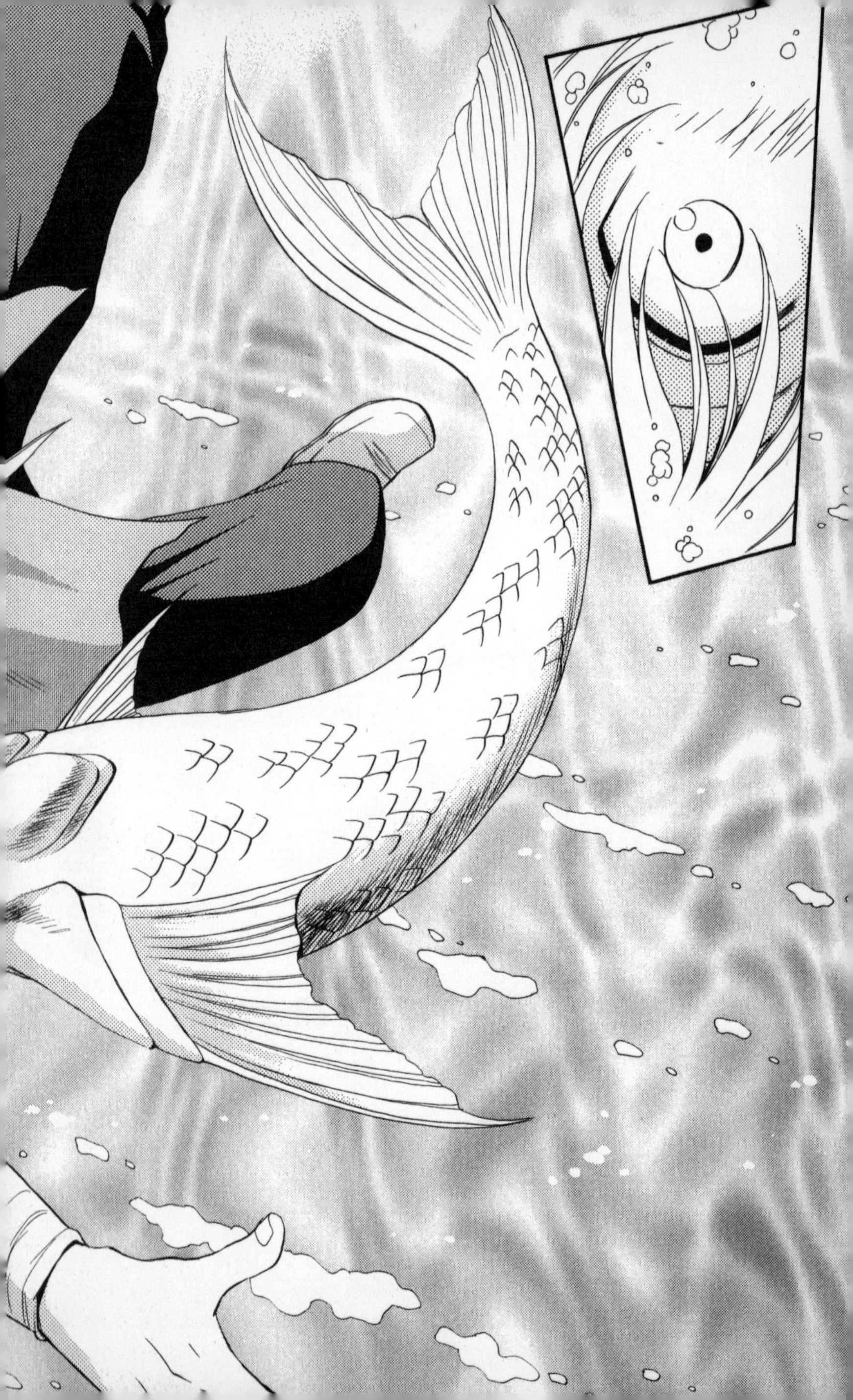

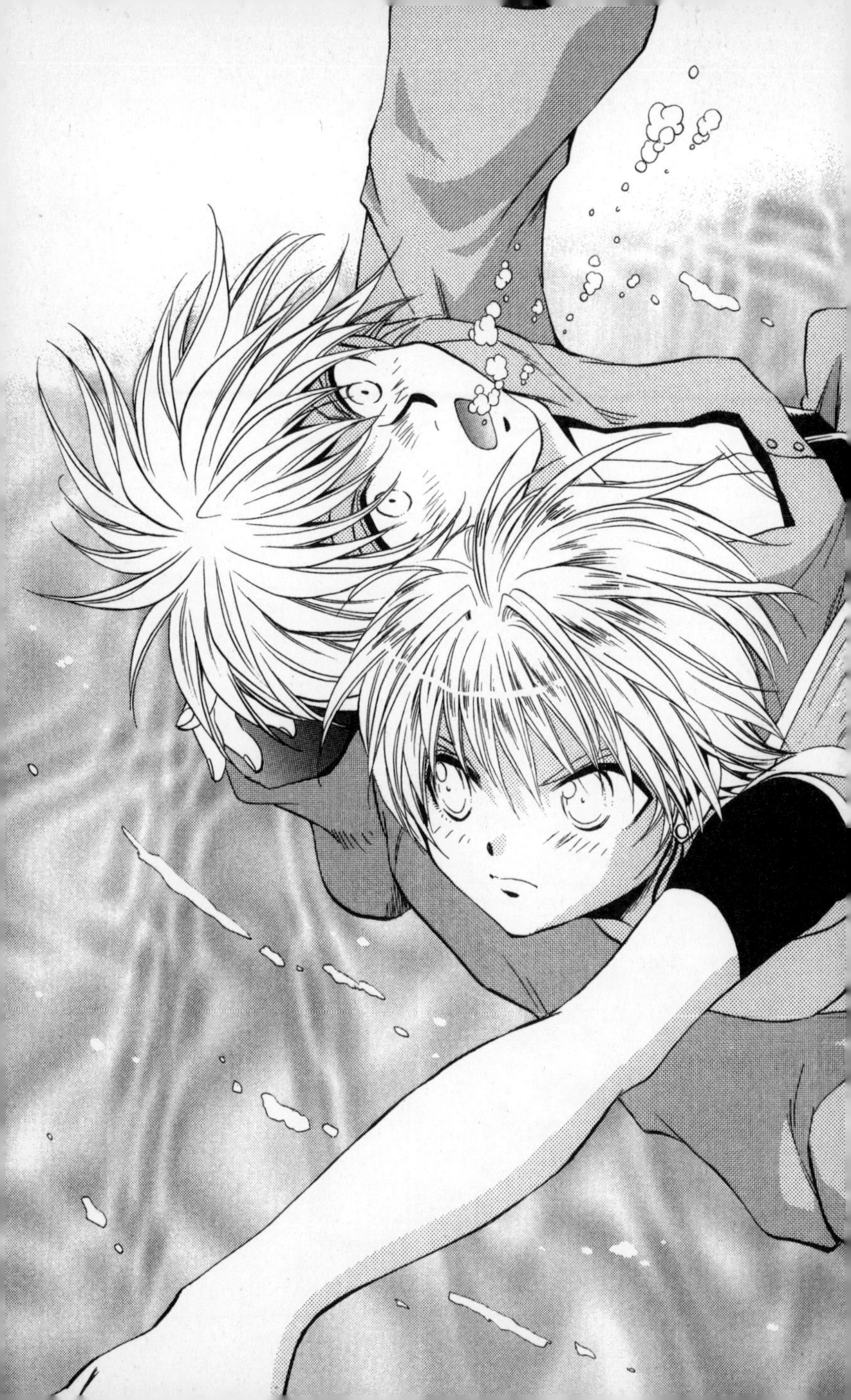

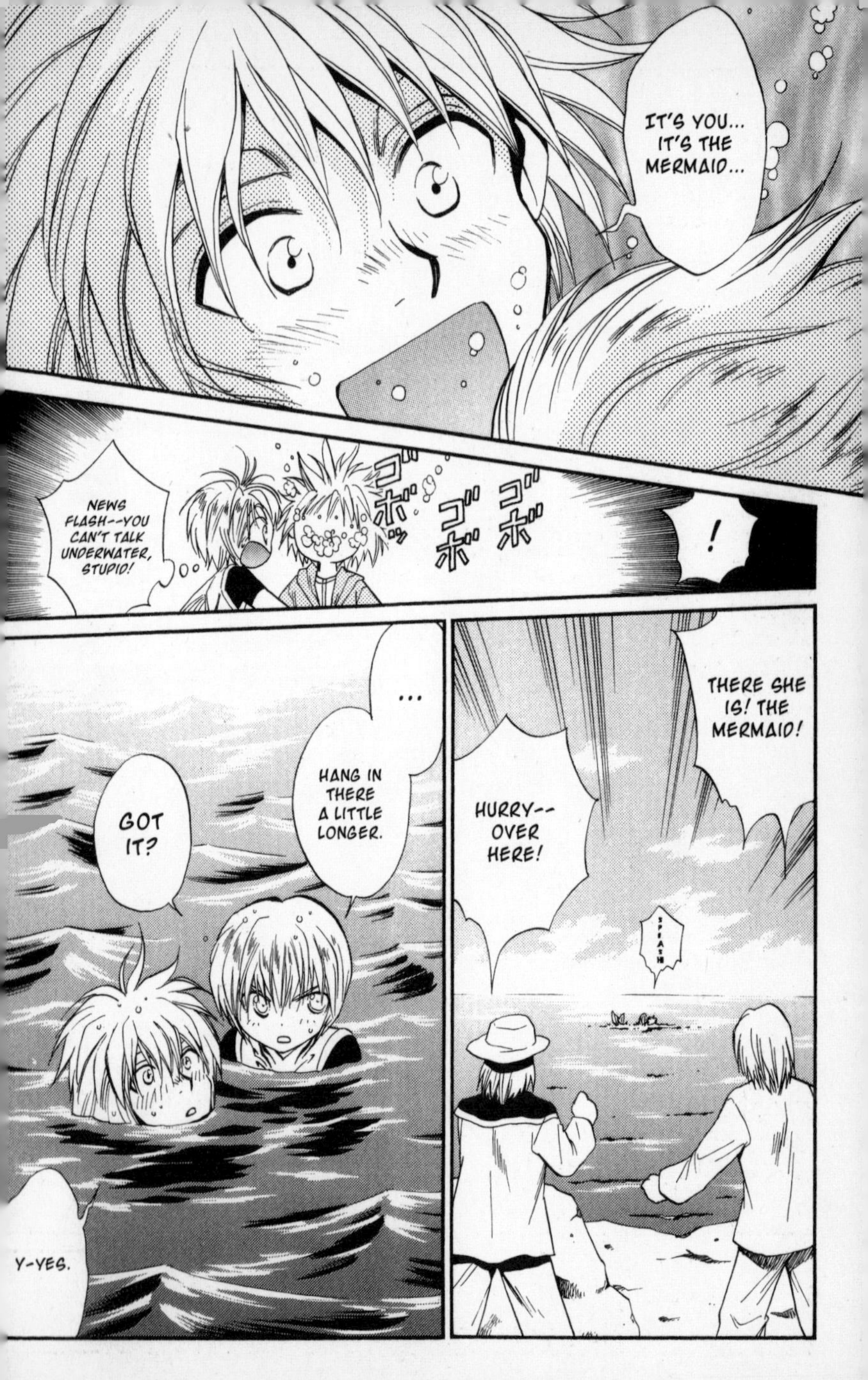
IT'S YOU... IT'S THE MERMAID...
!
ゴボ
ゴボ
ゴボッ
NEWS FLASH--YOU CAN'T TALK UNDERWATER, STUPID!
THERE SHE IS! THE MERMAID!
HURRY--OVER HERE!
SPLASH
...
HANG IN THERE A LITTLE LONGER.
GOT IT?
Y-YES.

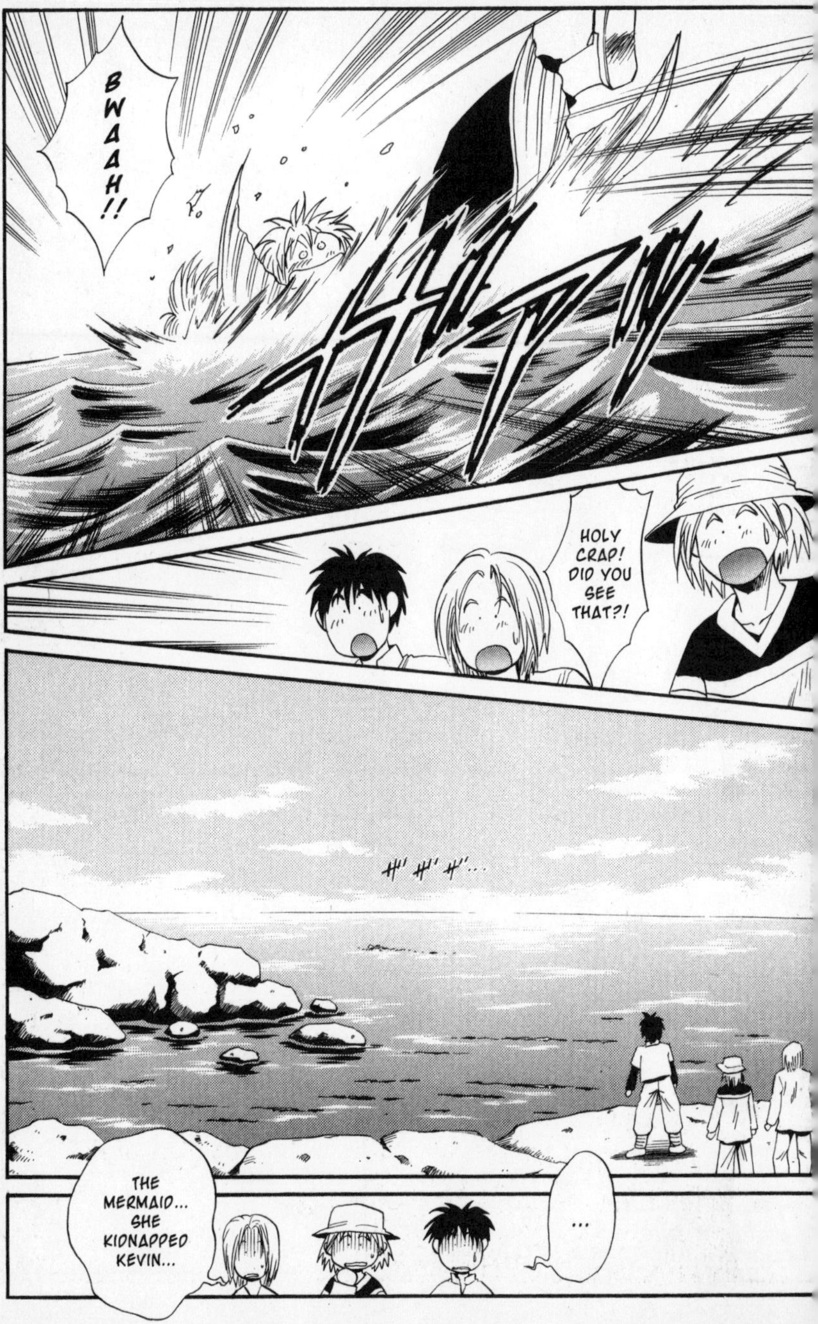
BWAAAH!!
HOLY CRAP! DID YOU SEE THAT?!
...
THE MERMAID... SHE KIDNAPPED KEVIN...

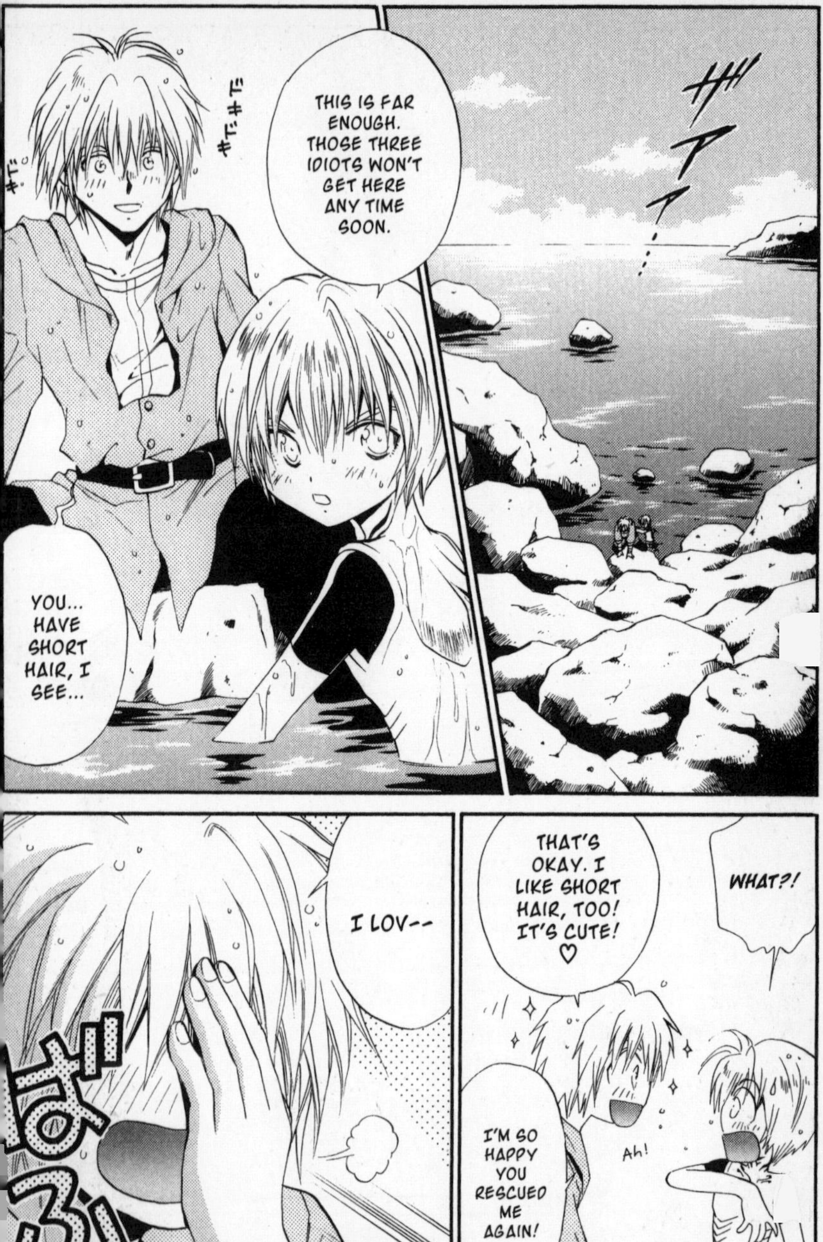
ザァァ…
THIS IS FAR ENOUGH. THOSE THREE IDIOTS WON'T GET HERE ANY TIME SOON.
ドキドキ
YOU... HAVE SHORT HAIR, I SEE...
WHAT?!
THAT'S OKAY. I LIKE SHORT HAIR, TOO! IT'S CUTE! ♡
Ah!
I'M SO HAPPY YOU RESCUED ME AGAIN!
I LOV--
ばふっ

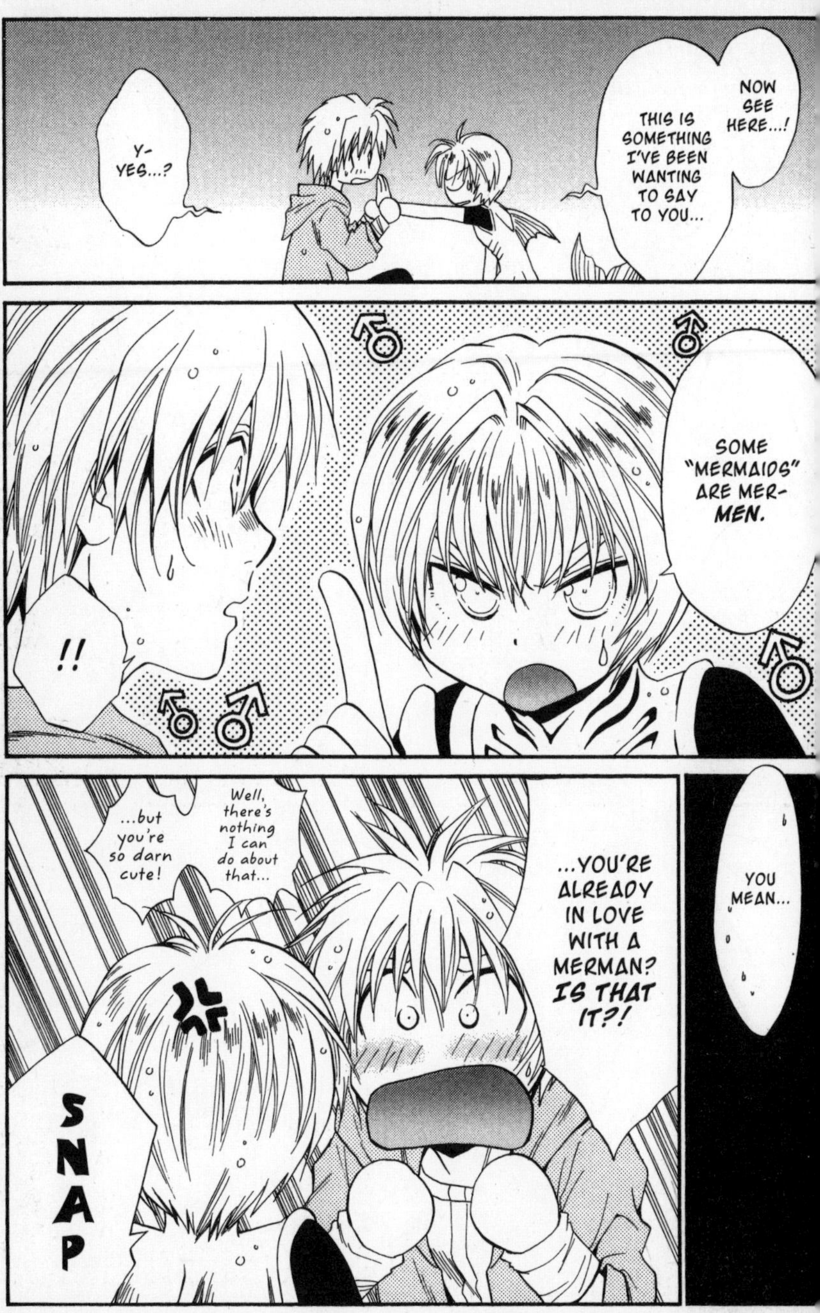
NOW SEE HERE...!
THIS IS SOMETHING I'VE BEEN WANTING TO SAY TO YOU...
Y-YES...?
SOME "MERMAIDS" ARE MER-MEN.
!!
YOU MEAN...
...YOU'RE ALREADY IN LOVE WITH A MERMAN? IS THAT IT?!
Well, there's nothing I can do about that...
...but you're so darn cute!
SNAP

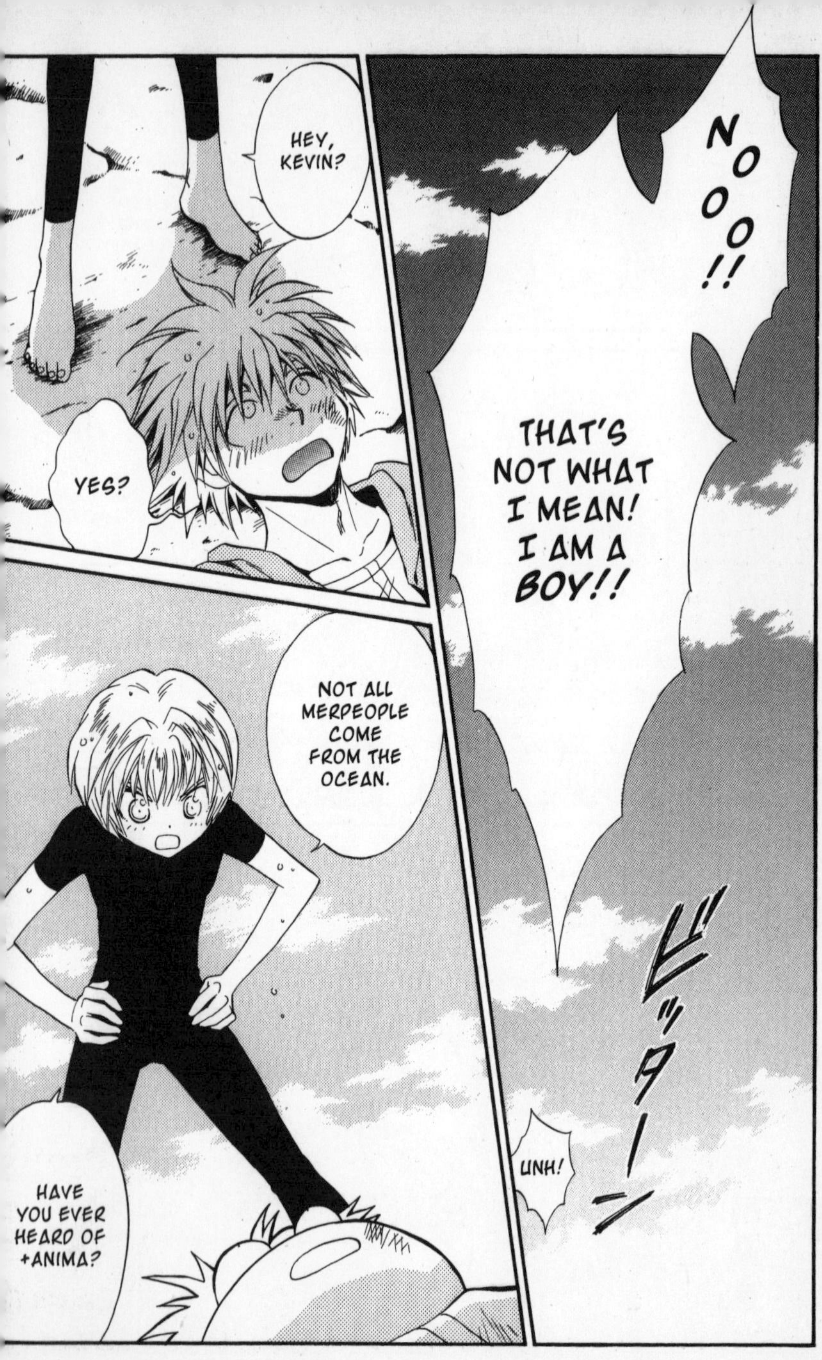
NOOOO!!
THAT'S NOT WHAT I MEAN! I AM A BOY!!
ビッターン
UNH!
HEY, KEVIN?
YES?
NOT ALL MERPEOPLE COME FROM THE OCEAN.
HAVE YOU EVER HEARD OF +ANIMA?

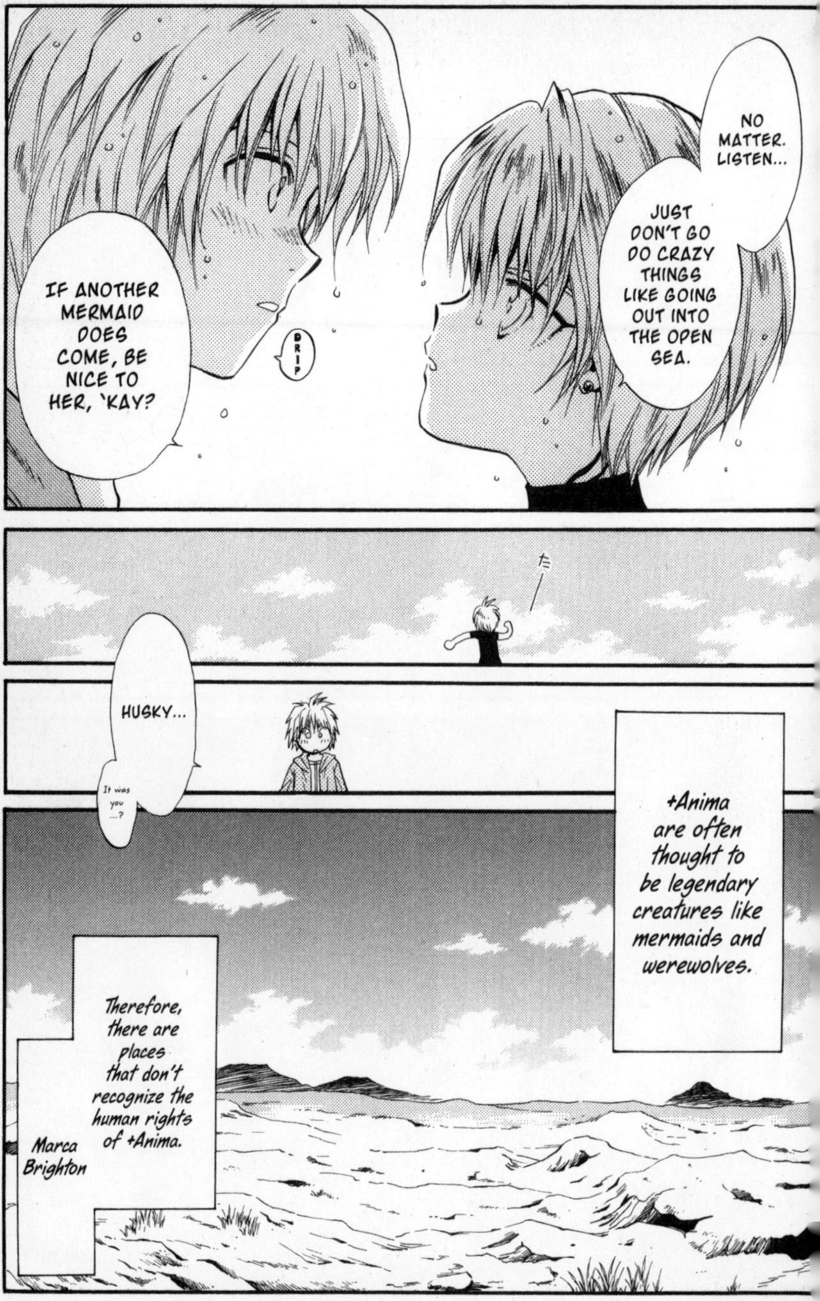
NO MATTER. LISTEN...
JUST DON'T GO DO CRAZY THINGS LIKE GOING OUT INTO THE OPEN SEA.
DRIP
IF ANOTHER MERMAID DOES COME, BE NICE TO HER, 'KAY?
た
HUSKY...
It was you ...?
+Anima are often thought to be legendary creatures like mermaids and werewolves.
Therefore, there are places that don't recognize the human rights of +Anima.
Marca Brighton

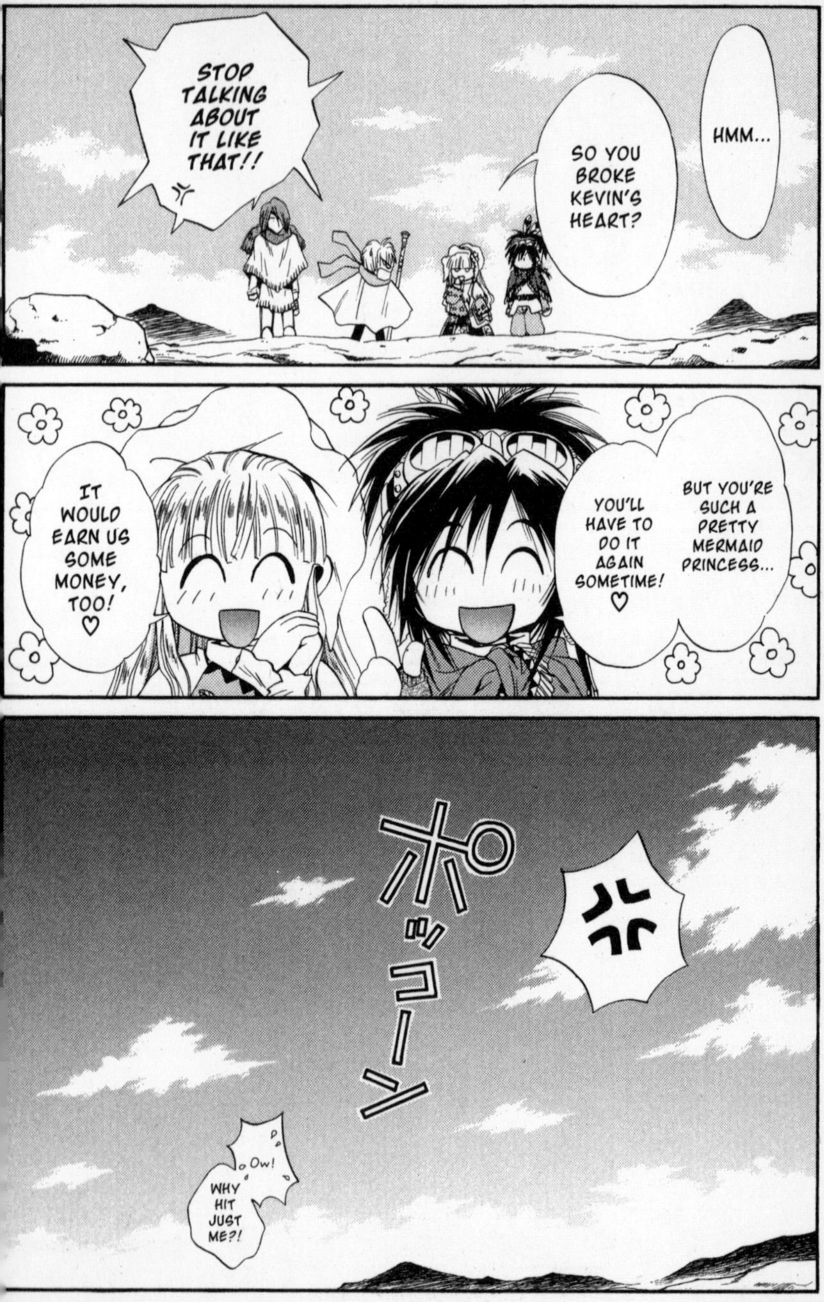
HMM...
SO YOU BROKE KEVIN'S HEART?
STOP TALKING ABOUT IT LIKE THAT!!
BUT YOU'RE SUCH A PRETTY MERMAID PRINCESS...
YOU'LL HAVE TO DO IT AGAIN SOMETIME! ♡
IT WOULD EARN US SOME MONEY, TOO! ♡
ポッコーン
OW!
WHY HIT JUST ME?!

Nicknames

Cooro
Teehee ♡
Eh heh!
Nana
Bear
Husky the Mermaid
WHY?!
Popular Name: Cooro Punishing Stick

A Natsumi Mukai Special Presentation

+Anima Backstage

Chapter 25: Teddy Bear

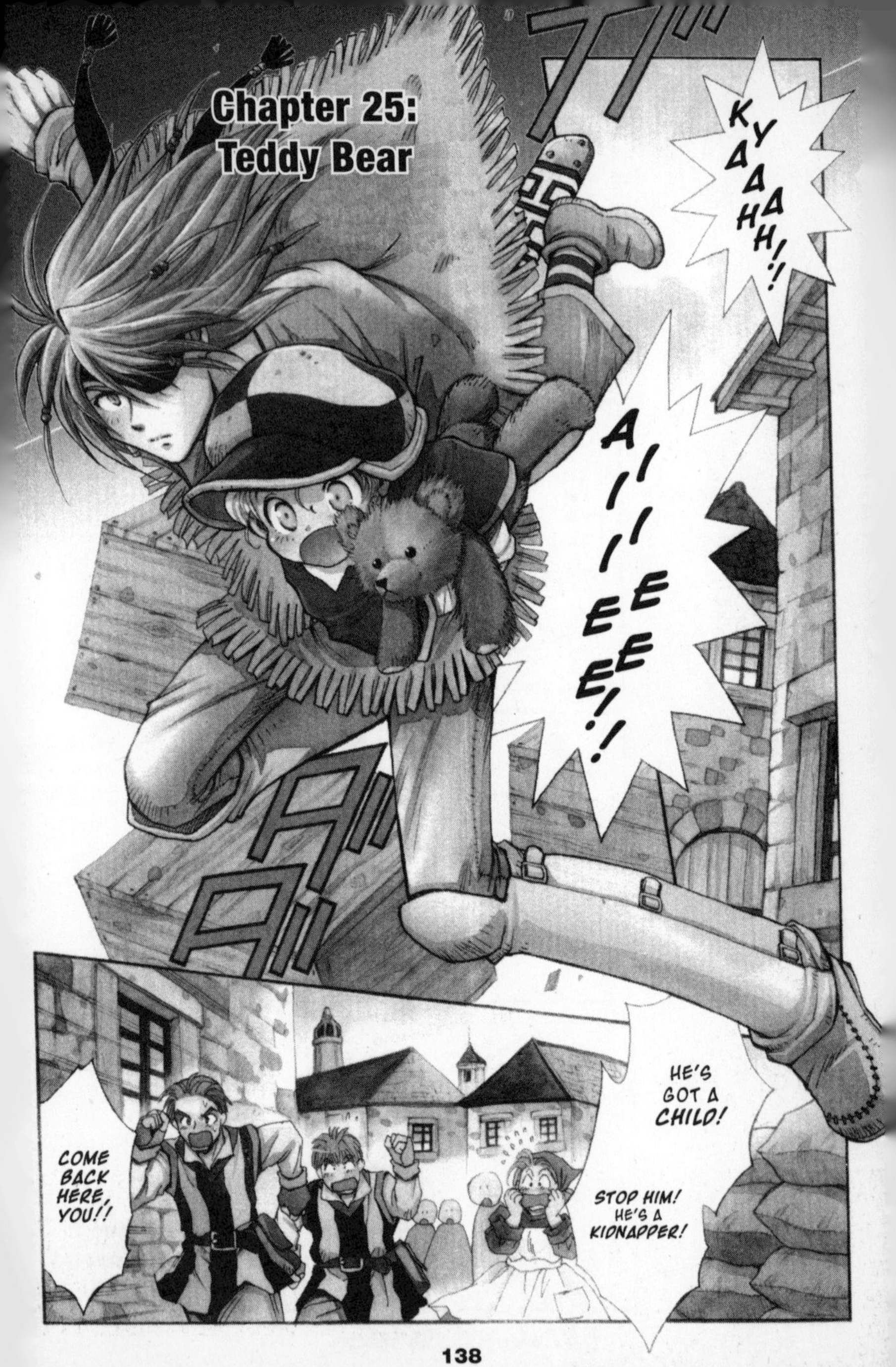
KYAAAHH!!
AIIIIEEEEE!!
HE'S GOT A CHILD!
STOP HIM! HE'S A KIDNAPPER!
COME BACK HERE, YOU!!

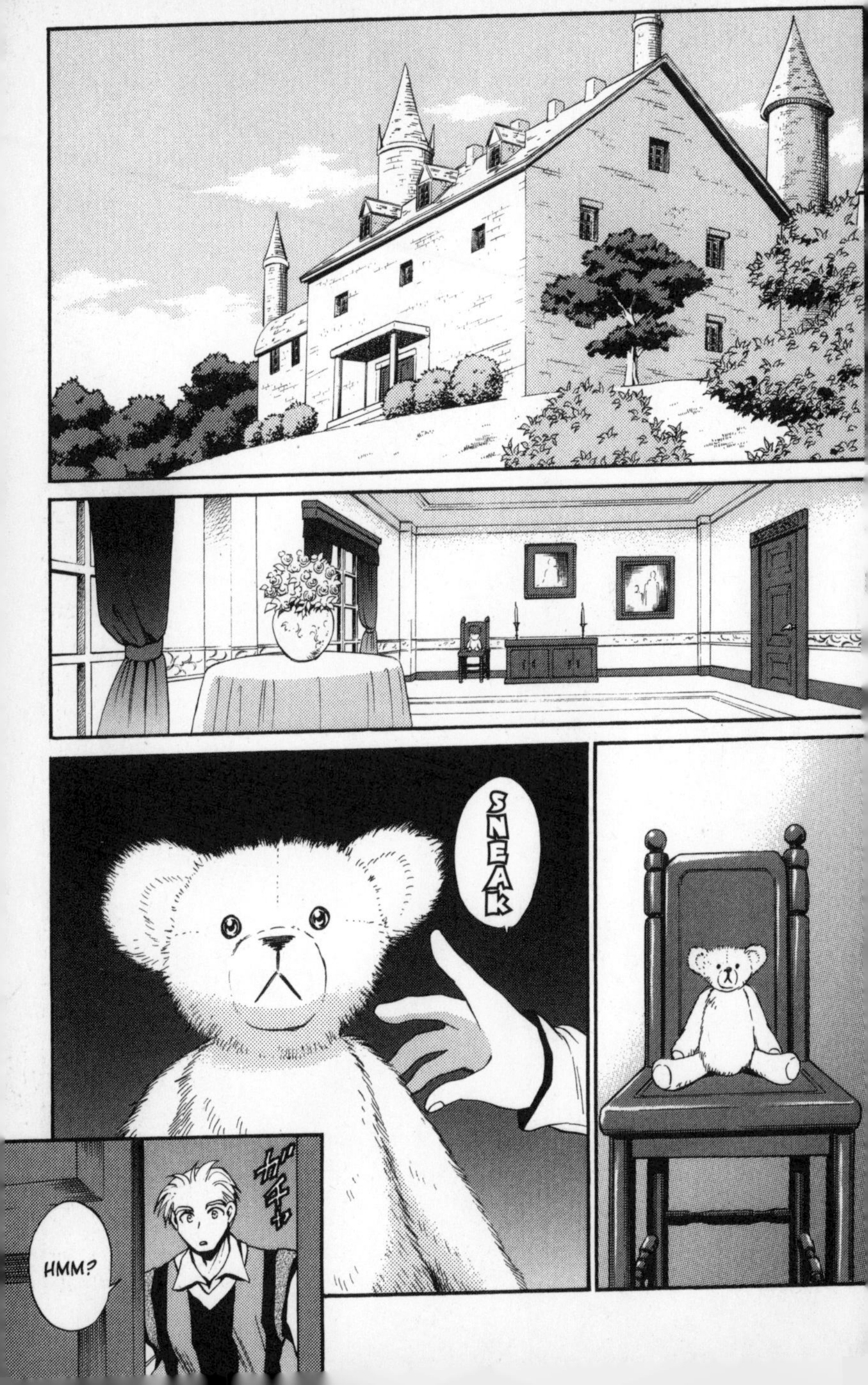
SNEAK
ガチャ
HMM?

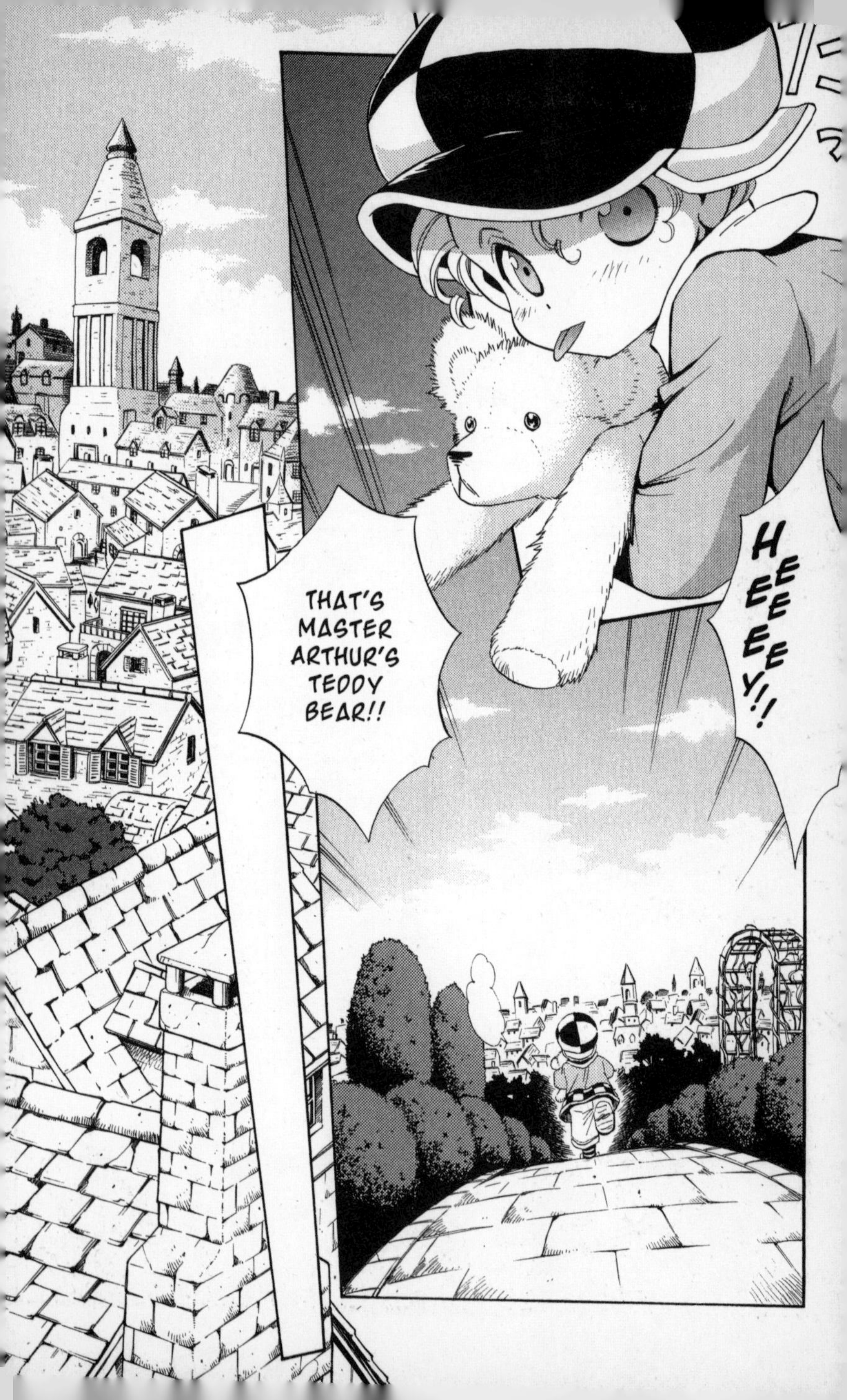
HEEEEEY!!
THAT'S MASTER ARTHUR'S TEDDY BEAR!!

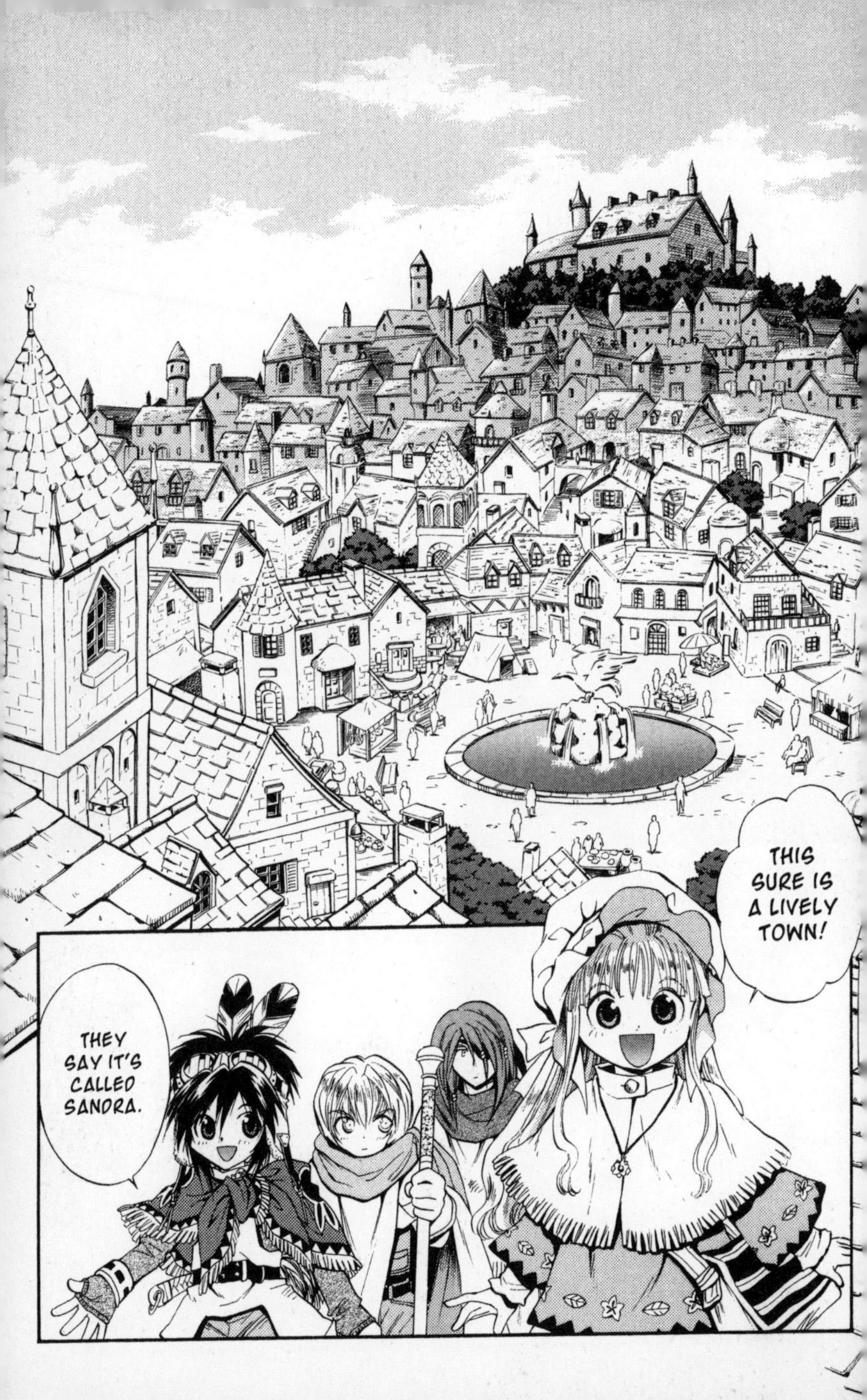
THIS SURE IS A LIVELY TOWN!
THEY SAY IT'S CALLED SANDRA.

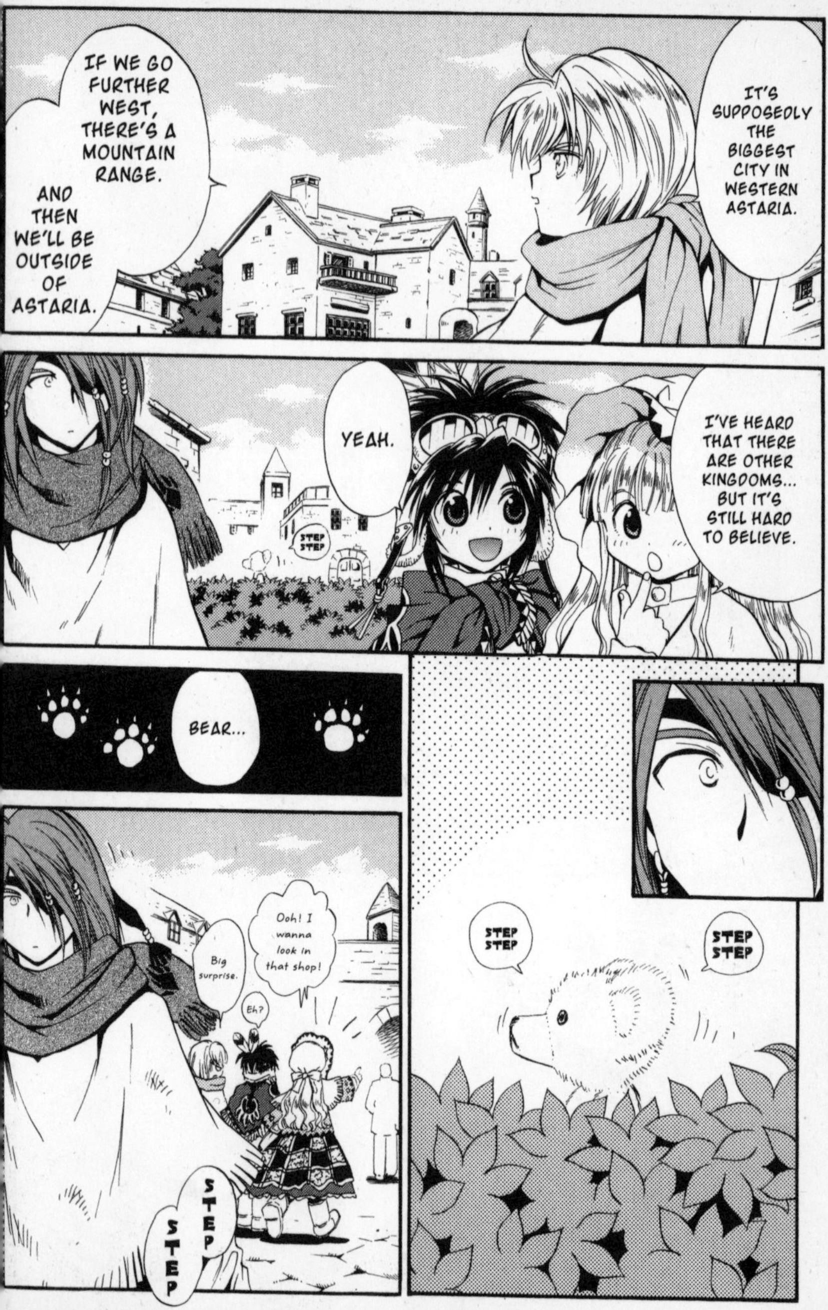
IT'S SUPPOSEDLY THE BIGGEST CITY IN WESTERN ASTARIA.
IF WE GO FURTHER WEST, THERE'S A MOUNTAIN RANGE.
AND THEN WE'LL BE OUTSIDE OF ASTARIA.
I'VE HEARD THAT THERE ARE OTHER KINGDOMS... BUT IT'S STILL HARD TO BELIEVE.
YEAH.
STEP STEP
STEP STEP
STEP STEP
BEAR...
Ooh! I wanna look in that shop!
Big surprise.
Eh?
STEP STEP STEP

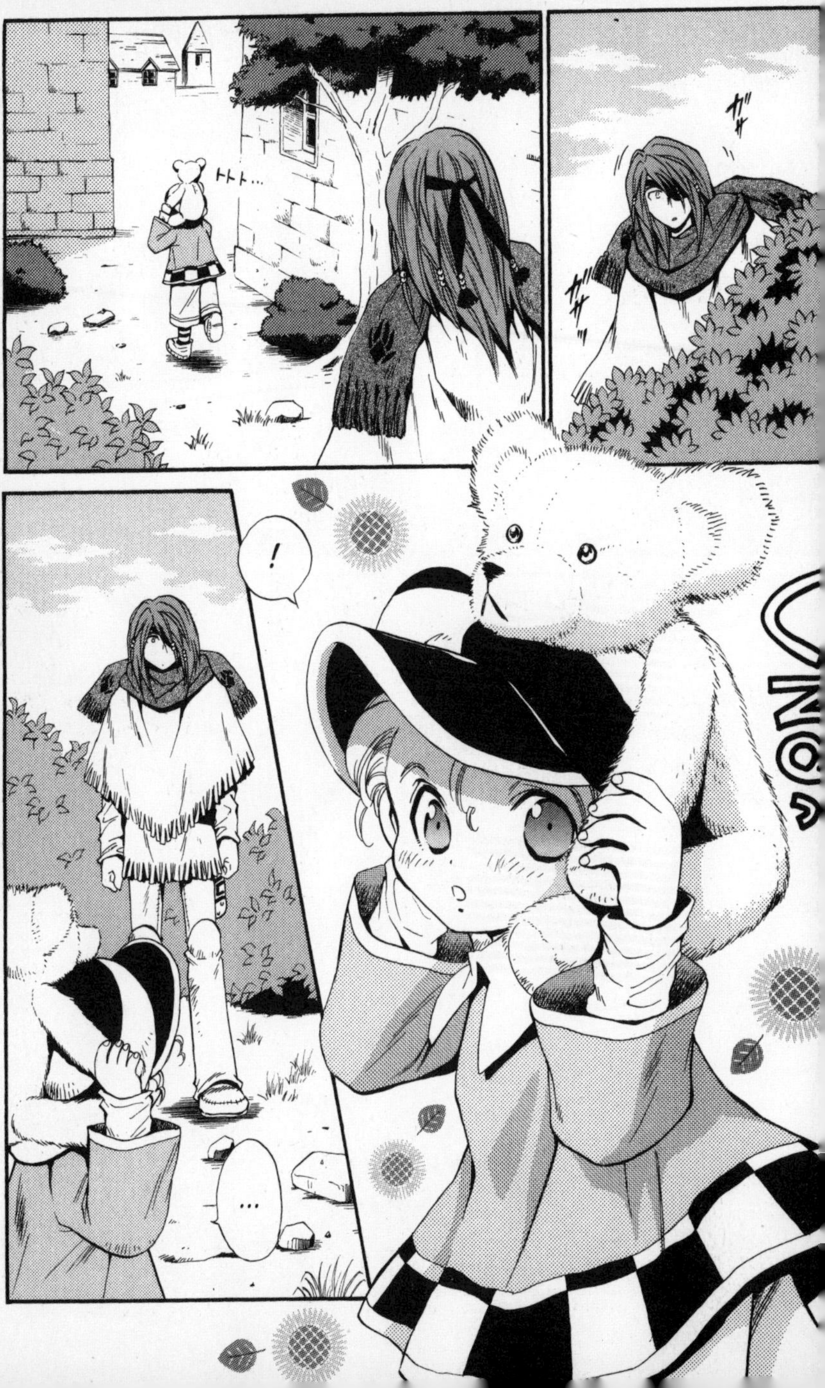

ガサ
ガサ
トトト…
!
…

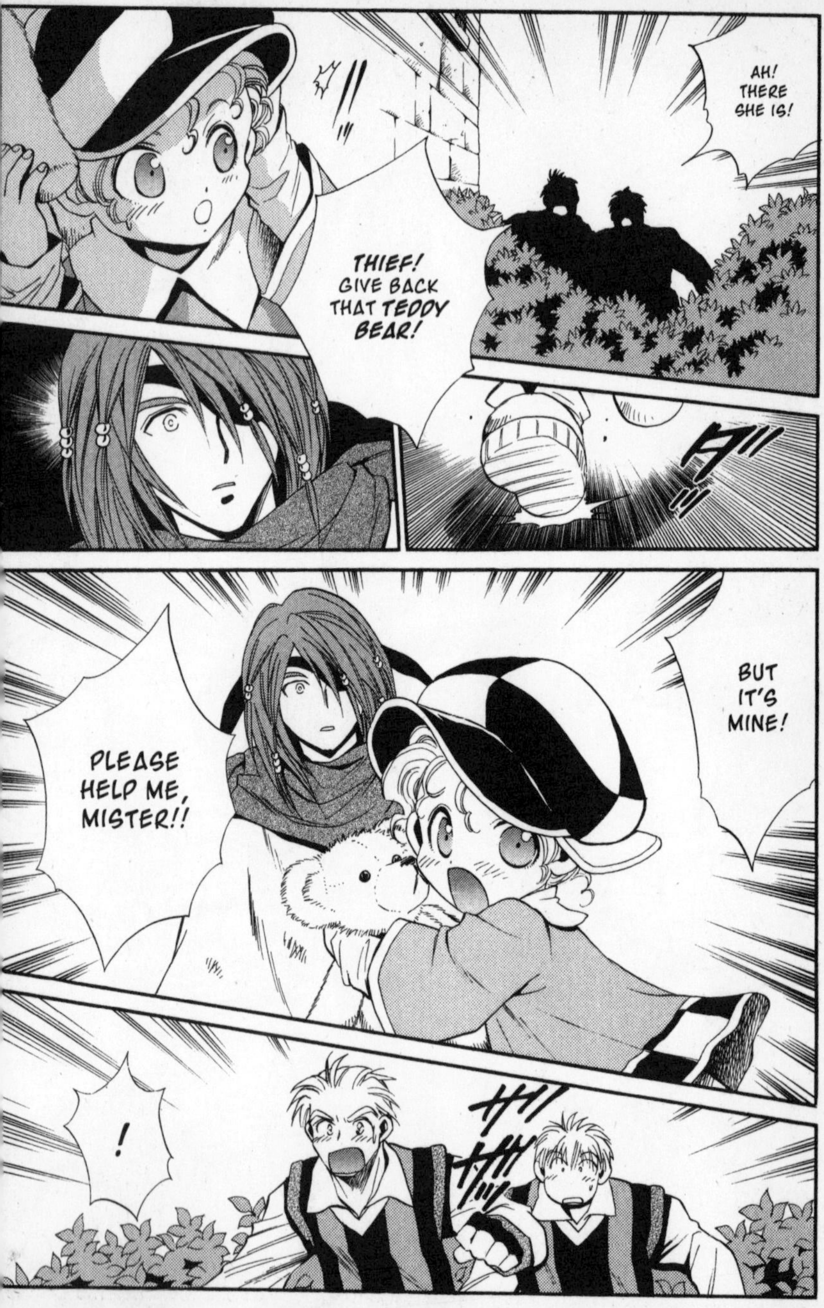
AH! THERE SHE IS!
THIEF! GIVE BACK THAT TEDDY BEAR!
BUT IT'S MINE!
PLEASE HELP ME, MISTER!!
!

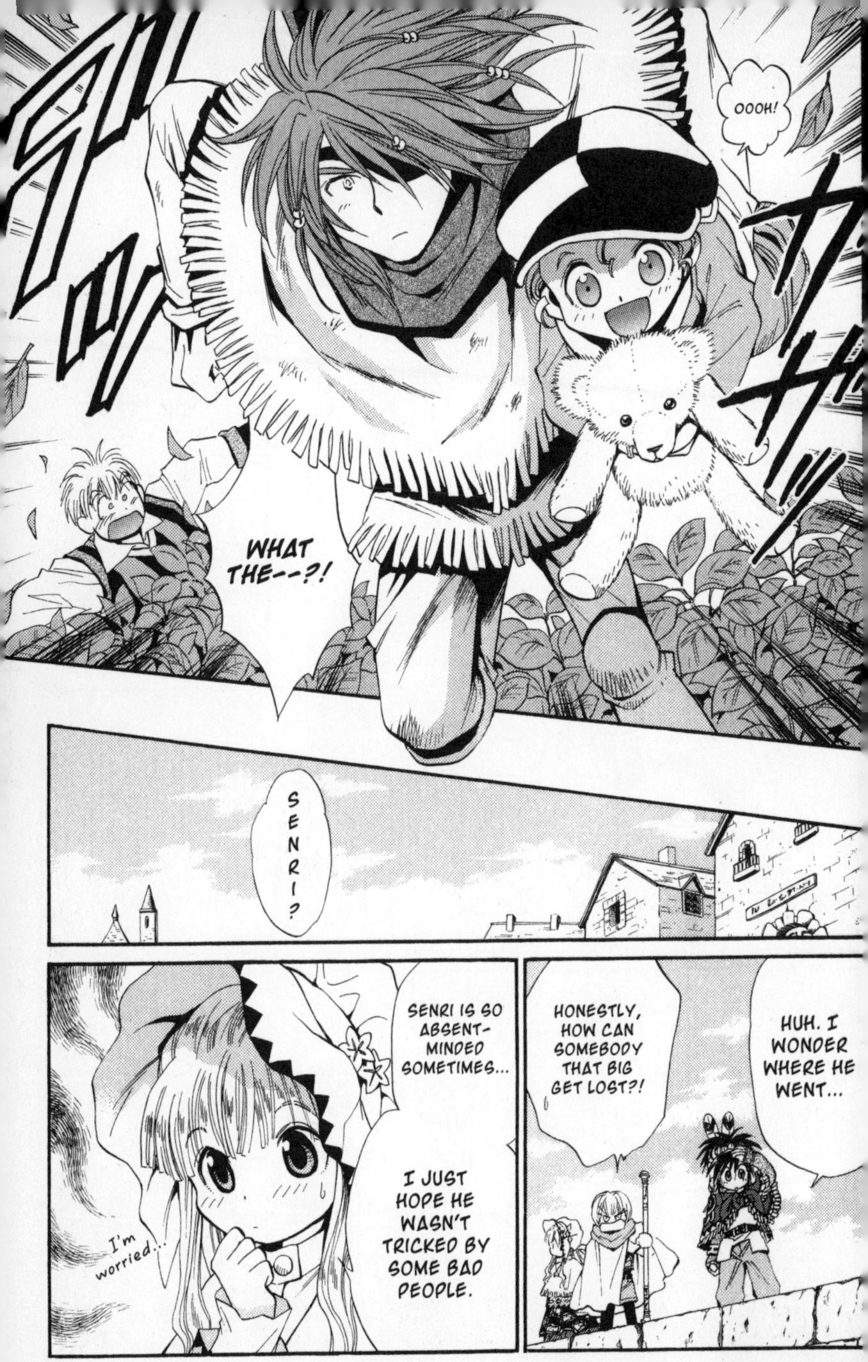
OOOH!
WHAT THE--?!
SENRI?
HUH. I WONDER WHERE HE WENT...
HONESTLY, HOW CAN SOMEBODY THAT BIG GET LOST?!
SENRI IS SO ABSENT-MINDED SOMETIMES...
I JUST HOPE HE WASN'T TRICKED BY SOME BAD PEOPLE.
I'm worried...

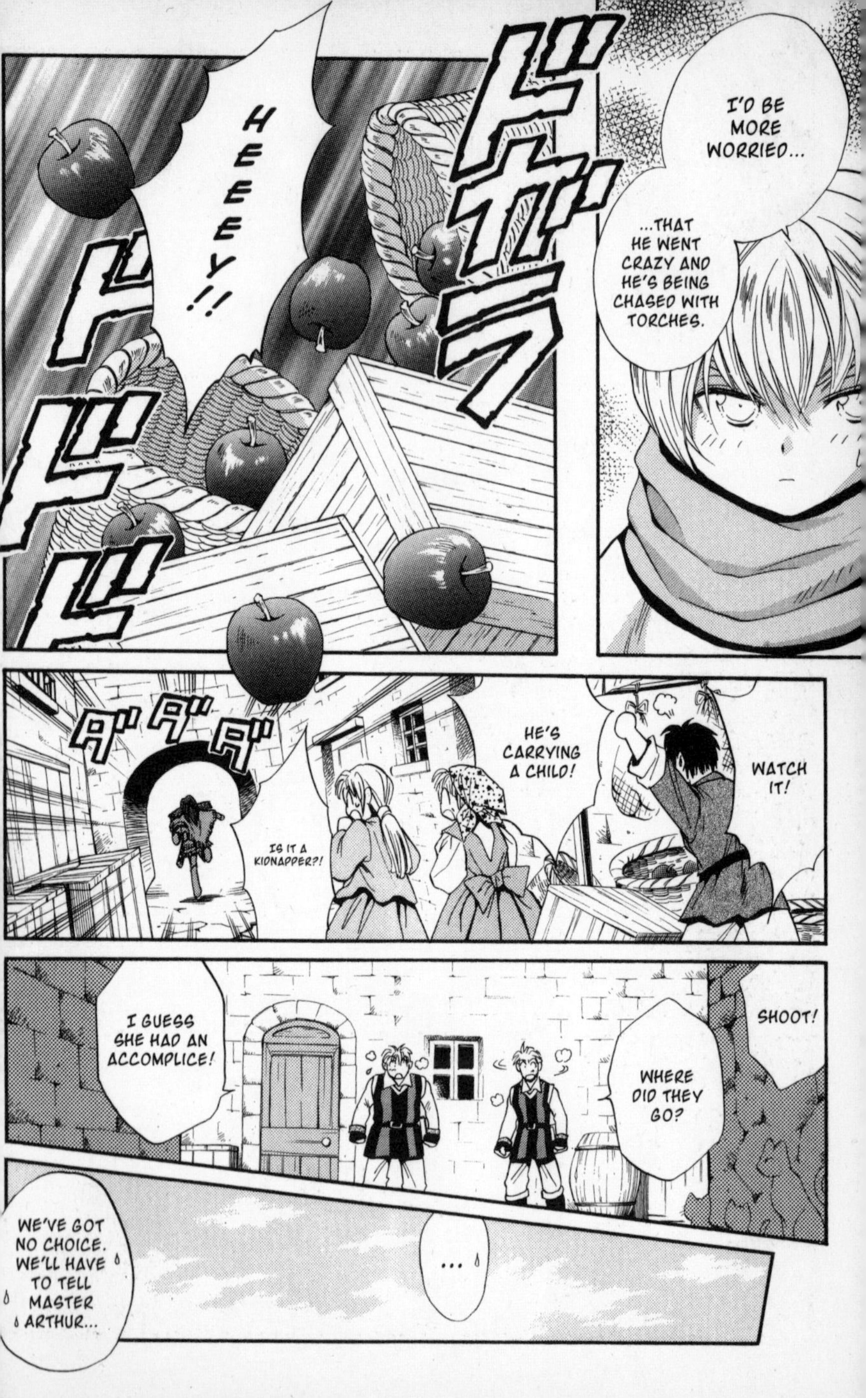
I'D BE MORE WORRIED...
...THAT HE WENT CRAZY AND HE'S BEING CHASED WITH TORCHES.
HEEEEY!!
WATCH IT!
HE'S CARRYING A CHILD!
IS IT A KIDNAPPER?!
SHOOT!
WHERE DID THEY GO?
I GUESS SHE HAD AN ACCOMPLICE!
...
WE'VE GOT NO CHOICE. WE'LL HAVE TO TELL MASTER ARTHUR...

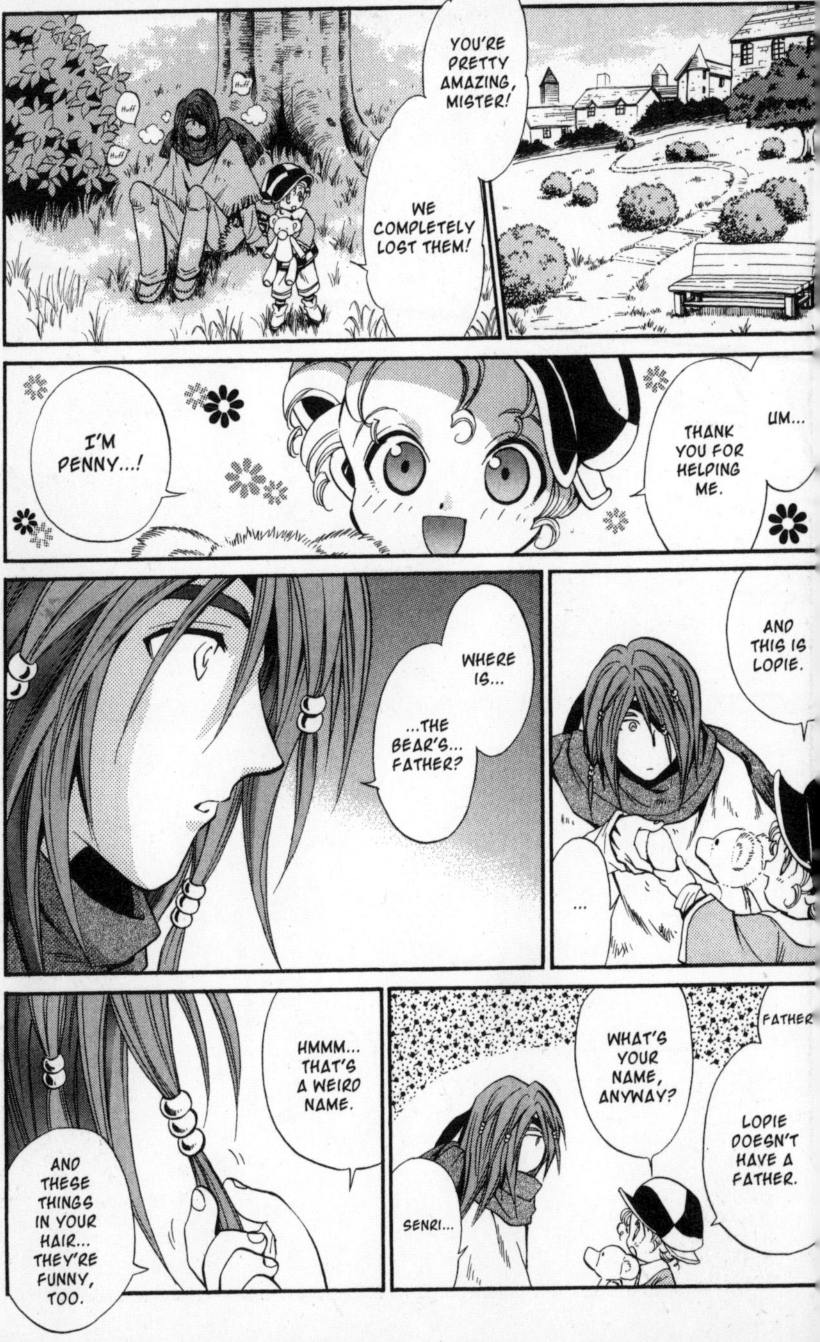
Huff
Huff
Huff
YOU'RE PRETTY AMAZING, MISTER!
WE COMPLETELY LOST THEM!
UM...
THANK YOU FOR HELPING ME.
I'M PENNY...!
AND THIS IS LOPIE.
...
WHERE IS...
...THE BEAR'S... FATHER?
FATHER
LOPIE DOESN'T HAVE A FATHER.
WHAT'S YOUR NAME, ANYWAY?
SENRI...
HMMM... THAT'S A WEIRD NAME.
AND THESE THINGS IN YOUR HAIR... THEY'RE FUNNY, TOO.

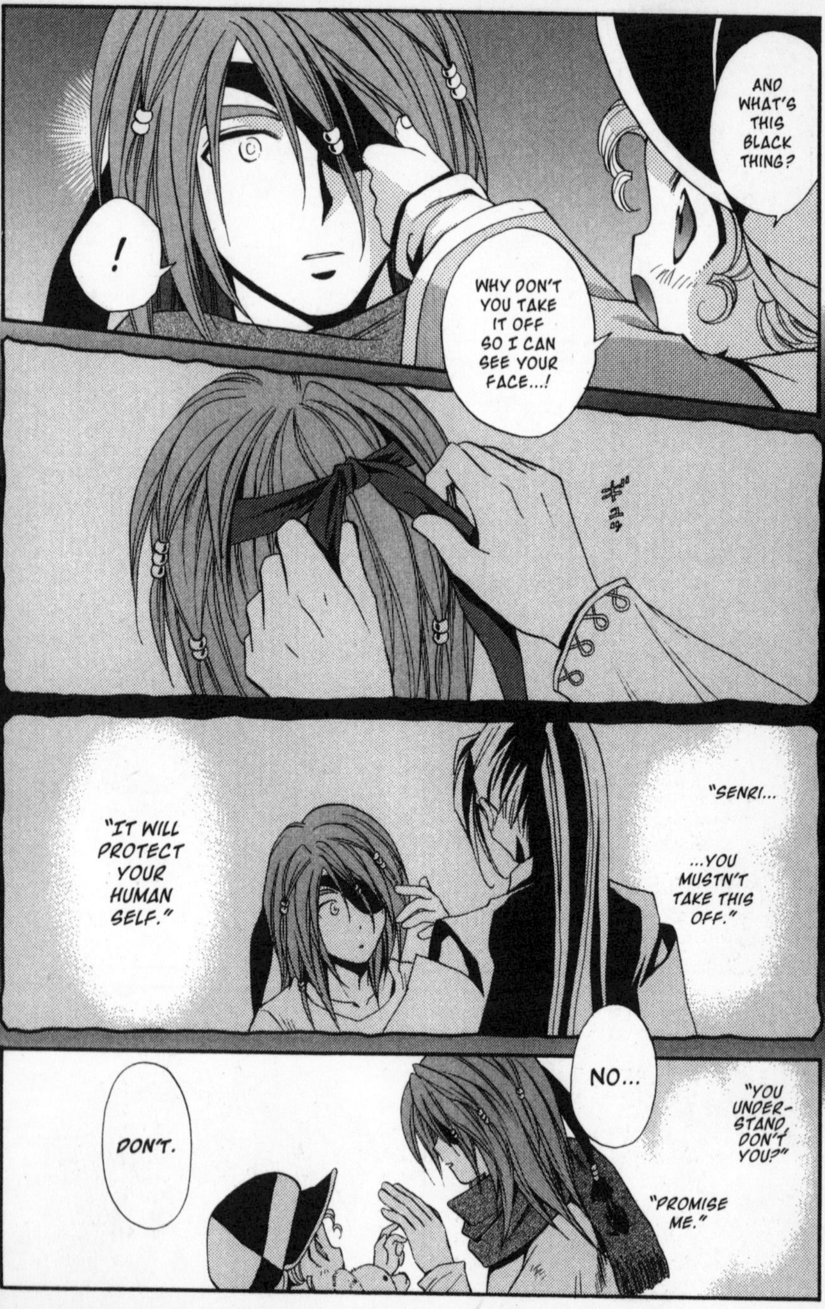
AND WHAT'S THIS BLACK THING?
!
WHY DON'T YOU TAKE IT OFF SO I CAN SEE YOUR FACE...!
"SENRI...
...YOU MUSTN'T TAKE THIS OFF."
"IT WILL PROTECT YOUR HUMAN SELF."
"YOU UNDER-STAND, DON'T YOU?"
NO...
"PROMISE ME."
DON'T.

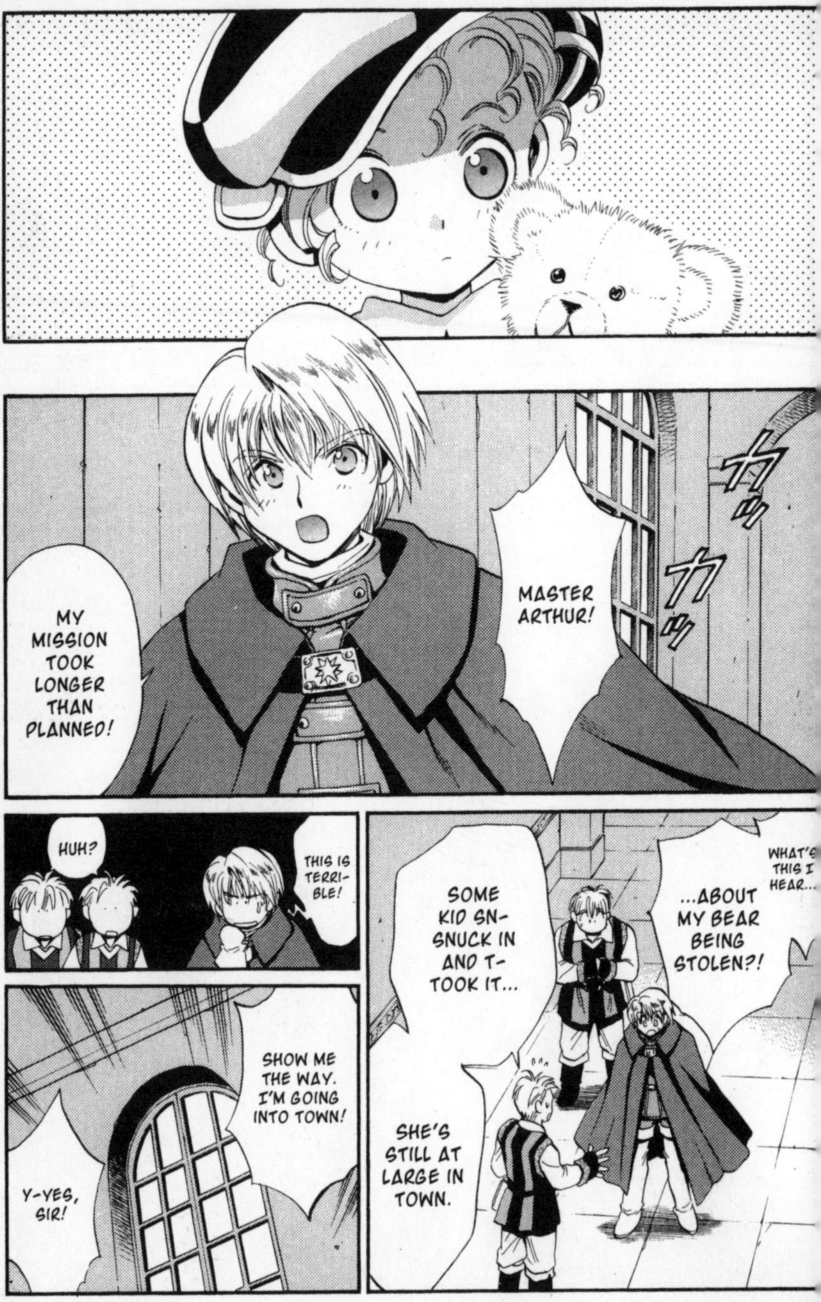
MASTER ARTHUR!
カッ
カッ
MY MISSION TOOK LONGER THAN PLANNED!
WHAT'S THIS I HEAR...
...ABOUT MY BEAR BEING STOLEN?!
SOME KID SN- SNUCK IN AND T- TOOK IT...
SHE'S STILL AT LARGE IN TOWN.
THIS IS TERRI- BLE!
HUH?
SHOW ME THE WAY. I'M GOING INTO TOWN!
Y-YES, SIR!

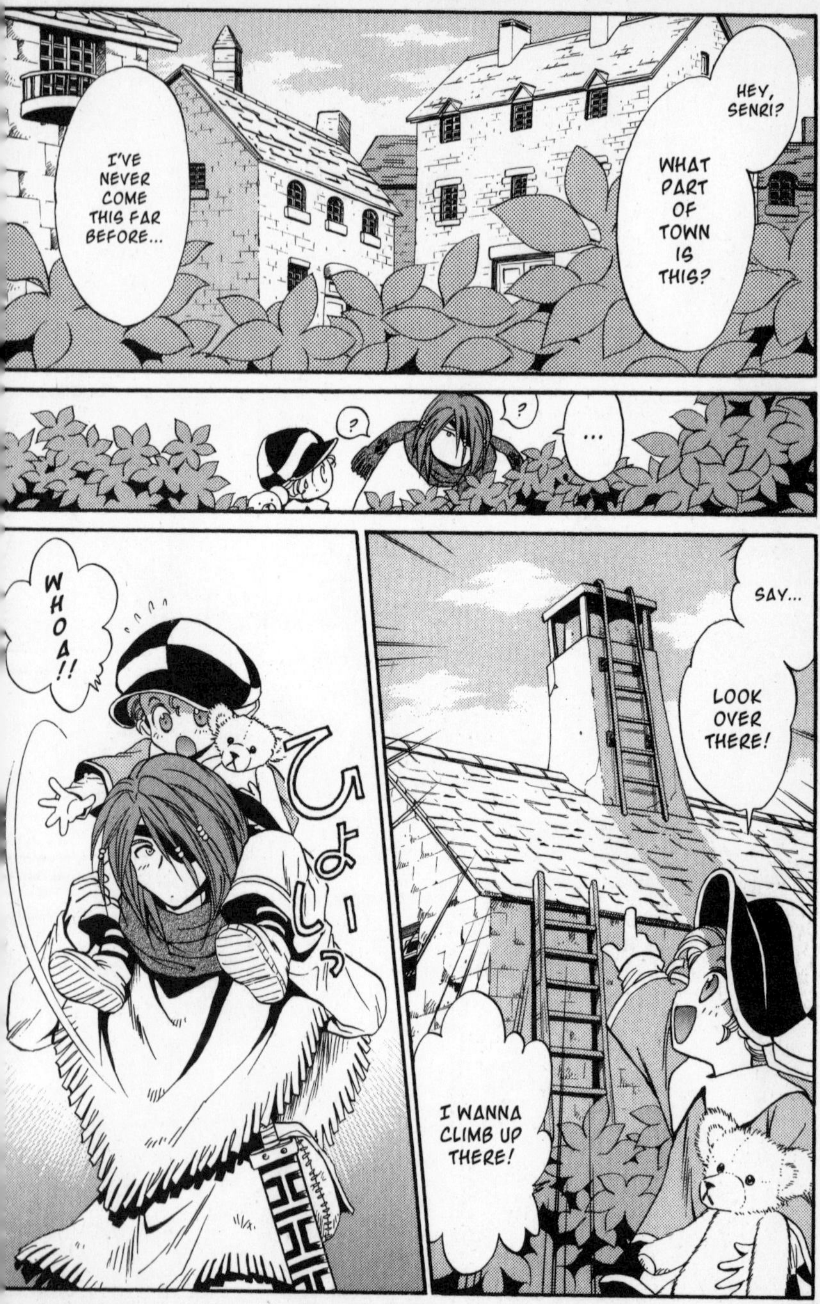
HEY, SENRI?
WHAT PART OF TOWN IS THIS?
I'VE NEVER COME THIS FAR BEFORE...
...
?
?
SAY...
LOOK OVER THERE!
I WANNA CLIMB UP THERE!
WHOA!!
ひょいっ

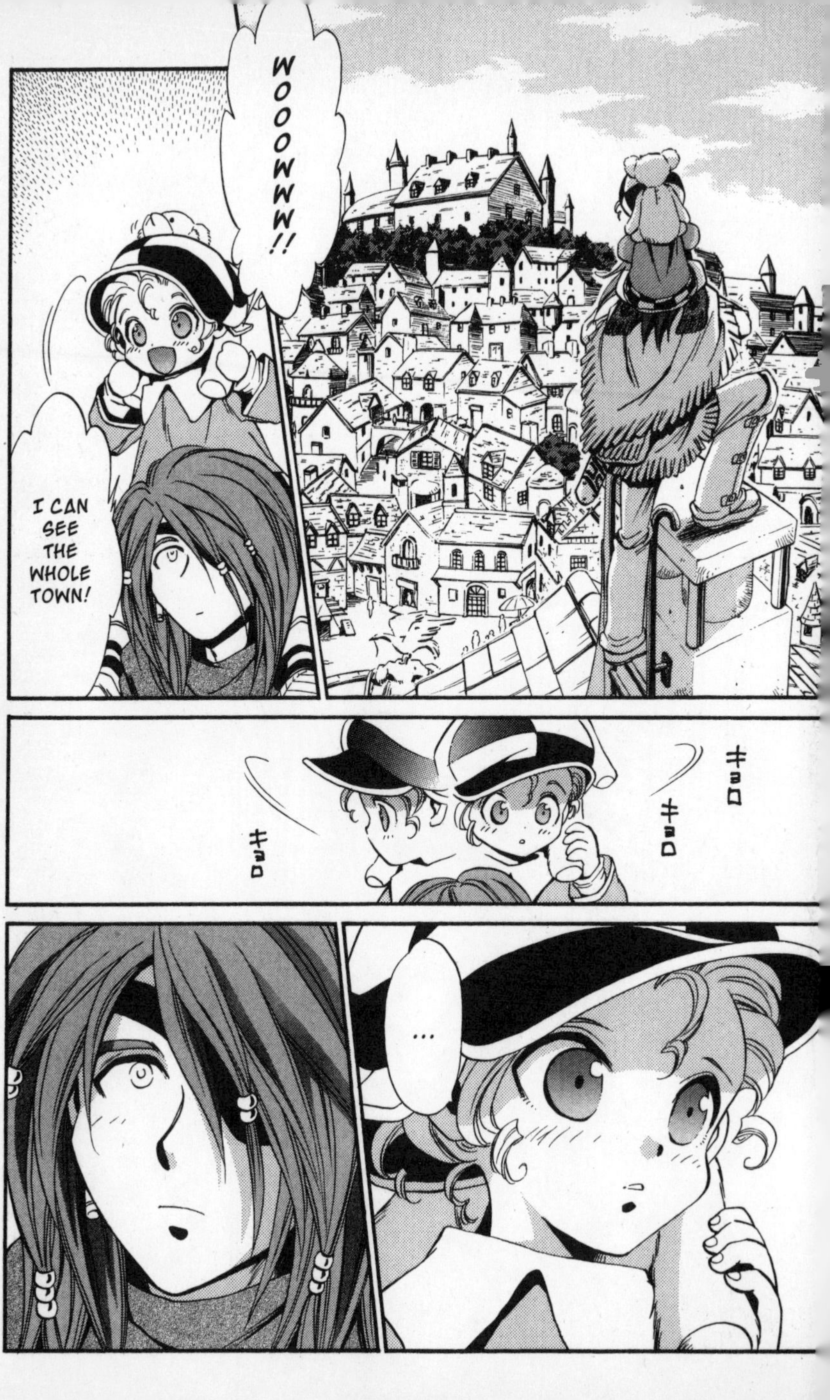
WOOOOWWW!!
I CAN SEE THE WHOLE TOWN!
キョロ
キョロ
キョロ
...

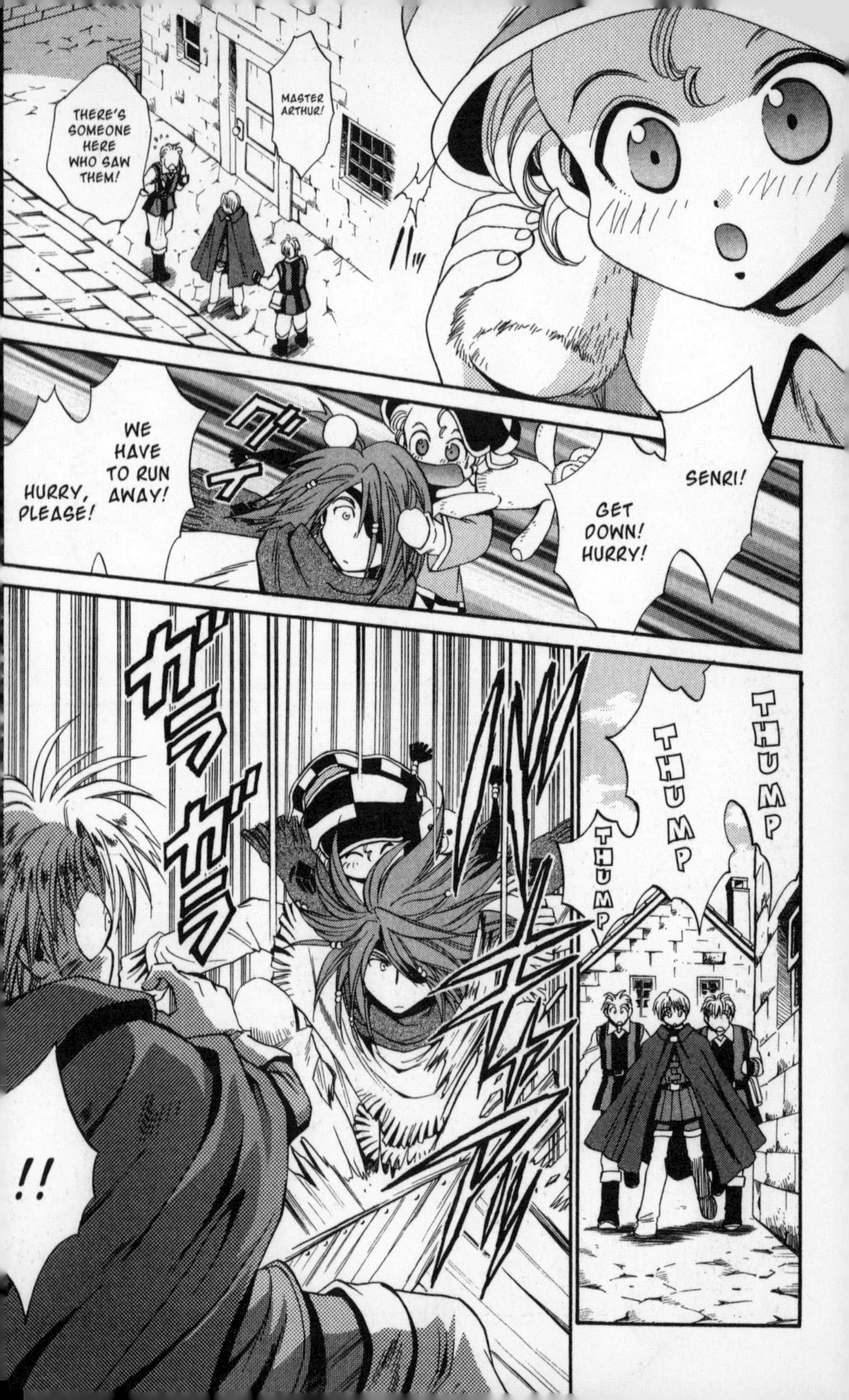
MASTER ARTHUR!
THERE'S SOMEONE HERE WHO SAW THEM!
SENRI!
GET DOWN! HURRY!
WE HAVE TO RUN AWAY!
HURRY, PLEASE!
THUMP
THUMP
THUMP
!!

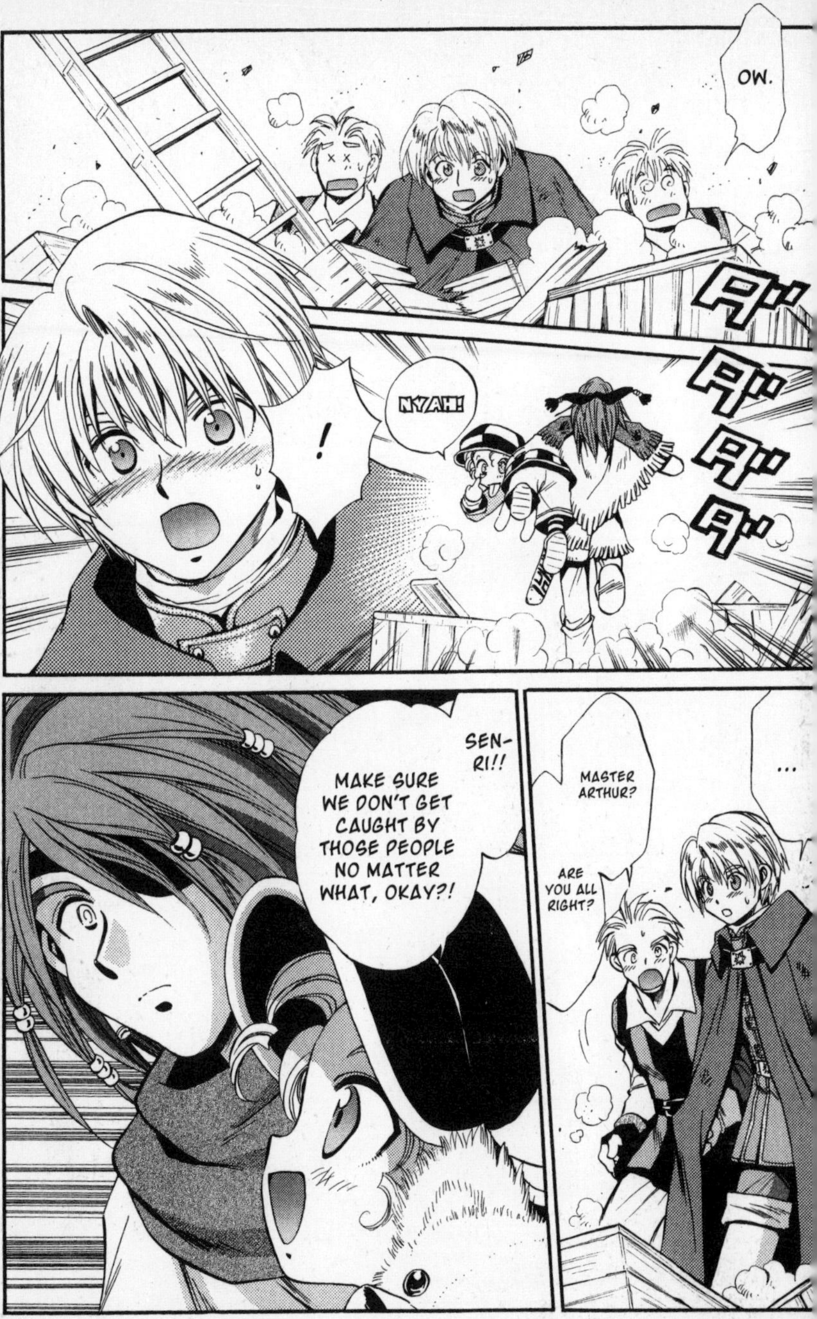
OW.
NYAH!
!
...
MASTER ARTHUR?
ARE YOU ALL RIGHT?
SEN-RI!!
MAKE SURE WE DON'T GET CAUGHT BY THOSE PEOPLE NO MATTER WHAT, OKAY?!

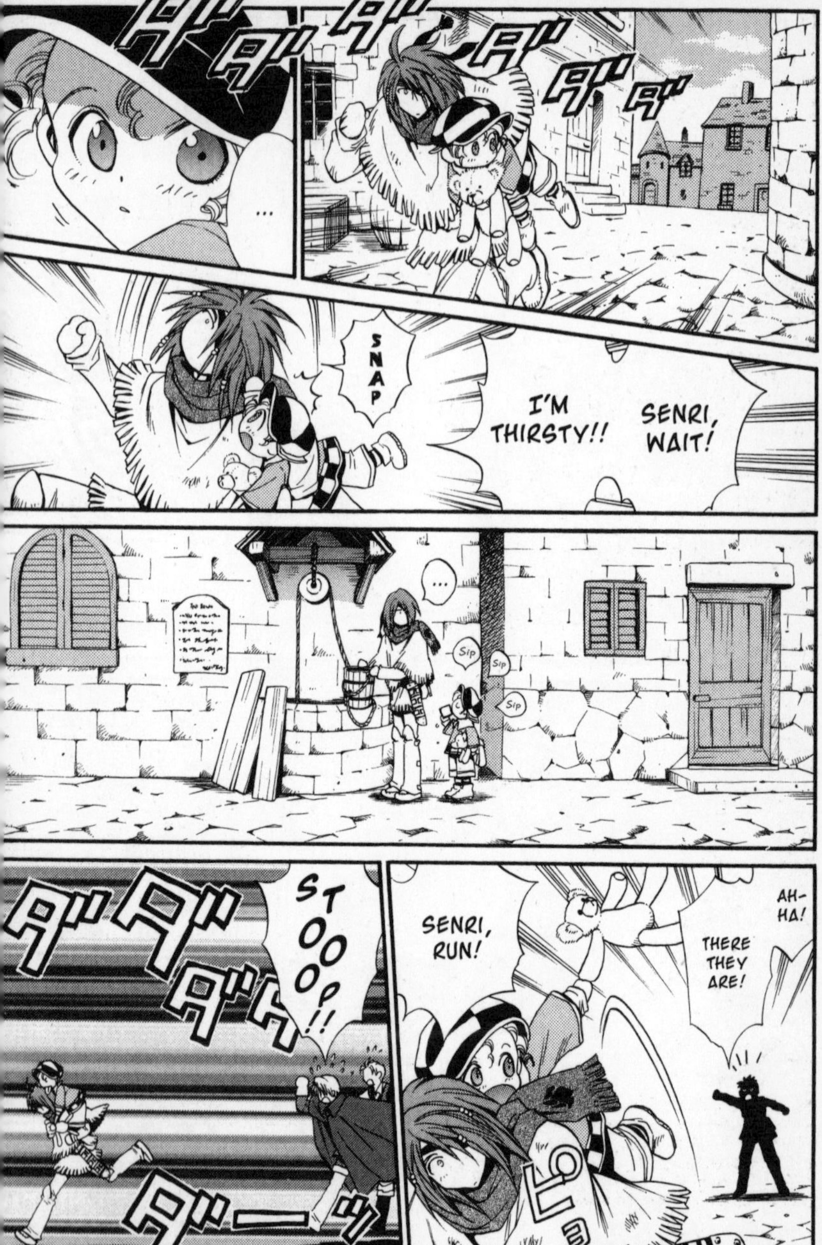
...
SENRI, WAIT!
I'M THIRSTY!!
SNAP
...
Sip
Sip
Sip
AH-HA!
THERE THEY ARE!
SENRI, RUN!
STOOOOP!!

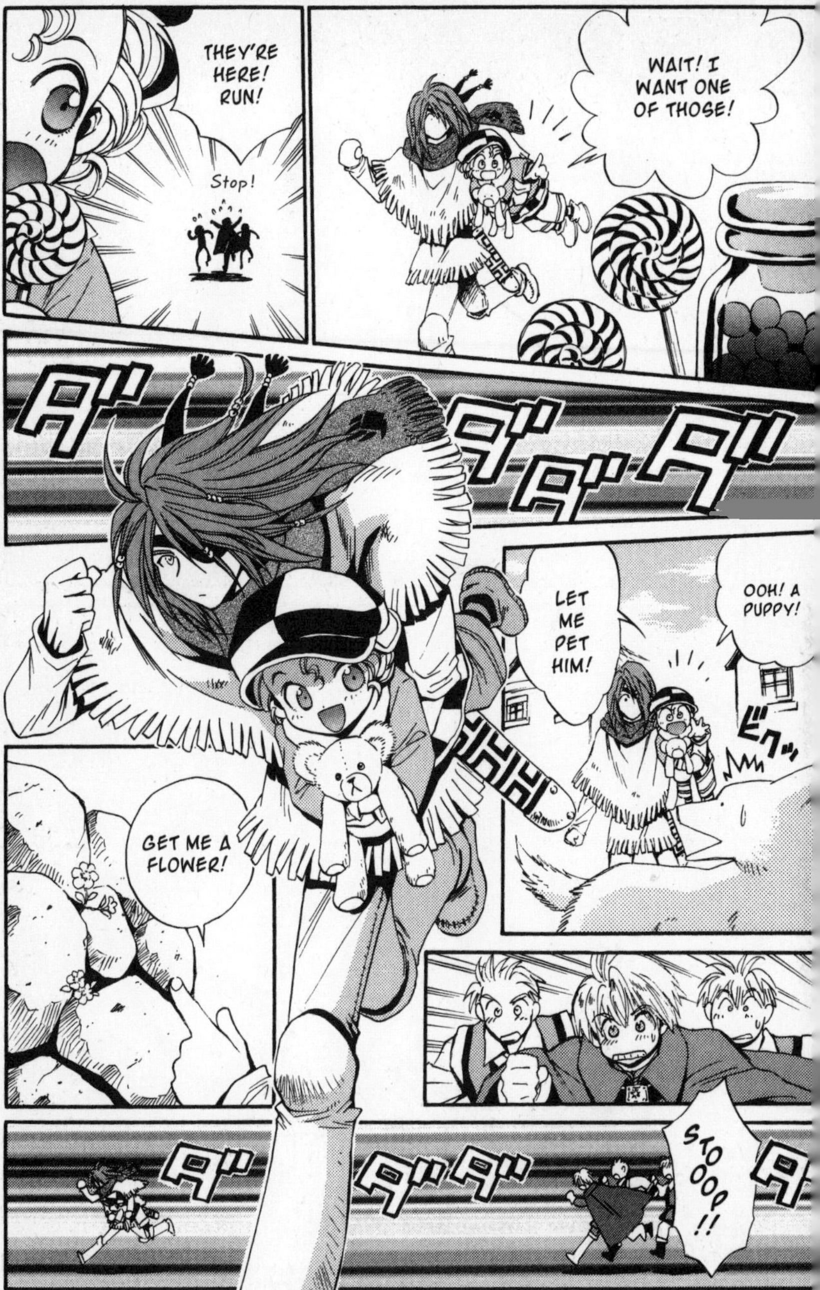
WAIT! I WANT ONE OF THOSE!
THEY'RE HERE! RUN!
Stop!
ダ ダ ダ ダ
OOH! A PUPPY!
LET ME PET HIM!
ビクッ
GET ME A FLOWER!
STOOOP!!
ダ ダ ダ ダ

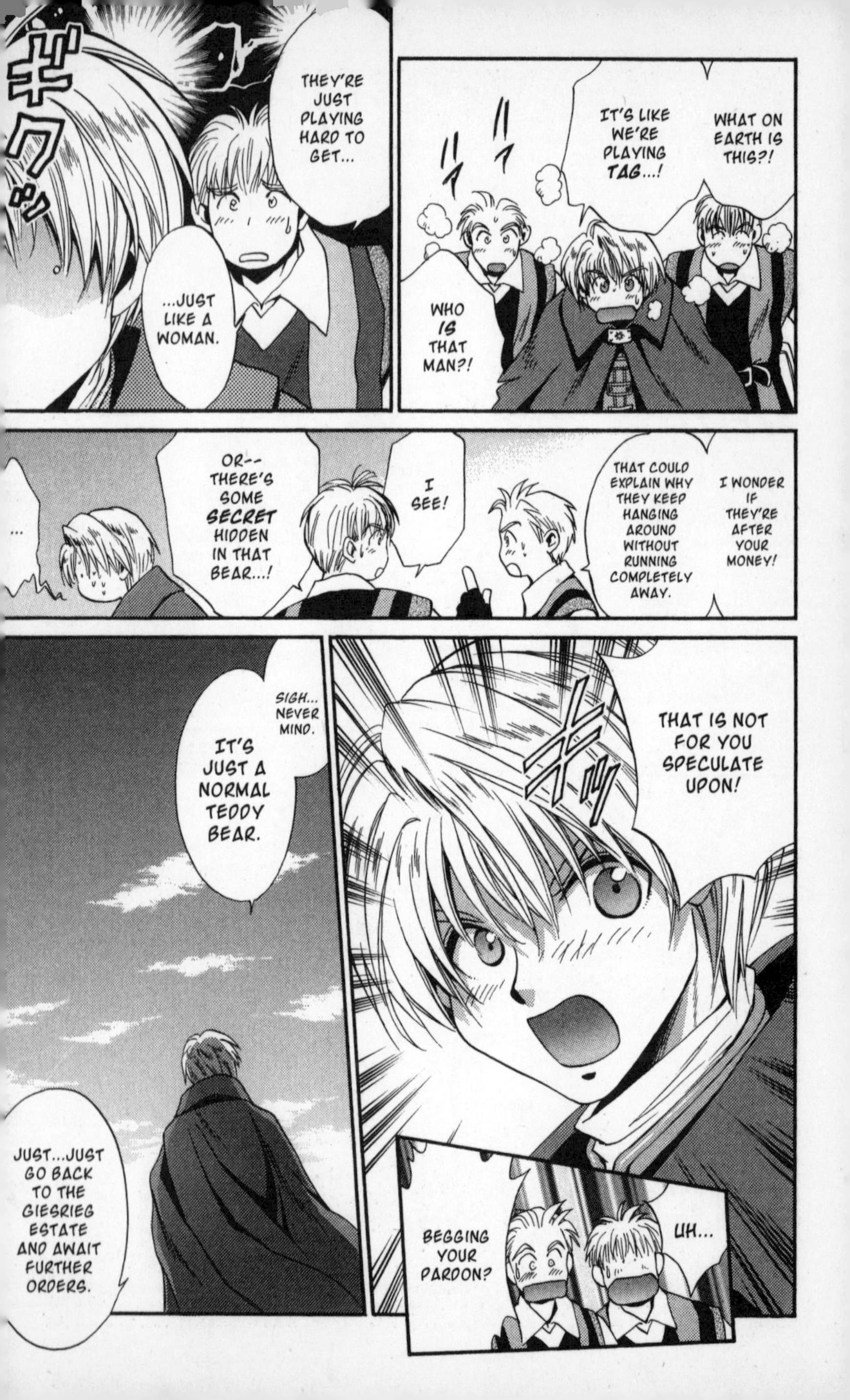
WHAT ON EARTH IS THIS?!
IT'S LIKE WE'RE PLAYING TAG...!
ハァ ハァ
WHO IS THAT MAN?!
THEY'RE JUST PLAYING HARD TO GET...
...JUST LIKE A WOMAN.
ギクッ
I WONDER IF THEY'RE AFTER YOUR MONEY!
THAT COULD EXPLAIN WHY THEY KEEP HANGING AROUND WITHOUT RUNNING COMPLETELY AWAY.
I SEE!
OR-- THERE'S SOME SECRET HIDDEN IN THAT BEAR...!
...
THAT IS NOT FOR YOU SPECULATE UPON!
UH...
BEGGING YOUR PARDON?
SIGH... NEVER MIND.
IT'S JUST A NORMAL TEDDY BEAR.
JUST...JUST GO BACK TO THE GIESRIEG ESTATE AND AWAIT FURTHER ORDERS.

LOOKS LIKE THOSE PEOPLE AREN'T COMING ANYMORE.

I WONDER IF THEY LOST SIGHT OF US...

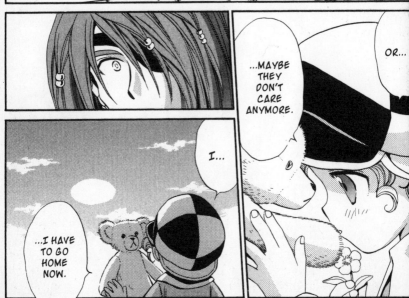

...MAYBE THEY DON'T CARE ANYMORE.

OR...

I...

...I HAVE TO GO HOME NOW.

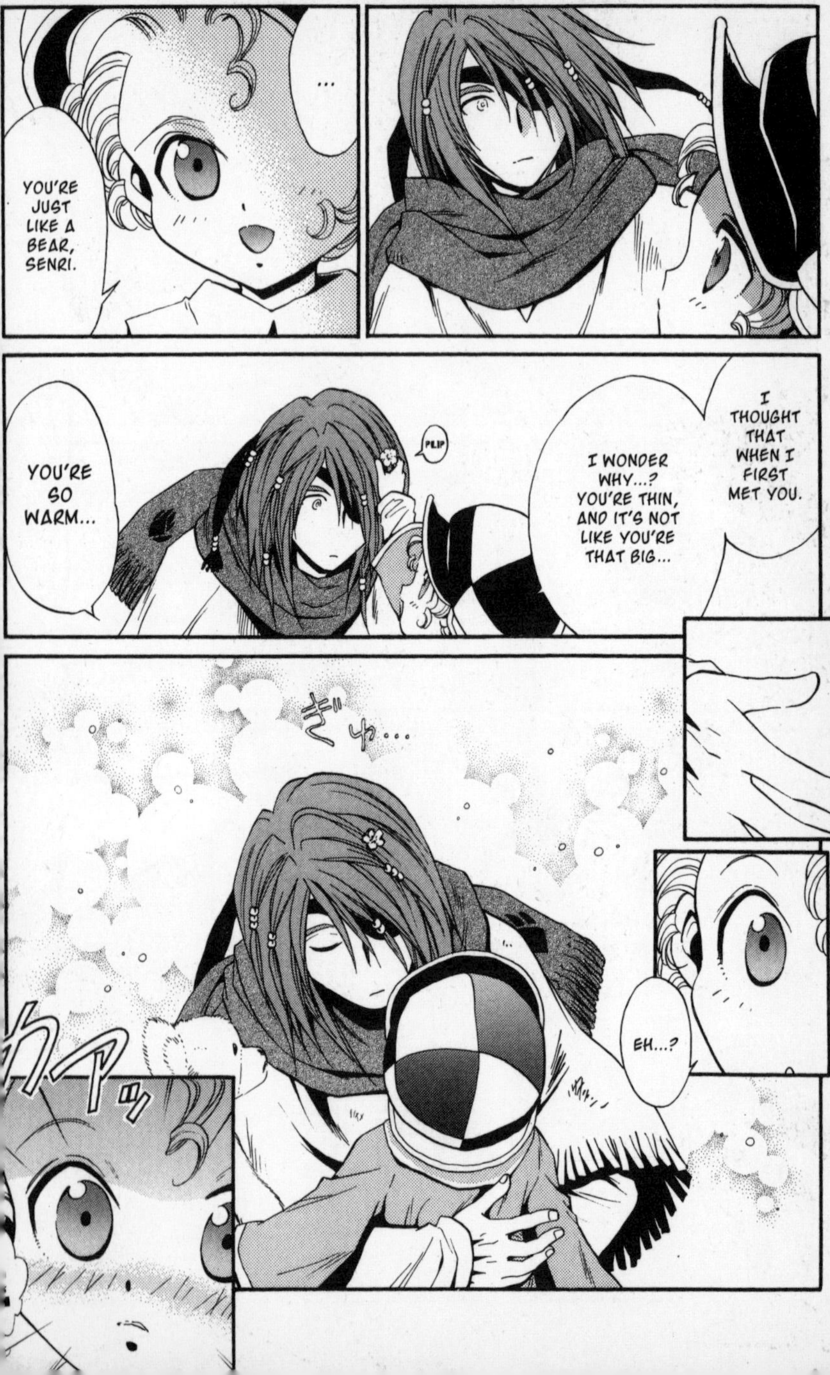
...
YOU'RE JUST LIKE A BEAR, SENRI.
I THOUGHT THAT WHEN I FIRST MET YOU.
I WONDER WHY...? YOU'RE THIN, AND IT'S NOT LIKE YOU'RE THAT BIG...
PLIP
YOU'RE SO WARM...
EH...?
ぎゅ...
カァッ

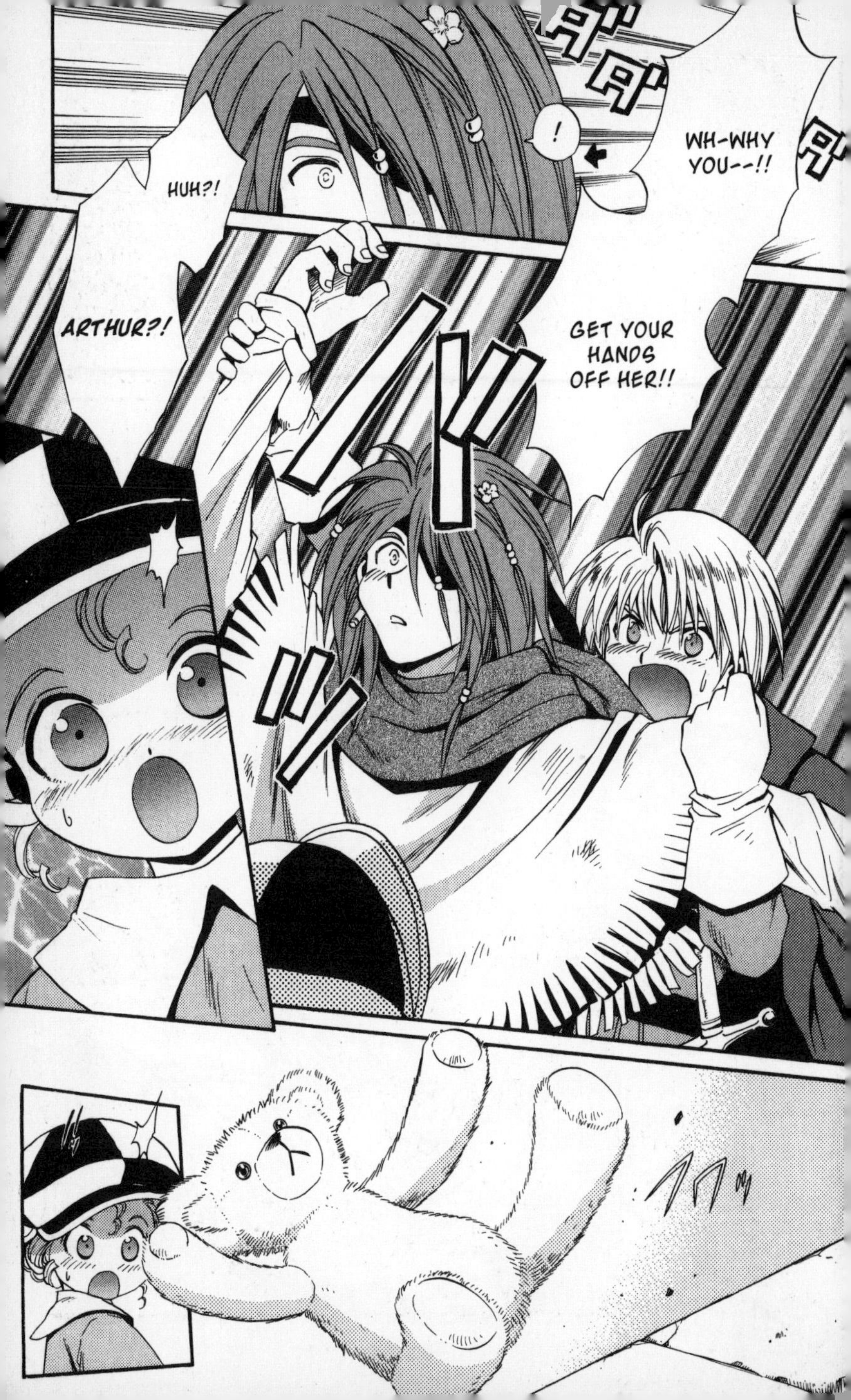
WH-WHY YOU--!!
!
HUH?!
GET YOUR HANDS OFF HER!!
ARTHUR?!

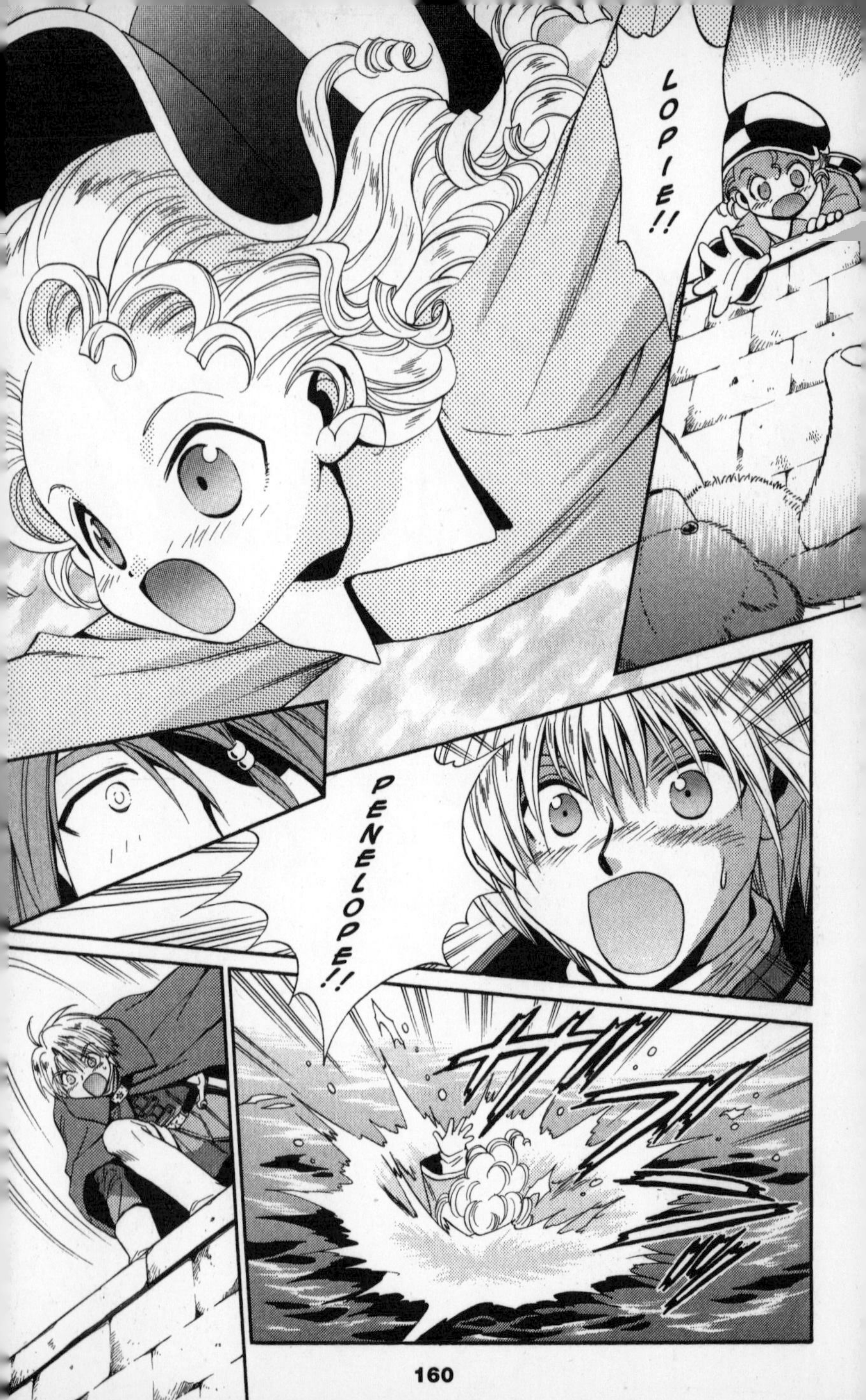
LOPIE!!
PENELOPE!!

PENELOPE... ARE YOU OKAY?

ARTHUR...

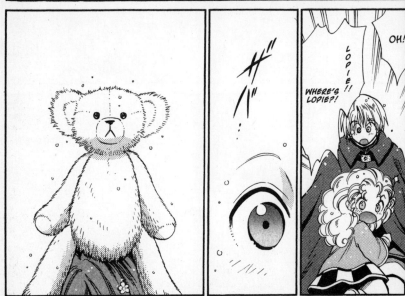

OH!

LODIE!!

WHERE'S LODIE?!

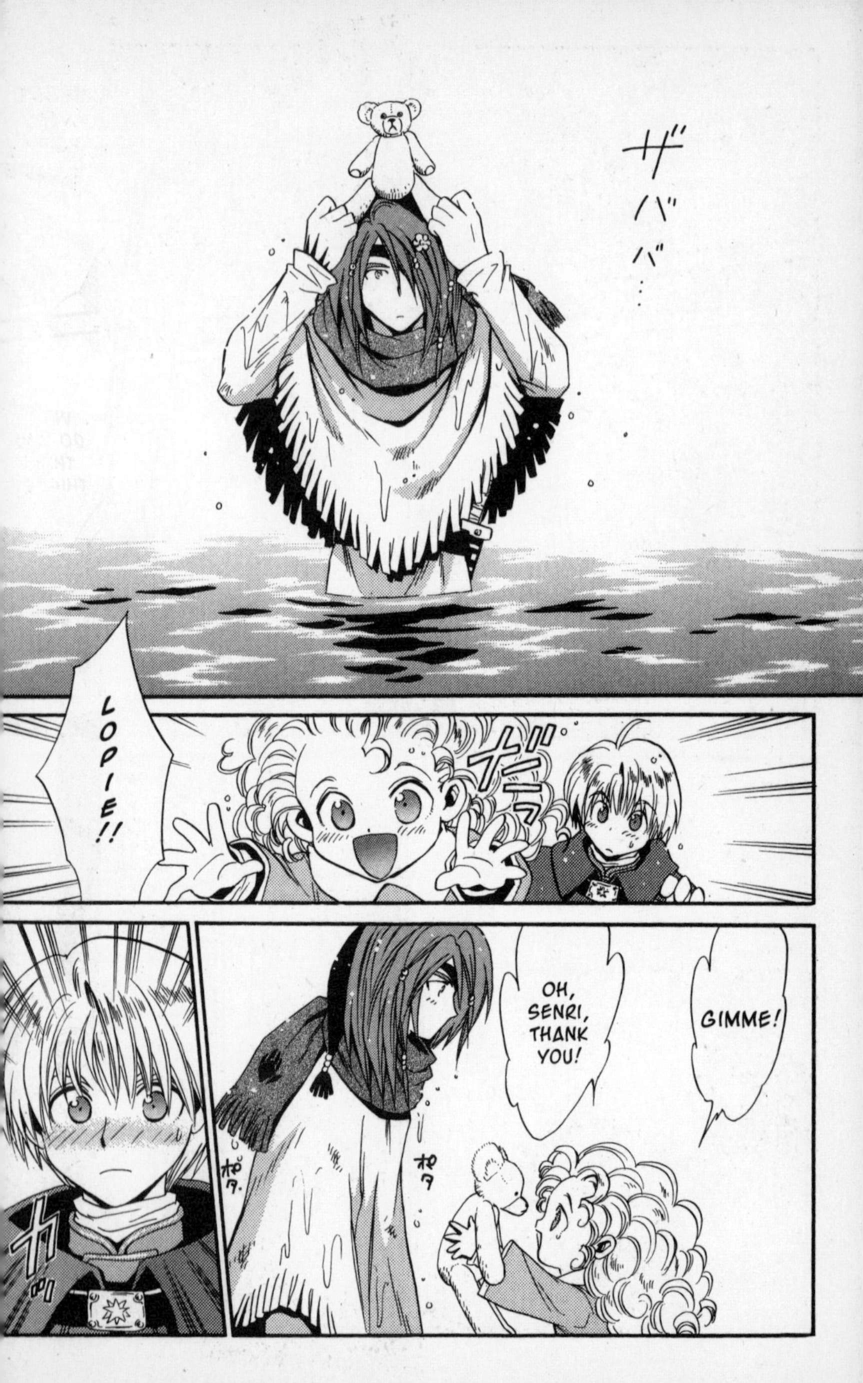
ザババ…
LOPIE!!
GIMME!
OH, SENRI, THANK YOU!
ポタ
ポタ

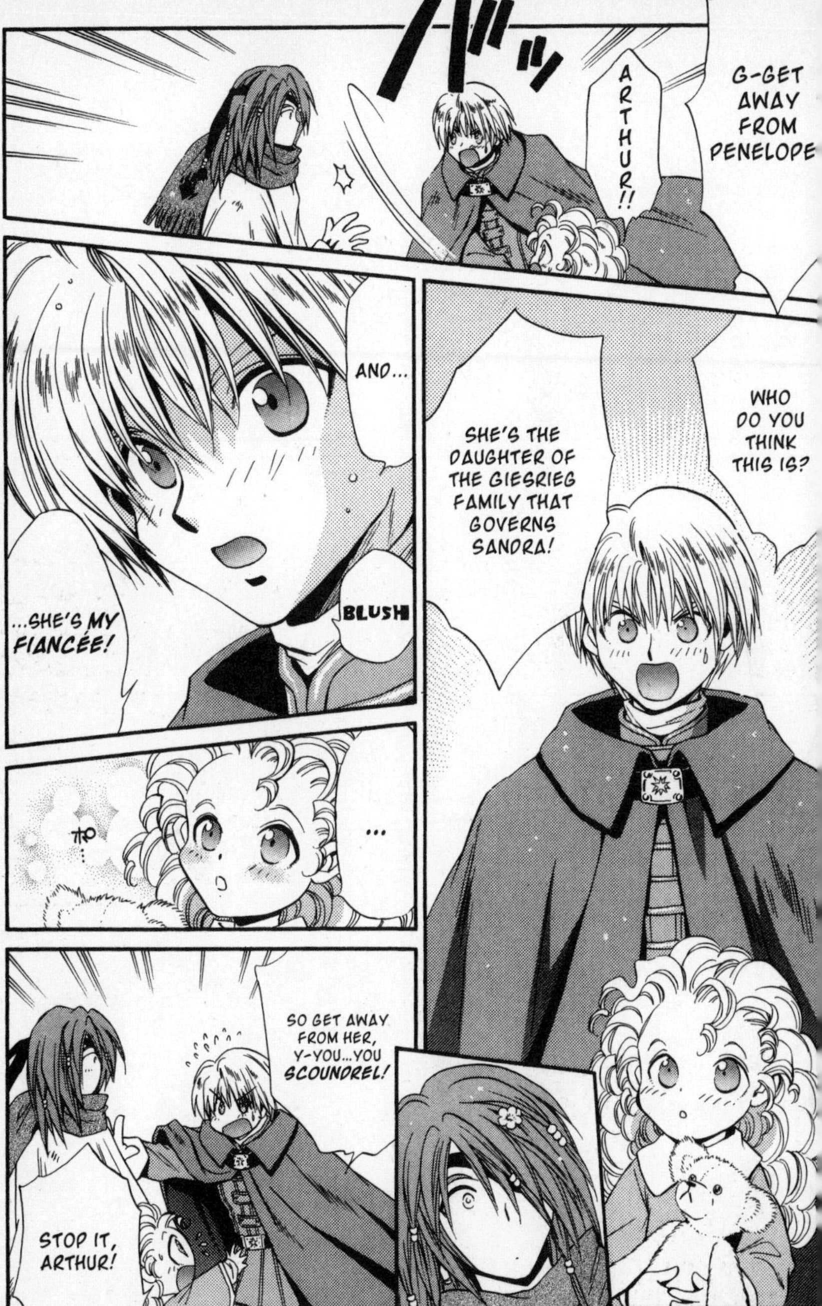
G-GET AWAY FROM PENELOPE
ARTHUR!!
バッ
WHO DO YOU THINK THIS IS?
SHE'S THE DAUGHTER OF THE GIESRIEG FAMILY THAT GOVERNS SANDRA!
AND...
...SHE'S MY FIANCÉE!
BLUSH
...
ポ...
SO GET AWAY FROM HER, Y-YOU...YOU SCOUNDREL!
STOP IT, ARTHUR!

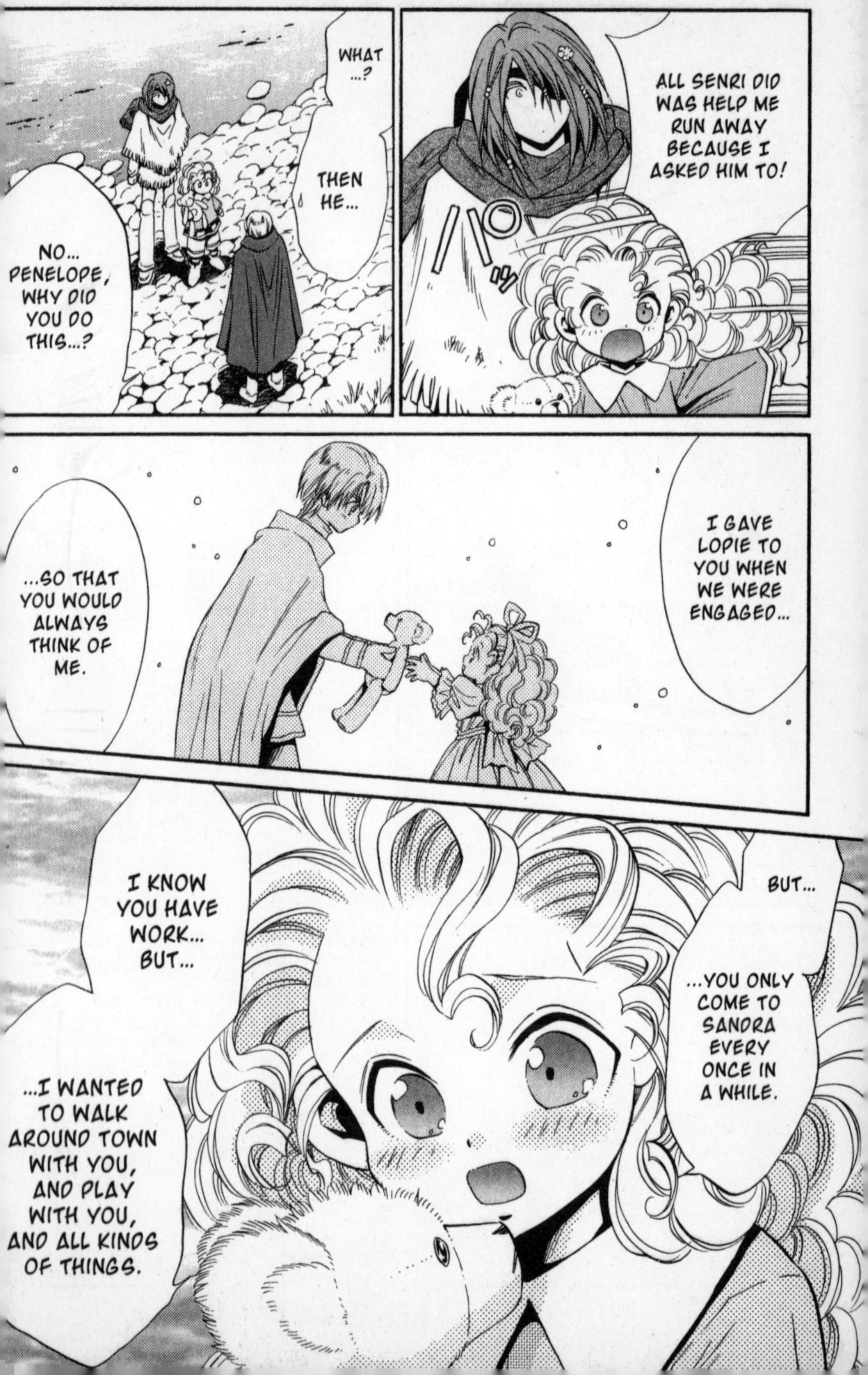

ALL SENRI DID WAS HELP ME RUN AWAY BECAUSE I ASKED HIM TO!
WHAT ...?
THEN HE...
NO... PENELOPE, WHY DID YOU DO THIS...?
I GAVE LOPIE TO YOU WHEN WE WERE ENGAGED...
...SO THAT YOU WOULD ALWAYS THINK OF ME.
BUT...
...YOU ONLY COME TO SANDRA EVERY ONCE IN A WHILE.
I KNOW YOU HAVE WORK... BUT...
...I WANTED TO WALK AROUND TOWN WITH YOU, AND PLAY WITH YOU, AND ALL KINDS OF THINGS.

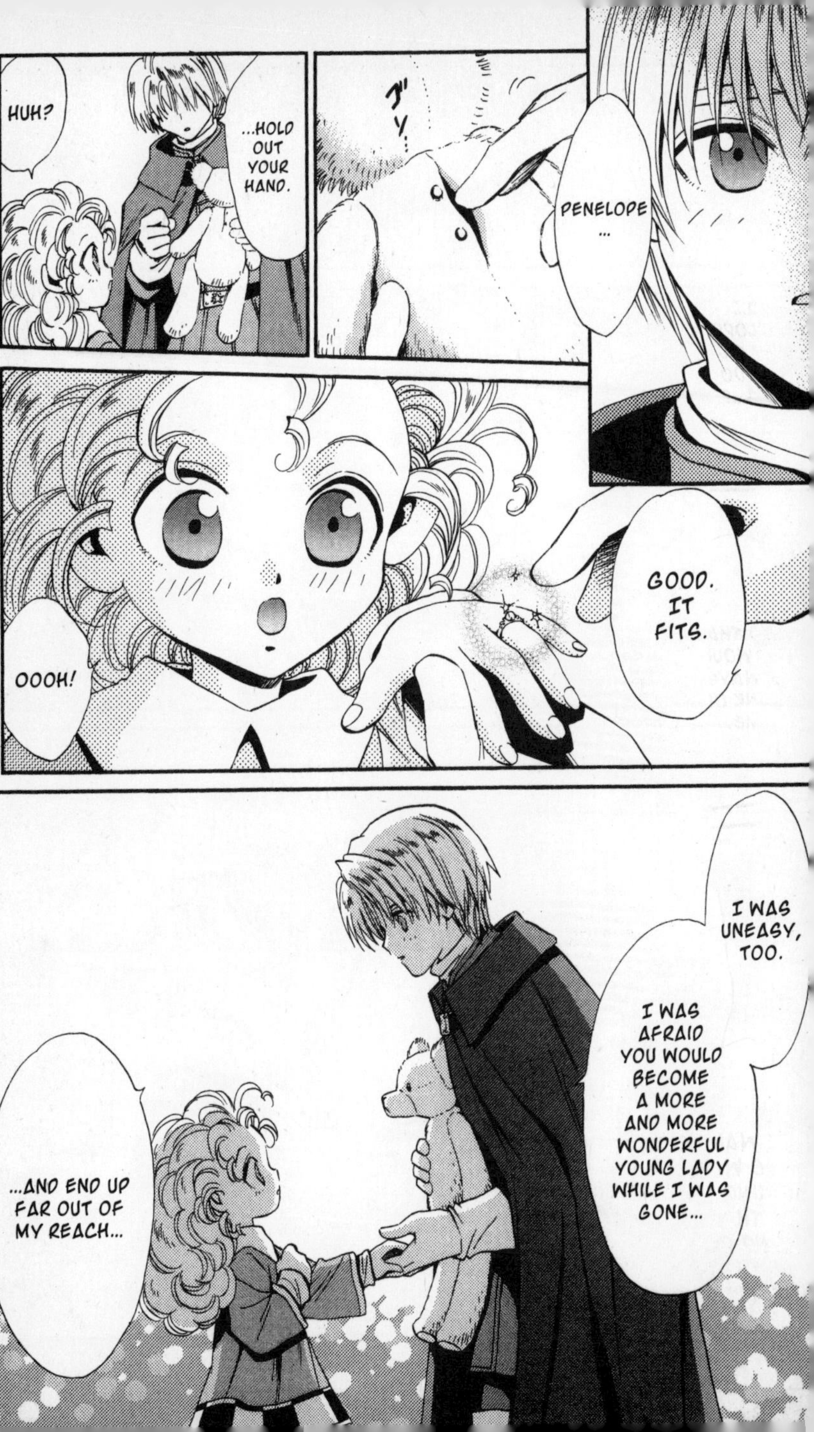
PENELOPE ...
ゴソ
...HOLD OUT YOUR HAND.
HUH?
GOOD. IT FITS.
OOOH!
I WAS UNEASY, TOO.
I WAS AFRAID YOU WOULD BECOME A MORE AND MORE WONDERFUL YOUNG LADY WHILE I WAS GONE...
...AND END UP FAR OUT OF MY REACH...

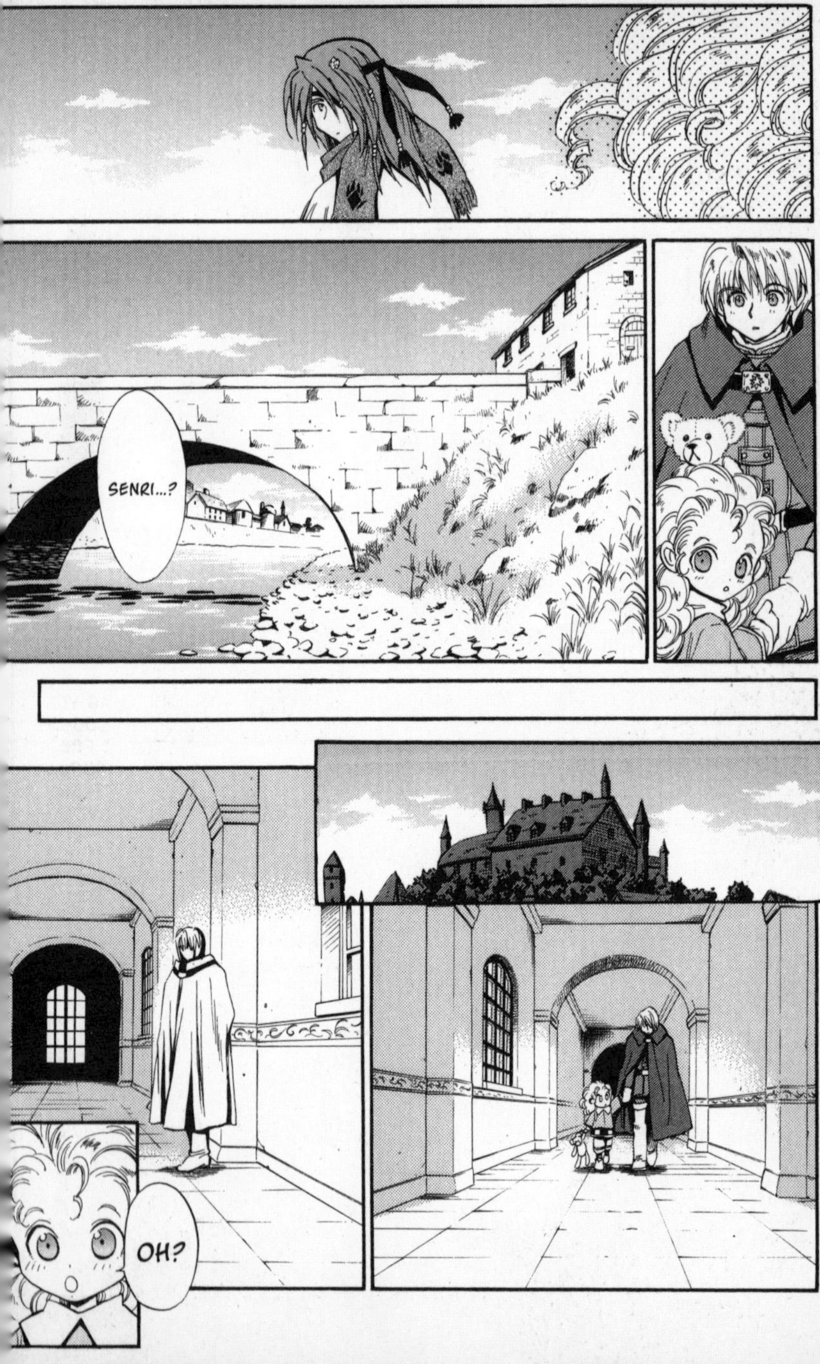
SENRI...?
OH?

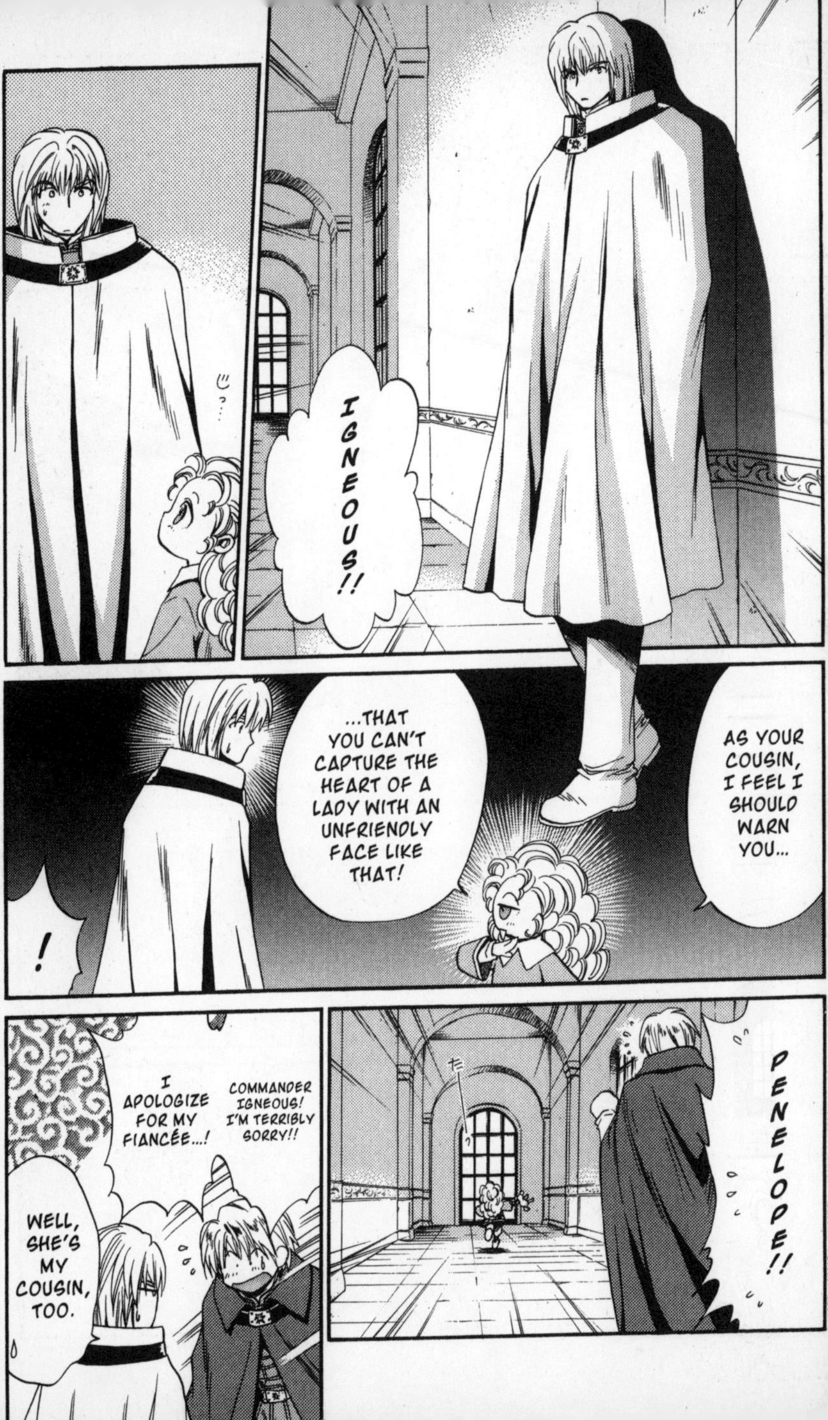
IGNEOUS!!
じっ…
AS YOUR COUSIN, I FEEL I SHOULD WARN YOU...
...THAT YOU CAN'T CAPTURE THE HEART OF A LADY WITH AN UNFRIENDLY FACE LIKE THAT!
!
PENELOPE!!
COMMANDER IGNEOUS! I'M TERRIBLY SORRY!!
I APOLOGIZE FOR MY FIANCÉE...!
WELL, SHE'S MY COUSIN, TOO.

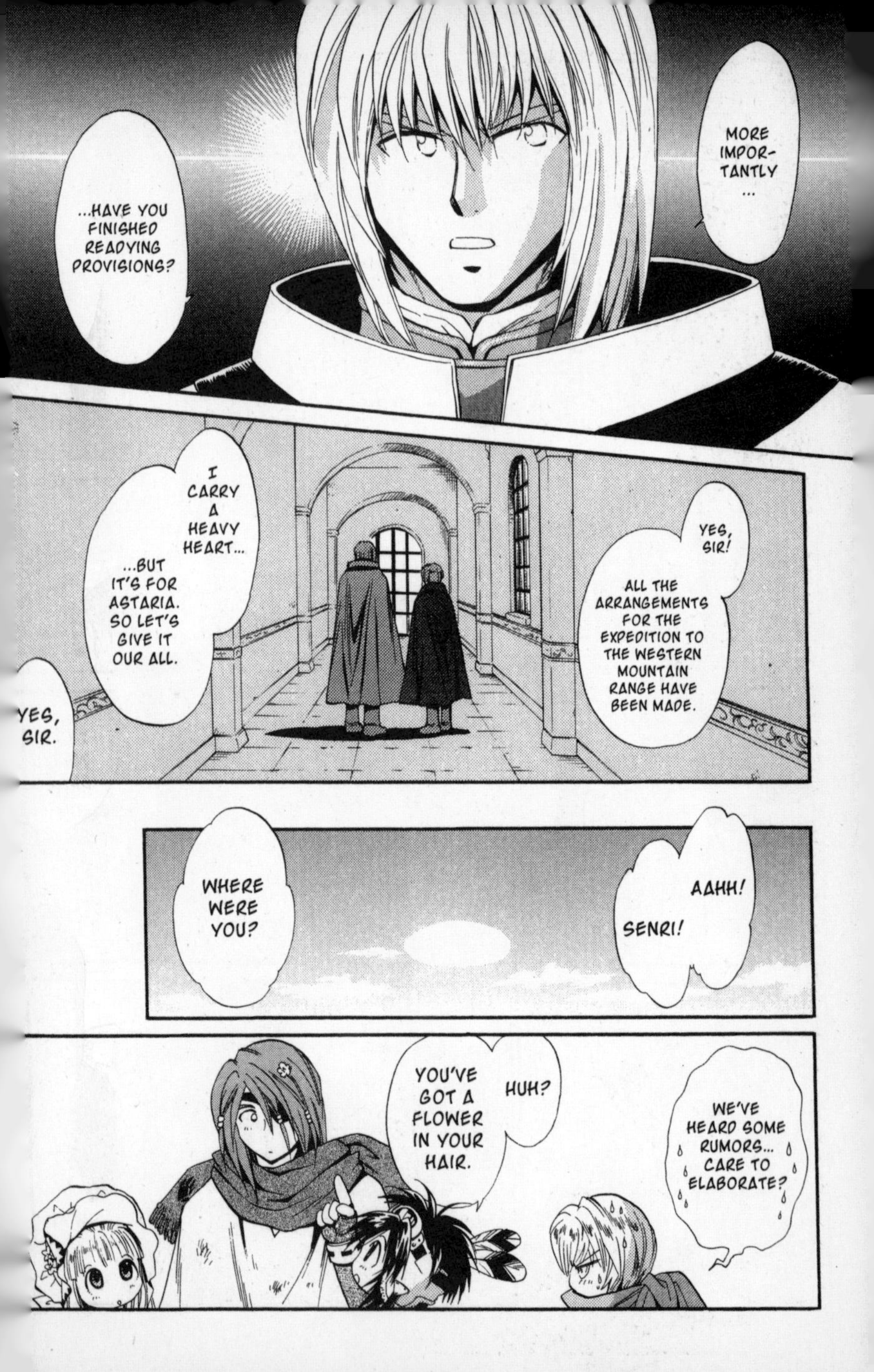
MORE IMPORTANTLY...
...HAVE YOU FINISHED READYING PROVISIONS?
YES, SIR!
ALL THE ARRANGEMENTS FOR THE EXPEDITION TO THE WESTERN MOUNTAIN RANGE HAVE BEEN MADE.
I CARRY A HEAVY HEART...
...BUT IT'S FOR ASTARIA. SO LET'S GIVE IT OUR ALL.
YES, SIR.
AAHH!
SENRI!
WHERE WERE YOU?
WE'VE HEARD SOME RUMORS... CARE TO ELABORATE?
HUH?
YOU'VE GOT A FLOWER IN YOUR HAIR.

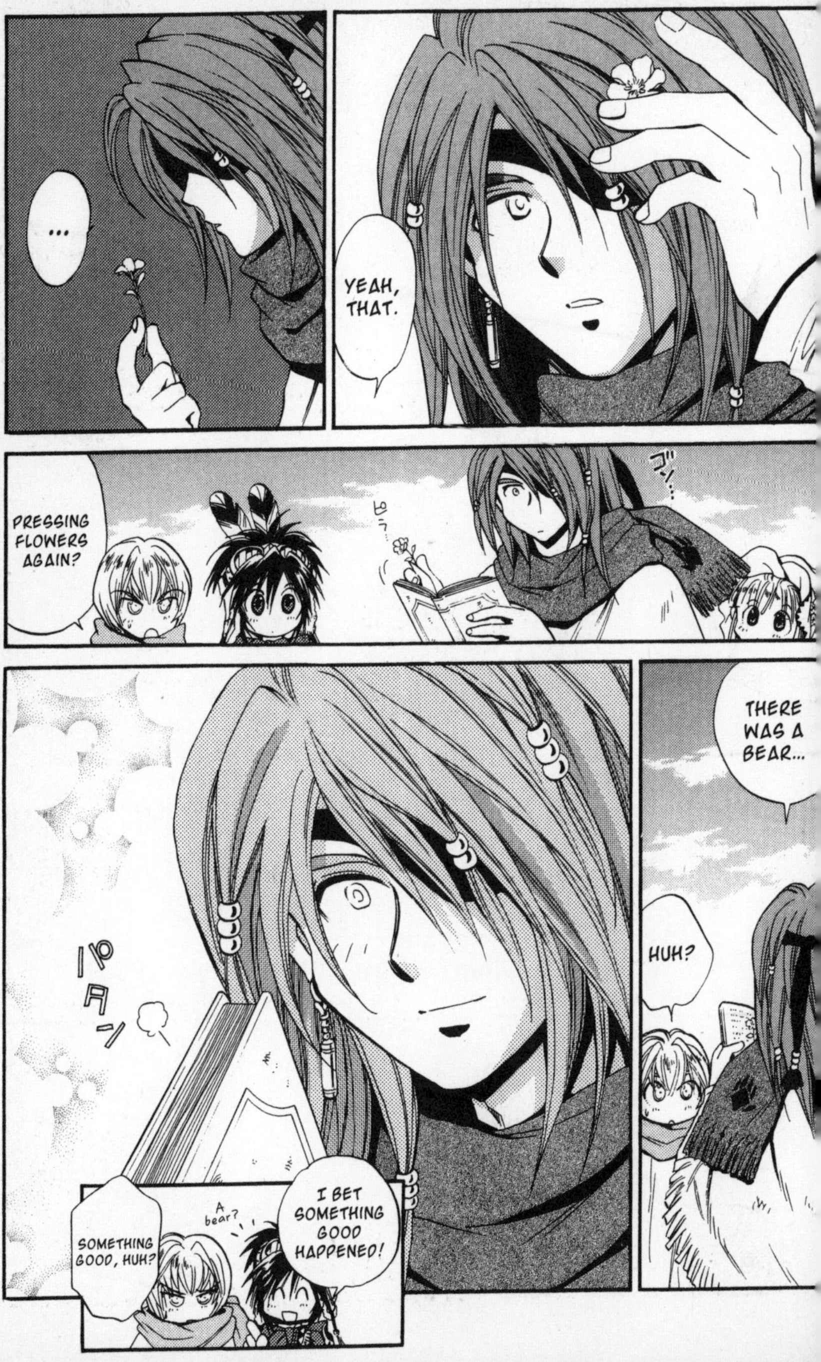
YEAH, THAT.
...
PRESSING FLOWERS AGAIN?
THERE WAS A BEAR...
HUH?
I BET SOMETHING GOOD HAPPENED!
A bear?
SOMETHING GOOD, HUH?

Rival of love?!

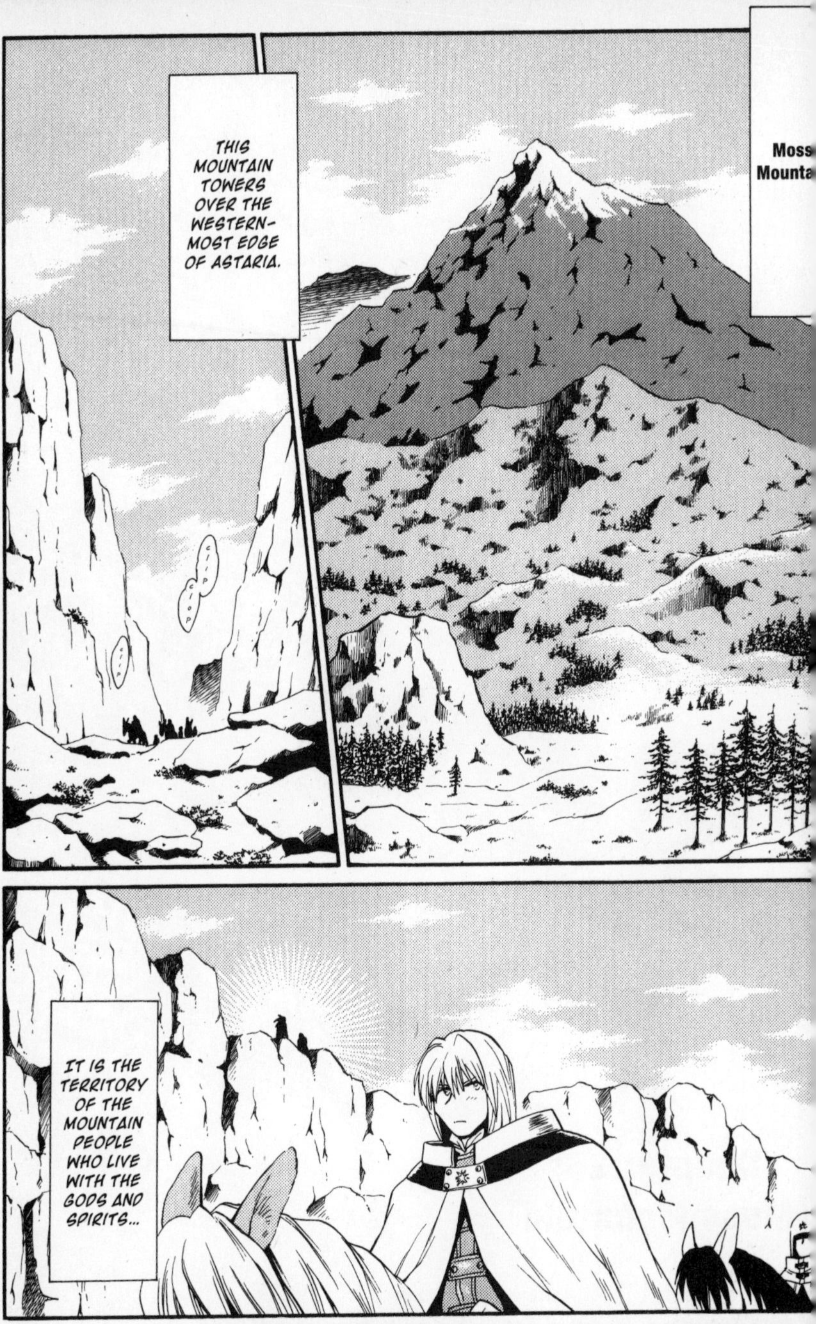

Moss
Mounta
THIS MOUNTAIN TOWERS OVER THE WESTERN-MOST EDGE OF ASTARIA.
IT IS THE TERRITORY OF THE MOUNTAIN PEOPLE WHO LIVE WITH THE GODS AND SPIRITS...

Chapter 26: Moss Mountain

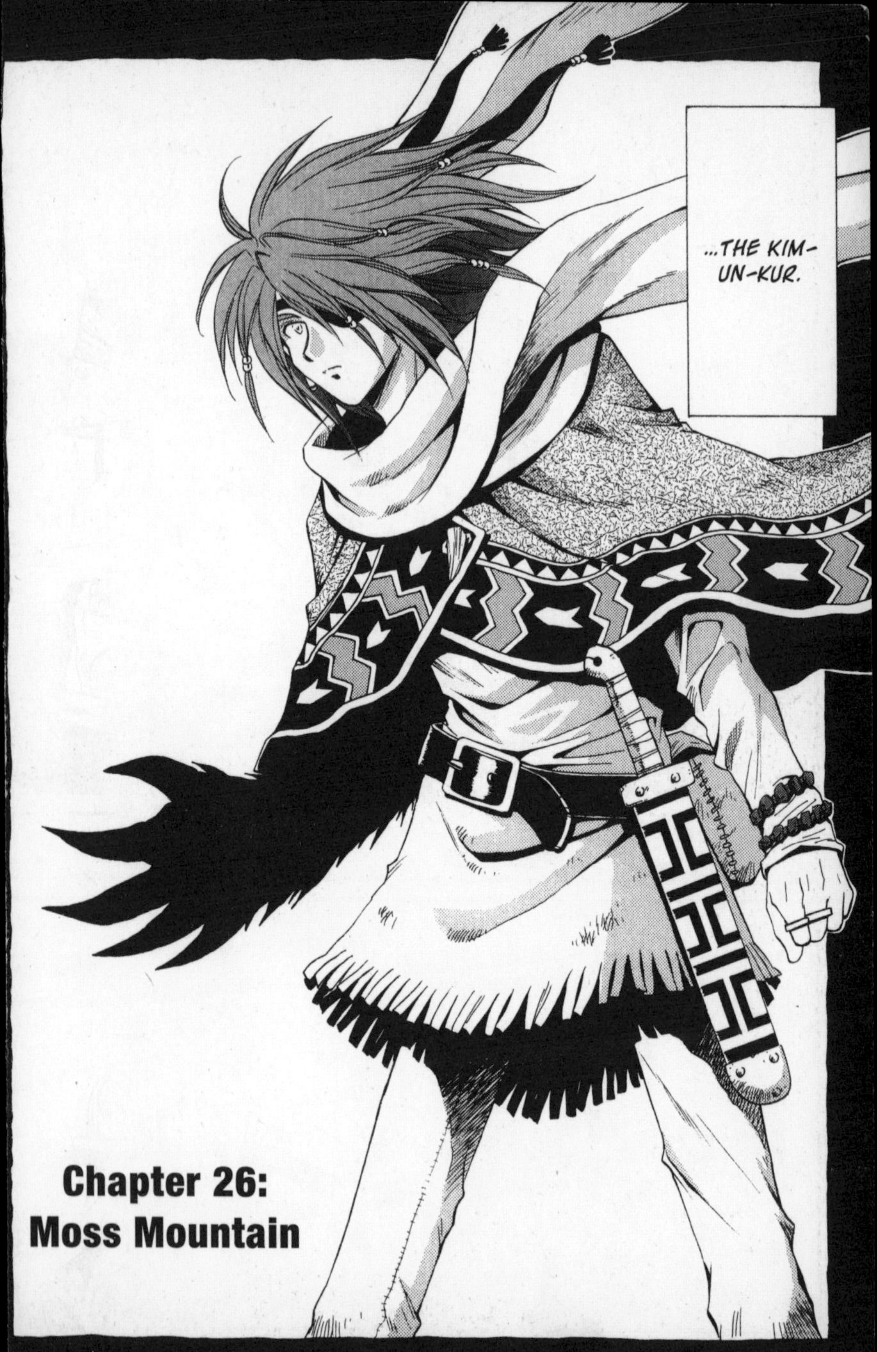
...THE KIM-UN-KUR.

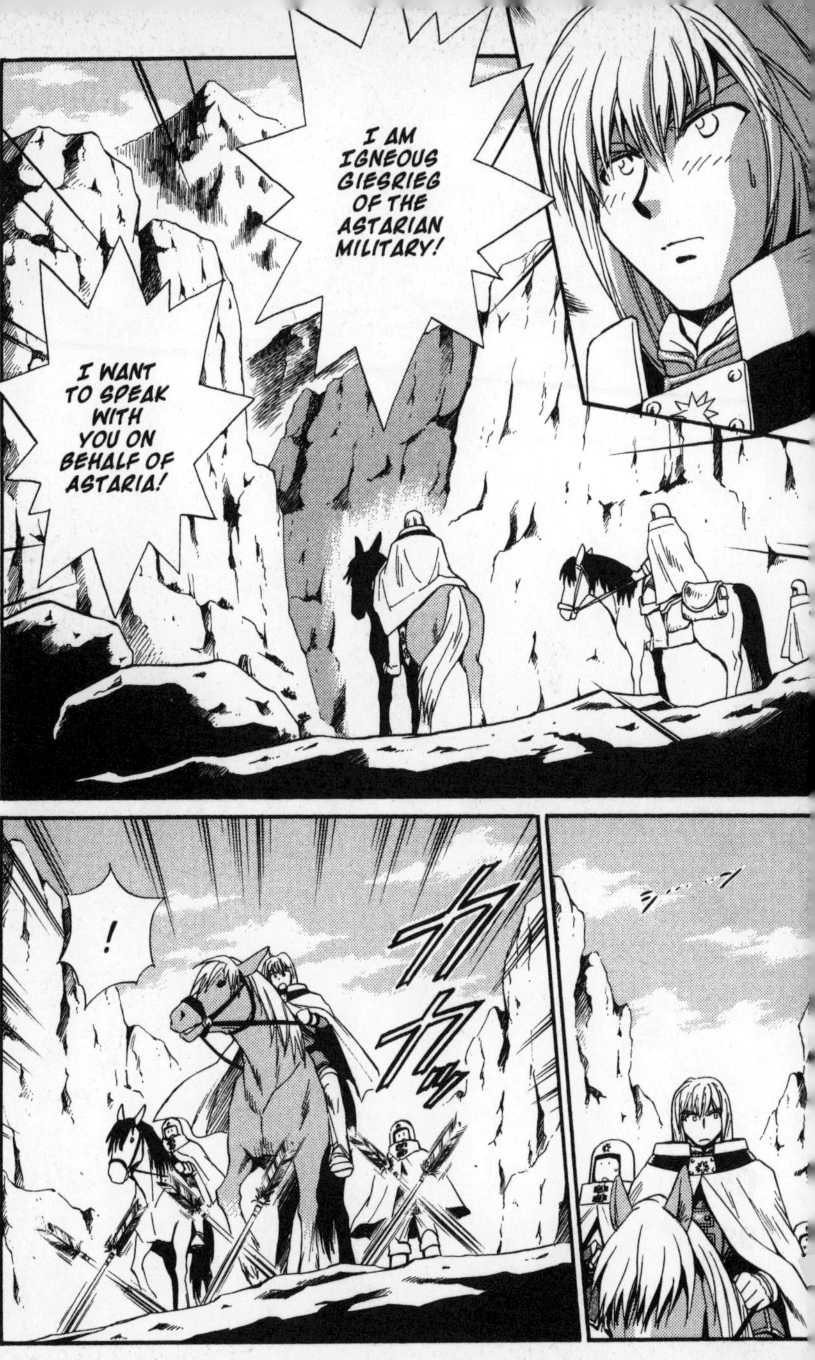
I AM IGNEOUS GIESRIEG OF THE ASTARIAN MILITARY!
I WANT TO SPEAK WITH YOU ON BEHALF OF ASTARIA!
!

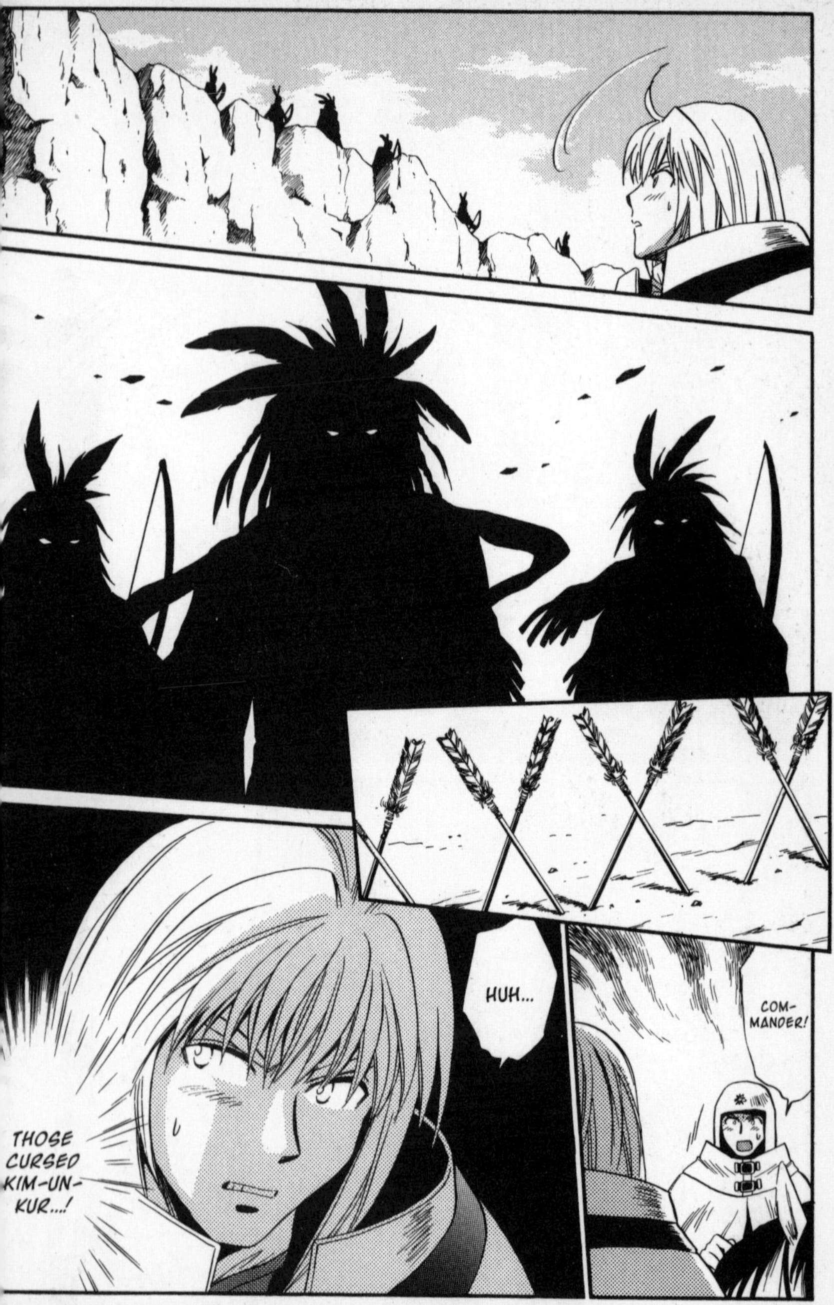

COM-MANDER!
HUH...
THOSE CURSED KIM-UN-KUR...!

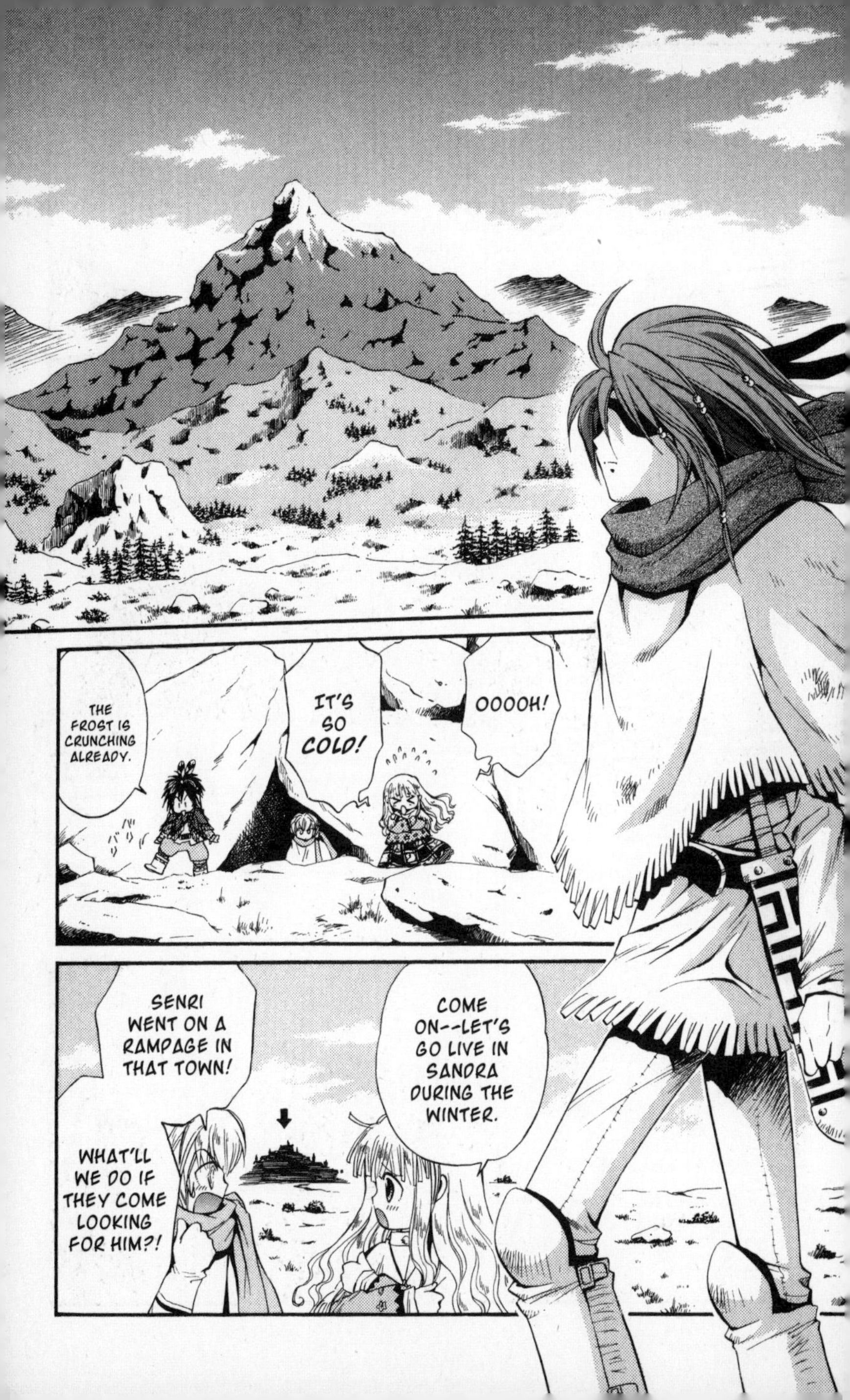
OOOOH!
IT'S SO COLD!
THE FROST IS CRUNCHING ALREADY.
COME ON--LET'S GO LIVE IN SANDRA DURING THE WINTER.
SENRI WENT ON A RAMPAGE IN THAT TOWN!
WHAT'LL WE DO IF THEY COME LOOKING FOR HIM?!

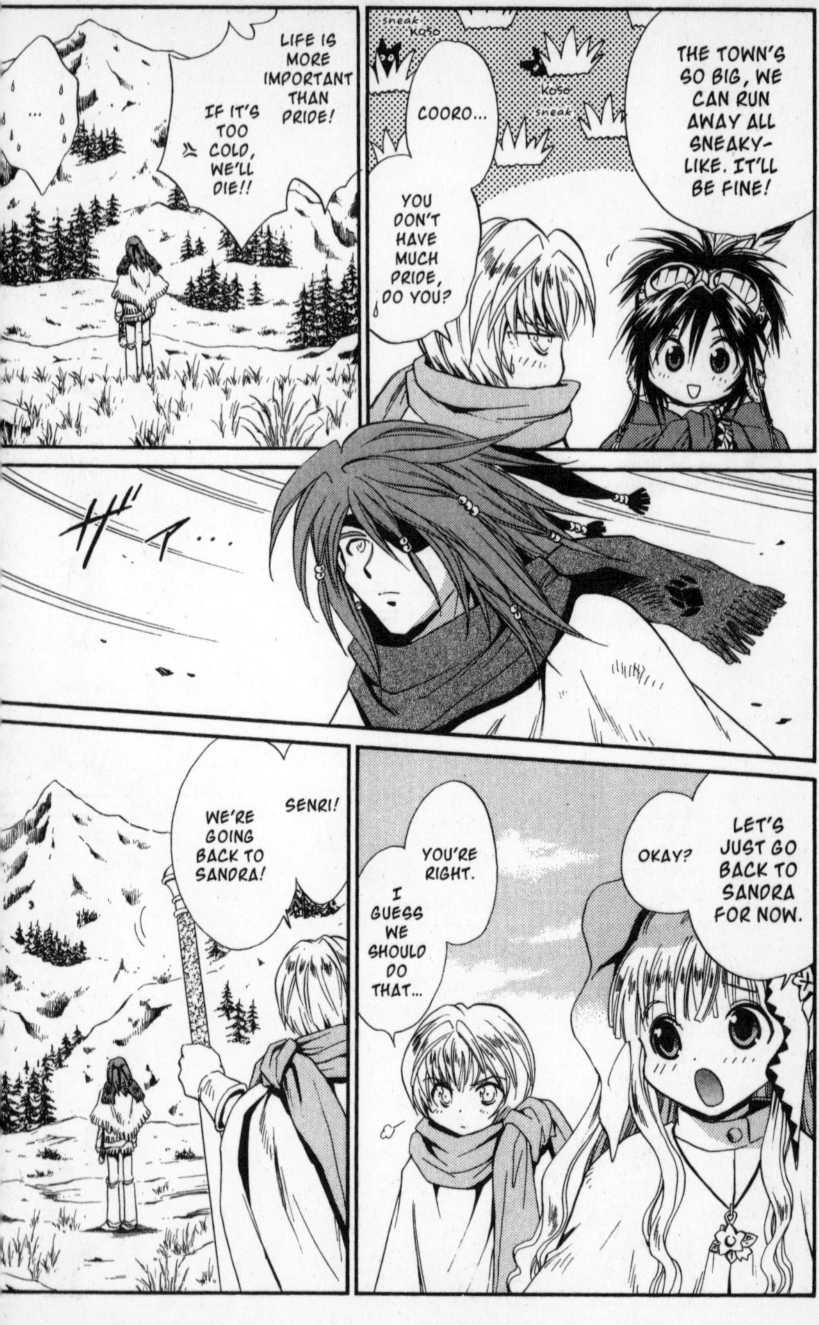
sneak koso
koso sneak
THE TOWN'S SO BIG, WE CAN RUN AWAY ALL SNEAKY-LIKE. IT'LL BE FINE!
COORO...
YOU DON'T HAVE MUCH PRIDE, DO YOU?
LIFE IS MORE IMPORTANT THAN PRIDE!
IF IT'S TOO COLD, WE'LL DIE!!
...
ザァ...
LET'S JUST GO BACK TO SANDRA FOR NOW.
OKAY?
YOU'RE RIGHT.
I GUESS WE SHOULD DO THAT...
SENRI!
WE'RE GOING BACK TO SANDRA!

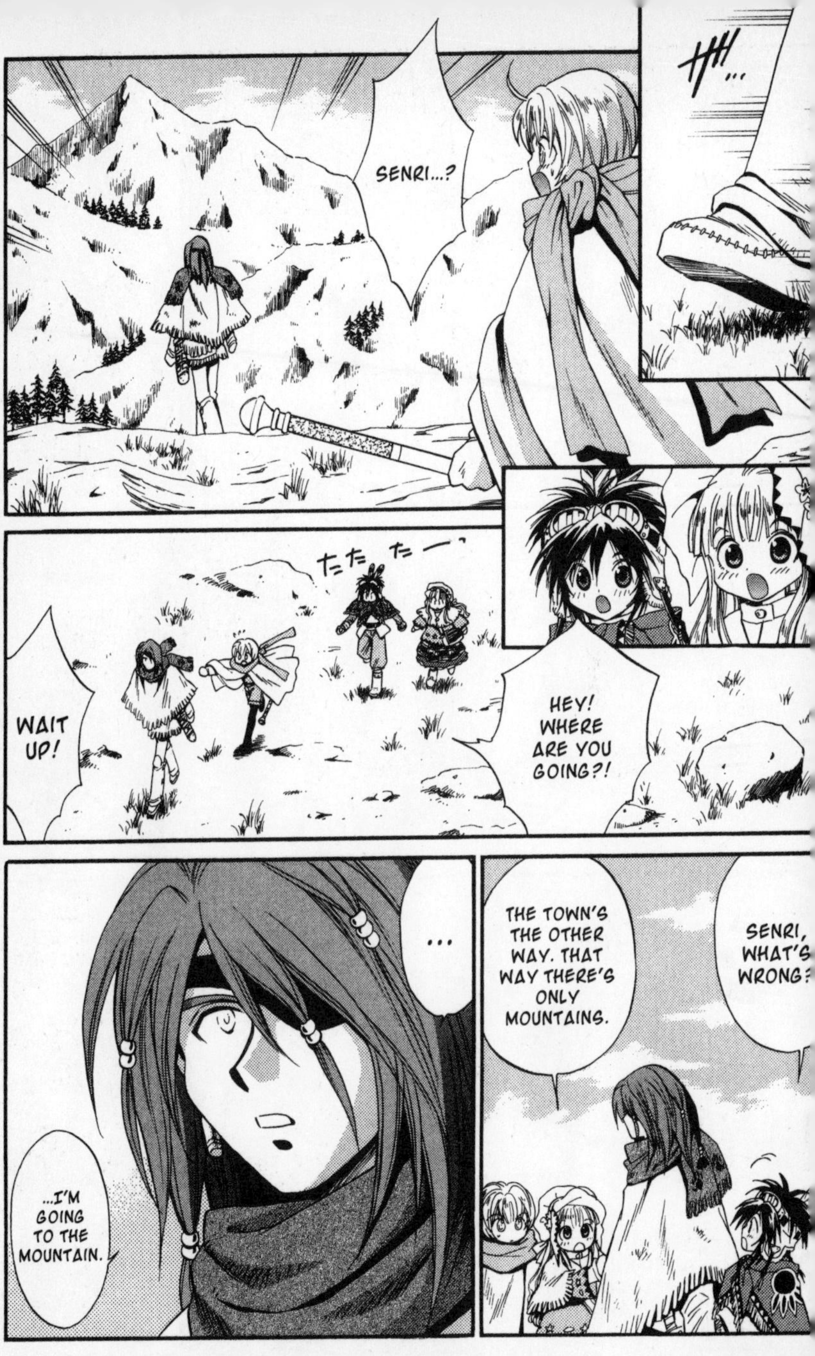
SENRI...?
HEY! WHERE ARE YOU GOING?!
たた たー
WAIT UP!
SENRI, WHAT'S WRONG?
THE TOWN'S THE OTHER WAY. THAT WAY THERE'S ONLY MOUNTAINS.
...
...I'M GOING TO THE MOUNTAIN.

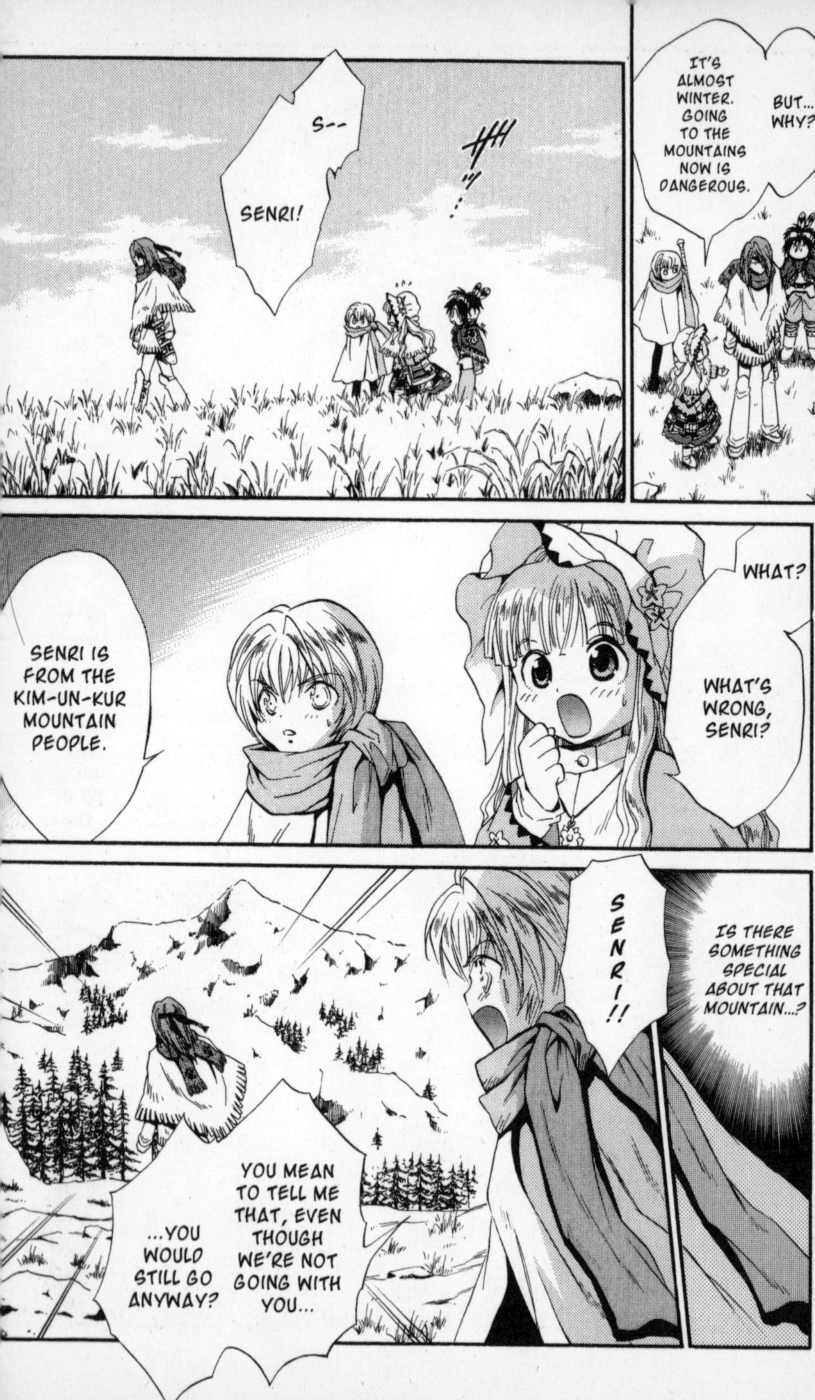

BUT... WHY?
IT'S ALMOST WINTER. GOING TO THE MOUNTAINS NOW IS DANGEROUS.
S--
SENRI!
WHAT?
WHAT'S WRONG, SENRI?
SENRI IS FROM THE KIM-UN-KUR MOUNTAIN PEOPLE.
IS THERE SOMETHING SPECIAL ABOUT THAT MOUNTAIN...?
SENRI!!
YOU MEAN TO TELL ME THAT, EVEN THOUGH WE'RE NOT GOING WITH YOU...
...YOU WOULD STILL GO ANYWAY?

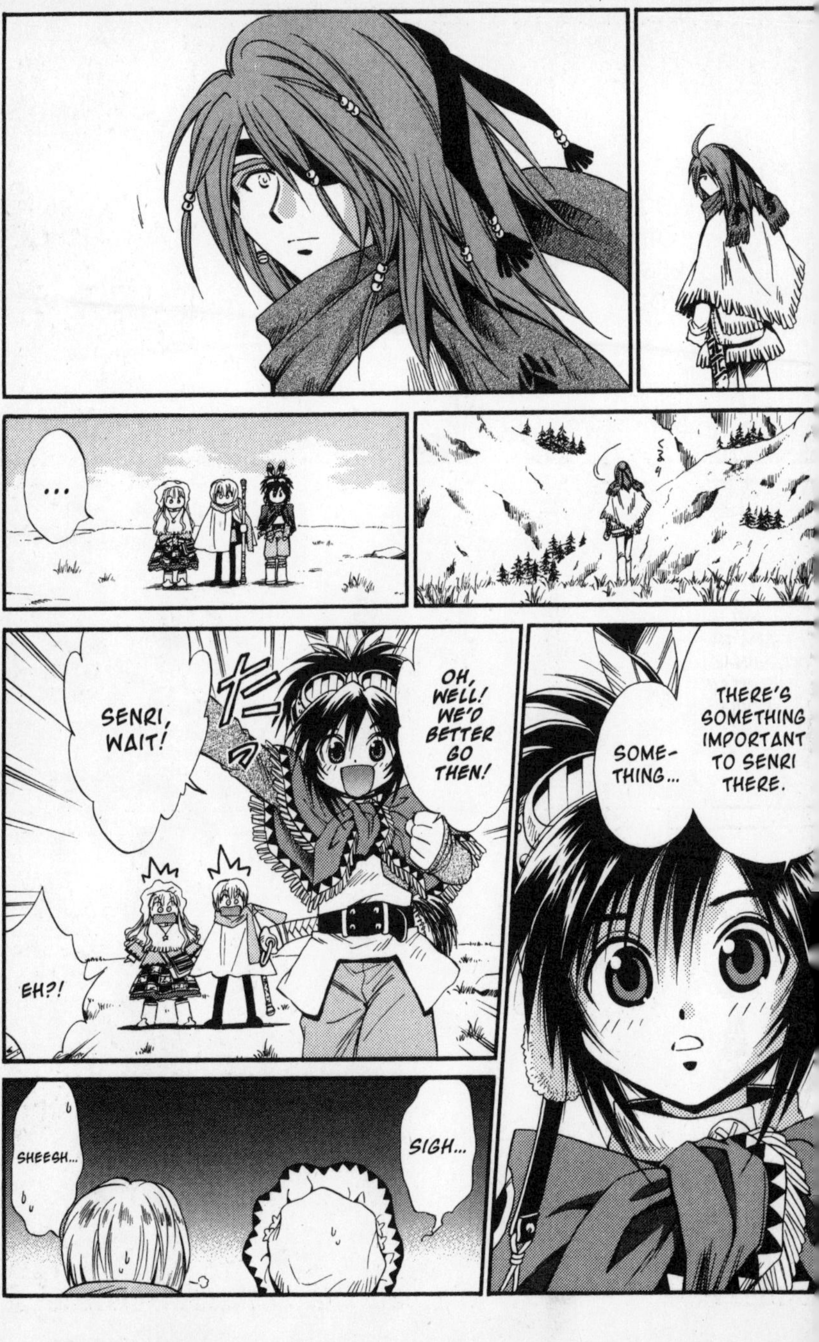
...
THERE'S SOMETHING IMPORTANT TO SENRI THERE.
SOME-THING...
OH, WELL! WE'D BETTER GO THEN!
SENRI, WAIT!
EH?!
SIGH...
SHEESH...

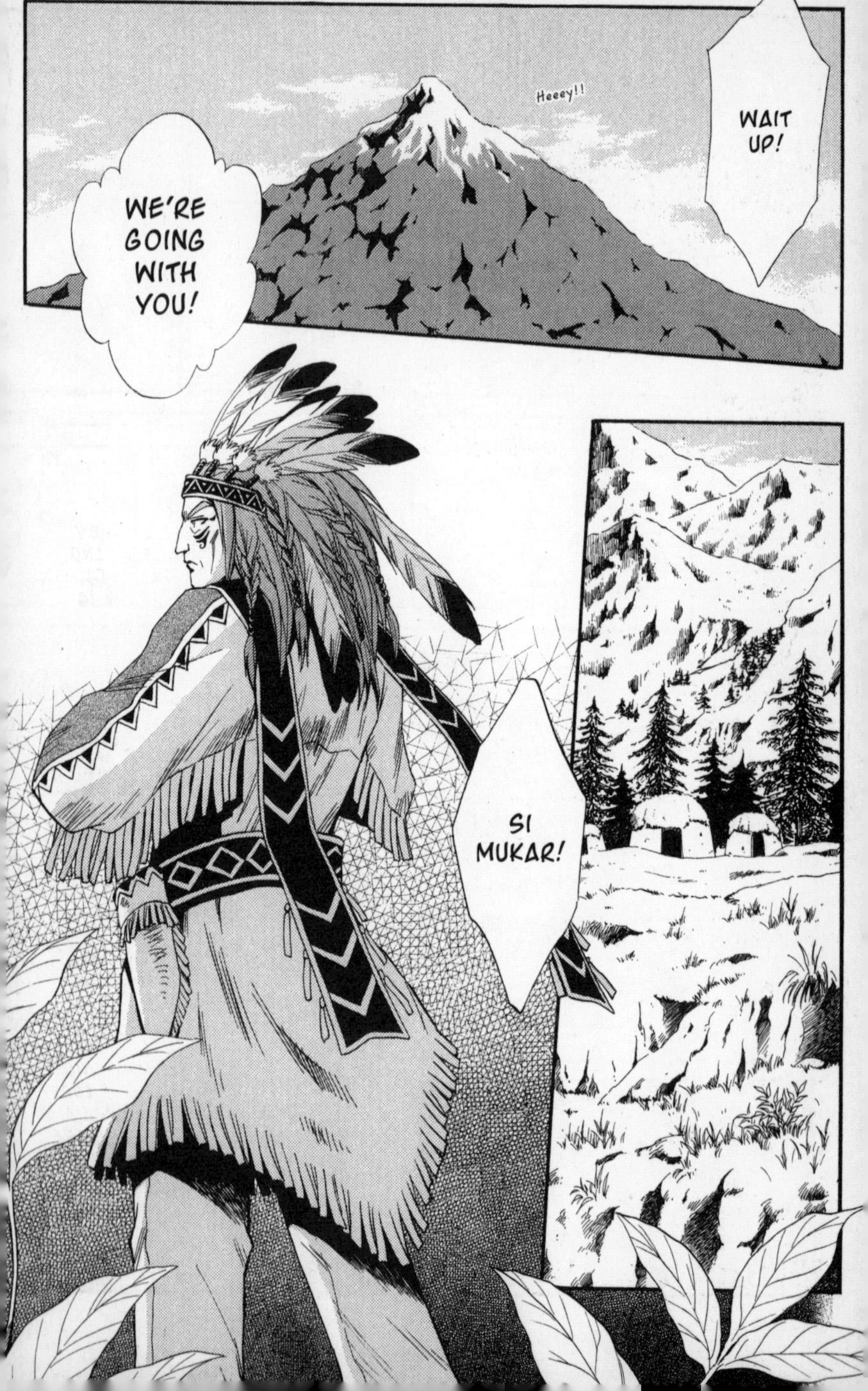
WAIT UP!
Heeey!!
WE'RE GOING WITH YOU!
SI MUKAR!

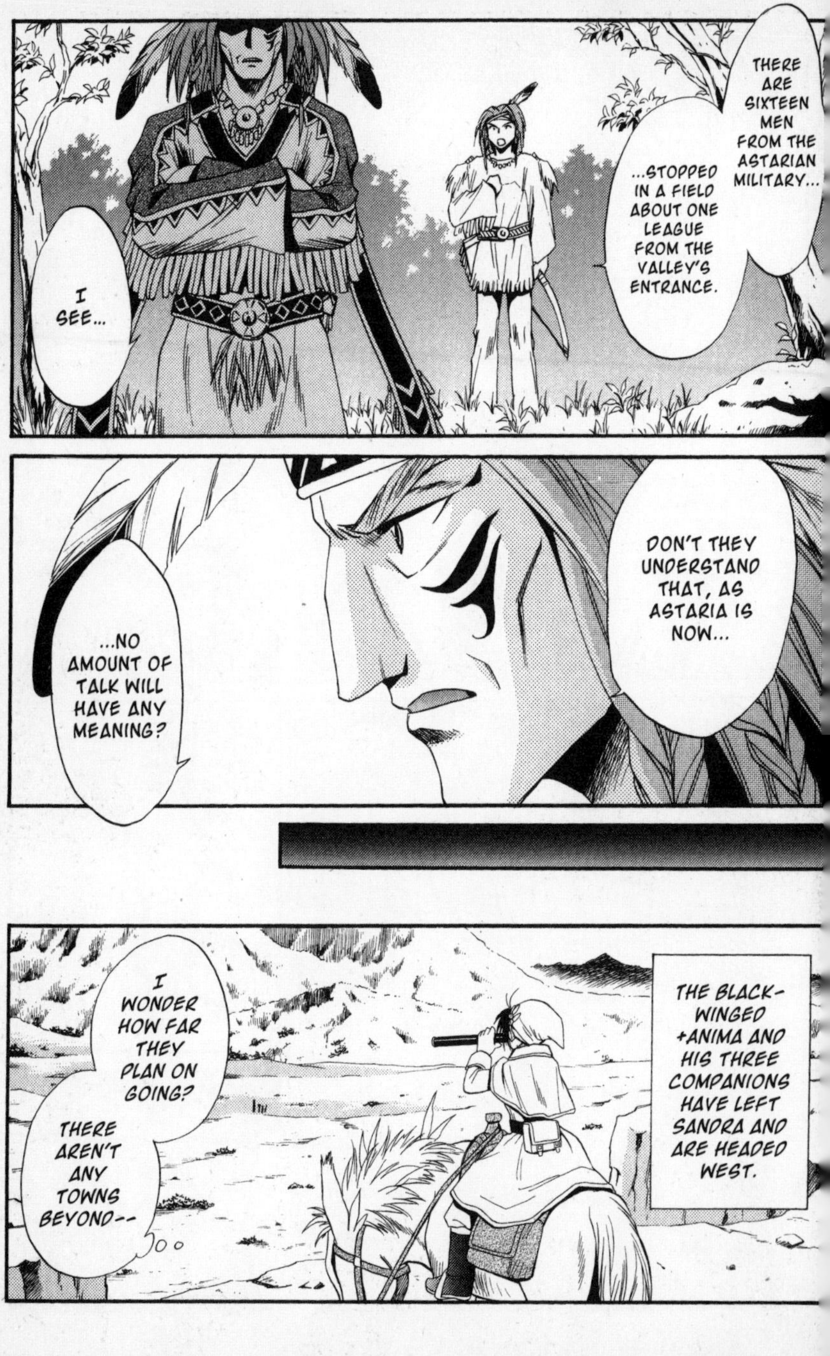
THERE ARE SIXTEEN MEN FROM THE ASTARIAN MILITARY...
...STOPPED IN A FIELD ABOUT ONE LEAGUE FROM THE VALLEY'S ENTRANCE.
I SEE...
DON'T THEY UNDERSTAND THAT, AS ASTARIA IS NOW...
...NO AMOUNT OF TALK WILL HAVE ANY MEANING?
THE BLACK-WINGED +ANIMA AND HIS THREE COMPANIONS HAVE LEFT SANDRA AND ARE HEADED WEST.
I WONDER HOW FAR THEY PLAN ON GOING?
THERE AREN'T ANY TOWNS BEYOND--

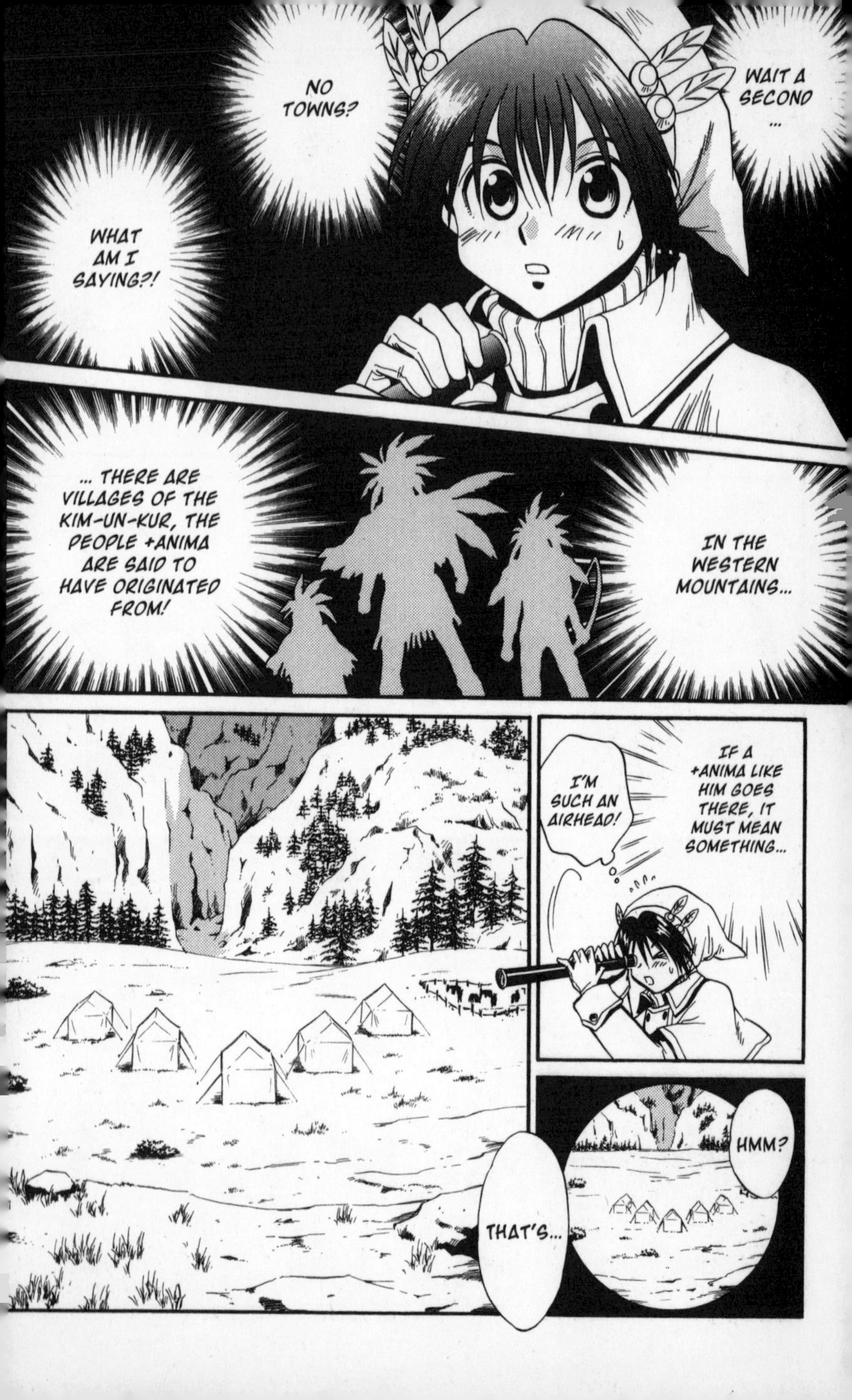
WAIT A SECOND ...
NO TOWNS?
WHAT AM I SAYING?!
IN THE WESTERN MOUNTAINS...
... THERE ARE VILLAGES OF THE KIM-UN-KUR, THE PEOPLE +ANIMA ARE SAID TO HAVE ORIGINATED FROM!
IF A +ANIMA LIKE HIM GOES THERE, IT MUST MEAN SOMETHING...
I'M SUCH AN AIRHEAD!
HMM?
THAT'S...

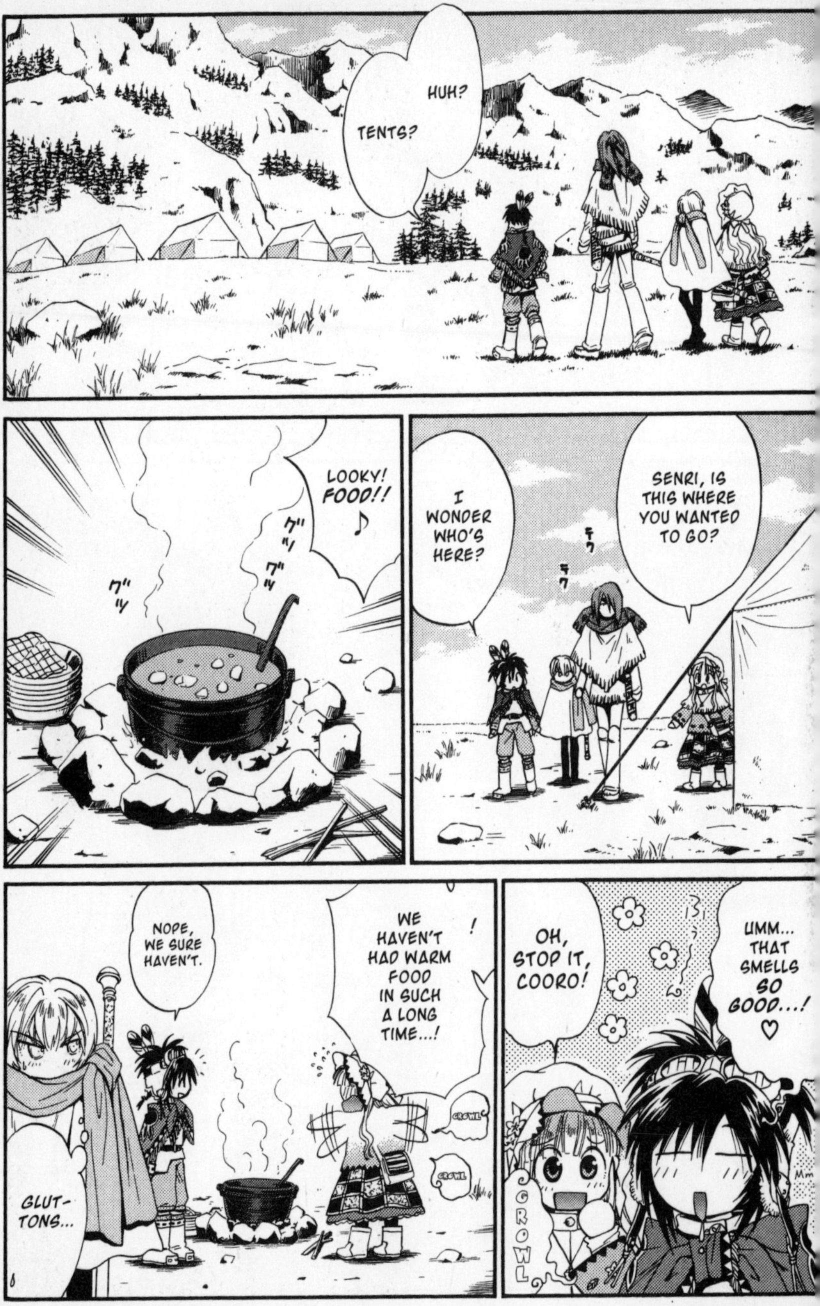
HUH?
TENTS?
SENRI, IS THIS WHERE YOU WANTED TO GO?
I WONDER WHO'S HERE?
LOOKY! FOOD!! ♪
グツ グツ
UMM... THAT SMELLS SO GOOD...! ♡
OH, STOP IT, COORO!
GROWL
WE HAVEN'T HAD WARM FOOD IN SUCH A LONG TIME...!
NOPE, WE SURE HAVEN'T.
GROWL
GROWL
GLUTTONS...

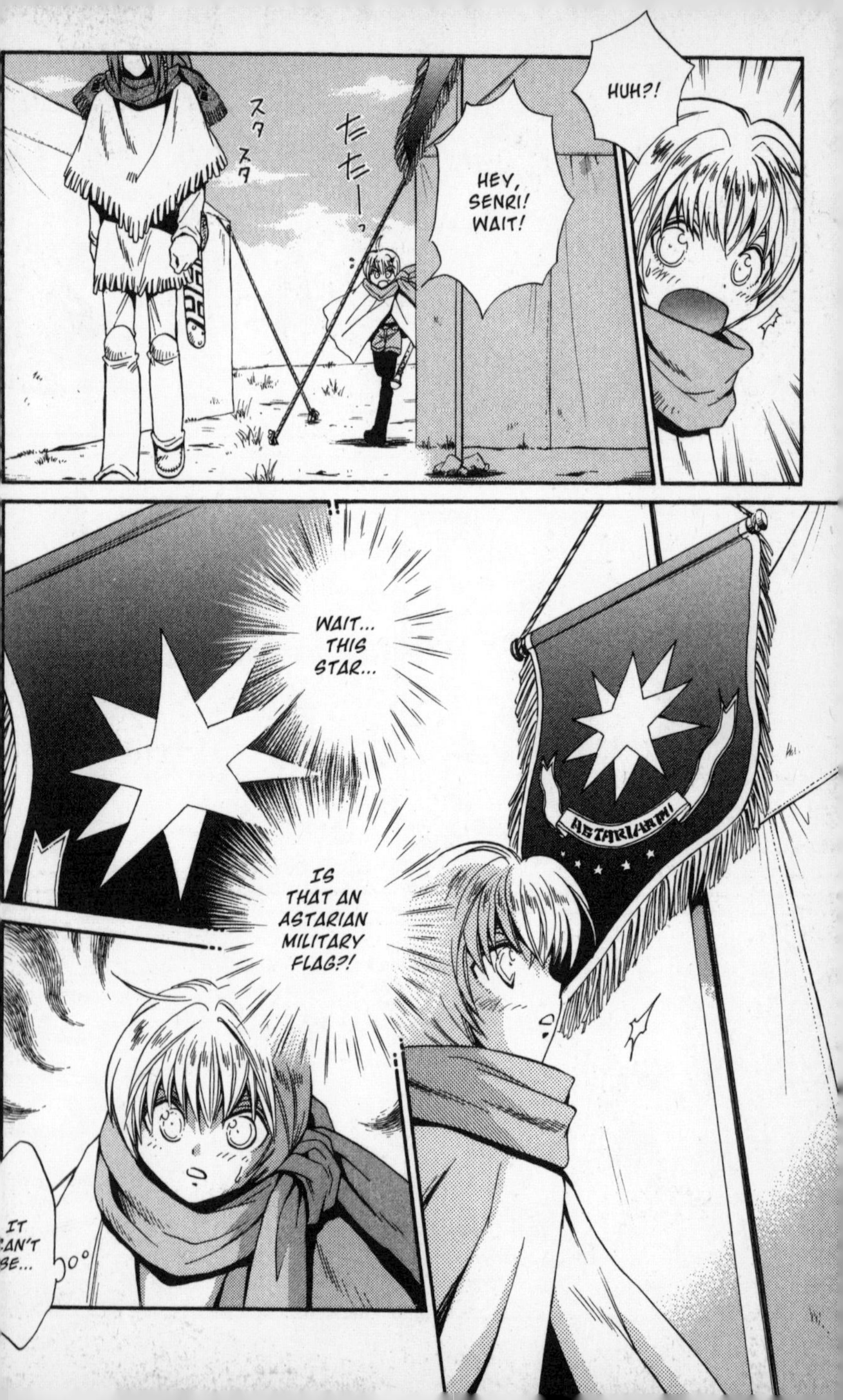
HUH?!
HEY, SENRI! WAIT!
たたーっ
スタスタ
WAIT... THIS STAR...
IS THAT AN ASTARIAN MILITARY FLAG?!
ASTARIA
IT CAN'T BE...

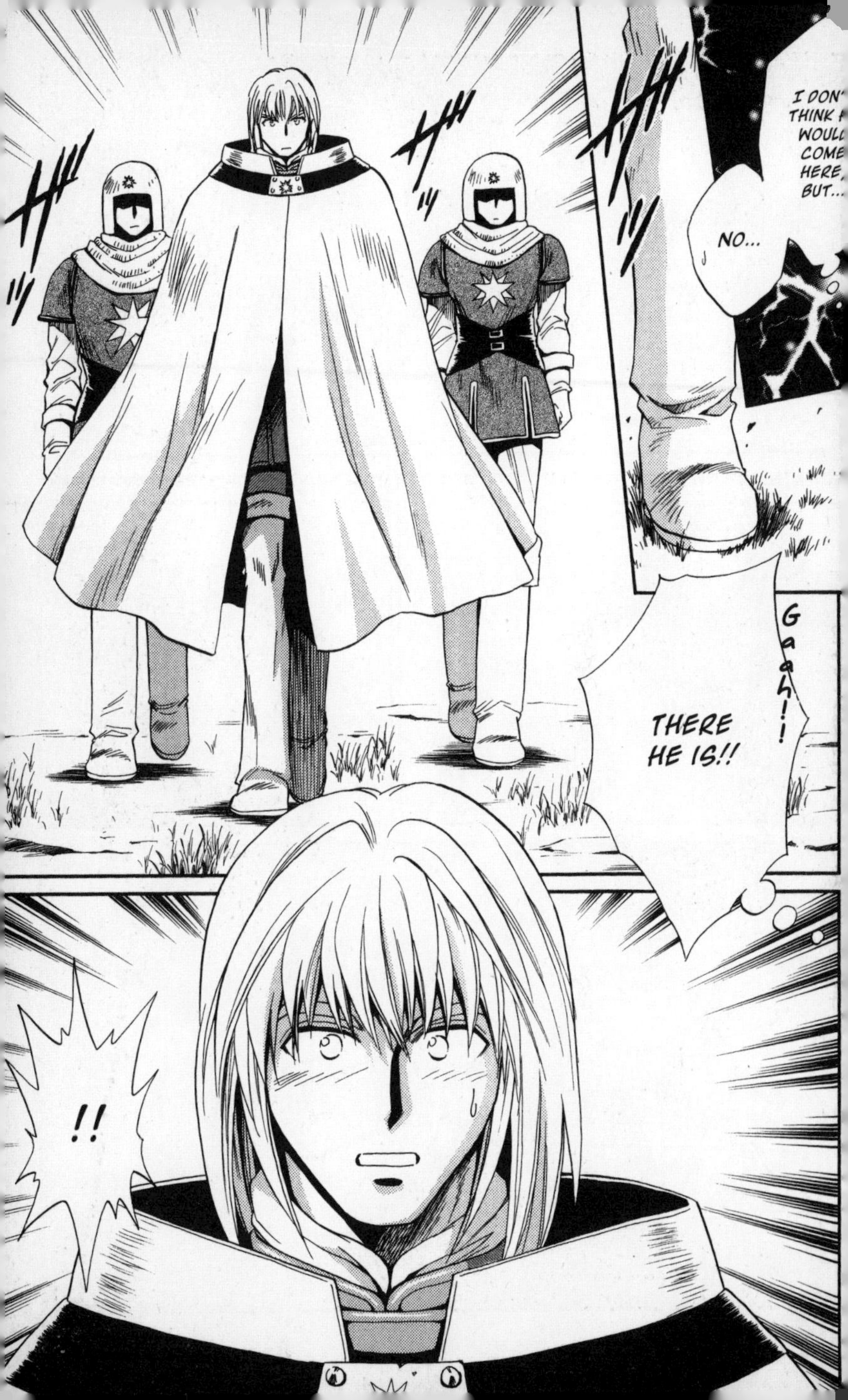
I DON'T THINK H WOULD COME HERE, BUT...
NO...
Gaah!!
THERE HE IS!!
!!

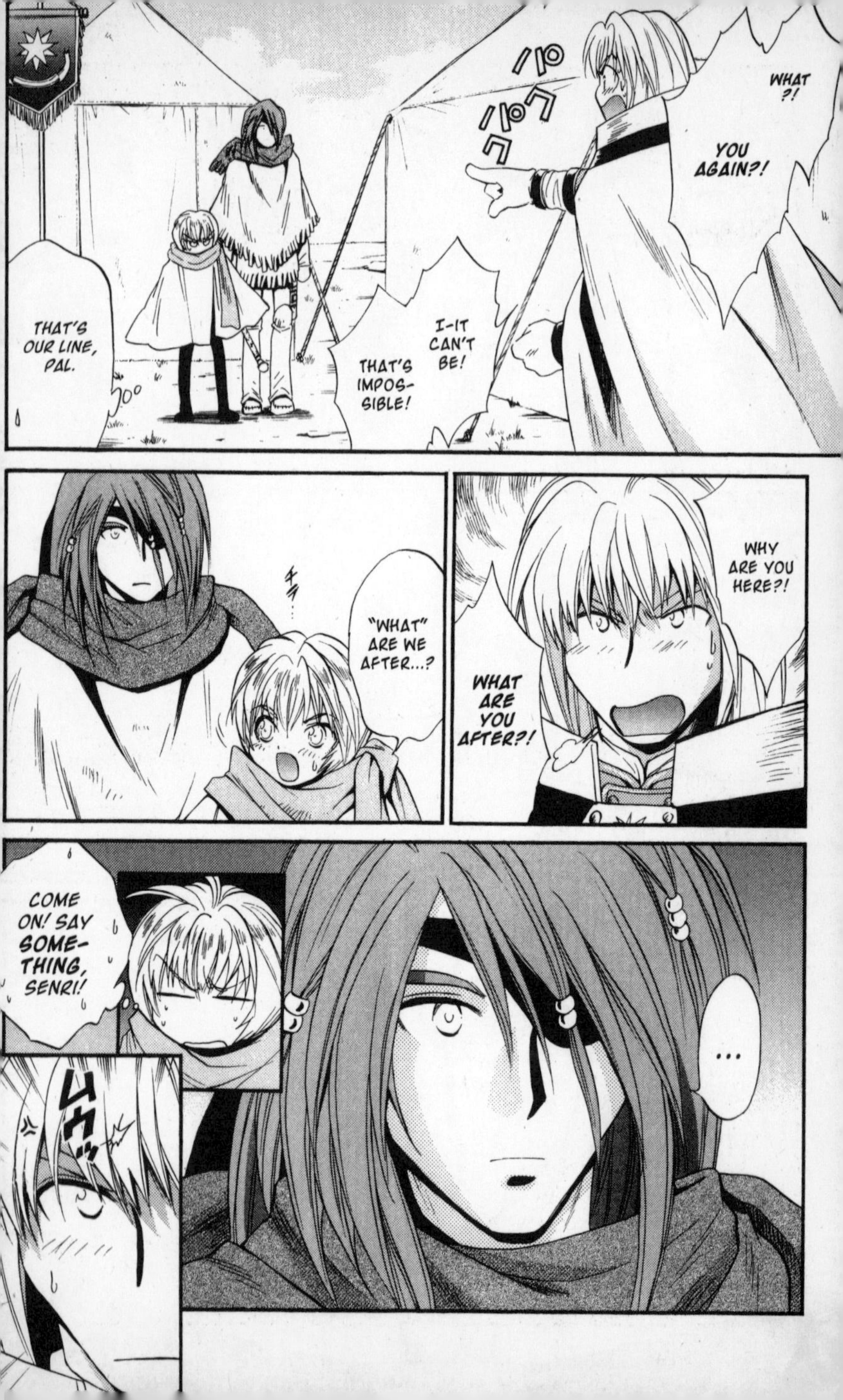
WHAT?!
YOU AGAIN?!
I-IT CAN'T BE!
THAT'S IMPOSSIBLE!
THAT'S OUR LINE, PAL.
WHY ARE YOU HERE?!
WHAT ARE YOU AFTER?!
"WHAT" ARE WE AFTER...?
...
COME ON! SAY SOMETHING, SENRI!

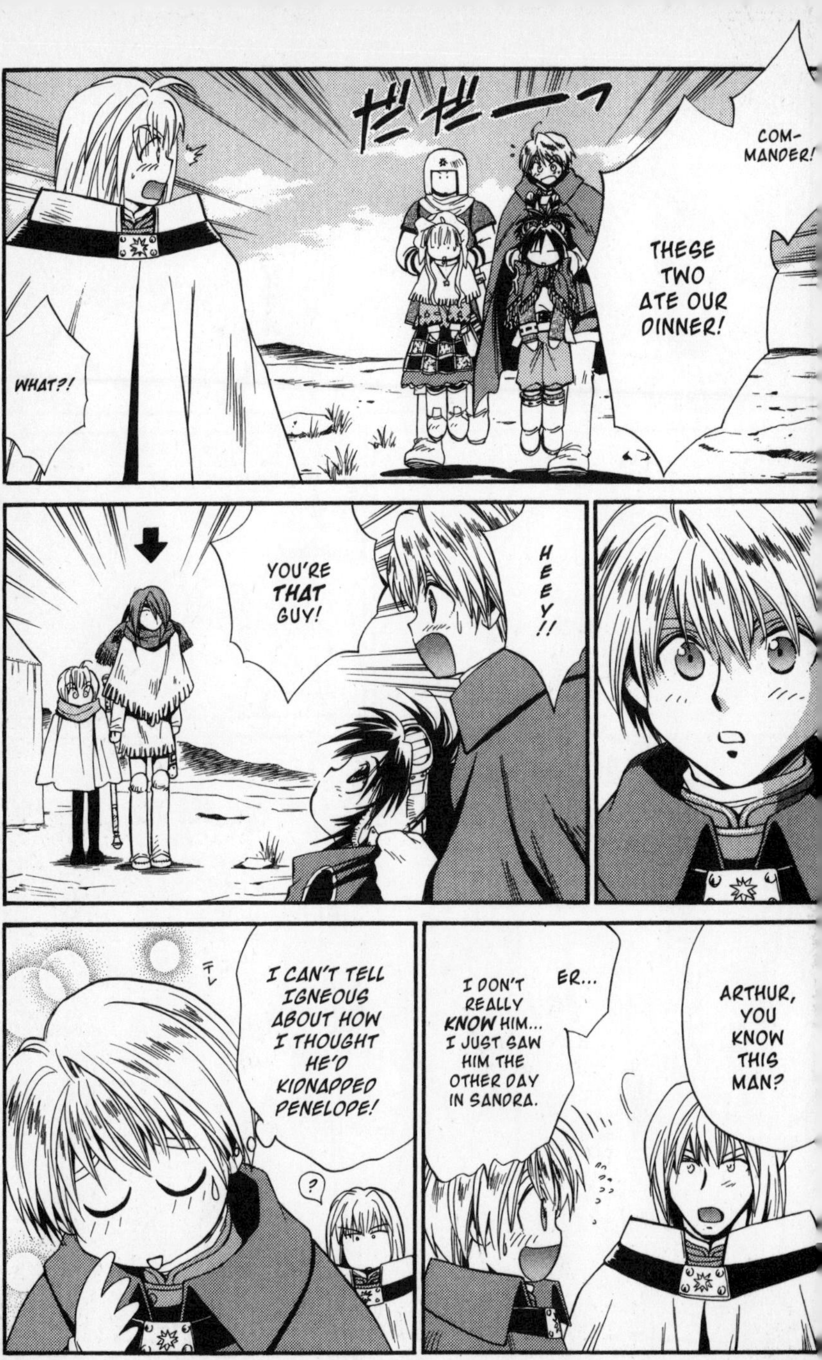
ザザーッ
COM-MANDER!
THESE TWO ATE OUR DINNER!
WHAT?!
HEEY!!
YOU'RE **THAT** GUY!
ARTHUR, YOU KNOW THIS MAN?
ER...
I DON'T REALLY **KNOW** HIM... I JUST SAW HIM THE OTHER DAY IN SANDRA.
テレ
I CAN'T TELL IGNEOUS ABOUT HOW I THOUGHT HE'D KIDNAPPED PENELOPE!
?

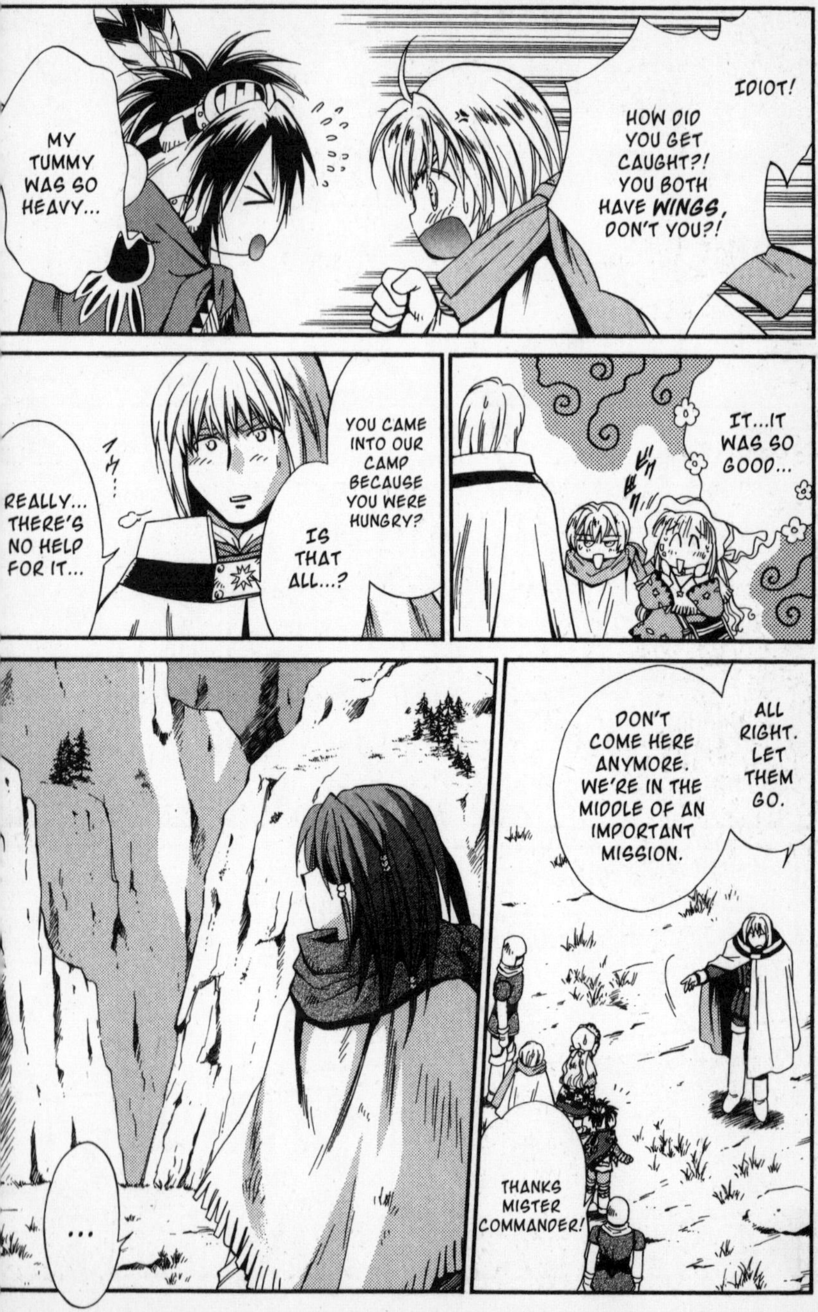
IDIOT!
HOW DID YOU GET CAUGHT?! YOU BOTH HAVE WINGS, DON'T YOU?!
MY TUMMY WAS SO HEAVY...
IT...IT WAS SO GOOD...
YOU CAME INTO OUR CAMP BECAUSE YOU WERE HUNGRY?
IS THAT ALL...?
REALLY... THERE'S NO HELP FOR IT...
ALL RIGHT. LET THEM GO.
DON'T COME HERE ANYMORE. WE'RE IN THE MIDDLE OF AN IMPORTANT MISSION.
THANKS MISTER COMMANDER!
...

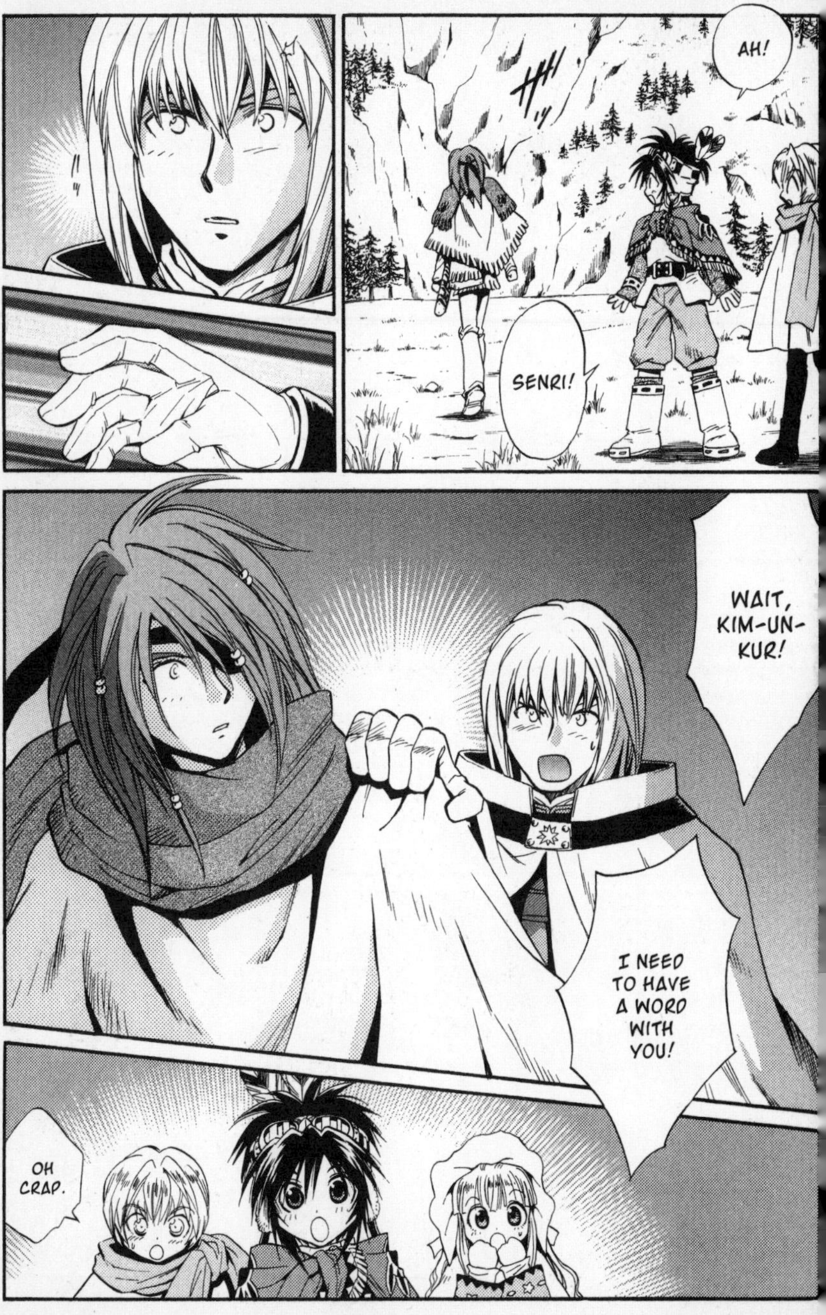
AH!
SENRI!
WAIT, KIM-UN-KUR!
I NEED TO HAVE A WORD WITH YOU!
OH CRAP.

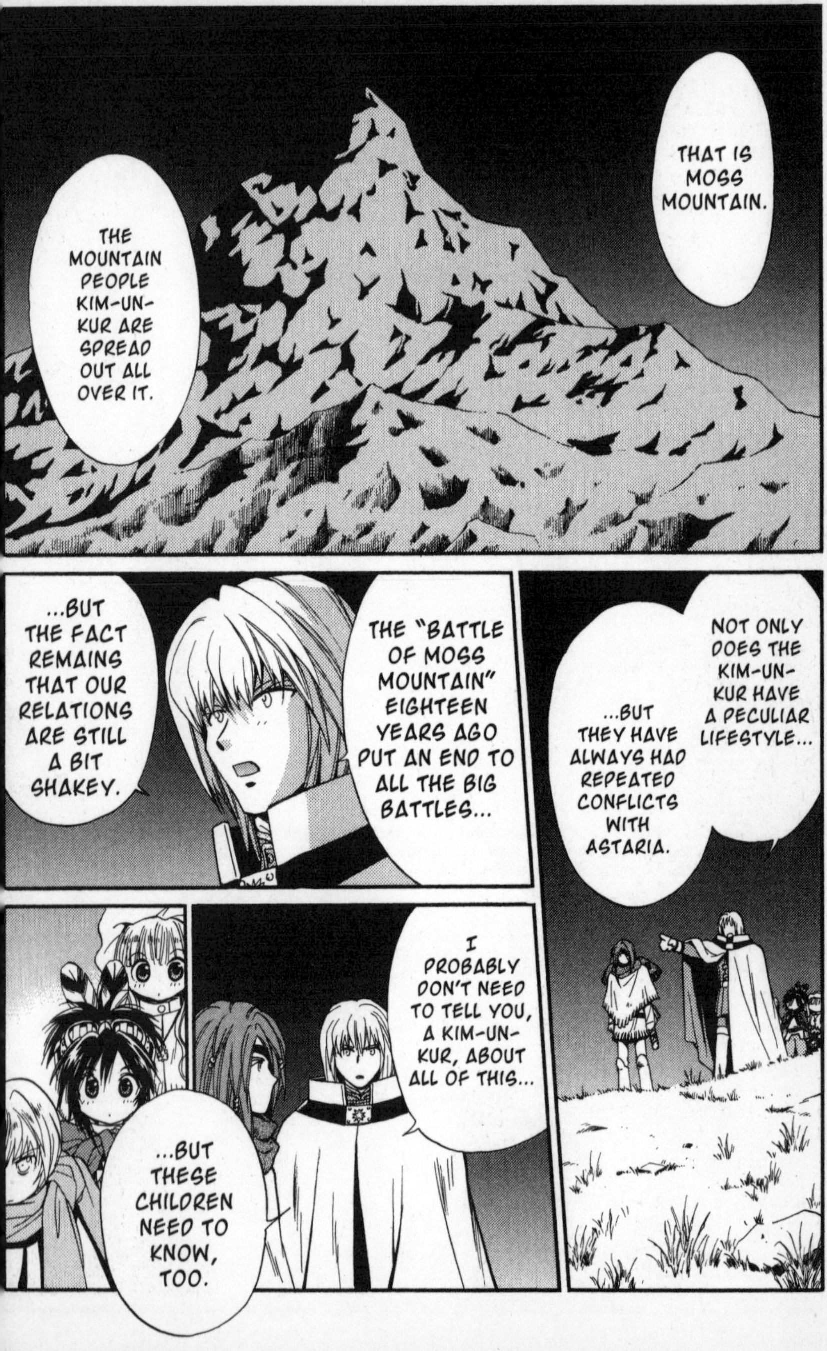
THAT IS MOSS MOUNTAIN.
THE MOUNTAIN PEOPLE KIM-UN-KUR ARE SPREAD OUT ALL OVER IT.
NOT ONLY DOES THE KIM-UN-KUR HAVE A PECULIAR LIFESTYLE...
...BUT THEY HAVE ALWAYS HAD REPEATED CONFLICTS WITH ASTARIA.
THE "BATTLE OF MOSS MOUNTAIN" EIGHTEEN YEARS AGO PUT AN END TO ALL THE BIG BATTLES...
...BUT THE FACT REMAINS THAT OUR RELATIONS ARE STILL A BIT SHAKEY.
I PROBABLY DON'T NEED TO TELL YOU, A KIM-UN-KUR, ABOUT ALL OF THIS...
...BUT THESE CHILDREN NEED TO KNOW, TOO.

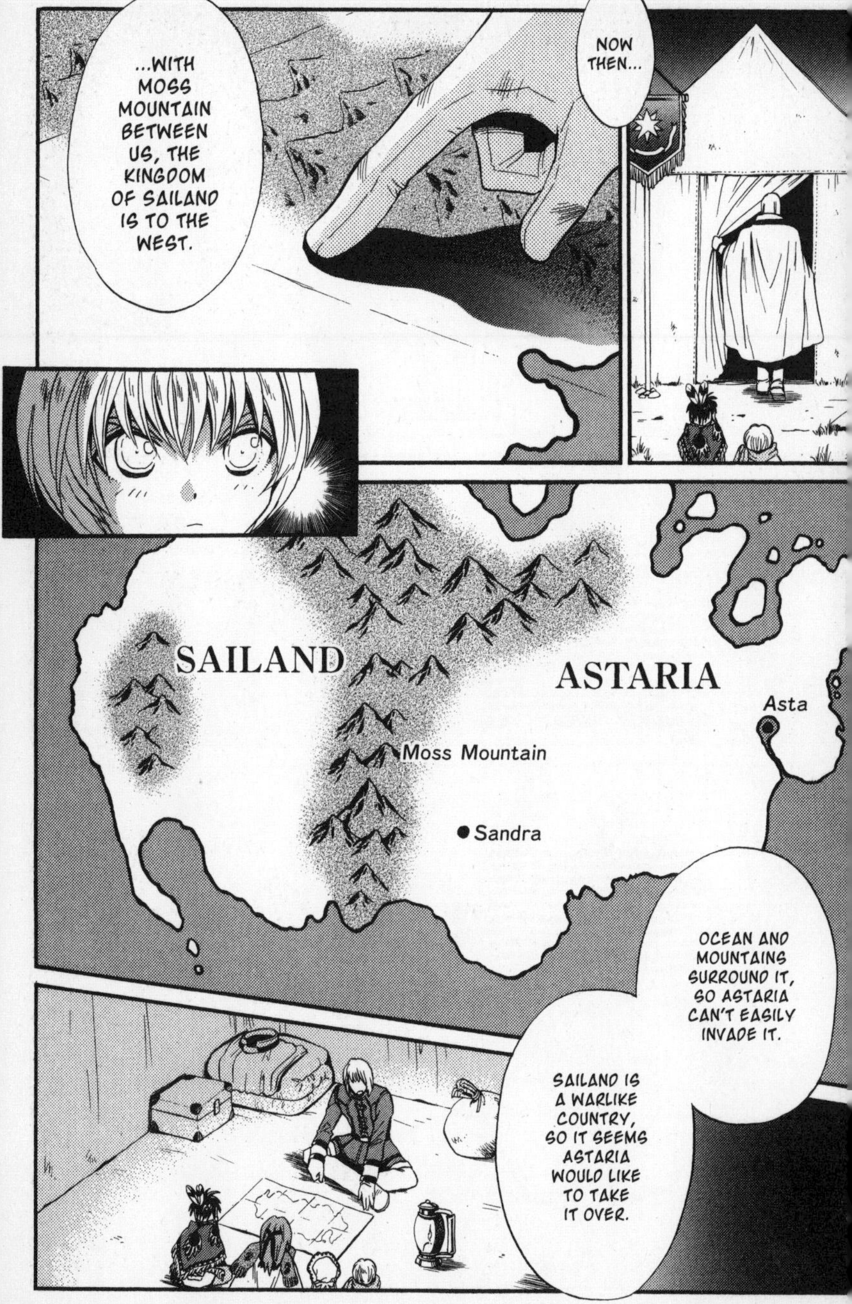
NOW THEN...
...WITH MOSS MOUNTAIN BETWEEN US, THE KINGDOM OF SAILAND IS TO THE WEST.
ASTARIA
SAILAND
Asta
Moss Mountain
Sandra
OCEAN AND MOUNTAINS SURROUND IT, SO ASTARIA CAN'T EASILY INVADE IT.
SAILAND IS A WARLIKE COUNTRY, SO IT SEEMS ASTARIA WOULD LIKE TO TAKE IT OVER.

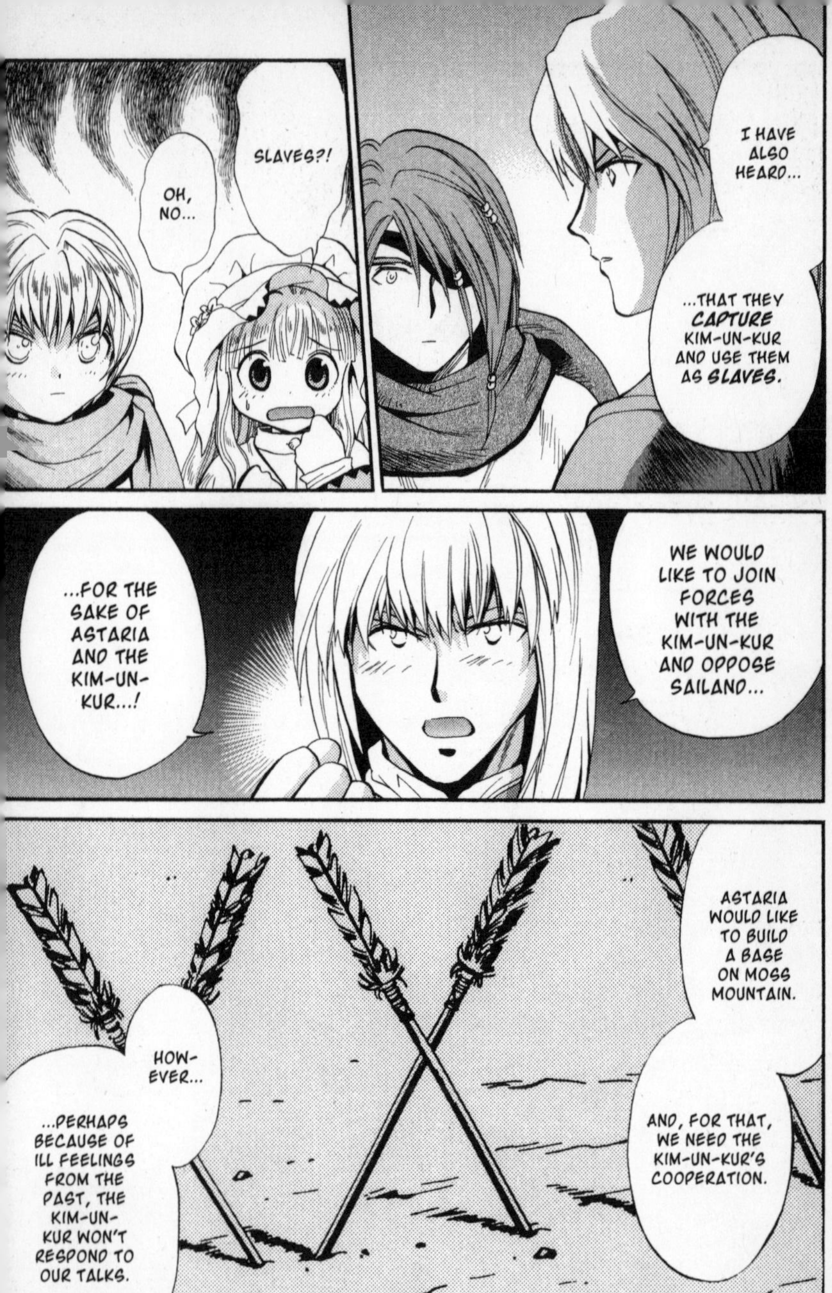
I HAVE ALSO HEARD...
...THAT THEY CAPTURE KIM-UN-KUR AND USE THEM AS SLAVES.
SLAVES?!
OH, NO...
WE WOULD LIKE TO JOIN FORCES WITH THE KIM-UN-KUR AND OPPOSE SAILAND...
...FOR THE SAKE OF ASTARIA AND THE KIM-UN-KUR...!
ASTARIA WOULD LIKE TO BUILD A BASE ON MOSS MOUNTAIN.
AND, FOR THAT, WE NEED THE KIM-UN-KUR'S COOPERATION.
HOW-EVER...
...PERHAPS BECAUSE OF ILL FEELINGS FROM THE PAST, THE KIM-UN-KUR WON'T RESPOND TO OUR TALKS.

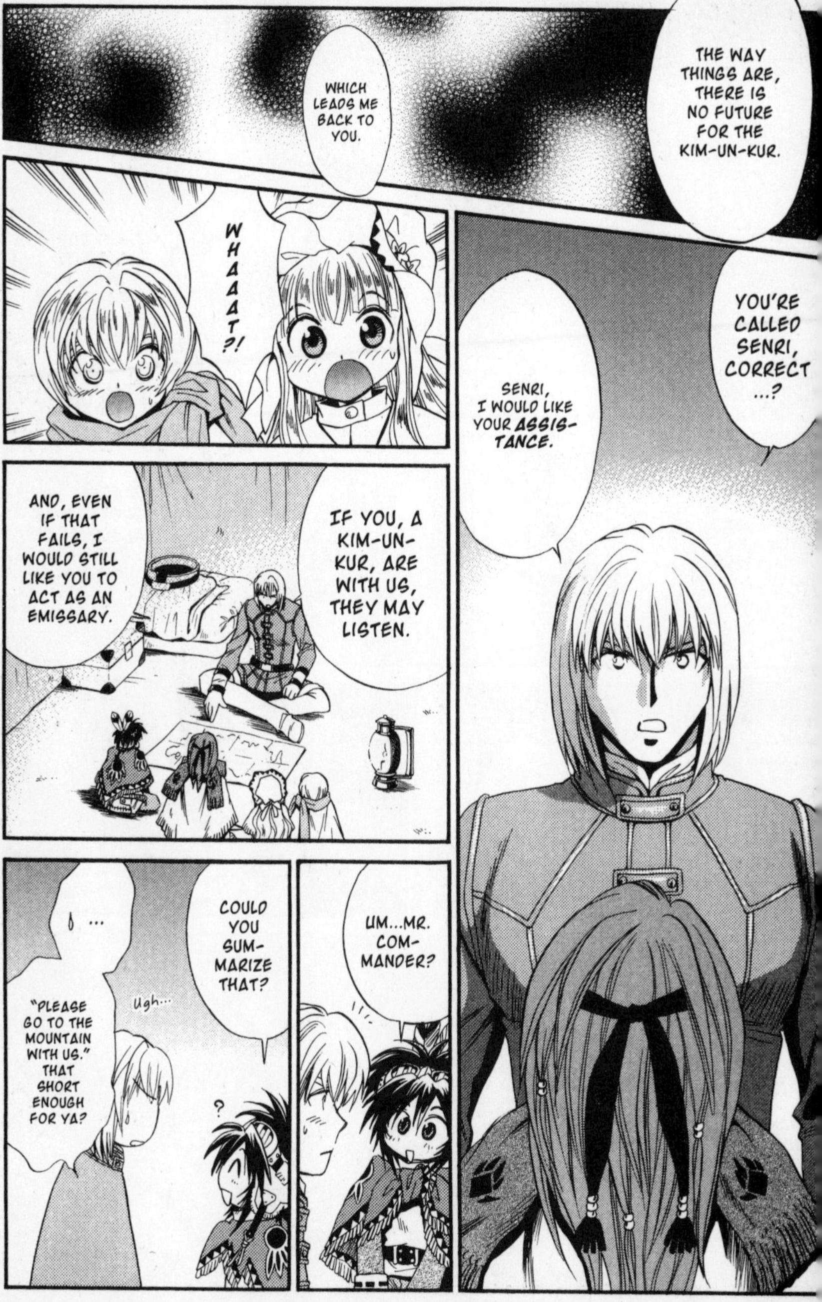
THE WAY THINGS ARE, THERE IS NO FUTURE FOR THE KIM-UN-KUR.
WHICH LEADS ME BACK TO YOU.
YOU'RE CALLED SENRI, CORRECT ...?
SENRI, I WOULD LIKE YOUR ASSISTANCE.
WHAAAAT?!
IF YOU, A KIM-UN-KUR, ARE WITH US, THEY MAY LISTEN.
AND, EVEN IF THAT FAILS, I WOULD STILL LIKE YOU TO ACT AS AN EMISSARY.
UM...MR. COMMANDER?
COULD YOU SUMMARIZE THAT?
! ...
Ugh...
"PLEASE GO TO THE MOUNTAIN WITH US." THAT SHORT ENOUGH FOR YA?
?

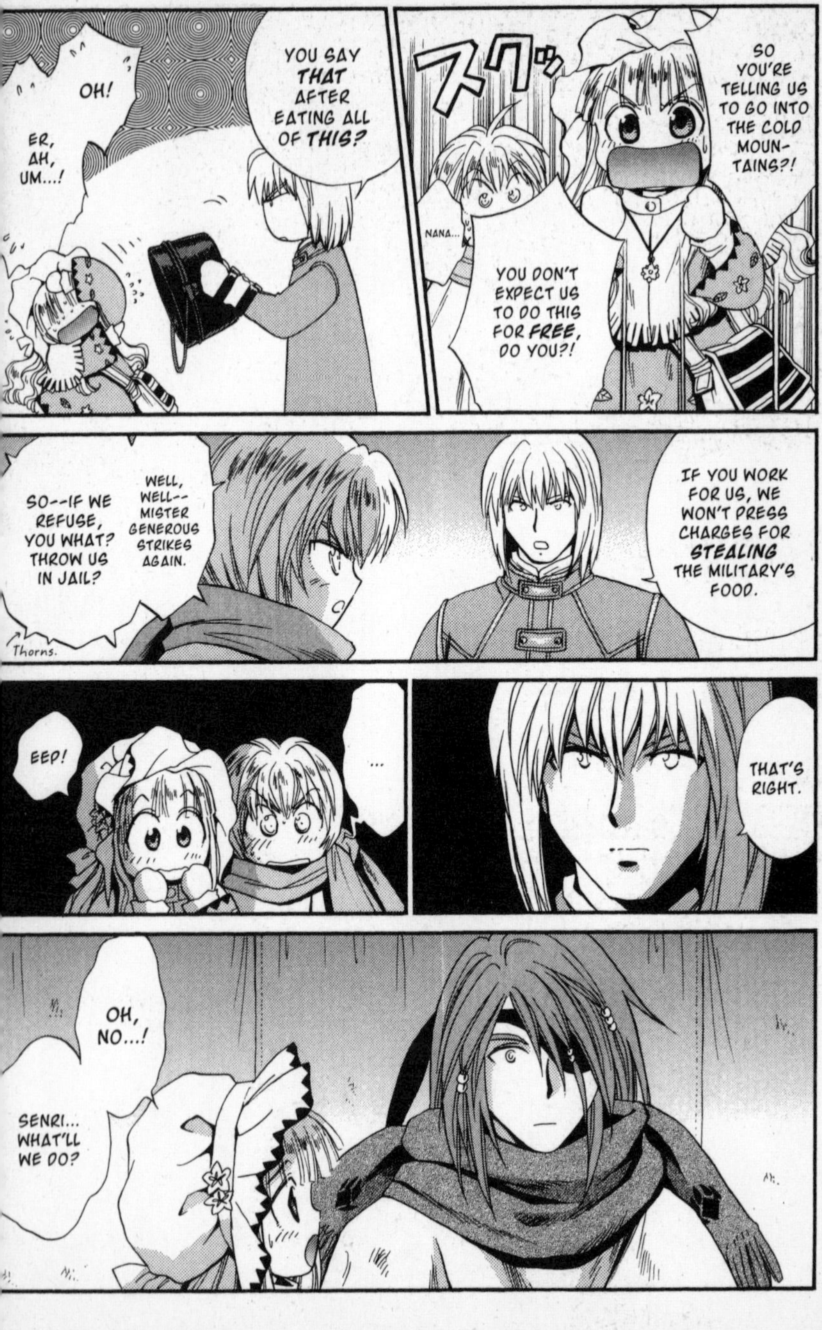
スクッ
SO YOU'RE TELLING US TO GO INTO THE COLD MOUN-TAINS?!
NANA...
YOU DON'T EXPECT US TO DO THIS FOR FREE, DO YOU?!
YOU SAY THAT AFTER EATING ALL OF THIS?
OH!
ER, AH, UM...!
IF YOU WORK FOR US, WE WON'T PRESS CHARGES FOR STEALING THE MILITARY'S FOOD.
WELL, WELL-- MISTER GENEROUS STRIKES AGAIN.
SO--IF WE REFUSE, YOU WHAT? THROW US IN JAIL?
Thorns.
THAT'S RIGHT.
...
EEP!
OH, NO...!
SENRI... WHAT'LL WE DO?

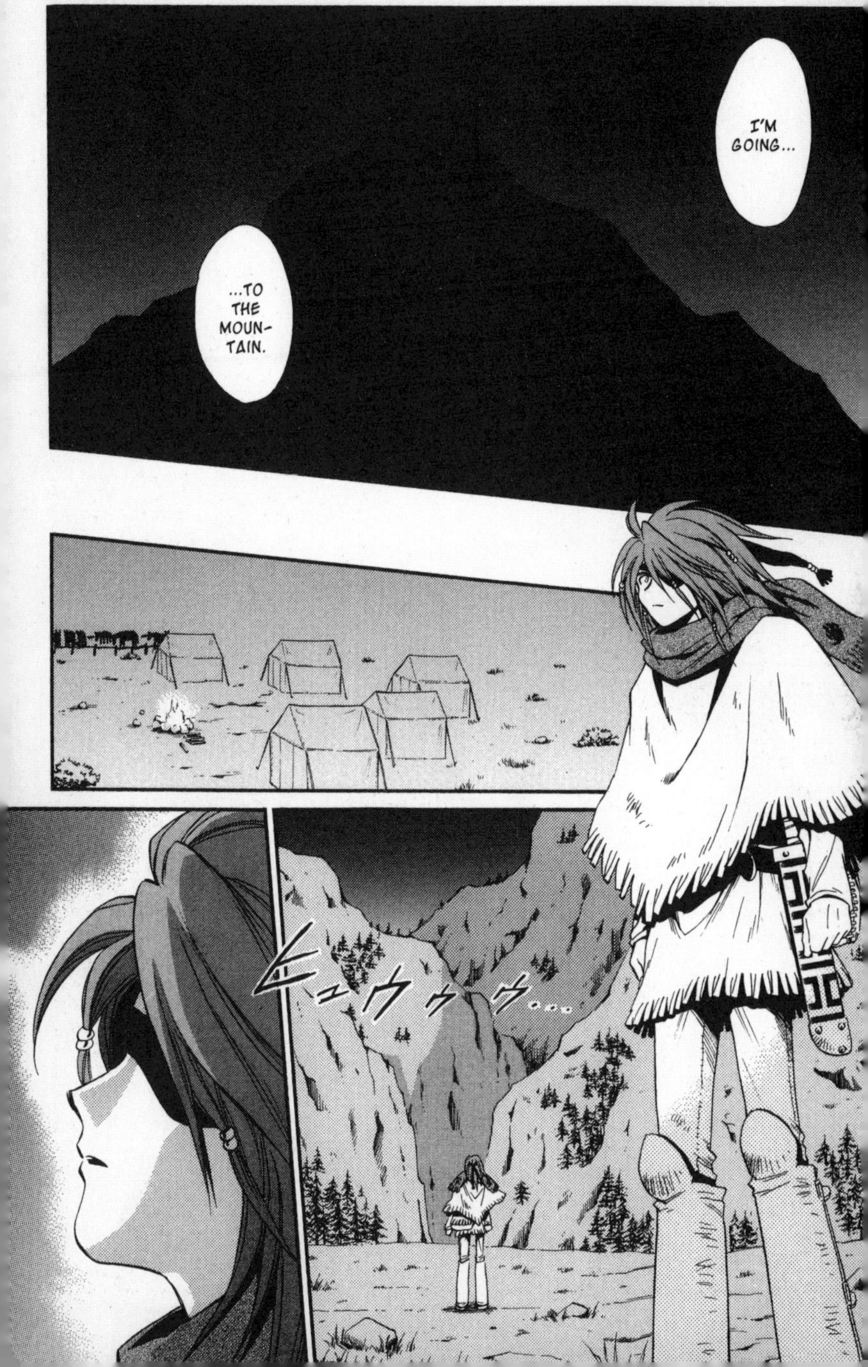
I'M GOING...
...TO THE MOUN-TAIN.
ヒュウゥゥ...

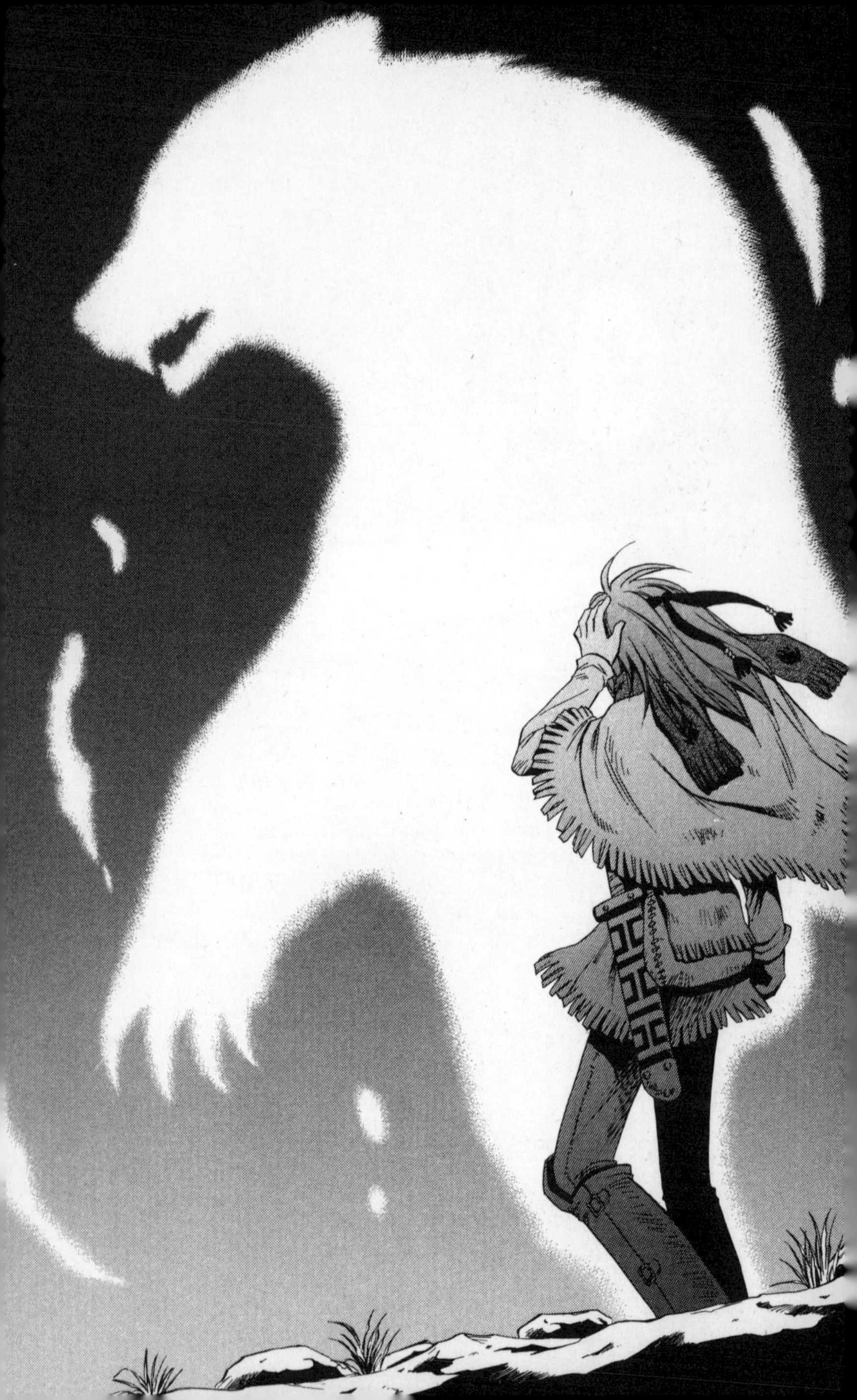

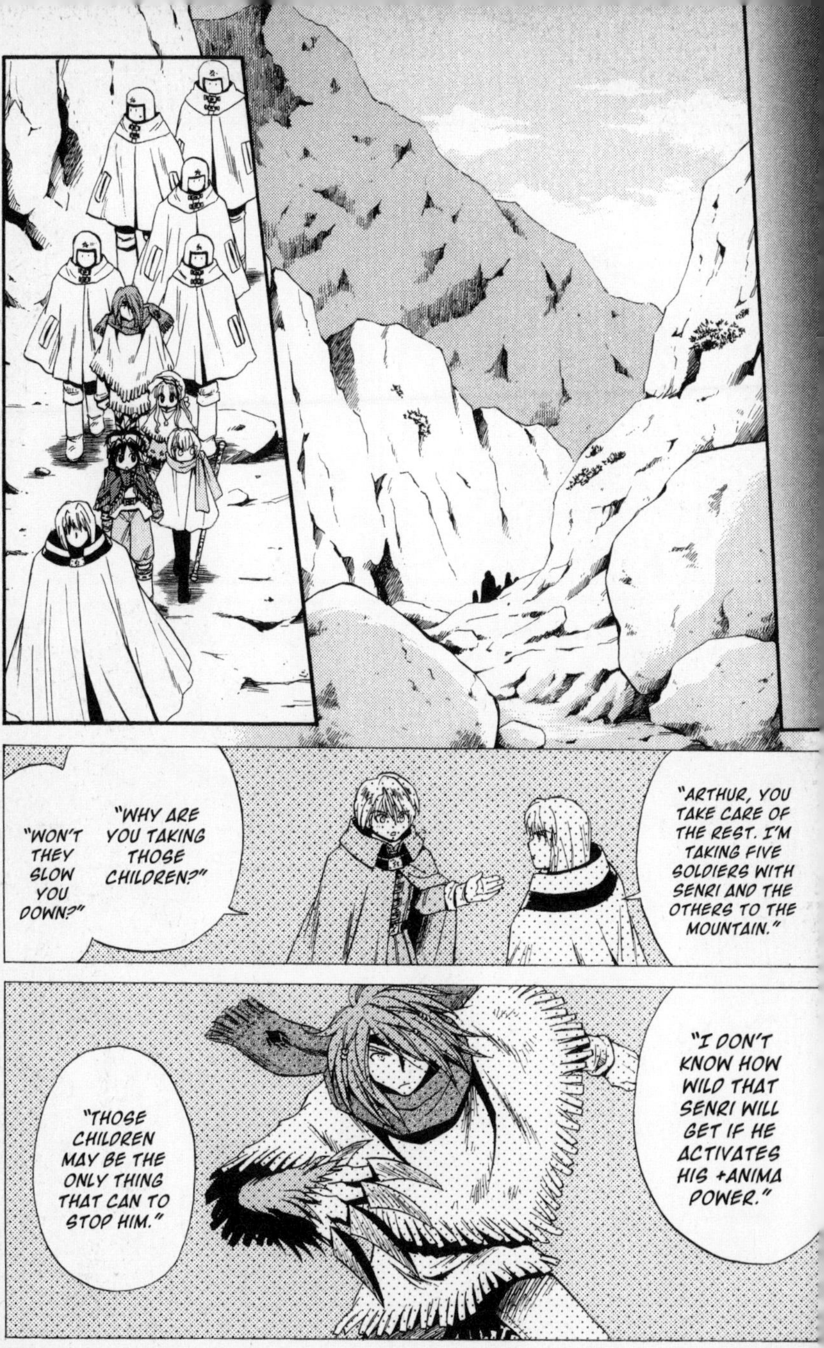
"ARTHUR, YOU TAKE CARE OF THE REST. I'M TAKING FIVE SOLDIERS WITH SENRI AND THE OTHERS TO THE MOUNTAIN."
"WHY ARE YOU TAKING THOSE CHILDREN?"
"WON'T THEY SLOW YOU DOWN?"
"I DON'T KNOW HOW WILD THAT SENRI WILL GET IF HE ACTIVATES HIS +ANIMA POWER."
"THOSE CHILDREN MAY BE THE ONLY THING THAT CAN TO STOP HIM."

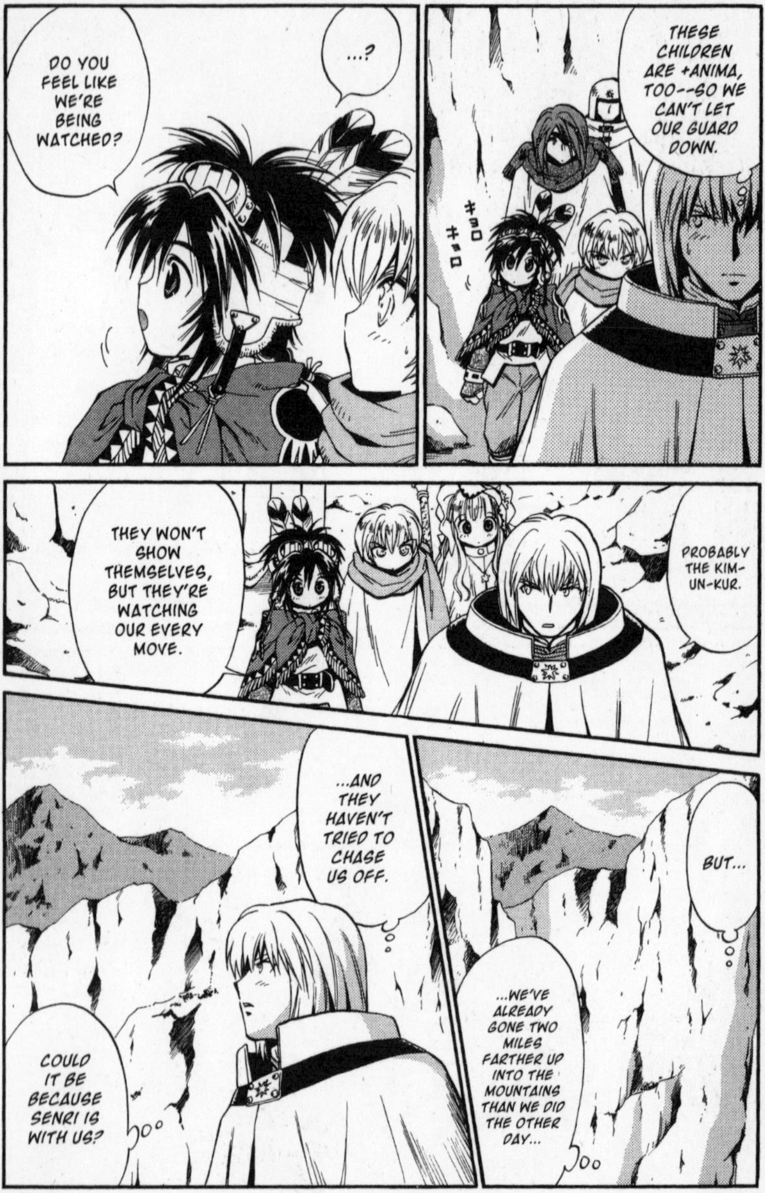
THESE CHILDREN ARE +ANIMA, TOO--SO WE CAN'T LET OUR GUARD DOWN.
キョロ キョロ
...?
DO YOU FEEL LIKE WE'RE BEING WATCHED?
PROBABLY THE KIM-UN-KUR.
THEY WON'T SHOW THEMSELVES, BUT THEY'RE WATCHING OUR EVERY MOVE.
BUT...
...WE'VE ALREADY GONE TWO MILES FARTHER UP INTO THE MOUNTAINS THAN WE DID THE OTHER DAY...
...AND THEY HAVEN'T TRIED TO CHASE US OFF.
COULD IT BE BECAUSE SENRI IS WITH US?

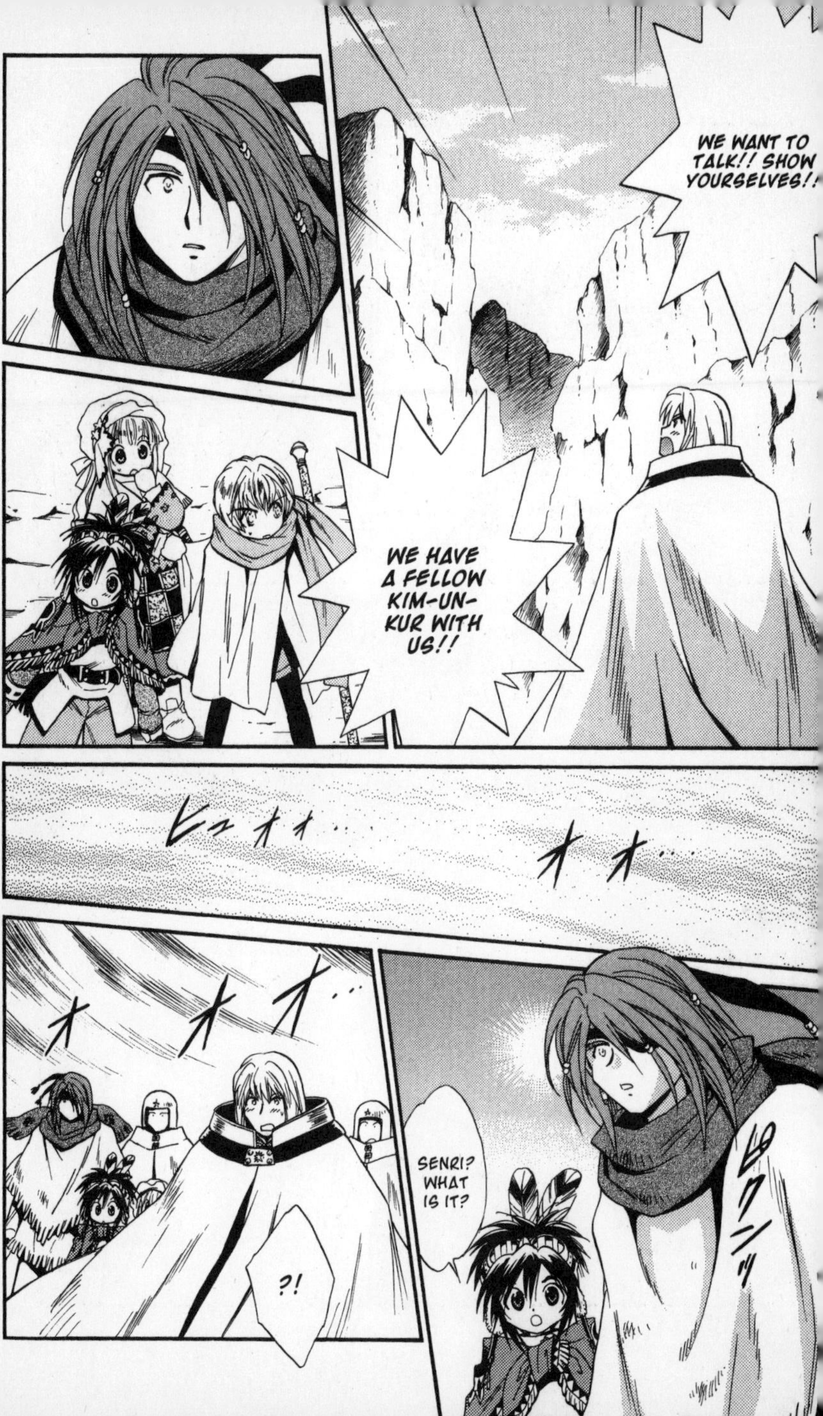
WE WANT TO TALK!! SHOW YOURSELVES!!
WE HAVE A FELLOW KIM-UN-KUR WITH US!!
ヒュオオ…
オオ…
SENRI? WHAT IS IT?
オオオ…
?!

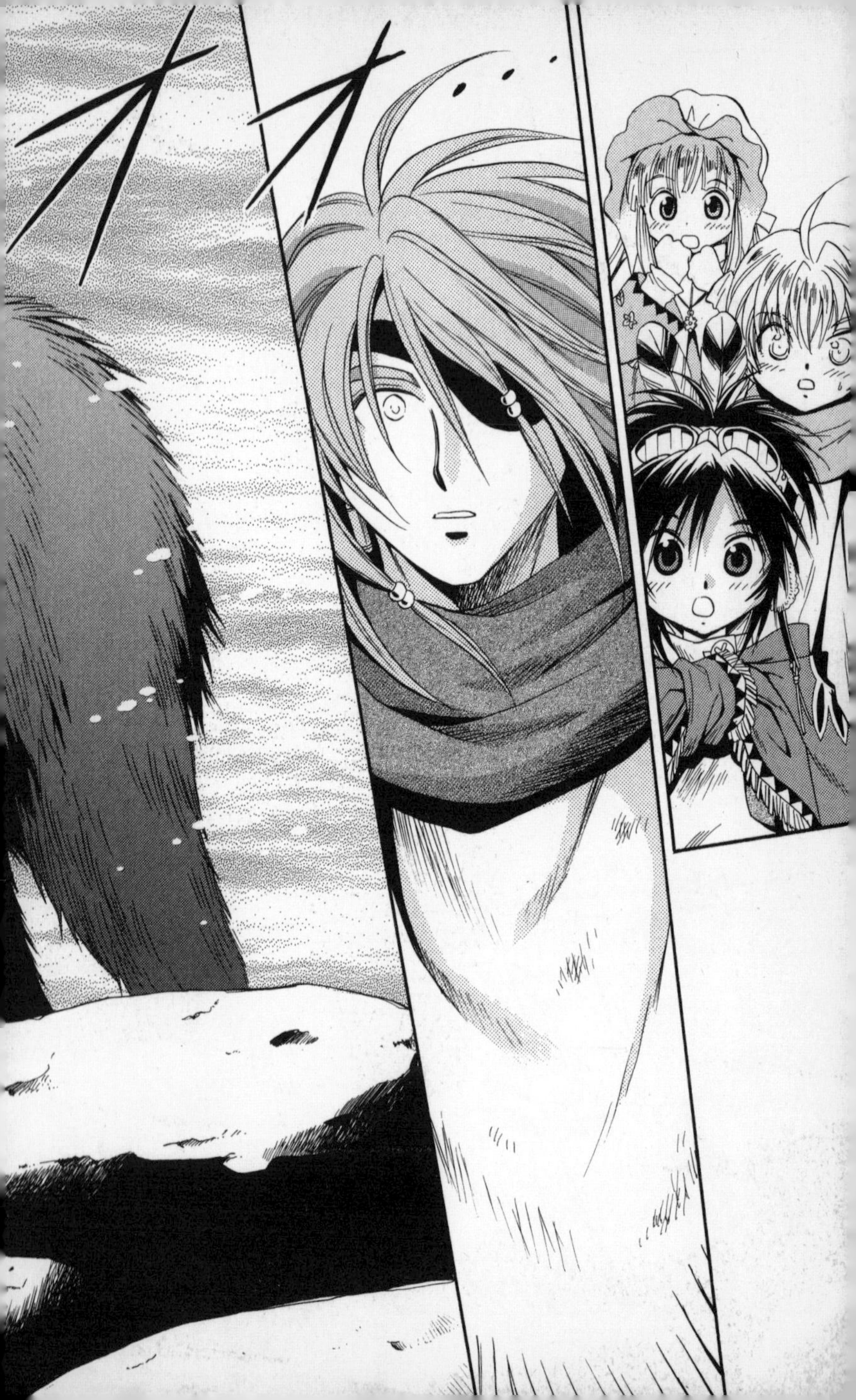
オオ
...

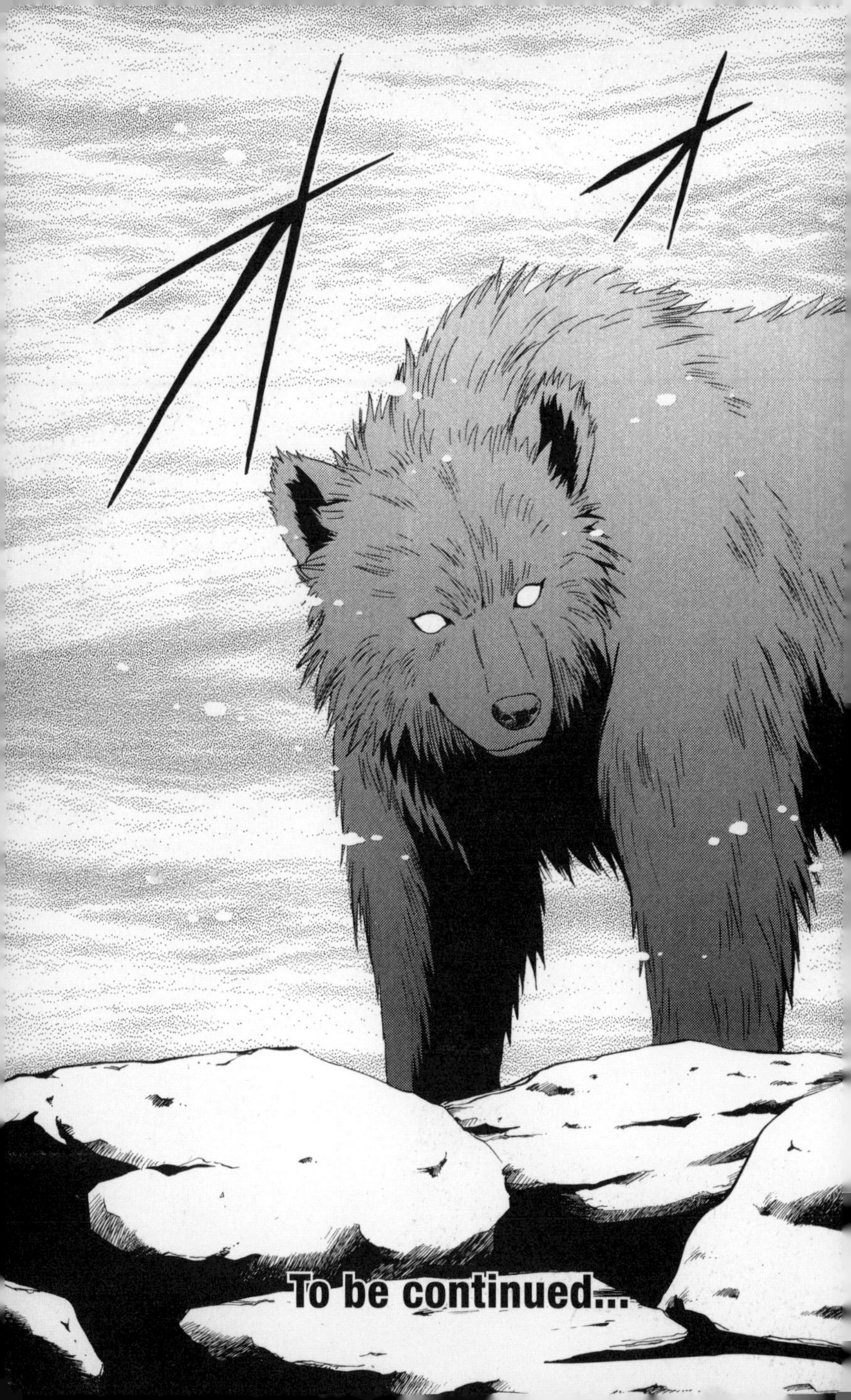
オオ
To be continued...

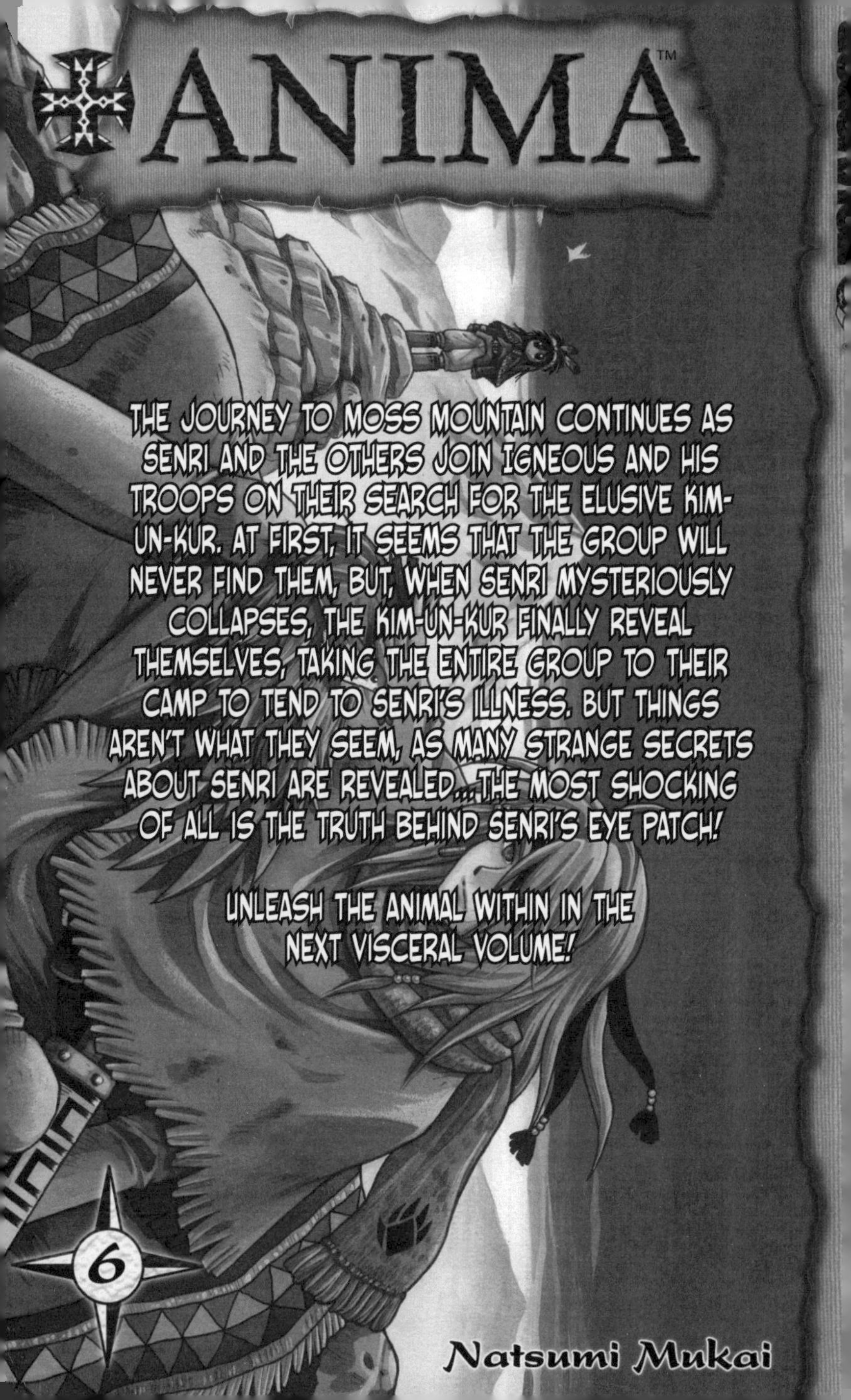
+ANIMA™
THE JOURNEY TO MOSS MOUNTAIN CONTINUES AS SENRI AND THE OTHERS JOIN IGNEOUS AND HIS TROOPS ON THEIR SEARCH FOR THE ELUSIVE KIM-UN-KUR. AT FIRST, IT SEEMS THAT THE GROUP WILL NEVER FIND THEM, BUT, WHEN SENRI MYSTERIOUSLY COLLAPSES, THE KIM-UN-KUR FINALLY REVEAL THEMSELVES, TAKING THE ENTIRE GROUP TO THEIR CAMP TO TEND TO SENRI'S ILLNESS. BUT THINGS AREN'T WHAT THEY SEEM, AS MANY STRANGE SECRETS ABOUT SENRI ARE REVEALED...THE MOST SHOCKING OF ALL IS THE TRUTH BEHIND SENRI'S EYE PATCH!
UNLEASH THE ANIMAL WITHIN IN THE NEXT VISCERAL VOLUME!
6
Natsumi Mukai

TOKYOPOP.com

WHERE MANGA LIVES!

JOIN the
TOKYOPOP community:
www.TOKYOPOP.com

LIVE THE MANGA LIFESTYLE!

EXCLUSIVE PREVIEWS...
CREATE...
UPLOAD...
DOWNLOAD...
BLOG...
CHAT...
VOTE...
LIVE!!!!

WWW.TOKYOPOP.COM HAS:

- News
- Columns
- Special Features
- and more...

THE MANGA REVOLUTION • LEADING
漫画
革命
LEADING • THE MANGA REVOLUTION

The Complete Epic Available for the First Time in one Ultimate Edition!

EXCLUSIVE

Eight full-color pages of new story from the original creators, preliminary sketches from the artist, and an afterword from Blizzard's Chris Metzen are included in this gorgeous compilation of the Sunwell Trilogy.

WARCRAFT
THE SUNWELL TRILOGY

ULTIMATE EDITION
RICHARD A. KNAAK • JAE-HWAN KIM

STOP!

This is the back of the book.
You wouldn't want to spoil a great ending!

This book is printed "manga-style," in the authentic Japanese right-to-left format. Since none of the artwork has been flipped or altered, readers get to experience the story just as the creator intended. You've been asking for it, so TOKYOPOP® delivered: authentic, hot-off-the-press, and far more fun!

DIRECTIONS

1
2
3
4
5
6
7
8
9
10

If this is your first time reading manga-style, here's a quick guide to help you understand how it works.

It's easy... just start in the top right panel and follow the numbers. Have fun, and look for more 100% authentic manga from TOKYOPOP®!

THE MANGA REVOLUTION • LEADING THE MANGA REVOLUTION • LEADING 漫画革命

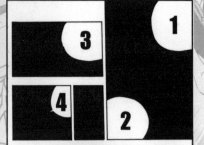